The Mental World
of Brands

The Mental World of Brands

Mind, memory and brand success

Giep Franzen
Margot Bouwman

With a foreword by Wendy Gordon

www.warc.com

**World Advertising
Research Center**

First published 2001

World Advertising Research Center
Farm Road, Henley-on-Thames
Oxfordshire RG9 1EJ, United Kingdom
Telephone: +44 (0) 1491 411000
Facsimile: +44 (0) 1491 418600
E-mail: info@warc.com

A CIP catalogue record for this book is
available from the British Library

ISBN 1 84116 081 4

Typeset in 10/13pt Sabon by Marie Doherty
Printed and bound in Great Britain by Cromwell Press, Trowbridge

Contents

Foreword   xi
Acknowledgement   xv
Introduction   xvii

Part One   The Brain and Memory

1   The Brain   3

    1.1   The brain   3
    1.2   Neurons   9
    1.3   Networks   13
    1.4   The origin of connections   17

2   The Cognitive and Emotional Brains   21

    2.1   Interconnectedness   21
    2.2   The limbic system: centre of emotions   22
    2.3   Unconscious and conscious emotions   26
    2.4   Information storage   27
    2.5   Emotional associations   30
    2.6   Emotional memories   34

3   Memory Processes   39

    3.1   The basic model of memory   39
    3.2   The working memory   39
    3.3   Consciousness   42
    3.4   Processing information   45
    3.5   Long-term memory   46
    3.6   Associations   49
    3.7   Epicentre and Gestalt   58
    3.8   Spreading activation   60
    3.9   Remembering   65
    3.10 The influence of cues   67

3.11   Recognition   69
3.12   Forgetting   70
3.13   The forgetfulness of the elderly   72
3.14   The complexity of memory processes   73

4   Memory Systems   75

4.1   Processes and files   75
4.2   Declarative and procedural memories   76
4.3   Habits   76
4.4   Explicit and implicit memory   77

5   Memory Representations   81

5.1   Analogous and propositional representations   82
5.2   Concepts: units of knowledge   83
5.3   Concepts and language   85
5.4   The meaning of words   88
5.5   The nature of concepts   90
5.6   Categories   91
5.7   Schemata: knowledge structures   95
5.8   The functioning of schemata   98

6   Associative Networks   101

6.1   Associative network models   101
6.2   Associative systems   104
6.3   Neural network models   105
6.4   Parallelism   106
6.5   Connectionism   106

7   The Development of the Brain and Memory   111

7.1   The embryonic stage   111
7.2   The origin of representations   112
7.3   Development phases   113
7.4   Children and brand names   122

Part Two   Brands and Memory

8   Brands in our Memory   129

8.1   Introduction   129
8.2   The influence of various elements of memory on brand choice 130
8.3   The brand as an associative network   144
8.4   Associations and brand functions   162

9 **Brand Awareness**   171

  9.1   Brands in memory   171
  9.2   Extent, intensity and breadth of the brand awareness   172

10 **Brand Meanings**   177

  10.1   Introduction   177
  10.2   Brand signs   184
  10.3   The origin of the brand and sub-brands   186
  10.4   Product-related brand meanings   197
  10.5   Situational meanings   200
  10.6   Symbolic meanings   200
  10.7   Perceived quality   211
  10.8   Perceived (relative) price   214
  10.9   Presentation   215
  10.10 Associations in advertising   215

11 **Brand Emotions**   217

  11.1   Introduction   217
  11.2   Emotions   218
  11.3   Brand emotions   228

12 **Brand Positioning**   231

  12.1   Introduction   231
  12.2   Categorisation   232
  12.3   Brand positioning   238
  12.4   Brand concepts   242
  12.5   Research practice   252

13 **Brand Attitudes**   269

  13.1   Attitudes   269
  13.2   Brand attitudes   274
  13.3   Influencing the brand attitude   276

14 **Brand Behavioural Tendencies**   279

  14.1   Habits   279
  14.2   The brand repertoire   282
  14.3   Duplication of brand purchases   288
  14.4   Market laws   291
  14.5   The connection between brand attitude and brand loyalty 294

15 Brand Relationships   297

    15.1   Introduction   297
    15.2   The psychology of a relationship   297
    15.3   Quantum theory   301
    15.4   Brand relationships   306

16 The Brand Representation   311

    16.1   Introduction   311
    16.2   The development stages of a brand representation   312
    16.3   Interconnectedness between the elements of the
             brand representation   323
    16.4   The saliency of a brand representation   325
    16.5   The brand image   326
    16.6   Brand equity   331

Part Three   Research

17 Visions on Brand Research   341

18 Research into Brand Representation   343

    18.1   Research practice   343
    18.2   The ideal research   344
    18.3   Forms of interviewing   349
    18.4   Aids   354
    18.5   Conclusion   364

19 Research into Brand Awareness   365

    19.1   Introduction   365
    19.2   Techniques to measure brand awareness   366

20 Research into Brand Meanings   367

    20.1   Introduction   367
    20.2   Techniques to measure brand meanings   367

21 Research into Brand Emotions   375

    21.1   Introduction   375
    21.2   Techniques for measuring brand emotions   376

22 Research into Brand Positioning   **381**

22.1   Introduction   381
22.2   Techniques for measuring brand positioning   382

23 Research into Brand Attitude   **393**

23.1   Introduction   393
23.2   Techniques for measuring brand attitude   394
23.3   Techniques for measuring brand preference   398

24 Research into Brand Behavioural Tendencies   **401**

24.1   Introduction   401
24.2   Techniques for measuring brand behavioural tendencies   402

25 Research into Brand Relationships   **407**

25.1   Introduction   407
25.2   Techniques for measuring brand relationships   408

26 Holistic Brand Research   **415**

26.1   Introduction   415
26.2   The free format method   416
26.3   The implicit method   417
26.4   The explicit method   424

27 New Forms of Research   **429**

27.1   Narrative   429
27.2   Observation   431
27.3   Panel research   432

28 Final Reflections   **435**

Appendix   437
Bibliography   439
Index   457

Foreword

For three decades, I have been a practising qualitative researcher, brand consultant and adviser to traditional marketing companies, experimental start-up businesses and service businesses bent on a mission to change.

I have always been passionate about trying to understand how ordinary human beings, like myself, think about, make decisions about and have feelings for brands. In the course of my work through face-to-face interviews, focus groups and observation sessions I have encouraged people to express their views about the way in which they respond, relate and react to brands in everyday life. I have accompanied people as they shop, go to the pub, eat in a restaurant or clean the toilet – all in an effort to find out how this thing called *brand* exists inside the mind.

Ordinary people are happy (for a fee) to play games personifying brands, creating brand landscapes with pens and scrap art materials, or choosing adjectives or sentences to describe a brand. They are able, usually, to deconstruct the behaviour that you have observed and explain why it is that they did what they did! They can look backwards and tell you all the reasons leading up to a decision-making moment; it seems logical and straightforward. They can even jump forward in time and construct explanations about whether a new idea will succeed or not.

I have often wondered whether or not any of these explanations and projections reflects what is really going on inside people's minds.

This unsettling thought has been reinforced by the observation that ordinary people often struggle to articulate how they think and feel about brands – even very familiar ones. They find it extraordinary that we professionals are willing to talk about a brand and its competitors for hours at a stretch and that we determinedly try to identify 'reasons why' behind brand choice.

Time after time I have been struck by an apparent paradox. What people tell me directly or reveal to me indirectly about a brand is complex and contradictory. There is all the richness of brand meaning available on the one hand, while on the other hand people explain their brand behaviour in terms of automatic habit, sudden impulse or indifferent inertia.

It is perplexing that the target market has a low recall of the advertising for a brand despite positive pre-test results, a heavy weight of advertising or a campaign that receives accolades in the trade press. It is odd that customers, even regular ones, show such a lack of brand loyalty and an ephemeral relationship with a service brand that they have used for years. It is surprising that consumers are so inert and resistant to change brands even when the product or service is not very good.

Contrast this with what is talked about in meeting rooms and on conference platforms around the world in an effort to manage brands more effectively. I have heard marketing and advertising experts talking authoritatively about separating rational and emotional components of a brand. I have sat at conferences where eminent researchers and thinkers have presented intelligent and rigorous diagrams about rigid brand structures – pyramids, diamonds, concentric circles and atomic models. I have read some of the vast literature on brand loyalty, on relationships, on how advertising works and on how it can be measured.

Marketing, advertising and research professionals continue to argue over the strengths and weaknesses of the large number of different theoretical models of brand motivation, attitude and behaviour. This happens because of the necessity for businesses today to predict the future and to measure the results of brand building investment.

The problem is that we have been searching for new ways of thinking in the same theoretical envelope. We try to look for new nuggets of insight about the 'consumer-brand relationship' in the same over-mined hole in the earth.

Giep Franzen's book guides us to a fertile and exciting new place to dig – the latest thinking in neuroscience and neuropsychology on how the brain works. I have experienced human behaviour many times as a qualitative researcher but have never been able to explain or substantiate why this should be the case until now. The challenges to conventional thinking come fast and furious. Here are five neuroscientific facts that made an impact on me:

(1) Thoughts are never separate from emotions and emotions never separate from thoughts. This is a neuroscientific fact. The brain is connected to the internal milieu of the body (influencing neurotransmitters, hormones and enzymes) as well as to the external world (sensory receptors). It is one system. Brands are coded in memory on a cognitive *and* emotional basis. They are inextricably linked, but it is emotional coding rather than reasoned argument that determines whether or not we take notice.

(2) Much about brand representation is beyond consciousness. This is a scientific fact. Most of the information we have absorbed over time is inaccessible. It is not even available to introspection. This challenges the assumptions we make that what people tell us (reveal to us) about how they perceive brands is 'the truth'. It is only the tip of the iceberg. We can conceptualise and hypothesise but we do not know.

(3) Recall is like a search engine. It is another fact that recall is only as effective as the cue given. Researchers use different accessing cues and therefore stimulate different parts of the brand associative network to come to mind. Therefore there is no right and wrong way to access brand memories. The capacity for brand recognition is infinitely greater than that for brand recall.

(4) We do not think in language. We think in 'mentalese' (a combination of sensory and symbolic codes). Language allows us to express our thoughts about brand meanings. Language is limited and words are laden with subjective meanings. That is why we find it so difficult to agree the definition of a brand positioning, brand essence, and brand personality profile or brand attributes.

(5) Research activates brand associations that may not be dominant or active in 'real life'. Associations can be induced. Sometimes the way in which people in qualitative research talk about brands and their relationship with them bears no relationship to measures of behaviour in real life.

In crowded and fast-changing global market-places, brand leaders and challenger brands must innovate continually in order to increase profitability. They must also differentiate or die. This means serious thinking for those of us professionally involved with brands and the way in which we create, reinforce, maintain and revitalise them.

Most importantly we need to remember that *brands only exist in the minds of others*. The brand in my mind is not the same as the one in yours.

There is much in this book to help you if you are involved with the way in which a brand gives cues to its customers – through its communications, its environments, its people and its products or services.

If you want a five-minute read about brands this is not the book for you! But if you are curious about brands and are prepared to think about what you know as well as explore what you do not know, this book will become a well-thumbed addition to your brand library.

Wendy Gordon
The Fourth Room

Acknowledgement

When writing this book we consulted numerous experts, some of whom provided us with information on specific subjects. Others offered their comments during the various stages through which the final text developed.

Needless to say, we are the only ones responsible for what has been printed. However, without the willing cooperation of those mentioned below, it would have been very difficult to bring our mission to proper completion.

We hereby wish to thank Reint-Jan Schuring (BrandmarC), Astrid de Jong and Reg van Steen (Centrum voor Marketing Analyses), Jos Ahlers (Consult/Y&R), Marjorie Dijkstal, Margriet van Eck Poppe, Goos Geursen, Gijs ten Kate, Andy Mosmans, Hans Ophof and Clary Veenstra (FHV/BBDO), Pim Asselbergs and Gé Derksen (IPM [Institute for Psychological Market Research]), Bert de Vries (Instituut voor Strategische Kommunicatie), Jan Bouts (Lowe Kuiper & Schouten/Nederlands Instituut voor de Publieke Opinie), Willem Brethouwer and Adriaan Lamme (MarketResponse), Frits Spangenberg (Motivaction), Rene Brounts (Ogilvy & Mather), Dr Dirk Sikkel (Tilburg University), Terry Häcker (Research International), Ron Walvisch (Saatchi & Saatchi), Erik Wünsch (Schaeffer Wünsch Has), Anjo Schreuder (Schreuder, Petrescu en Vunderink), Tijs Timmerman (SWOCC [Foundation for Scientific Research of Commercial Communication]), Dr Nico Frijda, Dr Jaap Murre and Dr Jeroen Raaijmakers (University of Amsterdam), Fred Bronner (Veldkamp/Marktonderzoek) and Richard Wolking (Wolking Research Strategy BV).

We would also like to thank Ruth Rose for her role in the translation of this book from the Dutch original.

Introduction

Just as the title suggests, this book is about brands. It starts with an introduction to neuropsychology and ends with a description of image research. In the intermediate chapters we attempt to convince you of the importance of emotions, the relativity of language, the fixedness of established brain positions and the inadequateness of analyses in the field of brand research. We do not define brands at any point in the book because there are many outlooks on brands, and definitions get formulated within all of these outlooks. We feel that a discussion on which is the right definition would only result in a veritable tower of Babel. For those enthusiasts who are curious as to the vision from which we have written this book, we would like to mention several elements that we consider belong in a good definition:

(1)   A brand exists only in the memory of people.
(2)   A brand is a sign of recognition (labels, names, logos, colours).
(3)   A brand evokes associations in people.
(4)   A brand is linked to commercially saleable goods or services.

Although brands have been an important phenomenon in our society for more than one hundred years, scholarly knowledge on the subject has been extremely limited until recently. On the one hand this is due to the status quo within the field of psychology, in which no consensus has been reached over many subjects. On the other hand, it has to do with the limited role that brands are granted in the study of consumer behaviour and in marketing. Even at the beginning of the twenty-first century, it remains true that the nature and functions of brands in the main standard works in the field of marketing hardly get any attention. In the familiar rows of marketing-mix variables (known as the 4, 5 or even more Ps), brands do not even appear. Thus marketing science implicitly considers brands as nothing more than identification means for the products and services of specific suppliers. Manufacturers of important brand name articles know better, though. To quote Polet, chairman of Van den Bergh Nederland, at the Unilever marketing day in 1993: 'Within Van den Bergh Nederland we sell brands, not products'.

Similarly, Vigeveno has written in the Unilever Policy Document: 'Unilever is in the business of marketing brands, not products'.

Most books on brands are written from a business economics perspective and deal mainly with brand management. We have chosen to write a book from a psychological perspective, in which we use mainly the hard neurological side of psychology in order to explain how brands are stored in people's memories. We have deliberately not made practical translations of the many facets of brand strategy. Practical translations are often personal and would obfuscate the fundamental character of this book. We only 'sin' in Part Three, when we give our vision of the ideal brand research.

In Part One we take you to the caverns of the brain. A growing insight into the biological foundations of mental brain functions gradually provides a framework for the study of perception, consciousness, learning, memory and recollections. We define learning as the processes through which we acquire new knowledge. Memory is a function of the brain with which we preserve that knowledge through time. Memory contains the processes with which that knowledge re-enters our consciousness. These processes have a central function for the understanding of our 'self' and the phenomena taking place in the world outside our own bodies. Part One also describes the associative network – a concept that advertisers and marketers have unconsciously borrowed from neuropsychology in order to describe a brand.

Part Two describes the brand-related information that is stored in people's memories. We have subdivided this profuse collection of information into what we consider to be seven logical groups. These seven groups will be discussed extensively, each in its own chapter. Needless to say, the idea is not for you to consider a brand as a sum of these seven components – a brand is much more than that. For this reason, when researching brands it is not good to measure the separate components of a brand and to add up scores. We have chosen to give the name of brand representation to the seven components together. This is somewhat different from a brand and also different from a brand image, as this part's closing chapter will prove. In the same chapter we give an overview of the large influence brands have in people's buying behaviour and the relatively considerable stability of long-existing larger brands.

Part Three is fully devoted to the way in which we can research brand representations. It gives an overview of the techniques applied in the world of market research. In this part we also present our vision of the ideal research on brand representation. This description will clearly show which phases of research in current practice are sometimes off the target and how this can be prevented. In short, we will point out the danger of the double-jeopardy effect in research results, the importance of base measurements, and the absolute need to expose the mutual connections between different variables and to link research results to brand use.

When writing this book we strove for completeness. We wanted to write a good, basic book on brands in the memory of consumers. This completeness has resulted in a book that can be read in several ways: from cover to cover, per part, even per chapter. The book also contains a large number of boxes with quotes from specialists in various fields. These boxes can be skipped or lightly skimmed over during reading. We ourselves have had much pleasure in the literature this book is based on and have enjoyed passing the most striking parts, as asides, on to you. With this book we hope to have contributed to the further deepening of the theoretical knowledge on brands and to have produced a practical guide for brand research as well.

Giep Franzen
Margot Bouwman

Part One
The Brain and Memory

'Life is all memory except for the one present moment that goes by so quick that you hardly catch it going.'

(Tennessee Williams, 1964)

Chapter 1

The Brain

1.1 The brain

The human brain is an object of around 1300 cc in size that weighs about 1450 g; it looks like a wrinkled walnut, feels like a fatty soft substance and has the colour of porridge. It does not have a shell to keep its various parts in place. It is a heavy mass of tissue with cavities, pleats and cracks. It consists of a large number of different interconnected structures that work together, each performing a specific function. MacLean (1973) characterises our brain as a triune, thus alluding to its structure and origins. Our brain can be seen as a fabric of three systems which represent our evolutionary phases: from reptile to mammal to human (Figure 1.1). These systems have different ages, strive

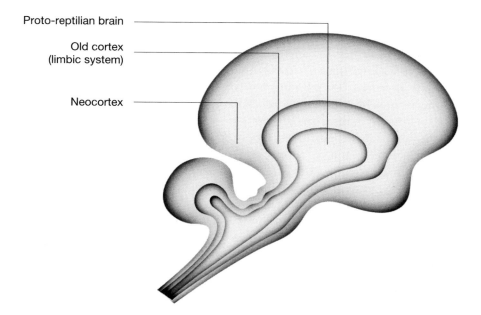

Proto-reptilian brain

Old cortex
(limbic system)

Neocortex

Figure 1.1 MacLean's schematic representation of the three parts of the brain that developed during evolution.

towards different interests, obey different laws and do not work well together. Globally summarised, we can link them to the features of instinct, emotions and reason (Vroon, 1991).

The innermost and oldest of the three brain parts (500 million years), the *proto-reptilian brain*, consists of the brainstem and the spinal cord. This part controls primary physiological needs such as drinking, eating, sleeping, waking, blood pressure, body temperature, bowel movements and regulation of muscle tone. It is assumed that the brain is geared towards achieving and maintaining an ideal balance situation within which processes take their course automatically in total regularity and order. When a disturbance occurs or there is an excess or shortage somewhere, the brain emits impulses to repair this balance. For instance, we become hungry or thirsty and we experience it.

The brainstem is believed to be the seat of our instinctive reactions. What instincts are exactly and how they materialise physiologically is still unclear. They are at any rate mechanical behavioural programmes that do not change with learning; our will has little or no grip on the compelling impulses that arise from them (Vroon, 1991). Within this context we can mention the tendency to play, the urge towards sexual experiences and towards activity or passivity. Instincts are psychic forces. Their connection within physicality is less clear than that of physiological needs. There is no unanimity among researchers on what instincts are and which instincts can be distinguished, but they do agree on the fact that they are innate. As we will see later, some researchers even claim that we are equipped with a language instinct. Instincts are mysterious. They cannot be reduced to elementary physiological needs. The tendency to avoid isolation and the urge to be with others and to conform to their behaviour is sometimes called the 'herd instinct'.

The second large part of the brain – brought about by evolution when mammals appeared 200 million years ago – is the *old cortex*. This old cortex contains what is known as the forehead brain and the limbic system (MacLean, 1973). This part houses mainly emotions, feelings and expressive reactions that are important to our preservation of life, such as happiness, anger, fear, sorrow, excitement and boredom. We share this middle part of our brain with other mammals (Vroon, 1991). This old cortex, also called paleocortex, is responsible for, among other things, deep-seated motivations such as women's need to nurture and men's need to protect and organise as well as fight and dominate. The limbic system is very sensitive to images and analogue communication. Images summon emotions in this system, and these emotions lead to behavioural tendencies. Analogue communication is related to the perception of postures, facial expressions, smells and sounds.

Finally, the third and largest part of the brain is the *neocortex* or cerebral cortex. This outer casing of the brain originated about 50,000 years ago. We can compare the evolution of the neocortex in computer terms with a continuous expansion of a central processing unit to which a memory with increasing capacity is added (MacLean, 1973). The neocortex is a layer about 1.5 to 3 mm thick with the dimensions of a dishcloth (40 × 40 cm), folded in such a way that it fits into our skull; this explains all the creases and pleats which are so characteristic of the surface of the human brain. It contains approximately 20% of all our brain cells. The brain cortex resembles a patchwork quilt made from many parts, and is the centre of higher brain functions like speaking and understanding language, thinking, reading, writing, mathematics, analysis, music, ethics, morals and all other specifically human capacities. It fulfils important functions in the materialisation of our behaviour and in the integration of various cerebral processes. The neocortex contains several areas that are specialised in performing certain specific functions, like processing visual information, awareness of touch, directing muscular movements and understanding language. Our sensory perceptions are integrated and interpreted there. However, large parts of the cerebral cortex do not have a clearly defined task: these are the association areas in which information is evaluated, selected and stored (McEwan and Schmeck, 1994).

Although it would be useful to distinguish the three large parts of the brain from each other, in reality they constantly function in a closely connected way. During evolution they blended into a new whole. Even though it may seem that we go through life calculating, reflecting and weighing things up, in reality we are considerably ruled by our emotions, which originate predominantly in our old cortex.

1.1.1 *Left and right brain half*

It is now accepted that a differentiation can be made between a left and a right brain half or cerebral hemisphere. Each brain half consists of four lobes, and each lobe houses various functions. The centres of vision are localised in the occipital lobe at the back of the brain. Below, the temporal lobe houses the functions for processing sound and understanding language. The parietal lobe, the upper part of the cerebral cortex, contains the centres for movement, orientation, calculation and certain forms of recognition. Finally, the frontal lobe accommodates the most integrated cerebral functions: self-consciousness, observation, the formation of ideas and the making of plans. The experiencing of emotions also takes place here (Gazzaniga, 1998).

These lobes are found in both brain halves. The temporal lobe is larger and more developed in the left brain half than in the right half (Kalat, 1995). This explains why language processing takes place in most people's left brain half.

The left brain half is logical, exact and geared towards detail. This half is constantly trying to analyse the meaning of perceptions, but cannot do this without the help of the right brain half. The right half has an eye for the whole and for coherence, while the left half wants precisely to untangle complicated patterns. The right brain half is dreamier and more focused on sensory

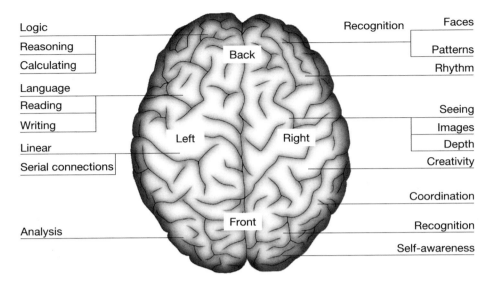

Logic

Reasoning

Calculating

Language

Reading

Writing

Linear

Serial connections

Analysis

Back

Left

Right

Front

Recognition   Faces

Patterns

Rhythm

Seeing

Images

Depth

Creativity

Coordination

Recognition

Self-awareness

Figure 1.2   Specialisations of the left and right brain halves.

perceptions than on abstract notions. It is more involved than the left half in processing emotional stimuli and in activities which involve relationships with others (Gazzaniga, 1998) (Figure 1.2).

The two halves are connected to each other through a thick fibre cable, the *corpus callosum*. This cable acts as a bridge between both halves and constantly sends information back and forth. Incoming information units are split up and sent in parallel to the left and right halves. Each brain half functions autonomously to a large degree, but the two halves also work closely together and combine their data (McEwan and Schmeck, 1994; Kalat, 1995). What is more, some functions – such as visual processes, touch sensations and motor control – are distributed over both brain halves.

Both brain halves are needed for the interpretation of a brand and the messages that a brand sends out. Roughly speaking, we can say that our left brain half processes the knowledge elements of a brand (how the brand name is written, which articles are sold under that brand name), and the right half processes the visual and emotional elements (how does it look, and do I like it?). In fact, neither brain half can perform these functions without the help of the other (Figure 1.3).

The locations of language functions (Pinker, 1994)

(...) Using tools that are getting more sophisticated each month, neurobiologists are charting vast territories that once bore the unhelpful label 'association cortex' in the old textbooks, and are delineating dozens of new regions with their own functions or styles of processing, like visual areas specialising in object shape, spatial layout, colour, 3D stereo-vision, simple motion, and complex motion. For all we know, the brain might have regions dedicated to processes as specific as noun phrases and metrical trees; our methods for studying the human brain are still so crude that we would be unable to find them. Perhaps the regions look like little polka dots or blobs or stripes scattered around the general language areas of the brain. They might be irregularly shaped squiggles, like gerrymandered political districts (...). There is already some evidence that the *linguistic brain* might be organised in this tortuous way. The neurosurgeon George Ojemann, following up on Penfield's methods, electrically stimulated different sites in conscious, exposed brains. He found that stimulating within a site no more than a few millimetres across could disrupt a single function, like repeating or completing a sentence, naming an object, or reading a word. But these dots were scattered all over the brain.

(...) A word is a bundle of different kinds of information. Perhaps each word is like a hub that can be positioned anywhere in a large region, as long as its spokes extend to the parts of the brain storing its sound, its syntax, its logic, and the appearance of the things it stands for (...). There are many computational waystations between the stimulus and the response. For example, naming an object involves recognising it, looking up its entry in the mental dictionary, accessing its pronunciation, articulating it, and perhaps also monitoring the output for errors by listening to it. A naming problem could arise if any of these processes tripped up.

1.1.2 *Brain modules*

The increased awareness that each brain half has a specialisation has led to a growing understanding of the modular structure of the brain as a whole. The brain consists of a fabric of various structures, each of which performs specialised functions. Within that modular system, the left brain half largely dominates important cognitive skills such as interpreting situations and working out solutions. It develops schemata (which we will discuss in section 5.7),

Outer side of the left brain half

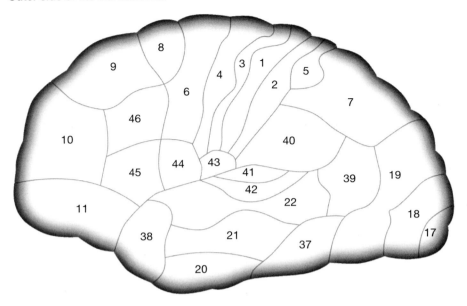

Cross section

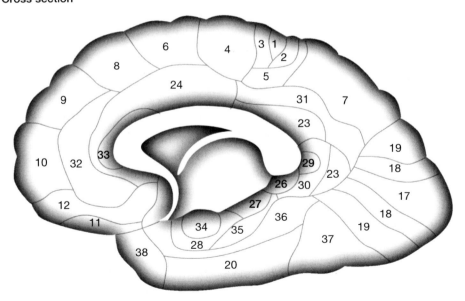

Figure 1.3 Brodmann's chart of the most important brain areas, put together on the basis of the characteristic cellular structure of the brain. It is an anatomical classification that does not actually correspond with the localisation of brain functions.

which it then consults in order to interpret incoming stimuli. The left brain half works progressively: it processes information step by step. The right brain half works more in parallel, perceiving a large number of non-verbal elements as a unit. This specialisation enables us to process two streams of information simultaneously and integrate them into one total impression.

Brand representations consist of connections between many different sorts of neurons which are situated in various brain areas and which perform different functions.

1.2 Neurons

Our brain contains approximately 40 billion (10 to the 11th power) brain cells, called neurons. Each neuron receives signals from other neurons and in turn sends signals to other neurons. A neuron consists of a cell body (the soma), with one fibre for sending (the axon), and several fibres for receiving incoming signals (the dendrite tree). These fibres are equipped with synapses (synapse comes from the Greek, meaning 'binding together'), a sort of terminal along which the connections with the embranchments of other neurons pass by. The axon also ends in ramifications which make contact via its synapses with the reception terminals of other neurons.

There are many sorts of neurons. No other type of cell has as many variations. Some neurons are small and simple, others look like large trees, yet others look like tightly closed bushes (Figure 1.4).

Nevertheless, every neuron has the same basic structure, whichever part of the brain it may be located in. Most neurons have between 500 and 6000 synapses, but there are also neurons with as many as 150,000 synapses (Kandel, Schwarz and Jessel, 1991). The average neuron of a two-year-old child has about 15,000 synapses. Our brain probably has a total of 10^{14} synapses. One single neuron can make direct or indirect contact with 50,000 others in order to send and receive messages. If we counted them at one synapse per second, we would only be finished in about 32 million years. An amount of brain as big as a matchhead already contains a billion connections. When we look at how these connections between individual neurons can be combined, the number of possibilities becomes hyper-astronomical – in the order of 10 followed by millions of zeros (Edelman, 1993). The totality of direct and indirect connections is far beyond our imaginative powers. This inconceivable number of brain cells, each with thousands of contact points, yields an unprecedented storage and processing capacity. If printed, the total amount of information stored in our brain could very well fill 20 million thick books (Holler, 1993).

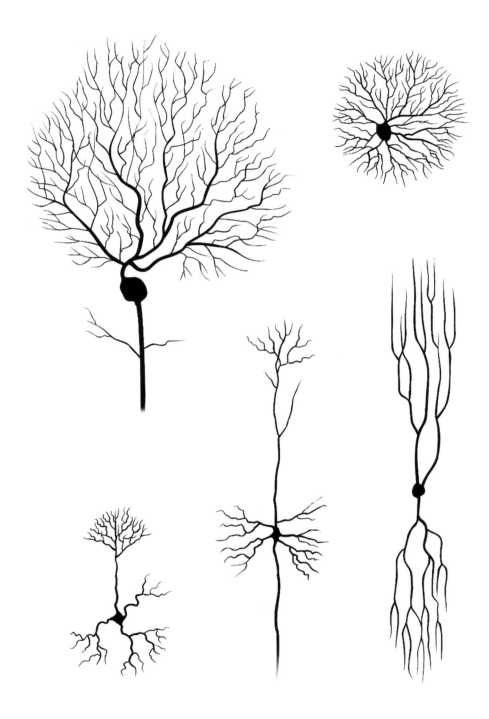

Figure 1.4 Types of neurons.

Neurons are not connected directly to one another – they are separated by the synapse. This is a crack of 10 to 50 nm (a nanometre (nm) is one billionth of a metre) that takes a central place in the transfer of information between neurons. When a neuron becomes active it sends an electrical impulse (50–500 Hz) called an action potential from the cell body, via the axon to the end of the neuron: the synapse. The action potential gives a change of 0.1 V in relation to the electrical charge in the state of rest of the axon and lasts about a thousandth of a second. If such an action potential is given off, the neuron is said to 'fire'. When the electrical impulse arrives at a synapse from the cell body, it causes the release of chemical substances – the neurotransmitter molecules – which are then allowed into the dendrite membrane of the following neuron (the postsynaptic membrane). Most neurons receive input via thousands of synapses and integrate them into one simple form of output: a new action potential. The cooperation of a stimulated neuron with many other neurons – which also have many neighbouring synapses, whether they do or do not release their own neurotransmitters – determines whether the following nerve cell will fire. The process is thus electrical–chemical–electrical (Figure 1.5).

Action potentials are all-or-nothing phenomena. The action potential is either there or it is not, and is always equally strong and lasts as long. No information can be passed on inside a neuron in the form of variation of the action potential. Action potentials cannot leap over from neuron to neuron either. The only function of the action potential is freeing the neurotransmitters – which are the real messengers in our brain – at the end of the axon (Schellekens, 1993). However, the electrical properties of neurons are as varied as their structure. Some neurons fire in a high, stable frequency, others fire quickly in the beginning and then slow down, and others fire in jolts. Each type of neuron has its own firing characteristics, but the faster a neuron fires signals, the greater the chance that it will activate its neighbouring cell.

It is estimated that between one hundred thousand and one million different chemical reactions take place for every minute of basic brain activity. These reactions use quite an amount of energy: while our brain constitutes 3% of our body weight, it is responsible for 30% of our total energy use in a body at rest. Synapses can be powerful or weak (a synapse is considered to be strong when it allows the neurotransmitters of the preceding neuron to enter more quickly). They have different 'firing dispositions'. The power of the synapse will determine whether and how easily an impulse crosses over to the next nerve cell. Generally speaking, a neuron sends only two types of message: stimuli (excitation), inciting the following cell towards activity, and restraint (inhibition), stopping or blocking the following cell's activity. If the totality of stimulus and restraint that a neuron receives via all of its dendrites exceeds a threshold value, it becomes active and either fires to other cells or curbs them. It thus follows that one synapse does not determine whether a neuron fires or

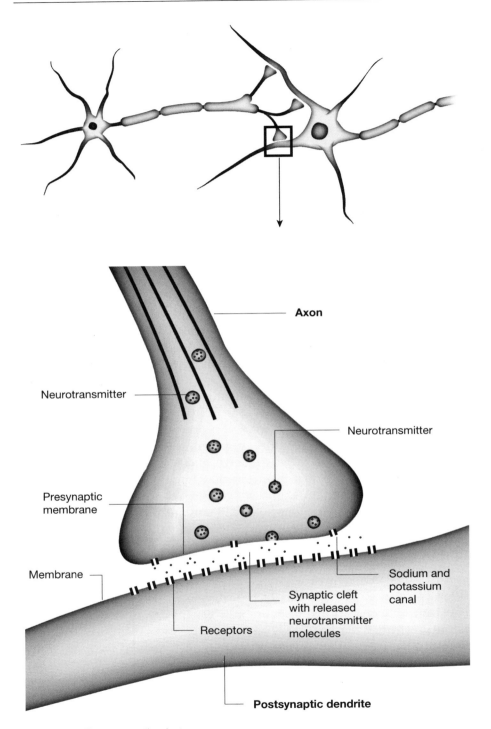

Figure 1.5   The connection between neurons.

Firedance (Carter, 1998)

How does the conglomeration of neuronal clumps and cat's cradle wiring actually do what brains do?

Essentially the neurons get fired up, joined up and dancing – on a huge scale.

The firing of a single neuron is not enough to create the twitch of an eyelid in sleep, let alone a conscious impression. It is when one neuron excites its neighbours, and they in turn fire up others, that patterns of activity arise that are complex and integrated enough to create thoughts, feelings and perceptions.

Millions of neurons must fire in unison to produce the most trifling thought. Even when a brain seems to be at its most idle a scan of it shows a kaleidoscope of constantly changing activity. Sometimes, when a person undertakes a complex mental task or feels an intense emotion the entire cerebrum lights up.

muffles: an integration of the positive and negative signals of all its dendrites takes place in the neuron, after which it either becomes active or does not. The interconnected neurons influence one another in many ways. One single neuron can fire several neurotransmitters that can strengthen or curb each other in many ways. The brain is thought to use about a hundred different neurotransmitters. Already 50 different neurotransmitters are known and new ones are constantly being discovered. Some are specifically geared towards direct communication via the synapse of one cell to the dendrite of the following cell. Others are spread through the brain fluid or the bloodstream and reach their goals that way. A number of transmitters influence different reception stations. No one has yet been able to fully fathom the whole process of sending and receiving (McEwan and Schmeck, 1994).

1.3 Networks

Neurons which are thus interconnected by means of synaptic transferable neurotransmitters form networks. Our memory consists of billions of these networks. 'We sometimes forget how complex our brain is', says Wytse J. Wadman, professor of neurobiology at the University of Amsterdam (Aan de Brugh, 1999), who always explains things to her students on the basis of 'the town'. Wadman illustrates: 'Let's say that I live in a town with 30,000 inhabitants. A phone line runs from my house to all the other houses. The same goes for each of those inhabitants: 29,999 telephone lines depart from

From Mars bar to electric impulse and back (Carter, 1998)

What makes sound sound, vision vision and smell smell? Wave amplitude and molecular structure? Think again. If one person experiences the effect of light waves as music and another tastes chocolate in response to the sound waves made by a spoken name, who is to say that light waves create vision rather than taste or that molecules, rather than sound waves, create smells? All we seem to have by way of authority on the subject is a majority vote.

Nonetheless, in a standard issue, one-sense-at-a-time brain, a particular type of stimulus consistently registers as sound while another is experienced as vision. How come?

The obvious place to look for clues is at our sense organs – eyes, ears, nose, tongue and somatosensory receptors in the skin. Each one is intricately adapted to deal with its own type of stimulus: molecules, waves or vibrations. But the answer does not lie here, because despite their wonderful variety, each organ does essentially the same job: it translates its particular type of stimulus into electrical pulses. A pulse is a pulse is a pulse. It is not the colour red, or the first notes of Beethoven's Fifth – it is a bit of electrical energy. Indeed, rather than discriminating one type of sensory input from another, the sense organs actually make them more alike.

All sensory stimuli, then, enter the brain in more or less undifferentiated form as a stream of electrical pulses created by neurons firing, domino-fashion, along a certain route. This is all that happens. There is no reserve

Contd

each house. That is a considerably complex network already. Of course, you could apply something similar over the whole planet with all its inhabitants. If you take 50 terrestrial globes, you will approximate the complexity of the brain.'

Each neuron participates in thousands of networks. These can involve connections between neurons with short axons in each other's proximity as well as connections over sometimes large distances via long axons. The total length of the axons that form circuits is calculated to be 10 million km (Murre, 1999). These circuits form systems with each other, which in turn form more complicated systems of systems. The brain as a whole is a super-system of systems (Damasio, 1995) (Figure 1.6).

The brain is connected to the outside world through specialised neurons which form the senses. These sensory converters supply the input to the brain, but the largest part of the brain receives input from only other parts of the transformer that at some stage turns this electrical activity back into light waves or molecules. What makes one stream into vision and another into smell depends, rather, on *which* neurons are stimulated.

In normal brains incoming sensory stimuli follow well-worn neural paths from the sensory organ to specific brain destinations. As the stimulus passes through the brain it is split into several different streams which are processed in parallel by different brain modules. Some of these modules are in the cerebral cortex – the wrinkled outer grey skin where sights and sounds are put together and then made conscious. Others are in the limbic system where the stimuli generate the bodily reactions that give them an emotional quality – the thing that turns noise into music and a pattern of lines and contrasts into a thing of beauty.

The cortical area for each sense is made up of a patchwork of smaller regions, each of which deals with a specific facet of sensory perception. The visual cortex, for example, has separate areas for colour, movements, shape and so on. Once the incoming information has been assembled in these areas it is shunted forward to the large cortical regions known as association areas. Here the sensory perceptions are married with appropriate cognitive associations – the perception of a knife, for example, is joined with the concepts of stabbing, eating, slicing and so on. It is only at this stage that the incoming information becomes a fully fledged, meaningful perception. What we now have in mind was triggered by stimuli from the outside world, but it is not a faithful reflection of that world – rather it is a unique construction.

brain, and in turn gives output to other parts without interference from the outside world. One could say that the brain is more in contact with itself than with anything else outside of it (Edelman, 1993).

The total system is in constant development. It continuously takes new forms. Neurons form new embranchments in their dendrites, and the strengths of new synapses and existing connections between neurons change. Within this context we speak of a plasticity or changeability of our brain. But the brain does not only create and select networks: it also rejects them. Only those connections which are reinforced by experiences retain their place (Suzuki, 1996).

The various types of neurons that are part of a brand representation form neural networks.

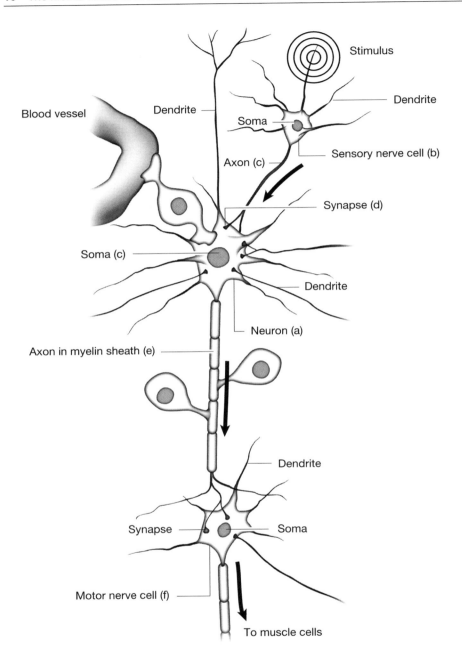

The central neuron (a) receives an impulse from the sensory nerve cell in the form of a sense (b). The axon of this cell (c) is connected to the central cell with a synapse (d). In turn, this synapse gives an impulse via an axon (e) to the motor neuron (f).

Figure 1.6   A neural circuit.

1.4   The origin of connections

Hebb (1949) contended that memory consists of synaptic connections which are the result of sensory perceptions of two phenomena in direct proximity to each other in time and space. 'Neurons that fire together, wire together.' The frequent repetition of the same perception results in the strengthening of the synaptic connection between the neurons. The firing threshold of the receiving neuron is thereby lowered, causing it to be activated earlier. He says that each new occurrence of the same phenomenon in consciousness, in the form of an activated memory or identical repetition of the same sensory perception, strengthens the unique capacity of the connection. When this takes place, neurons which were momentarily active towards one another ultimately form a stable, functional relationship. The number of dendrites connecting the neurons constantly increases (Hebb, 1949).

Each connection from cell to cell can be strong or weak, or assume any strength in between. The individual configuration of the connections, each with its own strong or weak characteristics, determines how a person reacts to sensory stimuli and to ideas stored in the system itself. The more frequently specific connections between neurons are activated, the stronger and more efficient they become. The term potentiation refers to the phenomenon in which the next time a neuron ensemble is stimulated, the response will become stronger than would be the case had it previously been stimulated less often. Connections which are no longer activated become gradually weaker. Repeated synchronous firing binds neurons together, so that the least or minimal activity in one cell will also activate all other cells connected to it. Repetition is essential to the development, strengthening and maintenance of the connections.

Neural brand networks consist of connections of varying strength. The more frequently specific connections are activated, the stronger they become. Connections which are not activated become gradually weaker.

The neuroscientist Stephen Rose (1992) gave a physiological substantiation of Hebb's theory. He devoted his whole life to the laboratory research of chicks in order to determine what exactly takes place in their brains when they make a memory. On the basis of that research we now know that the properties of certain specific brain cells change when an animal has a new experience which makes it necessary to adjust its behaviour in order to achieve a goal. These changes can consist of the growth of new embranchments in dendrites, an increase in the number of synapses or a change in the electrical properties of the cells. According to Rose, changes in the brain cells of chicks can be morphologically determined, for instance with an electron microscope, in terms of lasting changes in the structure of neurons and their mutual synaptic

Sensory perceptions lead to physical structures (Nash, 1997)

Of all the discoveries that have poured out of neuroscience labs in recent years, the finding that the electrical activity of brain cells changes the physical structure of the brain is perhaps the most breathtaking. For the rhythmic firing of neurons is no longer assumed to be a by-product of building the brain but essential to the process, and it begins, scientists have established, well before birth. A brain is not a computer. Nature does not cobble it together, then turn it on. No, the brain begins working long before it is finished. And the same processes that wire the brain before birth, neuroscientists are finding, also drive the explosion of learning that occurs immediately afterwards.

At birth a baby's brain contains 100 billion neurons, roughly as many nerve cells as there are stars in the Milky Way. Also in place are a trillion glia cells, named after the Greek word for glue, which form a kind of honeycomb that protects and nourishes the neurons. But while the brain contains virtually all the nerve cells it will ever have, the pattern of wiring between them has yet to stabilise. Up to this point, says Shatz, 'What the brain has done is lay out circuits that are its best guess about what's required for vision, for language, for whatever.' And now it is up to neural activity – no longer spontaneous, but driven by a flood of sensory experiences – to take this rough blueprint and progressively refine it.

connections. They can also be measured dynamically during the process of learning and recalling (activation), in terms of temporary local changes in the bloodstream and in the oxygen use of neurons. Finally, they can be measured biochemically and physiologically, for instance in terms of changed electrical properties of neurons.

Our memory is thus built not only by the formation of new synapses, but more particularly by changes in the efficiency of existing networks, via the long-term potentiation process described above. It is assumed that the formation of new synapses is necessary for the storage of new information in long-term memory, and that long-term potentiation is not only responsible for the connections in long-term memory but also attends to short-term storage.

Hebb's view is thus endorsed by Rose. It still forms the basis of current thinking about memory. At the same time, Rose left many questions unanswered. For instance: how many neurons and synapses are involved in a memory? Could we claim that one association equals one synapse? How is a memory delimited? But this is only half the story. Hebb's theory only indicates how learning takes place physiologically. However, memory is not only a question of learning, it is also a question of recalling, of retrieving stored information from long-term memory and bringing it back to consciousness. What neurobiologists do not even remotely comprehend is how the physiological and biochemical processes of this 'recalling' take place.

1.4.1 *The engram*

Despite the fact that modern research techniques have allowed us to gain a greater understanding of the location of processes in the brain, we have not yet managed to expose the neural basis of a specific memory in humans. This is called the engram: it is the permanent change in the brain resulting from a learning process. Many researchers equate this quest to the search for the philosopher's stone. Research such as a 30-year series of studies by psychologist Karl S. Lashley (1950) on the engram as a physical phenomenon produced nothing. His humorous conclusion at the end of this odyssey was that this series of experiments has yielded a great deal of information over what and where memory is not. Nothing specific has been discovered on the real nature of the engram. Whenever he reviews the evidence on the localisation of memory, he sometimes thinks that the inescapable conclusion is that learning is just not possible (Lashley, 1950).

The representation of a brand at a neuronal level is called a brand engram.

Chapter 2

The Cognitive and Emotional Brains

2.1 Interconnectedness

Our perceptions and memories are constantly linked to emotional reactions. Thoughts are never free from emotions and emotions are never free from thoughts. We could say there are two brains: a cognitive brain that knows, analyses, reflects, calculates, considers and takes decisions, and an emotional brain that reacts spontaneously, immediately and intuitively to perceived stimuli. Reactions to stimuli are always a combination of the two even when it comes to inner stimuli which are activated by the brain itself in the form of a continuous flow of successive thoughts. Emotions are essentially impulses towards behaviour ('movere' = Latin for move, 'e' = away, emotion thus literally being a 'movement away').

Cognitive and affective processes take place in various parts of the brain which in fact work closely together to lead us through life. Emotions feed the thought process and the cognitive brain evaluates and refines the output of emotions (Goleman, 1995). We could speak more of a bicolour single-lane road than of a two-lane road here (Figure 2.1).

2.1.1 *The thalamus: gateway*

Everything we see, hear, taste and touch comes from the senses into the brain through the thalamus. This is a structure located at the top of the brainstem. The thalamus is the gateway of all sensory information which is redirected from there to the appropriate parts of the brain for further processing. It is a sort of valve that controls the flow of sensory information (with the exception of that from the olfactory senses) through the brain. A large amount of that information ends up in the frontal lobe, the 'intelligent' part of the brain, where we make plans and take decisions (Carter, 1998). The thalamus is also involved in the awareness of certain stimuli to which the association cortex attaches a more precise meaning. The bottom of the thalamus is fused with the hypothalamus. This is a small organ that regulates important bodily functions

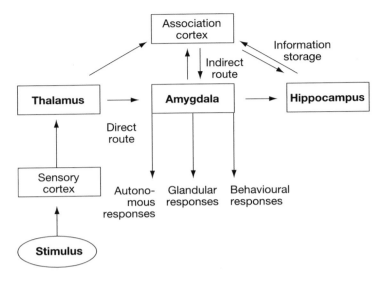

Figure 2.1   The route from stimulus to response.

such as changes in our heartbeat and breath, body temperature and water balance (sweat), which are coupled with severe emotional reactions. The thalamus is located close to the limbic system and has a direct link with one of its important elements: the almond nucleus or amygdala (Figure 2.2).

2.2   The limbic system: centre of emotions

The part of our brain that is responsible for our emotional reactions is the limbic system. The term limbic system was introduced by MacLean (1954). He linked it to the theory of evolution as the transition from the reptile brain to the mammal brain. All sensory stimuli that enter the brain via the thalamus pass one or several structures of the limbic system on their way to the brain cortex. As was briefly discussed in the first chapter, the limbic system forms the middle part of our brain, something we share with other mammals and which is responsible for instincts such as caring and playing. In a certain sense it is the power station of our brain – the place where the desires, motivations, emotions and moods that steer our behaviour are awakened. It is localised in the old cortex, which surrounds the brainstem (the word limbic stems from the Latin 'limbus', meaning 'ring'). It interacts constantly with that part of the brainstem in which our knowledge is stored and our thought processes take place: the association cortex. The limbic system is a very complicated body of interconnected structures that are responsible for our emotional reactions and also play an important role in the selection of stimuli for our attention and in

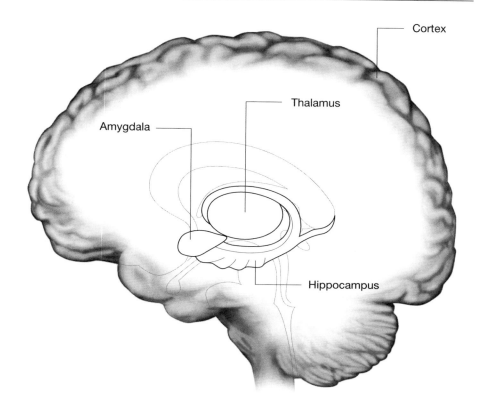

Figure 2.2 The cortex and the limbic system.

the formation of long-term memory. One of these structures, the almond-shaped amygdala (Greek for almond), seems to be especially linked to our emotional reactions. It is a small, insignificant-looking structure located deep in the innermost areas of our brain.

The assumption that only one system in our brain is responsible for our emotional reactions has now been abandoned (Bear, Connors and Paradiso, 1996). We know that the limbic system works closely with the neocortex, which evaluates and interprets stimuli and helps regulate emotions. The term limbic system remains in use, though, as a coordinating indication for the totality of elements that play a leading role in the experience and expression of emotions. Although by now a lot is known about the anatomy of the limbic system and the neural connections with other parts of the brain and the nervous system, much remains unclear with respect to the function of the system in the materialisation of specific emotions. This is an area of much scientific speculation.

2.2.1 *Amygdala: the sentinel*

Just as the thalamus can be seen as the gateway to all sensory information, we could characterise the amygdala as a permanent sentinel that carefully analyses every incoming signal and evaluates its emotional meaning. Incoming information that goes from the senses via the thalamus to the association cortex is converted into perceptions and interpreted there. It then moves on to the amygdala, which evaluates these perceptions and reacts to them with an emotion. There is, thus, traffic in two directions, going back and forth between the limbic system and the association cortex (see Figures 2.1–2.3). Any

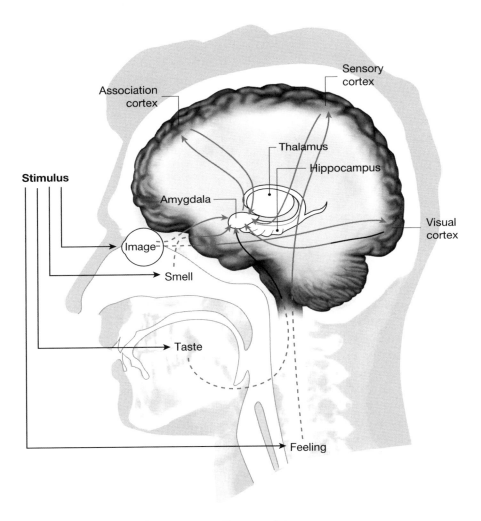

Figure 2.3 Connections from senses to the amygdala.

information processed by the 'conscious' brain is sent from the cortex to the limbic system to be evaluated emotionally. That reaction goes back to the cortex, where it is processed into a complex reaction.

LeDoux (1996) is convinced that some of the sensory perceptions go directly from the thalamus to the amygdala via a thick strand of nerve tissue, around the association cortex. This would enable the amygdala to react to perceptions directly, without intervention by the thinking brain. LeDoux received approval from various scientists. However, another group of scientists disagrees emphatically with the reasoning of LeDoux. They claim that interpretation (appraisal) is necessary for the conscious and unconscious experiencing of an emotion, and that this interpretation implies cognitive processing. For example, an object must first be interpreted as dangerous before the emotion of fear appears (Frijda, 1986; Lazarus,1991; Scherer, 1993; Frijda, 1998).

It is precisely on the issue of how the emotional brain exactly interacts with the cognitive brain that experts still remain in disagreement. Are stimuli always attached a meaning first, which is then evaluated (appraisal, in Frijda's terminology) on the basis of our interests, only after which we react with an emotion? Or is a direct emotional reaction possible without intervention of the cognitive brain? LeDoux (1993) thinks that incoming signals can follow two routes. He says that the direct link of the thalamus with the amygdala enables the amygdala to react first, even before the stimuli are analysed and interpreted by the neocortex. The signals that follow this route would contain the most elementary and potent visual images and sounds, to which the amygdala reacts as an alarm system. We would hereby be reacting on a first-impression basis to the most characteristic aspects of a stimulus, without weighing out the details against each other yet. This happens so fast that it occurs outside our consciousness and the control of our free will. We are overtaken by our emotions before we are fully aware of what is happening to us.

Ekman (1989) established, by registering changes of facial muscles, that such a primary emotional reaction takes place in a few thousandths of a second, and that the heartbeat and the blood circulation also react within fractions of a second. The emotional brain, which reacts immediately to sensory input, is also much faster than the rational brain. It precludes the deliberate analytical reflection that characterises the rational brain. As expressed by LeDoux (1993), 'You do not have to know exactly what it is in order to know it can be dangerous'. According to Ekman, the full heat of such a primary emotional reaction is very short, seconds rather than minutes. The limbic system is in many ways superior to the neocortex. It is actually faster – it reacts in thousandths of a second to a signal from the outside. This speed is accompanied by a large degree of certainty. Whereas the rational brain often needs a lot of time to arrive at a decision on the most sensible reaction to a situation, the emotional spirit reacts as an accurate machine. Even when the situation makes it possible to weigh alternatives calmly against each other, emotions can still have the greatest influence on the ultimate behavioural response.

All the information that enters through our various senses passes the amygdala, which takes care of the evaluation of the input of the senses and reacts permanently to it with an emotion. In turn, the amygdala sends signals to the autonomous nervous system, thus provoking reactions in remote places like muscles or the intestinal tract. This is how signals go to, for example, our facial muscles, thereby expressing our emotions, and to our vocal cords, making us speak in a higher voice. LeDoux (1993) argues that this is how the amygdala forms the core of a central network for processing emotional information and for the emergence of emotional memories. It probably also acts as a filter, thus allowing our attention to limit itself to stimuli with emotional relevance. It influences the arousal (degree of activation) and the process of paying attention. The amygdala also has access to more refined and processed information from subsequent processing phases and uses this to evaluate current information in the light of previous emotional experiences (Schacter, 1996). It is also responsible for the development of emotional associations, and steers our physical reactions. The amygdala thus plays a vital role in our mental life.

2.3 Unconscious and conscious emotions

The amygdala is thus involved on a permanent basis in processing information and in its emotional evaluation. We think of emotion as a feeling, but the word is misleading because it indicates only one aspect of emotion: awareness. In fact, emotions are not feelings but survival mechanisms embedded in the brain that help us escape danger or drive us towards things that may be advantageous to us (Carter, 1998). The literature sometimes compares emotions with colours. A reduced number of primary emotions blends in order to produce an infinite number of secondary emotions and shades. Several researchers claim to know which our primary emotions are. Chapter 19 will show that there is not the least concordance on the subject.

Complex emotions are refined reactions that only materialise after being processed in the cortex. Separate perceptions are combined there into one single integrated experience. Once the conscious brain perceives that an emotional reaction is desirable, it sends signals to the amygdala, which in turn drives the body to perform certain changes (Carter, 1998). The heart starts beating faster, our breath becomes irregular, sweat breaks out, in the worst case we scream or hit, and the body sends back the message: 'we have an emotion'. Becoming aware of these somatic reactions reinforces our emotional experience.

We are not aware of most emotional reactions: we cannot 'feel' the emotion. Most of our emotional life takes place in the unconscious. Emotions under the

> **The autonomy of emotions** (Le Doux, J. in: *Mapping the Mind*, Carter, 1998)
>
> Emotions are things that happen to us rather than things we make happen. We try to manipulate our emotions all the time but all we are doing is arranging the outside world so it triggers certain emotions – we cannot control our reactions directly. Anyone who has tried to fake an emotion knows how futile it is. Our conscious control over emotions is weak, and feelings often push out thinking, whereas thinking fights a mainly losing battle to banish emotions. This is because the wiring of the brain favours emotion – the connections from the emotional systems to the cognitive systems are stronger than the connections that run the other way.

consciousness threshold do have a large influence on what we perceive and how we react to it. They are at the bottom of the phenomenon of our selective perception. The emotional reactions that we do become aware of are, as it were, the tip of the iceberg. Frijda (1986) calls them pointers that stick out above the deep, continuous flow of our emotional reactions.

When confronted with brand signals (names, logos, folders, packaging, etc.) the meanings stored in the cortex are activated. The amygdala gets involved from here, reacting to specific emotions. This emotional reaction is always there, but can remain under the consciousness threshold.

2.4 Information storage

An extremely important part of the limbic system is the hippocampus (Greek for sea-horse), which is responsible for our memory storage. The hippocampus is a fairly large elongated structure, which takes up about 3% of the volume of the cortex. The hippocampus is bilateral and appears in both brain halves. It is linked to almost every part of the cortex and information constantly passes back and forth. The hippocampus temporarily stores perceptions and thoughts that have demanded our attention recently. During this time the hippocampus regularly sends the experiences back to the cortex, and with every repetition they are etched deeper into the cortex. Ultimately the memories are so deeply embedded in the cortex that the hippocampus is no longer needed to recall them. This is called long-term potentiation. The process of permanent storage can last as long as two years. Up to then the memory is vulnerable and can be erased very easily. The hippocampus works selectively; if all our perceptions

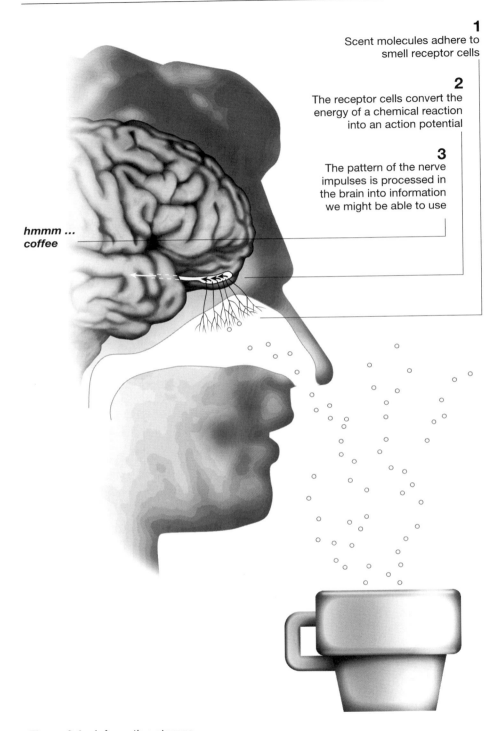

1
Scent molecules adhere to smell receptor cells

2
The receptor cells convert the energy of a chemical reaction into an action potential

3
The pattern of the nerve impulses is processed in the brain into information we might be able to use

hmmm ... coffee

Figure 2.4   Information storage.

were stored in our long-term memory, we would quickly suffer from a memory overload (Figure 2.4).

Physiological research, such as the previously mentioned studies of Rose (1995), indicates that during a few hours after performing a learning task there is an increase in the number of processes such as protein synthesis and mutual activation of a number of neurons. The brain changes as a result of this. New embranchments have been created in dendrites of several neurons in our brain. This is an indication that something has been fixed in our memory. This process lasts six to eight hours in chicks. Rose claims that sensory perceptions that are not moved from short- to long-term memory seem to get lost in chicks within eight hours.

Psychologists and neurobiologists have established that some of the existing networks in our brain show a greater resistance towards forgetting with the lapse of time. They called this consolidation. It can take the form of growth of new synapses, as the research of Rose showed. It can also take place through the strengthening of already existing synapses, which facilitates the crossing over of neurotransmitter molecules from one neuron to another. Nobody knows exactly what happens in the brain when a memory gets consolidated in the long term (Schacter, 1996).

The hippocampus seems to be particularly sensitive to new information. When the hippocampus responds to new stimuli the left frontal lobe is switched on, supplying a profusion of associations and knowledge in order to process the offered stimuli thoroughly. The hippocampus acts here as a sort of temporary depot or intermediate station for the new information, but is not part of long-term memory. The result of a damaged hippocampus is that new information is no longer recorded into long-term memory. The information that was already present before the damage does remain accessible.

The hippocampus seems to be involved in the formation of only knowledge-related memory (the declarative memory, see section 4.2). New information gets stored and organised there temporarily. The electrical signal in the receiving nerve cells of the hippocampus is thought to be strengthened by a repeated bombardment of neurotransmitters – the previously mentioned process of long-term potentiation. Recent research has shown that when the hippocampus is repeatedly stimulated by electrodes, it keeps firing even weeks after the 'bombardment' ends. The increased alertness of the hippocampus after repeated stimulation is believed to be an expression of the enduring changes in the synapses, which form the basis of learning.

Once the hippocampus fixes the new information, it can be transported to the neocortex. Little is known about how the hippocampus actually does this, although there are all kinds of hypotheses about it. One of them says that the hippocampus acts as an information file for the place where the memories are stored in the brain cortex – some kind of card-index box, as it were. Upon damage this function would be lost; the information file stops being refilled, therefore new information cannot be traced back in the memory anymore. Another theory claims that the hippocampus contains a type of abstract or rough draft of the information, from which links could be established with the more detailed information that is stored spread over the brain cortex. Many researchers believe that memory contents are consolidated through the hippocampus when sleeping in a dreaming state, though an exact description of the role the hippocampus plays in memory cannot yet be given. Recent research suggests that some memories can also be stored in the amygdala. LeDoux (1996) in particular thinks that these are unconscious memories of previous episodes which were accompanied by severe emotional reactions. The episodes themselves may be forgotten, but when the same experiences repeat themselves, the same physical effects can manifest without a person being able to place their origins: heart palpitations, wet palms of the hands, etc.

New information related to a brand arrives first at the hippocampus and is organised there. It undergoes consolidation. Other information can be lost.

2.5 Emotional associations

Although embryos have certain perceptions even before birth, the real development of our knowledge only expands following the first sensory perceptions immediately after birth. Each perception is accompanied with an affect or emotion. As our experience increases, the sensory perceptions form increasingly strong links with emotions. Although the amygdala is not seen as a primary location for the storage of memories, it is involved in providing emotional colouring to these memories. This dual coding of experiences is the key to an understanding of the role that emotions play in constructing and organising our intellectual capacities. Every sensory perception is coded (fixed in memory) on the basis of its cognitive properties and emotional qualities. Perceptions are attributed concepts such as large, soft, delicious, strong, etc. and at the same time pleasurable, unpleasant, exciting or calm. Each new confrontation with an identical or similar stimulus contributes to this emotional labelling.

Greenspan (1997) calls the system of associative connections of cues[1] with emotions our 'discrimination meter'. When someone is in a situation in which he is confronted with emotionally charged cues, he will tend to react with behaviour that is accordingly tuned to it. He does not have to think again every time how to react. In most cases he just 'feels' it. The affects he carries with

---

1   A cue is a stimulus that brings about a change in the nervous system. A differentiation can be made between external and internal stimuli. Examples of external stimuli are: a lion, a bang, a kiss, a brand, a smell. Examples of internal stimuli are: memories of situations and experiences.

Emotional associations organise the memory (Greenspan, 1997)

How can a handful of emotions organise so vast a store of information as is housed in the human brain? To fine-tune our selections, we modulate our emotions to register an almost infinite range of subtle variations and combinations of sadness, joy, curiosity, anger, fear, jealousy, anticipation and regret. We possess an extra-ordinarily sensitive 'meter' on which to gauge our reactions, and in a certain sense it almost possesses us. Anyone who pays attention to the subjective state of his body will almost always perceive within it an emotional tone, though it may be elusive or hard to describe. One might feel tense or relaxed, hopeful or fatigued, serene or demoralised. This inner emotional tone constantly reconstitutes itself in the innumerable variations that we use to label and organise and store and retrieve and, most important of all, make sense of our experiences. Our entire bodies are involved. Our emotions are created and brought to life through the expressions and gestures we make with the voluntary muscle systems of our faces, arms, and legs – smiles, frowns, slumps, waves, and so forth. The involuntary muscles of our guts and internal organs also play a role; our hearts might thump or our stomachs register the 'butterfly' sensation of anxiety. Affects such as excitement, delight, and anger are primarily controlled by the voluntary system. Others, including fear, sexual pleasure, longing and grief, are mostly involuntary. Some responses, like the intense fight-or-flight alertness stimulated by adrenaline, affect us more globally and belong to portions of the nervous system formed early in evolution. Those involved in social reciprocity, the ones that signal reactions and that negotiate acceptance, rejection, approval, annoyance, and the like, belong to more recently evolved parts of the nervous system and rely on the highest capacities of the cortex.

him from situation to situation tell him what he must think, say or do. They place a given occurrence or stimulus within the total emotional context of his life. This enables him to understand, distinguish, evaluate and react immediately in a manner relevant to him.

In the middle of this constant bombardment of external stimuli to which we are exposed, or thoughts which our own brain generates, we constantly have to make choices about which ones we will pay attention to and which ones we will ignore. The only way we can do that is by consulting our stored emotional experiences, thereby making the meaning immediately clear. There is a parallel between our senses and our emotional system in the sense that, just as our eyes perceive light and our ears sound, the emotional system perceives, as it were, the emotional meaning of a stimulus.

Brain activity made visible

The knowledge on brain processes has increased in the last few decades thanks to the availability of two new examination techniques, PET and MRI. In *Positron Emission Tomography (PET)*, a test subject is injected with a radioactive glucose that is transported by the blood to the brain. The more active a part of the brain is, the more glucose it uses up. The test subject sits on an adjusted dentist's chair and sensors are put on his head. These sensors register the sources of radioactivity and send the information to a computer, which produces an image. By exposing the test subject to various stimuli, a determination can now be made of which parts of the brain are activated by which stimuli. The PET images have a resolution of 5–10 mm. Therefore, they do not show the activity of individual neurons, but of groups of 10,000 neurons. Because the glucose is radioactive this limits the number of scans that can be made on individual test subjects. *Magnetic Resonance Imaging (MRI)* is a second examination technique that is used to get an insight into brain activity. It is based on measuring blood flows to and the amount of oxygen present in brain areas by using electromagnetic fields. The oxygen consumption of protons (nuclei of atoms) in the brain cells is influenced here by radio signals. The frequency with which this happens is called resonance frequency – that explains the name 'magnetic resonance'. An image of the spreading of oxygen in the brain is constructed with a computer. The amount of oxygen that is linked to the blood gives an image of the neural activity.

It is often assumed that emotional reactions always stem from cognitive evaluations. This certainly happens when we are confronted with situations and stimuli that we are encountering for the first time and for which we still do not possess reference frameworks. However, most of the time we deal with perceptions and experiences that have happened countless times before in our lives, and for which we fall back on the representations that we have formed of them in the course of time. In addition to cognitive information they also contain emotional associations. For this reason, when taking most decisions we do not have to first consider all the possible consequences of the various alternatives. We mostly follow our emotions first (colloquially, gut feeling or intuition) and may submit the results to further rational analysis.

Brands are coded in memory on a cognitive as well as emotional basis. The emotional coding of a brand determines, among other things, whether and to what degree we pay attention to the stimuli related to the brand (as in advertisements).

2.5.1 *Interaction between feelings and mind*

Although the existence of a direct route from the senses via the thalamus to the amygdala is controversial, there is a consensus that most sensory information is communicated first via the thalamus to the association cortex, which analyses it and attaches a meaning to it, and then involves the amygdala for an emotional evaluation. Next, the neocortex and the amygdala together orchestrate hand-in-hand our reactions to the stimuli that we receive, more slowly and deliberately than is the case with the direct route.

In this process, associations of a stimulus with a certain meaning precede our feeling. We are more conscious of our thoughts and a broader evaluation takes place. The rational brain lays logical links between cause and effect.

However, the world we live in is so complex that we almost never make purely rational considerations. Even the most intelligent among us do not manage with reason exclusively. The considerations that we have to make are much too complicated and our information fails. Furthermore, the various goals and values often conflict with each other and compete for priority in the decision-making process. This complexity does not release us from the need to take decisions, though, and our emotions help us out of trouble in all those situations. They act as heuristics. Heuristics are a way of taking decisions when there is no 'logical' solution available. Most decisions that we take in daily life and the standpoints that we take in all sorts of matters are based to a great degree on the application of emotions as heuristics.

In a way, the evaluations of the rational brain are only provisional: we are willing to adjust our evaluation when new information gives us reason to. In contrast, the emotional brain believes that its reactions are true. It sends signals that facilitate decision making by eliminating certain options. We are kept from them by emotional experiences or negative feelings, often without knowing what these are based on. Our emotions also see to it that we are convinced of certain views, regardless of whether they are 'true' or 'untrue'. A lack of emotional reactions can complicate decision-making to a high degree. It is difficult to decide what is true and who we can trust on the basis of logic alone. Some degree of gut feeling is always necessary. The emotional brain is thus just as involved in our decision-making process as the rational brain. They operate in close interaction with one another, intertwining their two ways of knowing in order to lead us through life. Our emotions feed the thought process, and the rational brain refines the input of the emotions. The thinking brain itself is often nothing more than the executing organ of our emotions. Emotions constitute an integrated element of the seemingly most rational decision making. Whenever thinking conflicts with emotions, emotions win.

Cognitive evaluations seldom lead to a balanced judgement over a brand. Emotional associations act as heuristics in the decision-making process. In choice processes they lead to a reduction of a number of alternatives and to an ultimate choice on the basis of gut feeling. A brand emotion is a dominant choice criterion.

2.6 Emotional memories

When a stimulus reminds us of a past emotional experience, the emotional brain reacts to it by activating the same feelings that accompanied the earlier experience. LeDoux (1993) believes that the hippocampus is responsible for storing dry facts and the amygdala for storing the feelings linked to it (Figure 2.5).

He distinguishes between 'emotional memories' and 'recalling emotions'. According to him, recalling an emotion is fixed in the hippocampus as a cold fact. Its nature is purely cognitive. We remember, for instance, seeing a television commercial for Good Year tyres in which a major traffic accident is only just avoided. We also remember that it gave us an oppressed feeling. But the memory of this is a cognition, fixed in the declarative memory (more in section 4.2), and has no emotional consequences.

When the emotional experience is also coded in the amygdala, the memory itself can be accompanied by an emotion. Not only do we remember the commercial – at the same time we have that oppressed feeling again.

Both the hippocampus and the amygdala work closely together, creating an integrated memory. Many emotional experiences are probably too subtle to be

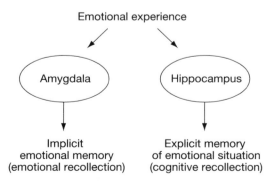

Figure 2.5   Two types of recollections of emotional experiences.

coded in the amygdala. The same appears to be the case for most brand stimuli.

Emotions for brands are probably more 'memories of emotions' – therefore of a cognitive nature – than 'emotional memories'. To the degree that the latter occur, they are probably relatively weak, more holistic affective reactions. The stronger the earlier emotional experiences, the stronger the imprint in our memory and the stronger the activated emotion when the stimulus enters our consciousness again. Affects influence the processing of information, the storage and organisation of material in memory, its activation in the form of memories and thoughts, and the decision-making process in all sorts of ways.

Experiences that are well retained in our memory are mostly those that were accompanied by emotional excitement. This releases a wave of neuro-transmitters which increases the firing speed of neurons. That increases the intensity of the perception and stimulates long-term potentiation. The mood of the person also plays an important role. Gloominess stimulates the memories of negative experiences like rejections and failures. Cheerfulness boosts memories of pleasant experiences like success and acceptance (Bower, 1992). The attention for stimuli is also influenced by our moods and their emotional associations. A dejected mood will make attention focus more on negative aspects of everyday occurrences that are associated with earlier negative experiences (Schacter, 1996). This leads again to the formation of negatively tinted memories. People who are in a positive mood are more open to the possibilities that present themselves, will more readily tend to consider new options, and are also more willing to see things in a different light (Isen, 1993). This greater receptiveness results in a person being more inclined to pay attention to material that is interesting or pleasurable to them, and to process this material more thoroughly and store it in memory. The representations are consequently more diverse and complex, while the number of connections with other representations – like situations and moments – increases. These representations are also better organised. Memories that are linked to positive feelings are therefore more easily accessible. It makes people see more similarities and differences with similar representations. For instance, it becomes easier to classify a brand somewhere (to categorise it, which will be discussed in more detail later) and to compare it with other brands. Decision making thus becomes easier.

It is precisely here that we could speak of the use of positive feelings as heuristics – the positive feeling associations acting as the dominant choice criterion. People take fewer arguments into consideration and increasingly follow their feelings. This happens mostly with relatively risk-free decisions such as the choice of frequently purchased daily consumption goods. However, people with positive feelings also seem to arrive at a faster decision in complex choice processes, like buying a new car (Isen, 1993). They are ready faster,

Playing chess is thinking and feeling (de Groot, 1997)

On 11 November 1997 the chess computer 'Deep Blue' beat world champion Gari Kasparov. 'How have the Grandmasters been able to hold back the victory of the monster for so long?', Dr A.D. de Groot has asked himself. 'This is due, among other factors, to the fact that chess is in essence not a calculation game, but a thinking game [...]'. In fact, mental activities like planning and taxing are often of an intuitive nature, among other reasons because, just like in the analysis behind the stack of arguments for and against striking, the decision comes about through an 'intuitive addendum'. How important taxing is, is shown by a beautiful statement by Jan Timman: 'The pondering of a chess player consists of taxations, threaded together by calculations.' Within this context, intuitive means: when in doubt about a choice – which is very common in chess thinking (and in life) – arrive at a decision by drawing from *ad hoc* general, *holistic* considerations which stem from *personal* experience and convert them into relatively *vague* suspicions ('feelings') over what is best. Such potential intuition can help the chess player enormously. Intuition is a secret weapon of the human expert – a weapon that cannot be converted into digital computer routines. How this works psychically and whether it can really help the human chess champion are still rather unusual, yet interesting questions for psychologists.

mainly because they eliminate unimportant criteria and more readily use their positive feelings as heuristics. Emotions as heuristics are thus practically always part of the game: they can act as the only criterion in simple choice processes, while in complex choice processes they see to it that the scope and complexity of the rational consideration remain contained within bounds, as indicated by Damasio (1995) as well. Positive feelings thus contribute to efficient decision making. People also tend to avoid unpleasant situations and information in order to give enough space to and protect their positive feelings. This happens, for instance, with brands they love – they do not really want to hear anything negative about them. Even in the event of imminent loss of something that is valued as positive, people try to protect themselves against it. The nature of our emotions and their meaning as brand responses will be discussed in more detail in Chapter 11.

People tend to protect their positive brand emotions – they do not want to hear anything negative about the brand they love.

Computers and the human mind (Greenspan, 1997)

'Proponents of the computer's ultimate ability to rival the human mind claim that inadequate capacity alone explains the failings of technology to replicate human consciousness to date. But they do not generally consider the most fundamental limitation of artificial intelligence: the computer's inability to experience emotion, and thus to use it to organise and give meaning to sensation, which remains simply inputs of data. No matter how sophisticated the technology may become, it is unlikely that a machine will ever acquire the emotional software possessed by a small child. Even a pet, despite the fact that its nervous system is in some respects quite different from our own, can respond in a more 'human' manner than the most brilliantly designed computer because it does feel affect and, to the limits of its ability, can learn from what it feels. No computer is likely ever to have anything like the uniquely human 'operating system' composed of feelings and reactions that would enable it to 'think' like a person. The basic element of thinking – the true heart of the creativity central to human life – requires lived experience, which is sensation filtered by an emotional structure that allows us to understand both what comes through the senses and what we feel and think about it as well as what we might do about it.'

2.6.1 *Body and mind*

For decades cognitive scientists assumed that the brain was an organ that worked in the same way as a computer. In particular Dennett, a renowned American philosopher, argued in his book *Consciousness Explained* (1991) that the human mind is an imaginary machine that can be likened to a computer. Almost at the same time, Damasio (1995), a neurology professor, convincingly proved in his book *Descartes' Error* the interconnectedness between feelings and reason, particularly by showing what goes wrong when that interconnectedness does not function properly. Dennett (1996) has now adjusted his standpoint considerably in his last book *Kinds of Minds*: the body has only one mind, and it influences our thoughts directly. He thus arrives at the place Damasio already was. Damasio (1995) postulates a theory of the 'somatic seal' – a kind of back-and-forth traffic between the body and the brain. In his theory, a perception of something or someone would first lead to a well-considered opinion. This opinion would cause an emotion. The emotion would then be experienced 'in the body', in the form of pleasant or unpleasant sensations and feelings. The body wires those experiences back to the brain, either in the form of a warning or a confirmation. In Damasio's vision, the somatic seal sees to it that the endless profusion of choices and their consequences are kept within bounds within the decision-making process. Damasio states that, when choosing, the calculation of all the possibilities leads again to new possibilities to be calculated, as a result of which we cannot manage with our reason alone. The somatic seal brings back the profusion of choices to manageable proportions. This curtailment increases the accuracy and effectiveness of our decision making. We thus make quicker decisions, 'listening' to our feelings (Visser, 1996).

Damasio's theory of the somatic seal brings down the computer metaphor. Cognitive science used to argue away the feeling and, with it, also the body as an influential factor in the taking of decisions. But it cannot be any other way: the cognitive and the emotional *must* be tightly intertwined. The countless connections and interactions between the emotional and the rational parts of our brain allow for an endless variation of human feelings. The brain forms one indivisible mechanism together with the rest of the body. Reason depends on our feelings, and our feelings depend on our reason. Damasio also believes that a human creature is ultimately a machine – only it is not a computer but a neurobiochemical machine.

Chapter 3
Memory Processes

3.1 The basic model of memory

In the course of history countless metaphors have been used to explain the functioning of memory. Plato saw memory as a wax tablet on which symbols were engraved. In his view, the differences between people depended on the properties of the wax. In the technological age, until recently people tended to liken the brain to a computer.

The most important question that kept minds wondering throughout the centuries was: how are the stimuli that reach our senses recorded in our memory? In the late 1960s, Atkinson and Shiffrin (1968; 1971) proposed a theory in which this occurs in three phases. First a sensory input is detained in the sensory memory (during fractions of a second up to about four seconds). A small portion of it ends up in the short-term memory, where it is stored a little longer (from a few seconds to about 12 seconds). Next, a small portion of this information goes to the long-term memory, where it is stored for a long time, sometimes for life (Figure 3.1).

3.2 The working memory

In past decades, the original idea of short-term memory as a temporary passive storage place for entering information has been abandoned. The current focus is more on the process of active selection and processing of information. Baddeley and Hitch (1974) proposed replacing the old concept of passive short-term memory with one of an active working memory. That is a complex system consisting of three components instead of only one storage unit. Baddeley (1990) called them the 'central executive', the 'phonological loop' and the 'visuospatial sketchpad' (see Figure 3.2).

The central steering element (central executive) is a system that controls the process of paying attention and is geared towards the selection of information. It monitors and coordinates the other two components. It is the most important component of the model because it is involved in every demanding task.

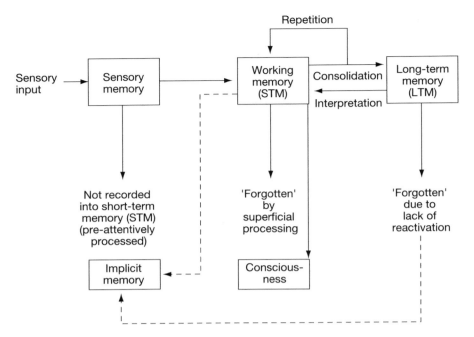

Figure 3.1   Basic model of memory.

The phonological loop, in turn, consists of two sub-components. One of them is the articulatory control system, which detains information temporarily by repeating it subvocally (the 'inner voice'). It holds, among other things, the words we are planning to pronounce. The second is the phonological storage system, which acts as the 'inner ear' (talking to yourself). Material which is present in the articulatory control system can be brought into the phonological storage system and carried back again from there. Together, these systems form a sort of circuit through which information can be held briefly and processed.

The visuospatial sketchpad receives information through the eye or from the long-term memory in the form of images. We can recall and inwardly see images from our long-term memory, or we hold images from our surroundings on the retina in order to process them and react to them. The visuospatial sketchpad can be seen as the inner eye.

Brain studies based on scanning have shown that these three elements can be traced exactly in the activities observed when people perform cognitive tasks. The places are shown in Figure 3.3. The idea of the central executive received much criticism later. It is very close to the concept of attention. It is a system that steers behaviour, holds objectives and resists distraction, as well as one of the elements of our cognitive system of which we know the least. It shows a great resemblance to the 'homunculus', the little person in our brain that steers everything – and whose existence is now generally denied.

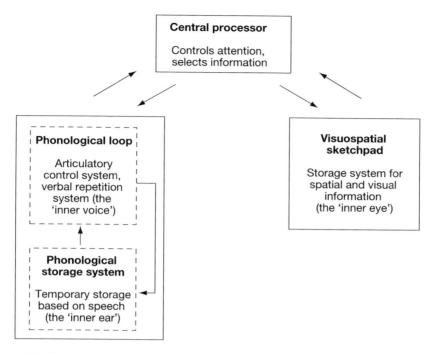

Figure 3.2 The working memory model (Baddeley, 1990).

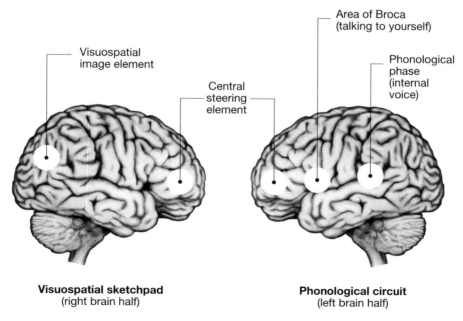

Figure 3.3 Structures in the working memory.

Richardson (1984) points out that an enormous range of simultaneous information processing takes place in our brain, making the exact function of the central executive unclear. The idea could seem as erroneous as the original concept of short-term memory. Against this, it stands to reason that there must be something else besides a number of memory processes that work independently of one another. It seems improbable for there to be no operating system that coordinates the individual mechanisms in their totality, but what it is and where it is localised in the brain remains completely unknown.

In spite of the fact that countless questions remain unanswered, the replacement of the idea of short-term memory as a passive storage place for processed information by one of an active working memory is now generally accepted.

The working memory can be seen as the place where the individual's inner self and the outside world meet. Because the capacity of our working memory is limited, this contact usually has a highly abstract character. When we observe something, not all our associations come into our working memory – only the impressions which have been processed after many steps into an abstract representation or scheme. We will go back to this issue in section 5.7. The working memory uses brain structures different from long-term memory. To form a durable memory, the incoming stimuli have to be processed thoroughly and connected to knowledge that is already present in long-term memory. This entails elaborate interpretation and coding. This is when selection processes start operating. What we already know determines to a high degree what we select and code. Things that already have a meaning for us provoke deep processing. This takes place in the left prefrontal cortex, the part of the frontal lobes directly above the nose. This deep processing is probably necessary for our capacity to be able to remember something in detail later on.

Brand stimuli in the surroundings and brand representations in the memory meet in the working memory. It is there that meanings from the long-term memory are drawn in order to interpret external stimuli. Because the capacity of the working memory is limited, not all brand associations are activated simultaneously – only a highly abstract representation.

3.3 Consciousness

That which is present in our working memory at a specific moment has a great chance of entering our consciousness as well. But consciousness and working memory are not one and the same. What is consciousness? Philosophers and psychologists have been trying to work it out for centuries, without having arrived at a consensus as yet. In a way, everybody really knows what consciousness is, but that does not mean that the phenomenon is scientifically defined and explained. It is especially unclear how consciousness is linked to other processes that take place in our brain. For a long time it was even thought that consciousness was the same as the totality of the processes in our brain. Detailed and systematic introspection would allow us an insight into everything that happens there. However, this thought was abandoned early in the twentieth century. Notably, Freud and Jung had already suggested the existence of an unconscious and a preconscious.

In the last 10 years several theories have been formulated to point to and explain consciousness. Crick (1994), in his book *The Astonishing Hypothesis: the Scientific Search for the Soul*, gives an overview of a number of the current theories on the phenomenon of consciousness. All of them share the common concept that whatever enters our consciousness is only a small part of all the processes that take place in our brain. We are consciously aware of the results of perception and memory processes, but have only a very limited access to the actual processes that cause these results. Some processes enter our consciousness, others do not. How does that happen? It is still a big mystery.

Johnson-Laird (1988), a cognitive scientist with a great interest in language, emphasises that there are millions of processes going on in the brain simultaneously, most of them inaccessible to our consciousness and thus also to introspection. He thinks that these processes are centrally steered in some way or other from within a high level in the hierarchy of the brain.

Jackendoff (1994), whom we will come across later in this book when discussing propositions, believes we have to see the experiencing of 'being aware of something' as an intermediate level between pure sensory perception of something and its high abstract representation in memory. Consciousness would be a level of representation located between the most peripheral and the most central representation levels. Jackendoff differentiates not only the brain and the mind, but even divides the mind into a computational mind and a phenomenological mind. This arrangement comes down to a division between unconscious processes and the conscious. That which we are conscious of is the result of unconscious background processes. Jackendoff says that there is an intimate relationship between the working memory and consciousness – in the sense that consciousness is fed from the working memory.

A third cognitive scientist, Baars (1988), introduced the idea of the global workspace – an area in the brain that is presumably linked to many specialised processing systems that are inaccessible to introspection themselves. Each of these systems is efficient in its own terrain, but not outside it. They can work together, but also compete for access to the global workspace. They interact in this working space until they reach concordance over one interpretation that enters our consciousness. Just like Jackendoff, Baars supposes a close relationship between consciousness and the working memory, in the sense that we are aware of certain elements in the working memory, but not all of them.

Kihlstrom (1987) proposes that we only become aware of an event when a connection is made between a mental representation of the 'self' and a mental representation of the event.

The conscious and unconscious aspects of our thoughts are sometimes described in terms of serial and parallel processes (LeDoux, 1996). Consciousness is a serial process that does things one after another, one by one. The unconscious brain, which consists of a large number of different systems, works more in parallel, doing all kinds of thing simultaneously. For this reason, some cognitive scientists have suggested that consciousness is a central processor of limited capacity sitting at the top of many specialised processors that work in parallel. Johnson-Laird (1988) believes that this central processor communicates its instructions in very abstract terms to the specialised processors, which convert them into detailed calculations, after which the results go back to the central processor, once more in abstract form.

Scientists do, thus, agree on the fact that not all the activities of the brain correspond with consciousness and that consciousness is an active process. They also agree on the fact that part of the working memory is involved in consciousness. Raaijmakers (1996) also says that language of which we are conscious, in the form of thoughts perceived in language, is the process of becoming conscious of background processes that are inaccessible as such. He believes the only possible explanation is the following:

- Information reaches our senses.
- It is processed by the brain, even up to a semantic level – without us being aware of it. All perception begins unconsciously.
- The processing of information is also unconscious – we only become aware of its end products.
- It is particularly those things to which we direct our attention that enter our consciousness: consequently, there is a system on top of the unconscious; at the higher level, some of it comes out as conscious.
- A lot of information is only processed unconsciously.

Raaijmakers remarks that several free speculative models have been developed on the manner in which consciousness processes are embedded in the brain. Some researchers believe that the emotional meaning of information is not necessarily the result of a process in which that information is first analysed fully (up to the meaning level), and then it is given an emotional value. Certain stimuli with a clear emotional meaning (e.g. facial expressions, sexual stimuli) may also activate the corresponding emotions via a separate, direct route. We actually do not know much about it. According to Raaijmakers, it is quite difficult to make a link between the results of neurological research on the one hand and psychological research on the other.

There is a general consensus, however, about consciousness working as a bottleneck. The early stage of information processing is mainly in parallel – many processes take place in our brain simultaneously. This is followed by a bottleneck situation: our consciousness can deal with only one or a few items at the same time. This happens through the filtering of information on those stimuli on which our attention is not focused. That attention shifts very quickly from stimulus to stimulus – and is therefore a progressive process.

3.3.1   *Does consciousness have a place?*

Scientific research indicates that consciousness stems from the activities of the prefrontal cortex, which – as was mentioned earlier – is located directly above the nose. This area is also responsible for the perception of emotions and the capacity of concentrating our attention on something (Carter, 1998). It is the only part of the brain that is not constantly occupied with processing sensory information. When the mind finds itself in a neutral state, that is the case with the prefrontal cortex as well. However, when we focus on issues, or when something happens in our surroundings that demands our attention, the prefrontal cortex goes into action and we suddenly become very alert. Attention, perception, self-awareness and reflection are all components of the process of becoming conscious. The nature of our experience depends on which components are involved in it. The prefrontal lobes are connected with almost all the other areas of the cortex, with which they exchange information, and they also have a direct connection with the limbic system, which is responsible, among other things, for selecting thoughts and perceptions that need attention and for ignoring others. A high degree of consciousness requires a high level of activity in the prefrontal lobes and intensive contact with a variety of other brain areas.

Our consciousness allows us only limited access to the processes that take place in our brain. Many background processes are inaccessible. Introspection does not really give us a glance into our own psyche – only information on what consciousness has selected. As a source of information on brand representations, it is limited.

3.4   Processing information

In order to clarify different types of sensory information Holler (1993) uses the metaphor of the newspaper editors. This metaphor is meant figuratively, but it is so enlightening that we are quoting it in its entirety:

The brain as an editorial staff (Holler, 1993)

'We can imagine the brain as a large editorial staff of a newspaper which is divided into five departments. The largest department is Seeing, followed by Hearing, Touching, Smelling and Tasting. Every department is subdivided into special sections. These sections have files filled with information on their own performance and that of the other sections. Every department works with specialised "sensory reporters" that deliver messages over events in the world: the "visual reporter" reports on images, frequencies and colours, the "audio reporter" on sounds and tones. The communication between sections passes through a secretariat which tests the character of a stimulus and determines whether the right route has been chosen. When that is the case, the secretariat passes the message on, and stores it in its files. If a similar message comes in, the secretariat knows which route is the most suitable for it. Although every section is specialised, it keeps files on almost every event in the other sections. Thanks to an extensive system of cross-connections and link positions, every section participates in every activity that takes place in the department. Every section can also fill in temporarily for another one. The task of the editorial staff is to make one useful, complete report out of the messages from the various departments. No single section is prepared to absorb information that does not contain a minimum degree of correspondence with previous messages. On the other hand, information which cannot be added to the already present information just like that, is much more stimulating for the activation and expansion of the system than the routine cases. When processing the daily incoming information, the secretaries of the section notice that certain information keeps coming

Contd

3.5 Long-term memory

In this book, which is ultimately about how brands are represented in our memory and how we can investigate that, we are interested mainly in long-term memory. For this reason, we will not delve any deeper into the processes of paying attention to and processing information. What we will ask ourselves is what happens in our brain when information from the working memory is taken to long-term memory. Repetition allows information that is present in the working memory to be stored there for a longer period of time. Repetition also increases the chance of information being transferred to long-term memory. Information which is not repeated fades away or is replaced by new incoming information.

back. This allows their dealing with this information to be increasingly faster and easier. This way, the secretaries in the rooms on the front side learn to process independently the information they have been assigned without having to find out again each time who is responsible. They can do this if the same information has come in at least seven times. The final report is never the business of a single section. This takes place in consultation between all the participating sections. The result is a pattern of actions that, together, become a "standard reaction process", a "style". If messages come in which have never been seen before, they are tested against the previously stored messages which offer a standard for all the interpretations. The more concepts a department knows, the sooner it can process messages it has never seen before. The "unconscious" brain processes our sensory perceptions according to the mechanism of stimulus and reaction. Here belong the organisational physical experiences as well as emotional reactions to sensory impressions. At a sensory and conscious level, our brain stores information from the moment it enters up to the moment of awareness. Important information is then placed in long-term memory. A condition for successful learning in humans is proper motivation. According to Pribam's theory of the storage and reactivation of memory, recollection occurs as a two-phased process. A stimulus – a sound, smell or representation – activates the memory processes of the short term. In these processes, the stimulus resounds in the infinite complexity of the connections stored in the brain until an association in long-term memory is formed. This correspondence between a sensory stimulus (cue) and a fragment of a stored memory starts the whole recollection. By activating just a single bit from a memory network, a recollection image can arise. People with good visual memories also have better access to long-term memory than other people.'

The transition from the working memory to long-term memory is called consolidation. Most of the information we process is *not* absorbed into long-term memory. That only happens with a small part of it, and only under certain conditions. Arousal, repetition, period of time elapsed since the processing (recency) and order of processing (primacy) play an important role. As we saw before, the amygdala and the hippocampus are particularly important here. But where is long-term memory localised? Where in our brain is everything stored? There is an increased acceptance that the storage takes place in the same areas where the processing of the sensory input also occurs. In particular, those areas in the cortex where visual and auditory information is processed would be the same ones in which visual and auditory memories are also stored. In a later stage, this information can be represented at a more

Memory and individual: one and the same (Carter, 1998)

The human brain holds billions of impressions, some fleetingly, some for a lifetime. We call them memories. Just as incoming sensory information is broken down, then rebuilt to form perceptions, so perceptions are broken down again as they pass into memory. Each fragment is sent off to storage in a different part of our vast internal library. But at night, when the body rests, these fragments are brought out from storage, reassembled and replayed. Each run-through etches them deeper into the neural structure until there comes a time when memories and the person who holds them are effectively one and the same.

abstract level in other areas of the cortex as well. It is assumed that it can take years before memories are sufficiently consolidated. Until that point is reached, stored information can be lost. If information were consolidated earlier, we would probably end up recording a large amount of trivial information – which would mean a waste of capacity and means. Consolidation allows us to sift the wheat from the chaff.

Most of the information we process that is related to a brand is not absorbed into long-term memory. That only happens with a small part of it, and only under certain conditions. Repetition is therefore essential. It can take years before brand associations are fully consolidated.

Is information that is already consolidated kept forever? Although this is not definite, and probably cannot be scientifically proven either, most memory researchers assume the permanence of long-term memory. In a survey of psychologists, 84% of them said they were convinced that once something is recorded in long-term memory it cannot be erased (Loftus and Loftus, 1980). They believe that whether we can regain access to something that is consolidated depends only on the right cues. In their opinion, 'forgetting' is not being able to find a memory that is still very much present. Bahrick and Hall (1991) speak in this context of a 'permastore' (similar to a 'permafrost' in arctic areas). They believe that it is true that not *all* the information that is already consolidated is kept for the remainder of a lifetime, but that that is the case for information which is deeply processed at the beginning and regularly retrieved. Connections can weaken due to the lack of activation, as a result of which they cannot be activated any more after an extended period of time. In reality, the old information is not accessible any more without there actually having been an active rupture process.

3.6 Associations

The current views on representations in memory are based in their simplest forms on a 2000-year-old theory on associations. These views assume that memory is built of neural connections that are the basis for mental associations between 'memory elements'. These connections (or associations) are the final products of learning processes. In fact, the nature of memory-related elements, the connections between them and the mechanisms which constitute the foundations for their emergence form the core of memory science. As we will see in the following chapters, it is an area with many speculative assumptions. No clarity exists on what a memory element actually is. Locke (1690) gave the name 'knowledge atoms' to the basic units of knowledge. Jackendoff (1994) speaks of 'conceptual primitives' which naturally raises the question of what a concept actually is. We will discuss that later. For a long time it was assumed, according to classical associationism, that the elements would be nothing other than direct representations of sensory perceptions.

Later, the insight was reached that memory can also develop meanings independently: this is called neo-associationism (see box overleaf). The most recent development is that of connectionism, which places an emphasis on the emergence of the connections in the brain. Connectionism is based on our current insights on the functioning of neurons, and attempts to arrive at representations over the emergence of knowledge by means of computer simulations. We will discuss this further in section 6.5.

The question of whether representations of brands in memory consist exclusively or predominantly of stored sensory perceptions, as classical associationism assumes, or also of meanings of a higher order – such as high, abstract values – as neo-associationism assumes, is certainly still very much alive. At any rate, stored perceptions seem to be more accessible than high abstract meanings. In research based on free association, they are activated more quickly and frequently. Respondents often have a lot of difficulty digging up more abstract meanings spontaneously, without any aids. This will be explored in more detail when discussing the hierarchy of meanings in Part Two.

Association is the phenomenon of one memory element being linked to another. When we talk about brands, associations are generally seen only in the narrower meaning of connections between knowledge elements while, in fact, the concept has a wider meaning: it involves anything that can be interconnected in our brain, thus also connections between brands and emotions/affects, attitudes and behavioural tendencies (habits). On the basis of this, Carlston (1992) formulated his theory of associative systems, which we will discuss in section 6.2. Figure 3.4 gives a very simplified representation of an associative network.

Classical associationism

Classical associationism is based on the premises that:

- There is an essential difference between memory contents and memory processes. When a person connects a meaning to a remembered event, it is assumed that the representation of the event is separate from the process of allocation of meaning.

- The memory file consists of fixed connections between units which are stored as direct representations of sensory perceptions.

- Once the information is embedded, it remains unchanged and cannot be erased. It is inactive. The connections can become weaker in time, but they cannot be broken off by the system itself. In that sense, the memory file is permanent.

- The stored units remain independent of other units; when perceptions are stored no interpretation takes place. Interpretation takes place later, on the basis of the stored perceptions.

- New information that conflicts with that which is already present in the file is absorbed but is less accessible during subsequent cognitive processes.

Neo-associationism

Neo-associationism, in contrast, is based on the premises that:

- Memory is not a passive file, but mainly a primarily active process. It interprets itself and constructs independent meanings on the basis of these interpretations. These are structured and complex yet largely unconscious processes.

- Whatever is absorbed into memory is not just a direct copy of reality, but an interpretation of it. Sensory perceptions are coded and stored, but are subordinate in our memory to the likewise stored meanings that are constructed independently through the cognitive system on the basis of perceptions and experiences. The memory content is the end product of thorough interpretation.

- Memory itself is an active dynamic system. It uses all the relevant knowledge and capacities when constructing memory files.

Contd

- These processes do not take place only during the processing of sensory impressions, but also when we recall information from memory and during the period of time between these two moments. The activity of memory is permanent: it goes on when the material is stored and is not limited to the moment of perception or recalling.

- The units that execute the construction activities are schemata: they take care of interpretations and giving meaning (we will discuss scheme theories in more detail later).

- The memory system as a whole functions by allocating its files higher order meanings. These act as a support for the construction processes. The system also strives constantly towards giving meaning and cohesion. Perceptions that correspond with the existing schemata are fixed better than information that does not fit.

- The strength of a representation is related to the degree to which its elements are logically interconnected. A wholeness of interpretation facilitates recollection.

- Components that are not important to the coordinating meaning of a representation are quickly forgotten.

- Information that does not correspond with the allocated meaning of a representation is eliminated. The neo-associationists (constructivists) thus assume that memory can change its own contents independently, and can even break off connections (there is no consensus on this issue). The hypothesis of permanent memory is rejected.

- When a representation is coherent, it is easier to derive forgotten elements from it than from material that shows less internal cohesion.

- Memory can supplement weak representations with other memory files when the situation requires it. This is a process of 'reconstruction'. In colloquial terms, it is known as 'guessing'.

- Components of a representation can be more easily remembered when they are associated with a higher meaning. When that is not – or not so much – the case, they are forgotten sooner.

- Memory is never the reproduction of a directly stored perception: it is always a reconstruction.

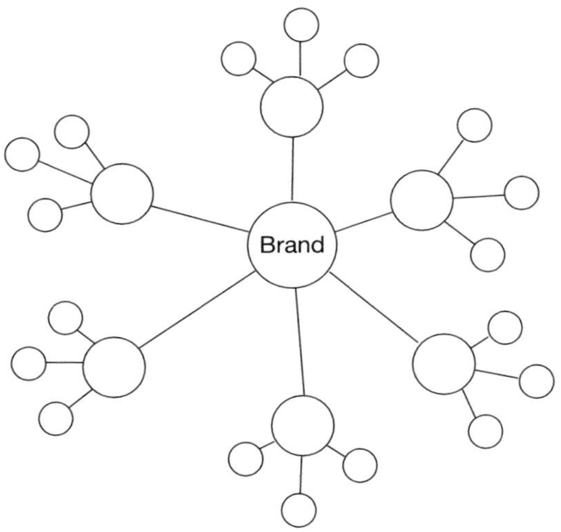

Figure 3.4   A schematic representation of an associative network.

3.6.1   *The strength of associations*

Connections between neurons have a certain strength which is determined, among other factors, by the speed with which a firing neuron releases a neurotransmitter in the synapse (exocytosis) and the absorption readiness of this neurotransmitter through the postsynaptic membrane of the fired neuron. The integration of all the chemical signals that a neuron receives via its receptors leads to one single response: the action potential. Associations are, in fact, activations of connections in the neural system. The strength of associations is a modification of the effectiveness with which neurotransmitters are released by the preceding neuron and allowed in by the following neuron. A schematic representation of association strength is given in Figure 3.5.

3.6.2   *Association laws*

Associations come about through the simultaneous perception of two elements or the thought of them as interrelated. In the course of time several laws have been formulated that constitute the basis for the emergence of associations and influence the association strength (Reber, 1997).

   The most general law is that of contiguity: elements that are perceived together in time (simultaneously) and space (contiguously) will be connected. A second important law is that of repetition (or frequency: number of repetitions per time unit): as elements are perceived increasingly together, they will be connected more often. As we observe 'Pampers', 'nappies' and 'dry bottoms' more often together, the connection between the three memory

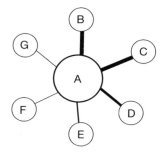

Figure 3.5 The strength of associations.

elements becomes increasingly stronger. A third law is that of similarity: stimuli that indicate the same thing will be connected to each other. Activating the element of Pepsi can lead to activating Coca-Cola.

A fourth connection is that of recency: those associations that are formed last will be the easiest to remember. We remember something more easily the more recently something such as the previous sensory perception, or the activation of the element in our thoughts, took place. This points to a gradual decrease in the strength of connections with time. Higgins (1987) adds to this the hypothesis that recency has more of an influence the more recently the activation took place, and that frequency has a dominant influence when the time interval is prolonged. When we have perceived very recently a brand that we knew but which we had not heard of for a long time (e.g. Chrysler), the recent perception can activate the thought of cars. But when we think of cars, the association with Volkswagen can be activated due to the fact that we have regularly heard or seen the two stimuli in a mutual connection throughout our lives.

Another law is that of vividness: unique exceptional associations are remembered more easily than less vivid ones.

The concept of laws is perhaps too optimistic a qualification for these relationships. All of these are factors that probably influence the strength of the associations, without there being any clarity as to the degree of this strength or how the associations interact. Their explanatory power – when they can be measured in sufficient isolation – is not great. The strength of associations is evaluated by looking at the frequency with which a stimulus invokes a response, and the speed with which this happens (the period of time between giving a stimulus and the appearance of the association response). This is done by researching brand awareness: after giving a product category cue, the order of associated brands and the period of time transpired between the cue and a named brand is used as a measure for the strength of the association from product to brand.

Associations – raw material of a brand (Carter, 1998)

Memory is many different things: it is the picture that comes into your mind when you think of the home you lived in as a child; it is the ability to hop on a bike and pedal away without working out how to do it; the feeling of unease associated with a place where something frightening once happened to you; the retracing of a familiar route; and the knowledge you hold that the Eiffel Tower is in Paris.

Not surprisingly, such a complex, multifaceted aspect of brain functioning is stored and retrieved in a different way, and dozens of brain areas are involved in a complex network of interactions. Little by little, though, the geography of human memory is becoming clear.

To understand memory you have to look at individual cells, because that is where memories are made. Whichever type of memory you consider, it consists of the same essential thing: an association between a group of neurons such that when one fires, they all fire, creating a specific pattern. Thoughts, sensory perceptions, ideas, hallucinations – any brain function (save the random activity of a seizure) is made up of this same thing. One pattern – a group of neighbouring neurons firing together in the auditory cortex, say – brings about the experience of a certain note of music. Another pattern, in a different area, brings about the feeling of fear; another, the experience of blue; another, a particular taste – a hint of tannin, say, in a sip of wine. A memory is a pattern like these. The only difference is that it remains encoded in the brain after the stimulation that originally gave rise to it has ceased.

Old, well-established associations of an element with other elements can exercise a negative influence on the emergence of new connections and the strength that these accumulate. The strength of previously acquired associations can make it extremely difficult to develop new ones. For instance, the Dutch brand Biotex (a biological detergent) is so strongly associated with the meaning of 'pre-wash' that it was impossible to develop a new association with the meaning of 'main wash'. For a newly introduced line extension, in spite of a very intense introductory campaign, the product had to be withdrawn from the market. This phenomenon is called 'associative inhibition'.

Repetition is essential to the development and strengthening of brand associations. The strength of connections decreases with time. New perceptions can force old associations to the background, but old, worn-out associations can inhibit or even block the emergence of new ones.

Figure 3.6   The direction of associations.

3.6.3   *The direction of associations*

An association is thus about a connection with two memory elements. This connection has a direction, from the preceding element to the following one. The connection is not necessarily reciprocal. The next element does not necessarily have to be linked to the previous one as well. To the degree that this may be the case, the strength of the two connections can differ (Figure 3.6).

A brand (e.g. Johnson's) can be connected to a product category (like suntan oil). But the opposite association, from suntan oil to Johnson's – if it is already present – will probably be a lot weaker.

A network of associations of a brand is thus a complete fabric of associations from other elements to a brand and from a brand to other elements – as is shown in Figure 3.7. In addition, each association has its own characteristic strength.

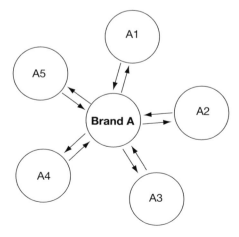

Figure 3.7   A system of associations.

3.6.4   *Mutual interconnectedness*

Elements that are connected to a brand can also be mutually interconnected. When dealing with primary associations, this can result in them being activated together. In Part Two we will analyse an example using the continental chocolate brand Milka, in which a number of primary associations (word brand, grammar, colour, brand logo/symbol, product) have such a strong mutual link as well that it can be brought from the long-term memory to the working memory as a unit (Figure 3.8).

3.6.5   *Association chains*

It is important to distinguish between direct and indirect associations. Direct associations are connections between two elements that do not transpire via a third element. For instance, we perceive an external stimulus and link it immediately with a meaning that is stored in memory. We see a pile of packages with 'Pampers' on it in a shop, and think immediately of nappies. Indirect association is about chains, with elements linked to each other via one or more intermediate elements. We think of babies and then of nappies, then of 'dry bottoms' and finally of 'Pampers', and write that last one on the shopping list. An indirect association can therefore come second, third or even later in a series of associations. (See the schematic representation in Figure 3.9.)

A third association form is the induced association, which comes about only after a stimulus and a task are presented. That could be, for instance, a

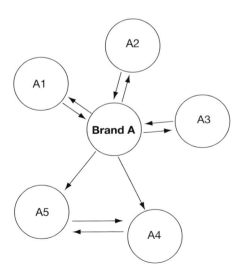

Figure 3.8   Mutual connection of brand associations.

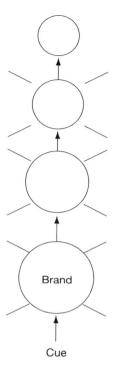

Figure 3.9 An association chain.

question in which the respondent's assignment is to link a brand with a specific meaning. A lot of image research is based on this: is 'Pampers' modern or old-fashioned? The fact that there is a great danger that only evaluations that come about merely on the basis of an assignment in a research situation are measured here, instead of existing connections, practically speaks for itself. Within this context we can make a distinction between autonomous associations – the connections present between two or more elements – and 'associations' that are the result of thought processes in which various concepts are linked to each other in working memory upon request.

A difference should be made between 'direct' brand associations and brand associations that are linked to each other via one or several intermediate elements. The chance of reaching a distant association decreases as the road that has to be travelled with activation becomes longer.

3.6.6 *Core associations*

Core associations represent the essence of the meaning of an entity. They are primarily defining characteristics (properties), on the basis of which we classify the entity in a category of similar entities. Heineken is a beer, just like the other big Dutch brands Grolsch, Amstel and Bavaria. Secondly, they are the characteristic properties of the individual entities in a category, on the basis of which we distinguish them from one another: Heineken is social, Grolsch is individual. We will explore this further in sections 8.3 and 12.3.

Core associations of a brand are those associations which represent the essence of the meaning of that brand.

3.6.7 *The scope of networks*

How extensive is the engram, or group of neurons, that a perceived entity – such as an object or a brand – represents? Biochemical experiments have shown changes in relatively large areas of the brain. Rose (1993) believes that a specific memory is not limited to a small group of neurons or to an individual component of the brain, but should be seen as a property of the whole brain as a system, even of the whole body. There is no single fixed storage space for information in memory. Memories are dynamic, are spread out through various parts of the brain, and are constantly made anew. It is assumed that the associations within the entity are stronger and more frequent than the associations outside it, between entities. The question is, though, what belongs in an entity? Is there a 'boundary' between the associations that represent an entity, and connections between this representation and other parts of the memory contents? What is mutually linked on a permanent basis in long-term memory, and which connections materialise *ad hoc* in the working memory, for instance under the influence of a specific set of tasks? Greenfield (1995) postulated in this regard her theory of 'Epicentre' and 'Gestalt'.

3.7   Epicentre and Gestalt

Greenfield (1995) proposes that a memory should be thought of as extremely variable combinations of neurons, which are activated temporarily from an epicentre. She depicts an epicentre as a relatively small combination of neurons that are more durably linked to one another (as also Hebb [1949] refers to). This specific combination of connections between neurons in various brain areas (representations of forms, colours, meanings, words, feelings, etc.) is activated in mutual connection. Other neurons are recruited from there. This activation (firing) occurs exceptionally quickly, within tenths of milliseconds. Within one second we produce millions of firing patterns in various circuits which are spread over a variety of brain areas. In analogy to the Gestalt theory, Greenfield gives the name of neuronal Gestalts to the ensembles of activated circuits. Neuronal Gestalts are short-lived and unique combinations of brain cells around an epicentre. An epicentre effectively activates such a neuron ensemble when it represents a moment-bound meaning for us. Consequently, a distinction can be made between more structural connections between neurons on the one hand, and more moment- and situation-bound *ad hoc* contacts on the other. The first are more permanent, the others extremely dynamic and temporary.

The scope of neuronal Gestalts is determined not only by the more durable connections, but surely also by the power of the activation which comes from the stimulus. According to Greenfield, the best way to depict a memory – and thus the consciousness of it – is as a stone that is thrown in a pond, causing the water to start moving in rings. The scope of the Gestalt is determined by the relative power of the stimulus constellation (epicentre) in competition with others. Groups of nerve cells in various areas of the brain fire simultaneously. 'It resembles an orchestra faced by a conductor,' says Bergsma (1996). The firing patterns of these various groups are linked to each other. As a result, we become aware of what we perceive. The scope of the epicentre and the strength of the mutual connections between the neurons that form part of it exercise a great influence on the formation of Gestalt and the process of awareness (which may or may not be a result of Gestalt formation). A very active group of cells, with many strong mutual connections, has a greater chance of recruiting a large number of cells for a Gestalt than a weak epicentre.

The general and permanent properties of the world around us are recorded in our brain by relatively durable and often strong configurations of synaptic connections. But what happens with one-time stimuli of a passing nature, with the constant flow of our sensory experiences? They are processed by one-time and mostly extremely short-lived contacts between various networks and leave no permanent traces behind. The more permanent connections do not change so fast. They are generally the result of repeated confrontations with the same stimuli. However, connections between different configurations can come about, change and dissolve from one moment to another.

A brand is represented in memory by a relatively small combination of neurons (the epicentre of the brand) that are connected to each other synaptically. They are activated in mutual coherence. From here, all other kinds of parts that constitute the associative network can be activated. The complete activated network is called a Gestalt.

The brain generally goes its own way, spontaneously and unpredictably. It does not wait for instructions or information from the outside. The millions of neural network connections whimsically connect all kinds of thoughts to each other. A Gestalt therefore is not a durable condition – on the contrary, Gestalt formation and the entry of certain Gestalts into consciousness is a continual process. Gestalts change constantly. The consciousness of them can change from one moment to the other, depending on the formation of new Gestalts. This constant change of Gestalts is a chaotic system in which countless influences lead to a certain result at a certain moment. Except for the durable connections between the neurons in a specific epicentre, there is little which is permanent in our memory. This explains how a single event can lead to very different interpretations, at the same time presenting the question of why it is precisely that one interpretation which enters our consciousness.

We should therefore not imagine memory to be a collection of simple and stable neural networks. Memory is a dynamic and extended system. Huge numbers of neurons perform in parallel in a staggering amount of combinations. It is also for this reason that we cannot compare human memory with the memory of a computer. The memory of a computer works with data; human memory works with meanings and context. Among other things, this means that every time we remember something we produce new memories. The next time that we remember the same thing, we do not remember the original perception, but the previous memory. We constantly reproduce our memories. Remembering is not like watching an old film passively, but actively reconstructing experiences from the past.

Greenfield's theory seems like a compromise between the schematic theories of psychology and the connectionist theories of computer science. The schematic theories assume that people give all sorts of data a more or less permanent mutual connection. It believes in a representation of information in memory through concepts and schemata, units that are stored as stereotypical representations of events or phenomena that return regularly. Connectionists also assume that fixed structures of connections arise which are formed and strengthened, as Hebb had already postulated. But their theory is ultimately about the 'weights' of the connections between the elements of representations. Consequently, the connections are not equally strong. We will discuss both theories in more detail later on.

What Greenfield in fact postulates is that there is a fixed connection between neurons (epicentres), and that from there temporary connections with other neurons or other epicentres arise on the basis of the situation in which people find themselves. However, this theory is still speculative. The question of whether something such as fixed association cores exist cannot be answered yet, according to Rose. And this is not the only question that remains unanswered. Questions such as 'Which connections are part of an epicentre?' and 'To what degree is that equivalent to the phenomenon outside our brain?' have not been substantiated empirically yet. Research on a brand must in any event make a distinction between the issues with which it is more permanently connected and associations that merely come about on the basis of a specific situation. This is especially crucial in image research. A great deal of research misses the intensity (strength) of the connections.

3.8   Spreading activation

A question that becomes inevitable is *how* other neuron ensembles are activated from an epicentre. To this end, the cognitive psychologist Quillian (1968) formulated the theory of 'spreading activation'. His ideas were elaborated further in 1975 by Collins and Loftus. Anderson (1983; 1995) used this theory as a basis for his model of memory and for developing computer simulations based on it.

The theory of spreading activation says that when our senses are confronted with a certain stimulus, a connection can be activated with specific neuron groups which represent this stimulus in our memory. Whatever is activated at first is therefore cue dependent. The activation then propagates itself along connections with other neuron groups (and the memories recorded in them) in

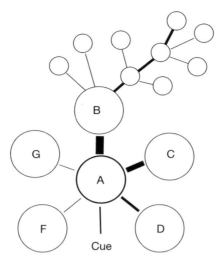

Figure 3.10 The spreading of activation.

the network to which this stimulus representation belongs. When A is reached, A is connected to B and if this connection is sufficiently strong, B is also activated (see the schematic representation in Figure 3.10).

This does not happen when there is no connection or when the connection is too weak. According to current insights, this is how activation spreads from an entry point through the system, decreasing exponentially with the covered distance and with time (Collins and Quillian, 1972; Anderson, 1984). The activation starts from entry point A, which is activated by the cue, and heads towards all the elements that are connected to A and whose connection strength exceeds a specific threshold value. It is assumed that the more connections that go out from an element, or the more the activation is divided, the weaker is the activation of the following element, and the longer it takes before a looked-for representation is reached in memory.

When there is only one connection from entry point A, activation chooses this route. The theory also posits that when there are more connections the activation is divided proportionately. In three connections of equal strength, each connection would receive one third of the activation (Anderson, 1976; 1984). This leads to the prediction that the more we know about something, the longer it takes to recall the information from memory – something that does not correspond with our intuition. In practice, it seems that connections do not often have the same strength (some information just gets more attention or is repeated more often). Subsequent experiments show that the prediction is correct for some tasks, but does not hold true for others (Reder and Ross, 1983). When looking spontaneously for a specific relationship between an item (such as a brand) and a property, the theory of Anderson seems to apply.

When evaluating the same reaction, greater knowledge leads to a quicker confirmation. Apparently, representations cannot be seen separately from processes.

Memories activated by external cues seem to enter our consciousness spontaneously, but we can also focus on looking for specific information in our memory. We ask ourselves questions like 'What was her name?'. This is a two-phased process. In the first phase, elements in the network are felt out from a starting cue, and in the second phase a decision is taken: this is what we were looking for, the goal has been reached, the sought-for memories enter our consciousness. Her name is Jean.

Which elements of a network are activated depends not only on the cue (or entry point), but mainly also on the number of connections and the relative strength of the individual connections within the network. A memory element such as a brand name can be connected to many others or to just a few. The connections can vary from very weak to very strong. The connections between two elements can be direct:

$$A \rightarrow E$$

but also very indirect:

$$A \rightarrow B$$
$$B \rightarrow C$$
$$C \rightarrow D$$
$$D \rightarrow E$$

In this case, the activation from A to E must move through B, C and D. Each subsequent element is activated on the basis of a connection with the preceding one. The preceding elements probably also have many connections with other elements, thus decreasing the chances of reaching goal E. Activation can also spread in other directions:

$$A \rightarrow B \rightarrow K \rightarrow Z$$

When the chain becomes too long, there is no activation.

On the basis of this empirical research, Ebbinghaus showed in 1885 that an activation of two elements that are directly connected to each other is quicker and easier than when the connection is indirect. Due to the gradual decrease of the activation, the chance of reaching more remote elements would become increasingly smaller. No conscious memory appears past a certain element in the chain.

There are various theories with regard to the chance of a specific element being activated. One of them posits that the more extensive a network with which a memory element (e.g. a brand) is connected, the greater the chance of it being activated. In an extensive associative network, as is undoubtedly the case with, for example, Philips in the Netherlands, there are more paths along which Philips can be reached. Few connections, for example with Duracell, make the chances of Duracell being reached correspondingly smaller. The chance of Philips being activated is thus greater than that of Duracell. In a nutshell, we will think more often of Philips than of Duracell. The course of the activation is also determined by the strength of the connection. Another theory postulates that automatic activation in particular moves on the basis of the relative strength of the individual connections. According to this view, the chance of activation decreases as the number of weaker connections in the network increases. The more extended a network is, the weaker the activation of elements within that network. There is probably a balance between the number of connections, which increases the chance of activation of a specific element, and the weakening that takes place as a result of an excess of connections. When too many connections have to be added to a network, it can become 'confused'. Consequently, when we think of batteries, chances are we will end up thinking of Duracell instead of Philips. This causes umbrella brands, which are connected to a large number of product categories, to have difficulty competing in sectors with strong mono-brands whose name is strongly associated with a product category.

Activation of a specific memory element, like a brand, depends on:

(1) The nature of a cue that reaches our senses: is it a cue that corresponds with the element itself (like the brand Grolsch)?

(2) The strength with which that cue itself is represented in our memory: how strongly is the concept of beer present in our memory?

(3) The number of connections of this cue in our memory with other elements; for instance, with which other brands is the concept of beer connected in our memory?

(4) The relative strength of these connections; for instance: how strongly is the concept of beer connected to brands like Heineken, Amstel, Grolsch, Brand, etc.?

(5) The length of the association chain between the representation of a cue and the element to be recalled (e.g. Grolsch).

3.8.1 *Automatic and strategic activation*

When confronted with external stimuli (an ad, a package on the shelf of a shop, etc.), incoming impulses initially spread automatically and unconsciously, from the senses via the thalamus to the long-term memory in the association cortex. It is assumed that when activation of an intersection exceeds a threshold value in an associative network (known as a node), the cognition recorded in it enters the working memory (Grunert, 1996). Since its capacity is limited, this happens only with the strongest or most familiar stimuli in our surroundings. The automatic analysis of these stimuli takes place on the basis of the relevance criterion. Fazio (1989) has suggested and empirically substantiated that there is an automatic activation of the attitude with regard to the stimuli in this phase. The principle of selective attention is based on the very first phase of unconscious and automatic spreading of activation.

The results of these automatic processes can lead to a focused conscious attention: these are strategic processes. The stimuli enter consciousness. From the objectives and interests of the individual in the given situation, the meaning of the stimuli is now analysed more extensively and they are thought about more deeply. It is assumed that automatic and strategic activation of memory contents is additive, and only those stimuli whose activation through both processes is the strongest enter consciousness. This explains why weaker stimuli also receive attention when they are extremely relevant. The 'cocktail-party phenomenon', which we will be describing, shows this. Relevance and attitude, two concepts that are hard to separate from each other, determine the degree of involvement in a stimulus. High involvement leads to more extensive strategic processes. Automatic activation is very influential in low involvement cases. It is assumed that the degree of activation that a stimulus node receives works as a heuristic[2] in the choice of brand. When a product is bought in the supermarket, the choice decision can be the result of a predominantly automatic activation of a brand name and the meanings attached to it. As will become evident in Part Two, in some product categories this takes place in a matter of seconds.

In a high involvement and a more well-considered choice decision, the degree of initial automatic activation of a brand can act as a heuristic in order to activate the knowledge (associative network) of it – whether or not it is in the strategic process – and process more external information about it. The probable result of a larger influence of automatic activation in a lower involvement is that only few elements (associations) in the network become activated. Analyses of brand studies in the sector of fast-moving consumer goods indeed show that a considerable portion of the brand choice can be explained with a very limited number of brand associations. The strength of the association of a brand with a product category and with one product characteristic can be the dominant influence on the brand choice in cases of low involvement.

---

2   In complex situations, an individual is not always capable of making a decision on the basis of an extensive information processing operation (the time may not allow it, or the person may not have sufficient information at her disposal). In such a situation, her decision will be reached on the basis of heuristics. Heuristics are rules of thumb that allow an individual to make decisions in an efficient manner; they cost little effort but usually produce good results. Consumers also use heuristics when making a shopping decision: they may choose the most popular brand.

The cocktail party phenomenon

Attention and perception emanate from a preceding process of unconscious automatic processing of stimuli present in the surroundings. When there is conscious (directed) attention, this entails that the senses have selected a stimulus from the total supply in order to focus the primary cognitive capacity on it. At the same time, other stimuli are processed automatically in an unconscious manner. When the brain thinks there is reason for it, primary attention is shifted to one of these stimuli. To illustrate this phenomenon, reference is often made to experiences at a cocktail party. Even when a person is involved in conversation with someone, he hears his name when it is mentioned somewhere else in the room. This can only be explained on the basis of the hypothesis that he is scanning all the other conversations in the surroundings simultaneously (unconsciously), therefore being able to detect the relevant information in them. The same occurs in a car, when one has to watch traffic, is talking to a passenger and is listening to the news at the same time. The shifting of attention from one stimulus to another is preceded by a process of simultaneous processing and analysis of relevance of all three information sources. Consequently, there is a parallel unconscious information processing which takes place automatically and is not limited in its capacity.

When there is low involvement, automatic activation processes have a large influence on the brand choice. Only a limited number of associations are activated here.

Activation of specific brand associations depends on the number of associations from a brand and the strength of the individual associations. The 'clearest' brands are those characterised by a number of direct, strong associations.

3.9 Remembering

Perceptions are not stored in long-term memory as one whole: they are first broken into little pieces and stored in different places of the brain cortex. They are subdivided into categories (colour, form, smell, meaning, etc.) and categorised in various networks. Those networks are interconnected. How it is exactly that we put those pieces back together to form a unified memory (the problem of binding) is one of the big mysteries of brain science. There is

Unconscious information processing (Grunert, 1988)

'It seems clear that the vast majority of consumer decisions are in fact not based on a large degree of conscious thinking (...). A lot of information processing is unconscious. To name just a few examples: the recognition of outside stimuli, and the decision to select them for conscious attention or not, are unconscious processes. The integration of new information with information already stored in memory is an unconscious process. Retrieval of information from long-term memory into working memory is unconscious as well. The basic pattern is clear: unconscious information processing sets the limits within which conscious information processing can occur.'

probably not one single place where everything comes together, but there is proof that the various elements of a representation fire in synchronised fashion. Images remain separate from words and sounds, but are brought 'online' at the same time.

Damasio (1995) posits that various elements of stored information are linked to each other in certain convergence zones. He imagines a series of this type of zone which is functional at different levels. Calvin (1996) imagines the zones metaphorically as operators in a telephone exchange who are organising a telephone meeting. Many researchers think that there is a type of index in the prefrontal cortex which points to the various sorts of information that are stored in separate areas of the cortex, and that all those networks are activated from this index. Either way, various parallel networks are somehow bundled, allowing perception of phenomena as wholes.

That which is stored is not a picture of something, but a program that records the perception. When recalling, this program ensures that the formed networks are activated. This produces a memory which is similar but not identical to the original perception. Visual memories go together with memories of sounds, words and emotional images. Stimulating a small portion of these memory contents can be sufficient to recall the other relationships as well.

There is a very close relation between the processing of information and the subsequent memory. Experiences that are deeply processed leave more bits and pieces behind in memory, allowing us to reach the network in many ways and arrive at a richer reconstruction of the original perception. Schacter (1996) says that our memories are largely our reconstructions. According to Semon (1909/1923), each memory can be activated by a few selective cues that match the original coding. He believes this is not about a literal correspondence, but about whether a cue can restore the subjective perception of the observed situation. Recalling visual information related to the physical context of events is important here. The subjective experience of remembering something almost always goes together with reliving an event visually. This is paired with the fact that visual perception and visual memory take place in the same brain structure. When visual stimuli are not processed deeply – for instance because we are performing two tasks simultaneously – something stays behind in memory which we can sometimes recognise later, but cannot recall. Its activation requires the cue to be equal to the stimuli of the original perception.

A memory resembles a chain with many different links (Bergsma, 1996). Once we get a hold of a certain number of links, a whole series of facts can be retrieved from the depths of memory. But the chance of a specific memory, such as a brand name, being activated decreases as the number of elements that have to be passed increases and the activation must consequently cover a longer path through the network.

3.10   The influence of cues

The stored information and the memory are not one and the same. That which is stored contributes to the memory but is only one of its elements. Another element is the supplied cue itself. The perceived cue goes together with the activated parts of the memory, thus creating a new unit that is different from its components. Cues also have a large influence on the memory. This comes to light particularly in psychoanalysis and psychotherapy.

Spence (1984) posited that, more than we realise, the past is constantly being reconstructed during the process of analysis, and the psychologist, who contributes to determine the form and contents of the memory, is an important component in the process of recalling. The words and phrases used not only activate a drowsy memory, but are also instrumental in giving form to what someone remembers and to its subjective experience. According to Spence, psychologists who react too enthusiastically to an isolated memory or feeling can be the cause of someone reconstructing a memory on the spot, on the basis of what has been left behind of a long bygone event. Market research also produces striking examples. The question 'Which newspapers are you familiar with?' leads to other answers than does the question 'Which newspapers are you familiar with, even if just by name?'. In the first case, 'being familiar' is interpreted as knowing well or reading. In responding to the second question, people mention all the newspapers they have ever heard of.

What is activated therefore depends in the first place on the cue. The better a sensory stimulus corresponds with the cue representation in memory, the more easily memory is activated. A cue enters a network at a certain point, after which activation spreads further from this point. Depending on the specific cue, yet another part of the network is activated. The more direct and stronger the connections from this cue are, the quicker activation takes place and the larger the part of the network that is activated. Different cues thus lead to different aspects and boundaries of memories. During the process of activation there is almost always a certain rustle, in the sense that elements for which we are not looking are activated. Connections that are too weak are not activated. We may have someone's face clearly in our minds, but cannot recall the person's name. Still, we try to find out the name by using the face to activate a context with which the name is connected. This context then works as a secondary cue, and activation takes a detour. When we try to recall a specific element, like a brand, we sometimes go through a whole series of search strategies. This happens especially when looking for brands in our memory. 'Name all the brands of espresso coffee you know.' We will probably arrive at a name first, and then at an image, colour or product to which it is linked. Then we see the product before our eyes, and get a special feeling about it. As we saw, the memory of a brand is not located in one place in our head, but is spread over various areas. That which acts up in our consciousness when recalling something is always cue dependent. Only certain connections are activated. A slightly different cue will lead to a different memory. The strength of the connection in our memory between the representation of a cue and other elements in a network determines whether something gets recalled, and *what* it is. The boundaries of the recalled elements are not accurate. Besides, most elements are also associated with elements outside the activated network. The boundaries of a memory are always vague.

In marketing we speak of an 'evoked set' with which we indicate those brands that enter our consciousness spontaneously with a specific cue. Evoking means bringing forward (this is different from the 'consideration set': those brands that we accept as candidates in a choice decision). The concept of 'evoked set' is used to indicate those brands that we associate spontaneously with a product category. In principle, though, there are countless different cues that can activate the memory of a brand. What is recalled exactly and which part of the associations enters our consciousness is closely related to the cue that reaches us from our surroundings at a specific moment. Depending on the intensity of the association between the representation of the cue in our memory and the brand name, the memory of the brand name may or may not be activated. The strength of this association determines the accessibility of the brand name in memory at that moment. This is an important fact when it comes to carrying out studies on brands.

In qualitative research on brand representations, the interviewer has an important influence on what the respondent recalls and on the subjective experiencing of it. The cues that the interviewer uses contribute to give form to what the respondent recalls. This can cause different interviewers to arrive at a diversity of conclusions when it comes to the contents of a brand representation.

Our working memory has a limited capacity. At a certain moment, only a few associations can be brought to consciousness simultaneously from the working memory. These are called salient associations. Which associations these will be depends on the stimulus, the context, and the number and strength of the individual connections. In different situations, at different moments and under the influence of different stimuli, many different brand associations can be activated. However, for most brands these will be a limited set of associations characterised by a relatively large intensity and accessibility. The more often these are activated, the more accessible they become.

3.11 Recognition

Countless studies have shown that our capacity to *recognise*, especially when it comes to previous visual perceptions, is practically unlimited. In the 1970s, Lionel Standing conducted an experiment in which he showed students a picture for 10 seconds. Each student was confronted with 10,000 different pictures. A week later the students were invited again. This time, pictures were shown in pairs, one from the first series of 10,000 and one new picture they had not yet seen. The assignment was to identify the pictures shown in the first series. Students seemed to be able to do this with an accuracy of 90%. We do not know how this process works in our brain, though. The experiment does show that our capacity for recognition is infinitely greater than our capacity to recall on the basis of cues. The study led to the conclusion that a solid representation of the previous perceptions has remained in memory, but that many of these representations are too weak to be retrieved later without external help. The larger the correspondence between a cue and a stored memory, the greater the chance that we can retrieve previous perceptions (Standing, 1973).

Recognition is based on the fact that we are confronted with a cue that is represented as such in our visual or auditive memory. Essentially, recognition is also recalling, but is based on a virtually full congruence of stimulus and memory representation. The fact that recalling requires so much more effort than recognition is ascribed to recalling being a two-phased process. In the first place, recalling requires a search for a specific memory element and then an evaluation of whether the activated element is also the one that was searched for. Recognition only involves the second phase. Consequently, recalling involves two fallible phases, recognition only one. But the generality of this theory seems too simple. The issue is rather how the representation of a cue and a sought-for element are connected to each other, directly or indirectly, via one or several intermediate stations. In a direct connection, a memory can come about as quickly as a recognition. However, when the connection is an indirect one, recalling elapses following a two-phased process.

Recognition can take place on the basis of pure direct familiarity, but this is not always the case. Sometimes recognition requires a process of conscious recalling – on the basis of which the determination is then made to define and recognise a cue. Mandler (1980) points out that recognition on the basis of familiarity is linked to the degree to which the elements of a stimulus are integrated. Pure repetition of exposure to a stimulus ensures that its various elements appear more coherent and integrated, due to which the stimulus becomes more familiar and is directly recognisable, without information processing. This process takes place automatically. The second form of recognition is closer to recalling, and needs information processing.

Our capacity for brand recognition is infinitely greater than that of brand recall. Brand recall strongly depends on whether a cue is connected to a brand directly or indirectly, via intermediate stations.

3.12   Forgetting

Sometimes we cannot retrieve from memory that which we are looking for. It is as if we forgot something. But what is 'forgetting'? As we showed before, most memory scientists assume the permanence of memory, believing that with the right cues, any element stored in long-term memory can be recalled again later. Against this stands the decay theory, which states that traces of memories that are not activated again decline in strength. With the progress of time, our memories would become weaker and weaker, and consequently more difficult to access. After a period of time they might even be completely lost, without there being an active rupture process. This theory is disputed. A new vision on forgetting is presented by Bjork and Bjork (1992), who posit that 'forgetting' is mainly related to processing (or repeating) new information that is linked to the memory. According to them, there is competition in memory between different memories. Old associations interfere with new ones and vice-versa. This interference can manifest itself in two ways, depending on the time relationship.

The first form is that of proactive interference, in which associations that are already present encumber the development of new ones. It is reflected in the refrain 'old dogs cannot learn new tricks'. The old tricks that the dog has learned interfere in the learning of new ones. This proactive interference is at its peak when two situations or two cues (such as two brands) show certain similarities. The cue that is most strongly associated with a meaning in memory encumbers the development of an association between a new cue and this meaning. In practice, this takes shape when, for instance, an attempt is made to link to another category a brand that is also very strongly associated with a certain product category. In the cigarette market, for example, brands are strongly associated with certain subcategories (Camel → plain, Marlboro → full flavour filter, etc.). The development of new associations like Camel → filter or Marlboro → light seems to be much more difficult because of the old association.

The second form is retroactive interference, in which recent experiences make it more difficult to recall something we have learned earlier. A new advertising campaign can encumber recalling the preceding campaign. In general, the concept of interference means that as the quantity of stored memory with regard to an entity increases, it becomes increasingly difficult to retrieve a specific item (Glassman and Geluk, 1998). As time elapses, experiences get mixed together and details disappear as a result of interference. Too many competing associations can result in an inability to recall certain information. The exact course of the interference process is not known yet. One of the assumptions is that an increased interference can lead to an actual destruction of older connections. But as has been said before, the prevailing view is that connections in long-term memory are permanent, and thus associations cannot be actively broken. Within this view, interference would be the result of competition between responses.

As a consequence, it is difficult to change brand associations that are already consolidated, certainly when they are worn in and very strong. The only process in which this can happen is in the development of new associations and their subsequent strengthening in such a way that they are activated earlier and more quickly than the older associations. Whether this will come to pass depends on the strength or intensity of the old associations and the power with which the new ones are developed. We get an idea of the degree of difficulty when we think about how much work is required to replace motor actions, old worn-in patterns, with new ones – for instance when we learn to work with new computer programs. Some connections can even take on a monopolistic character. In the Netherlands, there is such a strong connection between 'mineral water' and 'Spa' that connections between mineral water and other brands, like Sourcy (a brand of the Heineken company), cannot be accomplished easily, or at any rate will be considerably weaker. According to the theory of spreading activation, the activation will automatically propagate to Spa from the representation of mineral water.

Brand associations that are already consolidated in long-term memory cannot be broken off. This makes it difficult to change associative networks, especially when the individual associations are direct and strong. The only way in which this can happen is by developing new associations and not activating the old ones any more. The chances of success depend on the intensity of the old associations and the power with which the new ones are developed.

Retention functions (Anderson, 1995)

Memories seem to fade with the passage of time. The *retention function* demonstrates how memory performance deteriorates with the passage of time. All retention functions show the same basic form. Initially, forgetting is rapid, but memories continue to worsen, almost forever. Retention functions differ with respect to the scales on which they display these basic phenomena and they also vary in time spans over which they occur. The period of time over which forgetting is manifested is a function of the strength of the memory record and the sensitivity of the memory measure. The weaker the memory or the more sensitive the measure, the more rapid forgetting is (Figure 3.11).

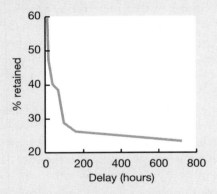

Figure 3.11 A graph of a 'retention function' (Anderson, 1995).

3.13 The forgetfulness of the elderly

About ten thousand of our neurons die every day but, since we are born with 100 billion neurons, at the end of our lives we have lost only 1% of our brain cells. With increasing age there is a shrivelling up of dendrites and axons. The brain also reduces in size and weight. When we turn 70 the weight has decreased by 5%, and by the age of 80 this becomes 10%. By the time we make it to the age of 90, our brain has become 300 g lighter. The hippocampus area is particularly affected, thus leading to memory loss. A weakening of the frontal lobe causes problems. It becomes more difficult to bring together the various elements of long-term memory and interpret new experiences: 'What is happening and why?' But part of the memory problems associated with age do not emanate from a weakening of existing networks; they are a result of a diminished attention when processing new information. Because the coding leaves much to be desired, our memory for recent experiences diminishes. We

Haitink's memory (Jansen, 1999)

In the March issue of the *Preludium* magazine, the renowned conductor Bernard Haitink confessed that he had forgotten that he had once given a performance of the *Six symphonic epigrams* by Willem Pijper, which he was to conduct in mid-March with the Royal Concertgebouw Orchestra. Haitink had received a score and a tape with a recording from Donemus, the documentation centre for Dutch music. To his surprise, the tape was of himself. 'This happens to me more often lately. It is probably not just becoming old, but the distance from the previous memories which has become so big. What's worse, in the Carte Blanche series I will be doing *La damnation de Faust* with the first orchestra I ever conducted, the Netherlands Radio Philharmonic Orchestra. I also didn't know anymore I had already done it. [...] When I opened the score I didn't remember it anymore. I have to relearn the whole piece again'.

remember fewer details and have to go more by our feelings and a sense of familiarity. A greater effort is needed for new information to be coded as well as retrieved later in memory. In contrast, our capacity to analyse stored information and draw conclusions is largely preserved.

3.14   The complexity of memory processes

The complexity of memory processes is enormous. Lay people usually have an oversimplified image of it. By applying new techniques for brain research, such as the PET and MRI scans, we are increasingly gaining insight into areas like the association cortex, where very specific processes take place. Electrical stimulation of minute areas can already lead to a disturbance of very specific functions, such as naming a simple object or finishing a sentence. Calling an object 'simple' already implies a number of very different processes. We first have to recognise the object, then find a suitable word for it, link the enunciation of that word to it and control its naming, so that we know this has been done properly. We might also write the word down and recall the spelling of the word (and all the letters that constitute it!), and steer our hands while writing. Such a simple action, to which we have never given a thought, appears upon reflection to consist of an arrangement of very different processes which we apply to a number of very different representations. We are still far removed from a detailed overview of how this operates exactly, but every day progress is made in the development of our knowledge on memory processes.

Chapter 4

Memory Systems

4.1 Processes and files

As long ago as the nineteenth century it became clear that damage to certain parts of the brain can result in a loss of specific memory functions. Experiments with animals have also revealed that different neural areas are responsible for different tasks. This led to the formation of the first theories on memory systems. Specific mental capacities were attributed to independent memory categories. Since then there has been a real explosion in the number of supposed memory systems that actually overlap with one another. To this day there is no certainty as to whether we can really speak of different systems, and if we can, how many there are and which ones we can actually distinguish.

When studying memory systems we should make a distinction between two important components. One is related to the representations of the world outside ourselves in memory, and we could compare it to a computer data file. The second component consists of the processes that operate this file, and is comparable to the software. The representations in the file do not acquire any meaning without the help of operations with which they can be processed and interpreted. On the basis of this elementary distinction, psychologists who specialise in the study of memory can be classified into two schools: the pure associationists and the constructivists, also called neo-associationists (Howes, 1990) (see the description in section 3.6). The hard-line associationists say there are two separate systems. The data file would consist merely of copies of sensory perceptions. Cognitive processes would consist of arrangements applied to that memory file, such as selection, combination, interpretation and deduction, at the moment a situation gives cause for it. The constructivists, in contrast, are of the opinion that the data file itself is the final product of active and dynamic cognitive processes. Rumelhart and Norman (1983) say that much confusion over memory systems is the result of a lack of recognition which is essential to representations and processes. One cannot be understood without understanding the other. Representation structures and interpretation processes are mutually intertwined. They say that when studying the way in which the world is represented in our memory, both should be seen as an indivisible twofoldness.

The first classification of memory in different systems was that of the declarative and procedural memories (Cohen and Squire, 1980). Declarative memory would consist of a memory for personal experiences (episodic memory) and one for facts (semantic memory). A new classification is that of explicit and implicit memory, introduced in 1985 by Graf and Schacter.

4.2 Declarative and procedural memories

We learn an unbelievable number of facts throughout our lives: Peking is the capital of China, mammals cannot fly, Guinness is a beer. We also store memories of events: last year we went on holiday to Tuscany, this morning I had Quaker cereal for breakfast. This memory for facts and events is called the declarative memory. We also learn to play the piano, write, drive a car and tie our shoelaces. The storage of those skills takes place in the procedural memory. This memory steers the muscular movements of our hands during typing as well as part of the automatic buying actions when we walk through a supermarket pushing a shopping trolley. It is expressed in every moment of our lives in the things we do, without us having to think about it consciously. These actions usually take place on automatic pilot. In the majority of the actions we perform we do not have to appeal to our conscious memory. Procedural memory needs a lot of time and requires many repetitions in order to learn something. During that learning process, the actions take place largely in our explicit memory, but at a certain moment they become programmed and move outside our conscious attention.

We then perform them without needing to appeal to conscious memory. Once they are programmed, they are not easily forgotten. Once we learn to skate, we will be able to skate away after years without any problem. Procedural memory plays a role in learning skills as well as in developing habits – the often repeated and mainly unconscious routine actions into which we slip back in our daily lives. The memory for skills like riding a bicycle resides in the cerebellum and the putamen, a structure located in the innermost depths of our brain.

4.3 Habits

The development of these habits is a learning process that takes place in a different area of our brain from that which processes information, separately from the hippocampus and the amygdala. It is non-cognitive, not based on knowledge or memories, but on the emergence of autonomous connections between a stimulus and a response. Mishkin, Malamut and Bachevaller (1984) say that habits, as we define them, remind us of automatic stimulus–response connections as they were already postulated a long time ago by behaviourist psychologists as the basis of learning. Behaviourists took concepts such as mind, knowledge and even memory out of their usual meaning. They directly oppose the theories developed later from cognitive psychology, whose explanations on behaviour are based precisely on those concepts. However, the possibility of learning being based on two very different systems, one on cognitive memory and the other on habit forming, could bridge the discrepancy between these two schools. When different neural mechanisms exist for both types of learning processes, behaviour could be a mixture of automatic responses to stimuli on the one hand and activities motivated by goals, expectations and knowledge on the other.

Deeply ingrained habits are stored in the caudate nucleus, which, like the putamen, is an element of the limbic system. Together they are called the striatum. This striatum directly receives projections from many areas of the cortex, including sensory information. It also has its own neural connections with other parts of the brain which control behaviour and movement. Neuroanatomically speaking, it provides a direct connection between a stimulus and those activities that are implicit in the concept of 'habit'; but it is with how memory and habits interact with each other in the adult brain that our quest really begins. It seems that most learning processes use both systems, but we know very little about how this functions (Mishkin *et al.*, 1984).

Habits, in the sense of automatic forms of behaviour, can be part of a brand representation. Consumer brand behaviour is then no longer the exclusive result of cognitive and emotional evaluations, but also of an automatic process from stimulus to response.

4.4 Explicit and implicit memory

When referring to memory, we think of the capacity to recall certain things consciously: numbers, facts, experiences, images, sounds and smells. Schacter calls that part of memory the explicit memory. It overlaps the concept of declarative memory. It is the memory of events that took place early in our lives, up to that which we experienced today (episodic memory). It is also the capacity of bringing very concrete things into our consciousness, such as what is a spacewagon (a new subcategory of cars with the Renault Espace as a prototypical example) and what is Weetabix (semantic memory). But this is only the tip of the iceberg we call memory. Large parts of memory function permanently, without our being aware of it. Schacter (1996) calls this part of memory the implicit memory. This comprises the procedural memory, although these two concepts do not completely cover one another. The term 'implicit memory' indicates all those memory functions that take place outside our consciousness. Not only does it include automatic action: it includes mainly those conditioned responses and all those sensory perceptions that are stored, as it were, unprocessed.

The term 'implicit memory' was introduced by Graf and Schacter (1985), after research had shown that the feelings and attitudes of people can be influenced by perceptions and experiences, especially those of everyday life, which they cannot explicitly recall as such, but which do have a certain influence on our subsequent perceptions and behaviour.

Schacter (1996) posits that this indicates the operation of a perceptual representation system (PRS). This system is specialised in the recognition and processing of exterior characteristics of objects and phenomena (visual forms, colours, sounds), but does not know what these mean or what they can be used for. No connections with semantic memory are established either, and the hippocampus does not seem to be involved. This is an extremely superficial processing of stimuli which can sometimes bring about very subtle changes: changes that we cannot bring into our consciousness, but which later influence our reactions to the same stimuli. Because these representations work outside our consciousness, we cannot resist them and it is difficult to understand the fact that we are influenced by them.

Schacter also points to research which shows that advertisements which we perceive only very superficially (we scan them but do not focus on them) and which we cannot recall, still exert an influence on our choice of behaviour. Subliminal perceptions, which last so briefly that they cannot enter

Implicit memory in advertisements (based on Perfect and Askew, 1994, in Perfect and Heatherley, 1996)

There are indications of the effects of advertisements in implicit memory. An experiment by Perfect and Askew (1994) showed that, after exposure to advertisements, the attitude towards these advertisements was influenced in a positive sense, even among respondents who could not remember having seen the advertisements previously. This corresponds with the 'mere exposure' effect that had been established earlier by Bornstein (see Franzen, 1992). A second experiment showed that, after exposing test subjects for 24 hours to newspaper pages, the advertisements that had been there but which they could not remember explicitly were evaluated more positively in a number of dimensions than a number of control advertisements which they had not seen earlier.

consciousness, also fall into this category. Schacter assumes that there is a considerable influence from implicit memory in our mental life.

When we switch into a deeper cognitive processing of stimuli, the hippocampus does become active. The perceptions are then connected to the knowledge that is already stored in long-term memory. A more durable memory is formed, which will form part of explicit memory and which contains the knowledge that we can later recall and convey verbally.

Implicit and explicit memory are connected with various areas in our brain. Explicit memory is mainly localised in the brain cortex (especially in the temporal lobe) and in the hippocampus. The cerebellum – a nerve centre in the back of the head which contains about three-quarters of all our brain cells (Murre and Sturdy, 1995) – seems to be especially important for procedural memory.

According to Lockhart (1989), when defining implicit memory people instinctively assume that explicit memory – and therefore conscious memory or recognition – is the standard. But why should it be this way? Why should it be special that our memory be influenced by an experience from the past that we cannot remember any more? Why should this not be the standard instead, and the explicit memory of a previous experience the special circumstance? Explicit memory may very well be overestimated because so much psychological research is based on introspection and therefore on explicit memory. According to Raaijmakers (1996), implicit memory is essentially simple: a person performs a task, based on a previous experience. The person cannot remember that previous experience, but the researcher does see its effect. In explicit memory the learning experience is always needed. In implicit memory it is not essential for the learning experience to have also been unconscious (implicit learning). The accomplishment in performing the task can increase without being reduced to previous experiences. When we sleep or are anaesthetised, a lot goes on in our brain as well.

In recent years, the classification into explicit and implicit memory has been the centre of interest, and opinions on the subject are mixed. Some memory specialists point out that if we count as implicit memory every influence on behaviour that is not accessible through memory or recognition, it follows that plants also have a memory (Roediger, 1990). A new school speculates that we should not think in terms of neurological systems that operate autonomously and independently from one another, as Schacter and others do, but rather of a multitude of memory components that are combined in different ways, depending on the specific task that is presented to the person. The performance of each task would lead to a task-specific fabric of the many different components. This fabric can be different for one task than for another (Witherspoon and Moscovich, 1989). Colheart (1978) points to the fact that certain processes whose operation has by now become clear consist of a considerable number of sub-components. Visual recognition of objects contains four independent sub-components, and recognition of faces contains as many as nine.

The representation of a brand can be partially implicit, in other words unconscious. Emotions and attitudes related to a brand are influenced by learning experiences that people cannot remember any more and which have not led to explicit cognitions.

Chapter 5

Memory Representations

Every individual has an unimaginable amount of information on the world and life stored in his or her memory. These mental ideas of the world of objects (a car) and events (a fair) are called representations. Rumelhart and Norman (1985) say on the subject that a representation is something that stands for something else. In other words, it is a sort of model of something it represents: we should make a distinction between a representing world and a represented world, and the representing world should in some way or other reflect some aspects of the represented world.

The question is how these ideas are stored and what is their form, so that when perceiving the world around us we can interpret and understand it. This book is ultimately about how brands are represented in our memory. In this chapter we will give an overview of the most important theories in the field of the nature and organisation of memory representations.

Perceptions and meanings (Carter, 1998)

The brain is a factory with many products. Its raw material is information: the length of light waves hitting the retina; the duration of sound waves pulsing in the ear; the effect of a molecule on the olfactory canal. From this the sensory part of the brain creates an idea of what lies outside. But that basic perception is not the brain's finished product. The final construct is a perception that is invested with meaning. The meanings we attach to our perceptions are usually useful: they transform mere patterns of light into objects we can use, people we can love, places we can go. But sometimes they are misleading: the pool of water in the desert turns out to be a mirage; the axeman in the dark corner a mere shadow...

5.1 Analogous and propositional representations

In the representation of each thing in our memory we can distinguish three different forms of cognition: analogous, verbal and propositional.

Analogous representations are the direct representations of external phenomena, i.e. the storage of visual, tactile, sound, taste and smell perceptions. These are representations of superficial characteristics of those things: how they look, how they taste, how they feel, how they sound, how they smell. They are non-verbal.

Verbal representations are linguistic. Pavio (1986) speaks of 'logogenes', words and sentences in memory which are also represented audibly (how they sound) and visually (how are they written, how do they look). He is the father of the theory of dual coding, which contends that there are two systems for information processing and storage – one verbal and one non-verbal – and that each one, in turn, consists of two subsystems. He calls non-verbal representations 'imagens'.

His theory ignores a third category, however, that of propositional representations. These are abstract and are related to the meaning of something: what it is, how it is, what it is for, how it works, what can be done with it. They represent what the things can mean to us, the activities for which they are suitable, the functions they have in them and the manner in which they express those functions. Within this context, Palmer (1975) made a distinction between intrinsic and extrinsic aspects of representations. A representation is analogous when our relationship with that which is represented is based on its intrinsic properties. Howe (1990) made a distinction based on Piaget and Inhelder (1973) between figurative and operative memory representations which appear to correspond with analogous and propositional representations. According to Piaget and Inhelder, both representation categories go together in an associative network of the phenomenon. When a memory originates, they work together and influence each other.

Rumelhart and Norman (1983) posit that the distinction between the analogue and the propositional is too emphasised. What is important is the relationship between the representation and that which is represented, and this relationship can have many different dimensions, therefore making several distinctions possible; for instance, that between declarative and procedural, in which the former stands for knowledge of facts and the latter for our behavioural programming: our 'knowledge' of how we do things, or deal with products. On the basis of this, Carlston (1992) developed the theory of associative systems, which we will discuss later.

Propositional representations are thus related to the meaning of the things. They are not words or sentences, but a sort of abstract 'knowing' what something is. Propositions are non-verbal and non-visual. They are the meanings that can sometimes be expressed by sentences. Children develop

Meanings and language (Einstein, 1956 in Greenspan, 1996)

The words of language, as they are written or spoken, do not seem to play any role in my mechanism of thought. The physical entities which seem to serve as elements in thought are certain signs and more or less clear images which can be 'voluntarily' reproduced and combined. There is, of course, a certain connection between those elements and relevant logical concepts. It is also clear that the desire to arrive finally at logically connected concepts is the emotional basis of this rather vague play with the above-mentioned elements. But taken from a psychological viewpoint, this combinatory play seems to be the essential feature in productive thought – before there is any connection with logical construction in words or other signs which can be communicated to others.

them from birth, even before they learn language. They are idea-like, regardless of the original perception modality (they are a-modal). They can be expressed in analogue form, for example in images, and can be described verbally, but sometimes we are unable to find the words or images that describe exactly what we think or feel we know, since we do not have the proper labels at our disposal. Propositions are independent from language. People who speak different languages can nonetheless still have formed the same propositions. A nice illustration of the difference between meanings and language was put into words by Albert Einstein (see above).

During our whole life we develop new propositions by constantly abstracting meanings from our sensory perceptions. The label often follows in the form of a new word. Sometimes that does not happen and we do not have the vocabulary to express those formed meanings properly. We can show the contents of our cognitive system very schematically, as in Figure 5.1.

5.2 Concepts: units of knowledge

As early as 1690, the English philosopher Locke put forward that the contents of our memory consisted of concepts. He imagined these to be basic units of knowledge, some kind of 'knowledge atoms' which, just like molecules, would be assembled into more complex knowledge structures. His idea wasn't that far-fetched. Three centuries later, the American philosopher Fodor came forward with the same idea, processed into his theory of Information Atomism. The belief that our knowledge consists, among other things, of concepts such as abstractions from reality is now commonly accepted. We develop the concept of 'dog' for the entity of dogs, so that we do not have to

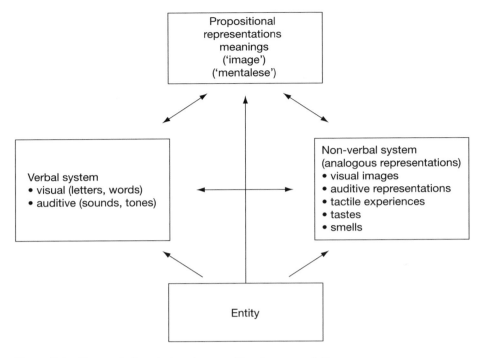

Figure 5.1 Non-verbal, verbal and propositional representations.

store a large amount of information for every type of dog or for every individual dog we know. The concept of 'dog' enables us to refer to that which Jack Russell terriers and mastiffs have in common. By identifying a Jack Russell terrier as a dog we allocate it a large amount of information (characteristics) that is included in the concept of 'dog'. By developing concepts, the amount of information from the world that is learned and remembered is reduced. Concepts make it possible to relate new perceptions to an earlier experience: when we see a chair of any type, we immediately know that we can sit on it and can somehow lean against it. If we did not have the concept of 'chair', then every chair we ever came across would raise the question of whether it is something one can sit on. A concept is therefore a body of characteristics or properties that apply to a series of individual entities and which exert an influence on our interpretations of and expectations over these entities.

We know concepts for objects with a practical function (such as 'chair'), for physical processes with a practical value (such as 'electricity'), and for simple actions of organisms (such as 'driving'). On the other hand, there are abstract concepts related to entities that are not directly observable (such as 'happiness', 'fear' and 'thought') (Van de Grind, 1997).

5.3 Concepts and language

Our mind contains an infinite amount of information units in the form of concepts, plus a collection of connections for combining them into increasingly complex knowledge and thoughts. Jackendoff (1994) calls these simplest knowledge units 'conceptual primitives', and the patterns that make combinations possible 'conceptual grammar'. Within this context, Pinker (1994) talks of 'mentalese'. He posits that every concept consists of three groups of neurons: one represents the individual item that is presented (e.g. Grolsch or Heineken or Twinings), another group the category with which the items are connected (beer, tea), and a third group the relationship between them ('is', 'resembles', 'is not', etc.). However, it should be noted that we now use language to indicate these groups, but these representations do not consist of language. The meaning 'Heineken = beer' is coded in our brain in a different way from in language.

There is, however, a close relation between concepts and the words that are used to describe them. 'Chair' is a concept as well as a word. As a concept, it is an abstract representation of a category of seats which have a number of common characteristics, thanks to which when we see one piece we immediately know it is a chair. The word 'chair' is only a verbal code we use to name the concept-category. In other languages people know the same concept but link it to a different code (for instance, 'stoel' in Dutch). It seems that living creatures that do not have a language capacity, like cats, can also

---

Concept-forming by pigeons (Gould and Gould, 1998)

Work on animal thinking has centred on birds and primates. One important line of evidence is the apparent ability of some animals to form concepts. The remarkable abilities of Alex the parrot, studied by Irene M. Pepperberg of the University of Arizona, provide one clear example. Another, involving pigeons, was pioneered by the late Richard J. Herrnstein of Harvard University. His technique was to provide lab-reared pigeons with a carousel of slides, half with some example of the class of target objects – trees, perhaps, or fish or oak leaves. The birds were then rewarded with food for pecking at any slide that contained, say, a tree. Learning was slow until the birds appeared to figure out what the rewarded slides had in common. Under some conditions, the pigeons would resort to memorising the full rewarded set of slides, revealing an astonishing ability to recall hundreds of pictures. In most cases, however, they caught on to the common feature, demonstrating their knowledge by responding correctly to an entirely new set of slides.

Language and vision as a window on thought (Jackendoff, 1994)

The basic reason for keeping language and meanings separate is that pretty much anything we can say in one language can be translated into any other, preserving the thought that the original language conveys. This means that thoughts can't be embalmed in the form of any single language – they must be neutral as to what language they are to be expressed in. For instance, the same thought can be expressed in English, where the verb precedes the direct object, and in Japanese, where the verb follows the direct object; hence the form to the thought must be neutral as to word order (...).

One language may have words for different things from another language, so that a simple word-for-word translation can't be done. (A case frequently cited is the alleged existence in Eskimo languages of words for many different kinds of snow, but no word for just plain snow.) Such gaps can usually be remedied by coining new words or borrowing words from another language.

If one is allowed to borrow vocabulary freely, any sentence of any language can be translated into any other language, with a few minor exceptions due to differences in grammatical structure. Moreover, these remaining differences can be explained to speakers of the languages being translated into. So differences in grammar do not reflect differences in the character of thought; the form of thought must be distinct from the linguistic garb in which it is clothed. The language we hear in our heads while thinking is a *conscious manifestation* of the thought – not the thought itself, which isn't present to consciousness.

We certainly have enough precedent by now for talking about completely unconscious parts of the mind. Still, it may seem counterintuitive

Contd

develop abstract concepts which enable them to interpret immediately very different specimens of one category.

People do not think in English or Dutch or Chinese. They think in connections between propositional representations, which Pinker calls 'mentalese'. Language is an instrument that makes it possible for us to express our thoughts – but the thoughts themselves are independent from language. Babies, although they have no language, still develop mental concepts. For instance, they already have a concept of 'dog' even before they learn the word 'dog' and its meaning. Above we include a description of the relationship between language, images and thoughts by Jackendoff (1994), professor of linguistics, and a pioneer in his contributions to the discussions on the connections between meaning and language.

that thought is unconscious. Two examples may help for now. First, consider the experience of bilinguals who can 'think in two languages'.

We would like to be able to say their thoughts are the same, no matter which language they are 'thinking in'. This is possible only if the form of thought is *neither* of the languages, and therefore something of which they are not conscious.

Consider the experience of suddenly arriving at a conclusion 'intuitively'. Surely thought has been taking place – it's just that we didn't have any awareness of it, and that's why we call it 'intuitive'. Only if thought is unconscious is such an experience possible.

When we don't think 'in a language', we often experience our thought as visual images, 'pictures in the head'. Could visual images instead be the form of thought? I don't think this is possible either. Who looks at them?

How could visual images clearly distinguish the thoughts expressed by sentences like, 'There's a bird in the tree', 'A bird was in the tree yesterday', and 'Birds like that tree'? What visual images convey the thoughts expressed by words such as 'justice', 'if', 'tomorrow', or, for that matter, 'thought'?

In fact, even simple visualisable words present a problem. For instance, the visual image that goes with 'dog' is of one particular dog – so how can it be the thought that encompasses the appearance of Collies, Dachshunds, St Bernards and Chihuahuas?

From these simple examples, we can see that visual images aren't adequate as a vehicle of thought. Rather, like things we say to ourselves 'in our minds', they're a way that thought can manifest itself in consciousness. Again, I urge the idea that thought itself is completely unconscious. I'll use the term *conceptual structure* for the form in which thoughts are couched. Like all the other kinds of mental information we've discussed, conceptual structure ultimately amounts to patterns of neural firings in the brain.

Hughlings-Jackson wrote in 1915 on the connections between language and propositions. He said we talk or think not just in words or signs, but in words or signs that point to one another in a certain way. Without a considerable connection between the elements, a verbal expression would be nothing more than a sequence of names, a collection of words that does not embody a proposition. The proposition constitutes the unity of language. Loss of language (aphasia) is therefore a loss of the capacity to proposition, and not only the capacity to proposition aloud (talking) but also internally or externally. The speechless patient has lost his language capacity in the full sense of the word. We do not talk only in order to tell other people what we think, but also in order to tell ourselves that we think. Speaking is a part of thinking (Sachs, 1989).

Language is therefore not only an expression of thoughts, but also that which makes thinking possible, and distinguishes thinking from non-thinking; it is an all-pervasive characteristic of the individual. Church (1961) says that, by learning language, the individual is changed so much that it can do new things, or old things in a new way. Language enables us to deal with things at a distance, to manipulate them without touching them. First of all, it allows us to deal with people and, through other people, objects. Secondly, we can manipulate symbols in a way that is impossible for the things they mean, therefore arriving at new and even creative versions of reality. We can verbally change situations which in themselves are difficult to change, we can isolate characteristics that cannot be isolated, we can connect objects and events that are widely separated from each other by time and space, and we can – if we want – symbolically turn the universe inside out (Sachs, 1989).

5.4   The meaning of words

People tend to see the meaning of words as objective data units that are fixed in dictionaries. However, the meaning of words is in our brain: what the dictionary contains is only an optimal reproduction of the meanings that were found in a specific culture at a specific time in many brains. The dictionary only tries to chart the situation in our brain as well as possible. A word in our brain is linked to a collection of meanings, all of which are part of Pinker's mentalese (1994). A word itself is part – probably the centre – of an associative network that extends over all sorts of areas of our brain and is linked to letters, sound, abstract meanings and sometimes the external manifestation of the things they represent.

We are brought up to think that words have exact meanings, and that inaccuracy is a sign of sloppy thinking (Jackendoff, 1994), but the fact is that almost every word we choose seems to present definition problems. Science is plagued by this. Even the most common words have many meanings in a dictionary, and the definitions that we find in different dictionaries are often very divergent. We have to give up the idea that we have an exact definition in our mind of the words that we know. Essentially, meanings are vague; this has to do with the way in which things are fixed in our memory in concepts as well as with the very meanings of the words. The concepts that constitute our mentalese consist of ideal cases as well as context-dependent grey areas. The meanings of the words are also vague. When attempting to make exact definitions, we try to have clarity on the contents of the concepts as well as on the words that express the meanings optimally. This is a whole process of puzzling that is constantly taking place in our brain, even as we write these words. Jackendoff (1994) asks himself why we think that words have exact meanings: probably because the word 'meaning' also expresses a concept. If we reflect consciously about it, we imagine it as an ideal in which everything is clean and clear. But why should 'meaning' be better defined than other words? Why shouldn't it be a bit vague on the edges? We might have to get a little used to the idea that 'meaning', by definition, is vague.

To summarise, we can now distinguish:

- An analogue representation of something: the representation in memory of sensory perceptions in the past
- A proposition, or a set of propositions, being the meanings that the analogue representations represent for us
- Word meanings: propositions in the form of or abstract mental descriptions of that which a word represents
- Analogue (visual and/or auditive) representations of words and phrases: what they look like, how they sound
- Mental words or phrases that describe the analogue representation
- Mental words or phrases that represent the propositions or meanings linked to the analogue representation.

Scientific integrity obliges us to note here that these theories are not uncontested. The question that keeps coming up is how propositional representations relate to classical association theories as they were discussed earlier in this book. Are propositional representation systems not mere systematic connections between elements, as was already assumed by the classical association theories? Yes and no, say Rumelhart and Norman (1983): they contend that the current representation models are indeed a formalisation of associations, but that here we are talking about a new association theory – neo-associationism (as discussed earlier, in section 3.6). The propositional representations differ in four ways from classical associationism:

(1) The associations have a direction. Associations from A to B are not necessarily the same as those from B to A.
(2) Associations are labelled. A and B can be associated with one another in many different ways. Different labels stand for different sorts of relationships (for example, 'is', 'can', 'resembles').
(3) A distinction is made between types and signs (between the general and the specific). This solves the problem of being able to activate a specific example of an item without confusing it with all other examples or with the generic scheme.
(4) A distinction is made in levels of representation. This allows the activation and processing of higher order representations. This difference was not made in the classical association theory, which was one of its shortcomings as far as its explanatory strength is concerned.

> A brand representation consists of a store of sensory perceptions (what it looks like, how it feels, how it smells and tastes, how it sounds, how it works) and of abstract meanings (propositions) – what its purpose is, what it means and what I think of it. This representation is independent of language. Language (words) only expresses the unconscious background activation of the representation.

5.5   The nature of concepts

How should we imagine a concept? We have already seen that it is an abstraction of a collection of individual entities that have a number of common characteristics. Frege (1952) made a distinction between the 'intension' and the 'extension' of a concept. With 'intension' he meant the properties that define a concept. Under 'extension' he included the collection of individual entities that fall under the concept (Figure 5.2). Later on, the concept of 'category' was used for it.

An example of a concept is that of a bird. It is probably linked to the following characteristic properties:

- Has feathers
- Has two wings
- Can fly
- Sings
- Has two legs
- Has a beak.

The concept contains a large number of different types of birds, from sparrows to chickens to ostriches.

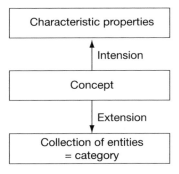

Figure 5.2   The concept according to Frege (1952).

For a long time, concepts were seen as stable structures in long-term memory. Barsalou (1993), however, is of the opinion that these are also temporary constructions in the working memory. He posits that parts of networks in long-term memory get activated as a result of the task a person is confronted with. Entities have many properties (associations), of which a situation-dependent subset is used in order to form a concept. In this vision, concepts are very flexible and come about *ad hoc*. A person who wants to lose weight will form a concept of low-calorie products in which light beer as well as low-calorie jams can be arranged. An entity can also fall under several totally different concepts. At the same time, associations vary in strength and so does accessibility. Strong associations within the same context lead to the formation of the same concepts. Consequently, there probably are relatively stable subsets of properties that are united in more permanent concepts in long-term memory, and very flexible *ad hoc* concept formation in the working memory – on the basis of the situation in which the person is and the task they are presented with.

A recent theory on the nature of concepts is that of 'psychological essentialism'. It suggests that concepts are determined mainly by their 'deeper meanings'. People develop heuristics based on the assumption that things with the same superficial characteristics also share the same deeper essences. The deeper essence would contain the substance of the concept. Concepts can thus be seen as combinations of external characteristics and deeper meanings: the analogue and propositional representations we have already discussed. A still more recent theory is that of 'informational atomism' by Jerry Fodor (1983), which sees concepts as information atoms – the cornerstones of our knowledge. The word 'apple' would be linked to a concept of 'apple' which is not to be further analysed, and – according to him – that is the end of it.

5.6   Categories

Collins and Quillian introduced in 1969 the assumption that concepts are organised in hierarchies. According to them, we can make a distinction between basic categories, supracategories above those and lower subcategories, sub-subcategories, etc. The basic categories contain most of the information about the objects that are classified in them. We can imagine having a category for 'furniture' with its subcategories of chairs, tables and cupboards. The category of chairs can in turn be subdivided into the subcategories of dining room chairs, living room chairs, office chairs, aeroplane seats, car seats, and so on. The category of living room chairs can also be subdivided into tub chairs, couches, etc. Within this hierarchical structure, chairs are the basic category, containing most of the information on all the objects that fall into it. The upper supracategory of furniture is too

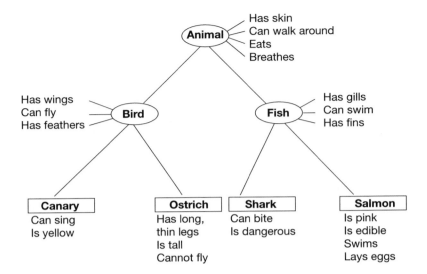

Figure 5.3 An example of a hierarchical concept (Collins and Quillian, 1969).

general, the lower subcategory of dining room chairs adds only one dimension to all the information that is already contained in the basic category of 'chairs'. In Figure 5.3, Collins and Quillian (1969) give an example of (part of) such a hierarchy.

Collins and Loftus (1975) later abandoned the strict hierarchical structures of concepts in our memory and postulated the theory of the spreading of activation, which we have already discussed (see section 3.8). This theory is based on the idea of distances between concepts that are linked to each other in networks. The closer the relationship between the concepts, the shorter the connection and the larger the chance that, when a concept is activated, the same will happen with the other concept. This theory, which has many supporters, is not wholly uncontested either.

The classification of entities into concept categories is done on the basis of their perceived properties, such as the physical manifestation, the functions they have for us, and the deeper (symbolic) meanings we allocate to them. On the one hand, the classification is based on natural, objective properties of things (birds have wings, fish have fins); on the other, they emanate from artificial (propositional) meanings they are given by people in a specific culture. Rosch and Lloyd (1978) posit that categories are neither 'natural' nor 'artificial'; they are rather always the result of an interaction between structural properties of the things as they present themselves to us in the world, and our human reactions to them, which for a large part are socially, culturally and situationally determined.

All entities in a category or subcategory have a number of common properties. An entity belonging in a specific category is determined by whether it contains these properties. How do we determine this? There are various theories about it. One of them says that an entity must have all the defining properties of the category. Another theory makes a distinction between two types of properties: defining and characteristic. The defining characteristics would then form the core of the concept and be shared by all members of that category. Characteristic properties allow for a larger margin: these are characteristics that the members can contain to a greater or lesser degree. Depending on this, they are better or less fitting specimens of the category.

Tverski (1977) postulated the contrast model, which suggests that an entity can also have properties that are not shared by the other members of a category. These lead to the entity being a less suitable representative of the category, or may even get in the way of its inclusion in that category. The assumption that a concept is determined by the definite properties that each member of a category should have has proved not to be sustainable. People are aware of the variety of examples within a category, and can evaluate them to the degree to which they are better or less suitable representatives of it. They can possess the properties of a category to a greater or lesser degree. A blackbird is more of a bird, so to speak, than a chicken or a penguin. This has led to the theory of typifying properties, in which every specimen has, as it were, a score for the degree to which it possesses each of the properties. According to this theory, those members of the category who attain a higher score for each of the properties are the most typical examples of that category: on the basis of cues, they are the members of the category most easy to recognise. Consequently, we also distinguish atypical members of the category – those specimens who attain a lower score on one or several properties, or who have contrasting properties.

Members of a category are therefore not always equivalent to each other. The series of entities in the category, classified from most representative to least representative, are called the graded structure of the category (Mervis and Rosch, 1981). Another theory says that each category in our memory is represented by an abstract prototype with which we compare an object. Yet another theory posits that there is no prototype, but that a category is merely a collection of individual objects. There is no consensus about this yet. According to the supporters of the prototype theory, a prototype can be defined as the most characteristic object in our perception of all objects in a category. Prototypes would help place individual objects into a category on the basis of similarities between the individual object and the prototype. Finally, the possibility has been proposed of using the most typical specimen in a category as prototype. Some memory scientists think that we do not have to choose between these possibilities, but that the various representational forms of concepts (properties, prototypes, specific specimen) work together when interpreting reality.

> Brands are or can be classified into concept categories that consist of product concepts or service concepts. This classification takes place on the basis of the degree to which the brand contains the typifying properties of the product concept. Based on this, it can be a prototypical specimen or a more or less suitable representative of this category.

5.6.1 *The development of categories*

Categorisation takes place as soon as young children start to know the world around them and have to process and store their perceptions into significant mutual relationships. In our younger years, these cognitive structures are still relatively simple, but as we learn they become more complex. This process takes place not only at a young age, but also in adults every time they are confronted with a new phenomenon. Initially, this leads to simple structures. As more information on a phenomenon is processed, the categories are increasingly differentiated and a more complex structure arises. We may assume that the product category 'passenger cars' is quite differentiated for most of us. Based on this, we can place almost all brands and types we know in a category or subcategory. In Part Two of this book we will give several examples. The moment the Renault Espace appeared on the roads, it was difficult to place it in an existing subcategory. By now we probably have formed a category of spacewagons, and elevated the Renault Espace into a prototype of this category. The category name is not established yet: another name is MPVs, or multi-purpose vehicles. There are new cars that do resemble the prototype but are much smaller, like the Renault Scenic. Is this a different specimen within the MPV category, or the beginning of a new sub-subcategory?

The same process is taking place now with the development of a product category such as computers. For most of us, this means a relatively small number of subcategories and a simple structure. This makes it difficult to understand all sorts of units that we perceive within the whole computer field, and to store our information in such a way that we can find our way around later on. Undoubtedly, the generations that are now growing up with computers will develop a more differentiated cognitive computer hierarchy with more subcategories.

5.7 Schemata: knowledge structures

Our knowledge contains more than just information regarding concepts and the hierarchies into which these are classified. We also need structures in order to be able to combine them into increasingly complex knowledge and thoughts. How should we picture these structures? It was Bartlett who, as early as 1932, came up with the 'scheme theory', which attempts to answer this. The theory is essential in current thinking about perceptions and memory. A scheme is a structured organisation of concepts. These concepts are linked to each other in a scheme, so that they represent more complex forms of knowledge in their mutual connection. These can be more complex objects (the kitchen), events (a picnic), actions (making coffee), values (power), or even political ideologies (liberalism). Schemes of objects are also called frames, schemes of actions are scripts. Schemata bear more of a resemblance to encyclopaedic knowledge than to definitions from a dictionary. A scheme arises on the basis of all the experiences that we have had with these phenomena. People cannot remember the individual memories any more, and what remains is a casing, a sort of map, and abstractions of all the perceptions. The specific experiences that have led to the formation of a scheme have been forgotten or completely relegated to the background. An integrated representation is formed in which the most relevant, the most characteristic information of all the preceding perceptions is encapsulated (Figure 5.4).

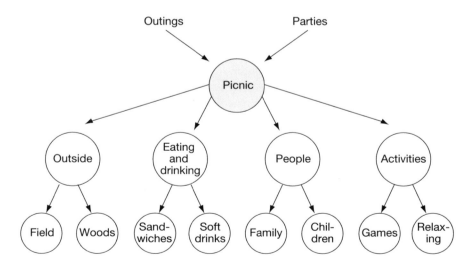

Figure 5.4 Picnic scheme. The scheme for 'picnics' consists of a number of subschemes such as those for the place in which we usually have picnics (a field or the woods), the food we eat (sandwiches), the people involved (the family) and the things we do (outdoor games). The picnic scheme can in turn be part of a more extended scheme such as 'parties' or 'outings'.

Once formed, schemata function as interpretation frameworks for subsequent perceptions of the same phenomenon. The process of interpretation implies the selection of relevant schemata; concepts perceived together activate schemata they are part of. The activated schemata colour our expectations with regard to the phenomenon and help us interpret the new perceptions. This is how our schemata interact with our sensory perceptions. The new perceptions, in turn, influence the already present schemata. These are constantly subject to change. They develop during our life, from primitive structures in young children to very complicated and subtle reference frameworks at an advanced age.

Schemata are the reason why we see things in the way that we do, which is often different from how others interpret the same perception. They function as selection filters for our perceptions and replenish them at the same time. We perceive a sensory glimpse of something, and at the same moment we have an awareness of the whole phenomenon. Because schemata are also interconnected through networks, they can activate each other, causing the meaning we give to a perception to be very varied and personal. Beijk and van Raaij (1989) say that without schemata, in which the constants of our experiences with the world are established, no significant perception is possible. Schemata also imply an attitude, in other words they often specify the nature of the relationship we have to the represented phenomenon.

In general, schemata consist of a configuration of subschemata. Every subscheme has subschemata, and so on (Rumelhart and Norman, 1983). Some schemata cannot be further dissected. Scheme theories therefore imply that memory consists of an infinite number of knowledge packages. Each package consists of a figuration of subpackages (concepts) that specify the constitutive components of the package. Rumelhart and Norman (1983) are of the opinion that our knowledge is fixed in schemata. A criticism of the scheme theory is that it puts a one-sided emphasis on the imperfection of memory, while in reality we are able to recall individual things, often to the smallest detail. Can we still speak of a scheme with such a detailed memory of one perception of one thing? For this reason, Schank (1981) posited a hierarchical structure for representations in memory that he called MOPS, or Memory Organisation Packets. The lowest level in this hierarchy would consist of the most specific representations of individual entities. At higher levels, the representations would increasingly become conceptual and scheme-like. According to this theory, the specific representations would not be kept for long – instead, they would be included in the generalised schemata.

Raaijmakers (1996) also believes that the concept of schemata should be reserved for the expectation patterns we have with regard to more complex phenomena and situations. They are based on many experiences in comparable situations. This leads to a sort of average experience, causing the emergence of a prototypical representation; for instance, what is a typical restaurant? In

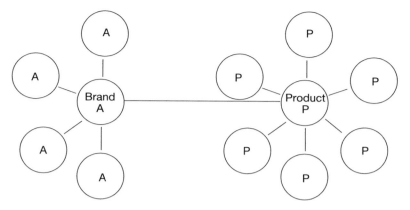

Figure 5.5 Brand and product scheme.

addition, says Raaijmakers, the separate phenomena and experiences are also stored. These consist not only of the common scheme with extra added information, but also of independent representations of the individual phenomenon. We therefore have a prototypical image of banks – a bank scheme – and, additionally, an independent representation of, for example, the Rabobank (a large Dutch cooperative bank). The Rabobank representation is not only a generalised bank scheme with specific additions, such as 'for farmers', but a specific representation of the Rabobank. The Rabobank representation is undoubtedly associatively linked to the generalised bank scheme and influenced by it. Figure 5.5 shows how a brand and a product scheme can go together in an associative network.

The generalised bank scheme is probably predominantly present in the representations of individual banks. The scheme theory, just like the SAM theory ('search of associative memory') of Raaijmakers and Shiffrin (1981), thus assumes a subdivision of memory into units (for that matter, Raaijmakers and Shiffrin speak again of 'images'). These units can be sounded during the search in our long-term memory. A scheme or image would be defined by the property of unit: during the search in long-term memory, the information that is activated is limited to the one that is 'united' in a scheme or image.

That which is recalled, however, is not the same as that which is present in memory – it is much simpler. The retrieval structure would only contain those aspects of the storage structure that are important to the search process. Many retrieval structures are supposedly organised in relation to moment- and content-bound information. The moment in which and the context within which we are confronted with a stimulus constellation therefore determine whether a specific scheme is activated or not. When a scheme is activated, a certain portion becomes available for evaluation and decision making. That portion is determined by the strength of the connections between the cue representation (a concept) and the other elements of the scheme that are linked to it.

The boundaries of the individual schemes are not exact – in fact, they are rather fuzzy. The various subcomponents of a scheme are in turn linked to subcomponents of other schemata. Raaijmakers and Shiffrin (1981) also assume that the connections of elements within a scheme are stronger than the mutual connections between various schemes. The capacity of our working memory is limited, and the processing of a limited and integrated retrieval scheme requires less capacity than that of the fully stored scheme. In short, during the search process in memory we only activate a retrieval scheme as a subset of the stored scheme.

5.8 The functioning of schemata

Alba and Hasher (1983) formulated a model on the functioning of schemata. According to this model, information processing takes place on the basis of the following five processes:

(1) *Selection:* only those aspects of incoming information which are the most important and relevant for the activated scheme are coded. No information or less relevant information is not coded.
(2) *Abstraction:* the selected information is not stored in terms of its superficial characteristics, but those of its meaning. The specific perception episode is forgotten, and what is left are the general characteristics of an entity.
(3) *Interpretation:* in order to understand incoming information, the relevant schemata in long-term memory are activated. We allocate properties to an entity on the basis of the general scheme.
(4) *Integration:* a new integrated memory representation is formed on the basis of the preceding three processes.
(5) *Normalisation:* perceptions and memories are adjusted to the relevant scheme so that they become consistent with it.

Here Alba and Hasher ignore Schacter's hypothesis (1996), which postulates that there is a perceptual representation system based mainly on recognition. Information processing would begin with it.

The model of Alba and Hasher would predict the best memory for information that, in correspondence with the expectations, is already decided in the scheme. However, Mandler (1984) contradicts this by positing that these expectations are precisely the cause of there being no, or less, attention paid to that which is already known. It is the scheme that enables the recipient to focus her limited capacity precisely on the new, unexpected aspects of an object or situation. It is those deviating, more bizarre recollections in memory that are in the foreground – not the everyday ones. Both theories are probably valid: in order to understand information, the relevant scheme must be present. At the same time, continued attention depends mainly on the new and unexpected aspects of our perceptions.

Schemata can also result in our allocating wrongful meanings to our perceptions. We fill our initial (and often partial) perceptions of an entity with the meanings that are already decided in the relevant scheme, while these are not present in the perceived entity. We also ensure our schemata are consistent: we make our perceptions correspond with our previous experiences, as they are summarised in our schemata.

Brands people are confronted with are interpreted on the basis of expectation processes we have with regard to similar entities, or schemata. People allocate properties to a brand on the basis of the general scheme of a category to which a brand belongs.

Chapter 6

Associative Networks

6.1 Associative network models

Cognitive scientists attempt to convert their theoretical insights on specific cognitive processes into computer models. Models based on the fact that representations in long-term memory are organised in mutually interconnected complexes are called associative network models. According to these models, representations (e.g. brands) can be understood as complex systems of associated elements in which each individual element is presented by a node (a junction in an associative network). The connections between these elements are depicted as operations. A representation of 'apple' is linked to the meaning 'round' by a connection with the name 'is'. Associative networks assume that:

(1) Entities (like brands) are presented by a content-free but accessible central node that is connected in a network with nodes that represent other meanings.
(2) The nature of these connections can differ. They can represent very general relationships (for instance, brand A being associated with product B, or brand A resembling brand B), or more specific relationships (for instance, brand A is coffee).
(3) The activation strength of the nodes as well as that of the connections between the nodes can differ.
(4) Learning takes place by adding new nodes or by changing the strengths of the existing connections between nodes.
(5) Various memory effects can be modelled by spreading activation from a specific node through the network.
(6) The way in which the spreading takes place can be influenced by various factors, for instance the number of intermediate elements from the point of entry up to a specific node.

Rumelhart and Norman (1983) posited that associative network models may very well form a useful basis for further theory forming, but that they are too simple in many respects. They have shortcomings, especially in the area of 'understanding understanding'. They believe a new approach is necessary in order to make the representation of more holistic units and more complex relationships between them possible.

Associative network models are rather vague on what it is exactly that nodes represent (characteristics, concepts or schemes), and how these representations are mutually interconnected and organised in a structure we call a network. Some theoreticians assume that each element in a network is directly linked to a central node. Others assume that there are associations between the elements. Yet another possibility is a structure in which individual associations are connected with coordinating categories of meaning. These distinctions are mainly relevant to the understanding of the outlining meanings and the possible relationships between individual associations. Figure 6.1 gives an overview of three different possibilities: Saab would be directly linked to the (higher) meanings of 'individualistic' and 'technological', which can in turn be associated with, for instance, 'creative people' and 'special' respectively. In principle, the reverse order is also possible. Saab → creative people → individualistic. The third possibility is for Saab to be directly linked to each of these meanings.

Little is actually known on the structure of associative networks. One of the possibilities is a hierarchical coherence in which meanings of a lower order are linked to meanings of a higher order. Product properties would be linked to product advantages, and in turn these would be linked at a higher abstract level to psychosocial meanings. In the example of Saab, such a hierarchy could look like this:

Saab → turbo → technological → creative people → individualistic

In laddering research, which we will discuss in section 20.2, we do find an association order of the concrete and specific to the more abstract and general, but that could be a consequence of the research method used.

Lawson notes that the theory of spreading of activation based on the relative strengths of the individual connections (see section 3.8) is probably an adequate idea of things for the process of automatic, unconscious information processing, but has its shortcomings when it comes to explaining the more strategic processes of information processing. Little theory forming has taken place on this subject. The big question is, if memory storage is organised (which is what we assume for the time being), how does this take place? Are individual associations organised in categories, and can we distinguish types of categories? Is it the case that, for instance, associations of a brand with concrete product properties are organised in a more general category that represents something like an advantage for the users? Are properties such as 'bodywork construction', 'crushable zone', 'anti-jamming system' and 'side impact bars' part of an organisation that carries the label of 'safety' when it comes to automobile brands? As plausible as it may seem, we just do not know.

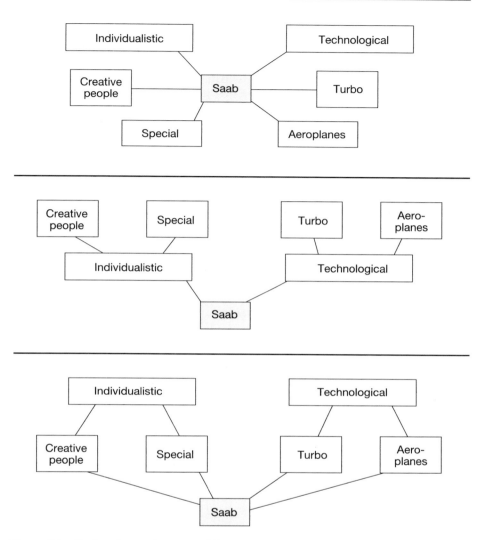

Figure 6.1   Saab scheme: three possibilities.

Lawson (1998) suggests nonetheless a structure in which universal consumption properties would be present in every associative network, next to specific properties per product category. Universal properties could include, for instance, perceived quality, price and convenience, and product-specific properties could include taste (in foodstuffs) and style (in decoration products). Lawson also assumes that brands are present in the experienced consumer in the form of such a knowledge structure with evaluations, just as they can be seen in research in the form of rankings and ratings. These evaluations would therefore not come about when given cause, for example during the cooking process or in an interview situation, but would be already present *a priori*. The authors believe these evaluations are part of the knowledge structure of the consumers who use certain brands. At the same time, however, this is least of all certain for brands of which people have no experience.

> The association of a brand with a product is different from that of a product with a brand: associations have a direction. Brand associations also have a label ('is', 'can', 'resembles', etc.).

6.2 Associative systems

When we recall someone's face, what we really recall is the eyes, the nose, the mouth, the hair and the fact that everything goes together. In turn, this visual memory goes together with the memory of the sound of the voice and the emotional image we have of someone. The memory of a small part of these relations is enough to recall the others as well (Bergsma, 1996). Carlston (1992) adds that associative networks contain a variety of representational forms, i.e. not only the cognitive, as we previously discussed. By representational forms we understand the totality of elements that are linked in our brain with a specific concept, thus cognitive representations, associated emotions and feelings, and attitudes and behavioural tendencies. Carlston labels his view 'associative systems'. He developed his theory especially with regard to the representation of persons in our memory. Carlston's system theory attempts to expose the connections between the various forms of representations and connect them with their origin. In this theory, passive perception would lead mainly to representations of visual phenomena (the previously mentioned analogue representations) and categorisations. Behavioural interaction would lead to episodic imaging and relationship orientations, emotional involvement would lead to affective relationships and evaluations. Within this associative system theory, the relative saliency of various representational forms and the strength of the intermediate associations are also stressed. A specific behavioural tendency can therefore influence the structural and emotional association categories. A conscious memory is the product of the cooperation between the various subsystems in the brain. The brain somehow has the capacity to keep up exactly with which fragments belong together (Bergsma, 1996).

Consequently, a brand does not sit as a complete entity in a single location in our brain, but is spread over the brain in the form of a large number of association categories for the many facets of which it consists. And when we recall the brand at a certain moment under the influence of a specific stimulus, it is present in our consciousness in one respect only.

Brands are present in our memory in the form of an associative network. This consists of the totality of responses that are connected to the brand, which include superficial characteristics (sensory representations), abstract meanings (propositions), emotions, attitudes and behavioural tendencies. A brand representation is spread over the brain in the form of the various association categories of which it consists.

6.3   Neural network models

Concepts and schemata, as discussed in the previous chapter, were seen as local representations. A localised storage of a concept as a whole and separate from other concepts was assumed. For a long time there was no clear picture of how the representation was structured at a neural level. It was unknown whether a concept such as a grandmother was represented by just one neuron (a 'grandmother cell'), which was itself connected with cells representing concepts such as a grandfather. After everything that has been discussed, it is clear that this is not very likely. The gradually increasing availability of insights into neuronal processes has led to new theories on the neuronal basis of representation. What they have in common is that they are based on distributed representations in which the same neurons form part of several representations. To elucidate, we offer an analogy with a digital watch. Instead of the individual figures as we know them in a classic watch, here use is made of a single network that consists of seven units. Each unit takes part in the production of each figure, only by being 'on' or 'off'. We could also say that the representation of a figure is distributed over all seven units, and that no single unit represents one of the figures selectively (Figure 6.2). The representation of an entity in memory, such as a concept, is imagined in a similar way, and is called distributed representation.

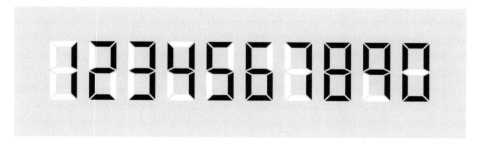

Figure 6.2   Seven units form the basis of digital numbers.

6.4 Parallelism

Our brain is not just a sort of tape recorder that stores unprocessed sensory stimuli. We apply all sorts of processes to the stimuli that reach us. We select sensory perceptions, modify them, interpret them and react to them. To that end, we send our perceptions through all sorts of configurations of synaptic connections. That does not take place serially, as with classical computers, but in parallel, or simultaneously, and we do this at an unbelievable speed. A personal computer takes a quarter of an hour to perform 100 billion individual calculations, but our visual system alone can do that in one hundredth of a second. All those calculations are performed in parallel. The brain in its totality performs 100 trillion calculations in the same one hundredth of a second. A personal computer would need about a week to do that. From each eye alone, millions of axons run to our brain, all of them simultaneously active. This parallelism recurs in practically every part of the whole system. Most of these parts are specialised in dealing with various sorts of information. The original idea of full distribution in information processing has been abandoned, and it is now assumed that the various parts of which a perception consists (visual images, sounds, tactile, smell and taste experiences, words) are processed simultaneously in different modules and are combined somehow into a whole.

This clearly explains how difficult it is to copy the processes that take place in our brain with computers and computer programs. Not even taking into account the fact that it is already complicated to imitate the behaviour of a single neuron, the fact that this neuron maintains extremely individual connections (with different strength/weakness charges) with as many as 10,000 other neurons makes this a nearly impossible task.

6.5 Connectionism

Classical computers carry out processes consecutively. With new generations of computers it has become possible to perform all sorts of calculations simultaneously, as does the brain. The past decade has seen the beginning of the development of computer programs that would be a reproduction of certain very specific processes that take place in the brain. They are based on the principle that knowledge is not stored *in* certain neurons, but in the *connections between* countless spread neurons. For this reason they are known as connectionist models. They are also based on a parallel process in which large numbers of neurons are simultaneously active. Connectionist models are also called parallel distributed processing models (PDP) or neural network models. The indication of neurons is replaced here by that of nodes, but the term synapses is used again for the mutual connections. This is how neural networks are developed which are imitations of specific processes such as the recognition of faces, reading printed text, distinguishing sounds and converting text into speech. Connectionist network models have the following characteristics (Eysenck and Keane, 1995):

(1) The network consists of neuron-like units that are linked to each other, causing a single unit to have many associations with other units. These units are called nodes.
(2) Units influence each other by activation or blockades.
(3) A unit integrates the input of all incoming connections and produces a single outgoing response to another unit when the common input exceeds a threshold.
(4) The network as a whole is characterised by the properties of the units that constitute it, the manner in which they are connected, and the rules that are used to change the strength of the connections.
(5) Networks can consist of different layers: a layer of input connections, one or more layers of 'hidden units', and a layer of output units.
(6) A representation of a concept is stored as a spread pattern of activation in the network.
(7) One and the same network can contain mainly different representations without them necessarily influencing each other.

There is uncertainty about the degree to which these neural network models are a mirror of what really takes place in our brain. There seems to be disagreement between cognitive scientists and computer engineers. Cognitive scientists look for a theoretical psychology. The computer engineer tries to make computers do useful things. Cognitive scientists consider neural networks, and the more recent connectionism, as metaphors for brain functioning rather than as brain models. However, optimistic supporters of connectionism see it as a true reproduction of what takes place in our brain, but this could be an overestimation. According to Damasio (1995), these models and our brain processes have nothing whatever to do with each other!

Let us imagine that these models at least show how networks *could* work, even if they are not exact reproductions of what occurs in our brain. At the very least, they lead to informed speculations on the actual nature of memory processes (Aleksander and Morton, 1993). They teach us to understand how networks could function in general, how they become specialised for specific tasks, and how various networks with very individual properties could interact with one another. McClelland and Rumelhart (1986) suggest that a complete model of a memory consists of a network of similar models. They assume that these models are mutually interconnected and that some receive input from the senses, others receive it from each other, and that they analyse each other's output. A 'mental state', a concept that is probably synonymous with the

The human brain and the computer (de Man, 1995)

'What do we do besides eat, drink, sleep and procreate?', asks Jos de Man (1995). 'We tell stories of dreams and desires, of black holes and galaxies, of love and death, of the excellence of our performances and of brands. The "stories" make no sense, i.e. we cannot prove them. They are always partly irrational. We express them in a language that is open to several interpretations, and the misunderstandings are innumerable. Why is that? Because it is seldom that we think rationally and logically. A mathematician does that now and then, when he concentrates very intensely and has nothing else on his mind. But by and large, thinking does not give us the mathematical certainty that a computer delivers. The brain is also involved with many other things – with intentions and ambitions, for instance. We want to know or achieve things. Those intentions and ambitions are unavoidably coloured by emotion. The purely calculating person does not exist. We are driven by instincts and impulses. The person does not resign himself to reality, he lets his imagination free. The brain makes unimaginable associations, linking memories to a picture or the smell of a flower. It wavers and doubts. Even when it is really thinking, i.e. when it is trying to form an opinion or draw a conclusion, in no way is it as accurate as a computer. The computer is sure of its business, but the person is wiser. He knows that there are no certainties, except for mathematical or trivial ones.' Computers can help us learn to understand better certain processes in our brain, but they will never be able to do what our brain can.

previously discussed Gestalt of Greenfield, is a pattern of activation of various models. Mental states are constantly alternating mutually as a result of sensory input. The total mechanism (system) is based on change of the weights of the connections between the individual units.

Neural network models are based on our current assumptions regarding the functioning of neurons and on what we can imitate with computers. But many neurons that are associatively linked to each other have functions that computers cannot handle – at least, not yet. This applies especially to the whole emotional system in our brain. Therefore neural networks can, at best, give an impression of the possible functioning of certain parts of our brain.

How can we connect the scheme theory with that of distributed representations on which connectionism is based? Just like Piaget, Hinton (1989) posits that there does not have to be a discrepancy here, but that representations in a network at a high abstract level, like the propositional representations, can go together with propositions of a lower, more concrete level, like the analogous ones. The analogously distributed representations have the advantage that they can be activated directly: they constitute the basis for the perception and recognition process, as we previously discussed. The activation of propositional representations does require conscious memory, and usually happens indirectly, through activation of the analogue. We could characterise the distributed analogue representations as the microstructure of a scheme, and the propositional representations as the macrostructure, or (as we already mentioned in previous explanations on brands in memory) the substructure and superstructure of a cognitive structure.

Chapter 7

The Development of the Brain and Memory

7.1   The embryonic stage

At birth a baby's brain weighs only 25% of that of an adult. It is assumed that all the neurons are already present in the brain of a baby. During the child's development the form, density and dimensions of the connections between the neurons change. The speed with which connections materialise also increases.

We can distinguish three phases in the development of our memory (Bergsma, 1994). The first connections between nerve cells materialise during embryonic development under the influence of genetic programming. In the second phase, these connections are accurately adjusted; this happens especially during the so-called critical periods of our early childhood years. Certain stimuli become necessary in order to arrive at an optimally functioning nervous system. The third phase has to do with learning during the rest of our lives. New connections arise constantly between neurons and neuron groups, and the strength of mutual connections is regulated on the basis of new experiences. Learning processes go on throughout our lives, from the development of memory as children to its decline as we get older (Figure 7.1).

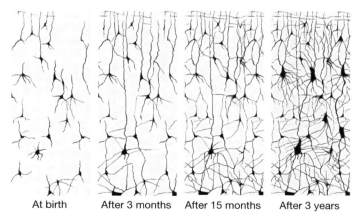

| | | | |
| At birth | After 3 months | After 15 months | After 3 years |

Figure 7.1   Growth of the neural network.

The formation of the brain begins only a few weeks after an egg cell has been fertilised. Every minute, cell fission results in about 225,000 neurons in the brain cortex alone. The brain mass expands further in the first few months. Cells move over long distances, sometimes right across other groups of neurons, and acquire a very specific task. This is how brain areas with very specific functions are formed. The number of connections between the neurons also shows an explosive growth at this stage. Axons grow towards other neurons and form synapses with the dendrites of these neurons. To achieve this they sometimes have to cover distances that are the microscopic equivalent of kilometres. They are also guided by growth cones in the genes that are equipped with capacities comparable to radar and sonar. They search in their surroundings for the presence of certain proteins. Some proteins attract axons, others have a repelling effect. This is how, before birth, the circuits are formed which are necessary for sight, smell, hearing, taste and touch, language and motor skills, and all other elementary capacities of the brain – as a sort of blueprint. The connections that have come about in the embryonic stage are refined after birth by the permanent flow of sensory perceptions.

7.2 The origin of representations

Although experiments indicate that embryos already have certain perceptions that are stored in memory before birth (Schacter, 1996), newborn babies probably do not have many representations of the world outside their bodies in their memory. Generating brain patterns from sensory experiences and structuring them occurs mainly during the first five years of life. A representation of the mother's breast in memory probably arises very soon after birth. Every bodily touch ensures the formation of a new pattern in the brain. Three days after birth, a baby reacts differently to the voice of the mother than to an unknown voice. Very young children can store details of objects in memory, together with some context information. Implicit memory, in which perceptions are still recorded unprocessed, is already functional. Two months after birth, motor memory is so developed that babies can suddenly reach out to an object and grab it. After four months they see depth. After nine months they show the first signs of explicit memory. After twelve months the language centres produce the first words. After thirteen months, procedural memory also becomes active and successions of events get stored. Afterwards, the capacity to recognise and recall increases constantly. The first years of life are crucial to a good development of the brain. Babies who have rich experiences produce rich brains (Nash, 1997). Babies who do not play a lot or who are not touched very much develop brains that are 20–30% smaller than normal for their age. At around the age of three this becomes difficult to change.

In a certain layer of the visual cortex, the number of synapses increases from 2500 to 18,000 per neuron within six months. On average, neurons have 15,000 synapses after the age of two years – twice as many as those of adults. This allows for an enormous flexibility. Perceptions are established extremely quickly in increasingly complex circuits. A baby who sees a dog for the first time is not capable of relating it to anything. What is formed quickly is a first rough visual representation of the dog in memory, but the dog has no meaning for him yet. As the child develops, he comes into contact with more dogs. Connections between neurons gradually develop which are representations of these confrontations. The first rough sketch is filled with more and more details. A core representation (concept) also arises in which the most specific characteristics of the phenomenon 'dog' are embedded. At a certain moment the phonetic word 'dog' also gets connected to the visual image of 'dog'. When the child starts reading and writing later on, the way of writing the word 'dog' will also form part of this. As the child becomes older, the representation will expand further and the connections will strengthen. The countless synaptic connections are increasingly filled in and their strength is modified so the child learns to function increasingly better in his physical, social and moral surroundings. When the representation of 'dog' is activated, a moment-bound memory arises that can take many different forms. From the entry cue, many different groups of neurons are recruited into a memory. This is how the largest part of the embranchments of neurons, which link them to each other, are formed during the first five years of life.

Around the tenth year of life the biggest sprint of growth of the brain comes to an end. A second large change occurs now, and it resembles some kind of large cleaning process: the brain reduces, as it were, connections or synapses that are not used or used very little. At age twelve, only one third of the synapses that were present at age two remain in the visual area of the brain cortex. Only those synapses that are strengthened by repeated activation will be kept. It is the initial overproduction of synaptic connections, followed by the breaking off of those not used, which leads to the steady patterns in our brain (Nash, 1997).

7.3 Development phases

In the 1920s, Piaget was the first to chart the cognitive development of children. His theories were adjusted later, mainly by Case (1984; 1985), on the basis of new insights into the cognitive processing of information and the influence of the social environment on the development of cognitive capacities. Case emphasised the development of mental blueprints to solve certain types of problems. While growing up, children become more and more efficient at dealing with their previously learned cognitive skills, which allows more room to become free in their working memory, thus enabling them to handle increasingly complex tasks. Case also focused his attention on the gradual formation of myelin isolation around axons and dendrites, which allows activation to move more quickly through the networks. This could benefit the efficiency of memory functions.

Greenspan (1997) points out that Piaget has largely ignored the role of emotions in the development of our mental capacities. The experiments of Piaget were related mainly to the development of the relationship of the child

---

Development of the concept of 'love' (Greenspan, 1997)

Viewing intellect as based on emotion gives a new perspective on the process of learning to abstract. From this novel vantage point, the ability to form abstractions is actually the ability to fuse various emotional experiences into a single, integrated concept. The abstract concept represented by a word like *love*, for example, begins to be formed not from any dictionary definition but, quite literally, in the heart. A baby may well first know it as hugs and kisses and a readily accessible nipple. Over the next few years, she learns that it also has to do with admiration, security, pride, forgiveness, the ability to recover from anger and retain a sense of security. The concept soon widens to include aspects of companionship, a variety of pleasures, and the demands of loyalty. The child learns that disappointment and dissension don't seem to destroy it. In adolescence, sexual longing is added to the mix, along with jealousy, perhaps, and pride. In adulthood the concept broadens further to encompass a sense of commitment and the willingness to work hard to sustain family life. As our emotional experience and the richness and reach of the loves we can feel continue to grow, so does our understanding of love. Where once it was an undifferentiated sense of well-being, it can unfold into a wide spectrum of loves – brotherly, erotic, filial, maternal, altruistic. It encompasses the devotion of a long-married couple, the inseparability of army buddies, the intimacy of best friends, the ecstasy of romance, the poignancy of posthumous memory, the awe and reverence a believer feels towards God. The concept of love can thus become very complex and abstract as we incorporate into it many challenges in many contexts: fulfilling our responsibilities, seeking our happiness, coping with loss and disappointment, coming to terms with other people's vulnerability and fallibility. To the concrete thinker, love is hugs and kisses and happiness. To the abstract thinker, it is far less simple, a many-layered formulation acquired gradually from life's experiences.

with the physical objects of her surroundings and the emergence of their categorisations. What Greenspan emphasises is that every perception also causes an affective reaction, and that there is a constant 'dual coding'. Piaget particularly emphasised learning by doing, but did not realise that doing leads as much to emotional reactions as to perceptual, motor and cognitive reactions. According to Greenspan, it is emotional associations in particular that organise our experience and behaviour. The affects that we carry from situation to situation tell us what to think, what to say and what to do. Emotional experiences are based on the formation of abstract categories, such as those of love.

At any random moment of our lives we must decide to which of the stimuli that surround us we will give our attention. Which are relevant, which are not? The only way to determine this is to consult our own 'catalogue' of physical and emotional experiences. They tell us what is important in a given situation. This is followed by a continuation of the attention and interpretation.

The thought process, as Greenspan (1997) proposes it, consists of two components: an emotional structure that organises facts, events and ideas and which is first 'consulted' before we attach values and meanings to something. This leads to an intuitive inner reaction based on emotions. This reaction then goes through a logical analysis on the basis of which we arrive at a more refined weighing and evaluation. Greenspan thus believes that the first ideas that we have about a stimulus are determined by affective categories that would form the organising architecture of our mind. He places the mental development from babies to infants completely in this perspective, saying that the deepest layers of our mind are formed by our perceptions and their close relations, affects and emotions, which are the product of our very first relationships. These early affects develop via a number of stages, each with its own goals, which are covered during the first four years of life. The development of the mind is by no means hereby completed, but the basis would be solidly rooted. On our way to adulthood, these are the foundations that are built on.

When perceiving and identifying a brand, the first reaction is probably an affective one. This can lead to a continuation of attention and processing. More refined weighing and evaluation can take place later.

The following box describes the development phases of memory and the mind, free from their scientific labels and based on the descriptions of Piaget, Case and Greenspan. Reference is also made to the theories on the emotional development that children go through (Harris, 1989; Greenspan, 1997).

The development phases of the child

From birth up to the age of eighteen months
In the first year of life, the behaviour of a baby is not guided by thinking but by inherent motor reflexes. Patterns do get perceived in the hotchpotch of sounds, images, smells and tactile perceptions. In this very first phase, mental representations of things in the life of the child are already formed, on the basis of its earliest physical perceptions. Newborns are capable of storing and recognising auditive stimuli. Twelve hours after the first contact, they already seem to recognise the mother. The memory for visual stimuli is already active in the first months. After two months, recognition of visual stimuli matures, although its precision is more limited than in older children. After three months a baby begins to laugh at bystanders. It learns to look and glance at things. After the fourth month, babies begin showing focused behaviour: they start to focus on things and events outside their own bodies. Between the fourth and eighth months, babies begin to coordinate their sense of touch and their visual perceptions. They start grabbing things they see. When they are seven months old, babies can already look around and localise objects that are out of sight – they can remember, for instance, absent toys. By now the baby is developing the capacity of having contact with others in its surroundings. The presence of other people is emotionally registered. Around the age of eight months, the first intentional communication also takes place. The child gradually learns certain motor skills: it discovers how physical objects react to its actions, and distinguishes between cause and effect. At the end of this phase, it is not yet capable of representing objects and events in the form of thoughts without having been confronted with the object or event. Each perception goes together with an affect or emotion. The baby reacts with an emotion to the physical effect that stimuli have on it: a blanket feels soft and is pleasant, a voice sounds loud or is unpleasant. Mother's cheek feels soft and nice. As the experiences increase, sensory perceptions become more solidly linked to emotions. A dual coding acts up (Greenspan, 1997). As children grow, their emotions help them to an increasing degree to give significance to situations with which they are confronted.

The 'dialogues' between the baby and the parents initially take place by means of facial expressions and gestures. The baby gradually develops a sense of 'self', and begins to make a distinction between 'you' and 'me', but is still fully egocentric: the world revolves around its own needs and motivations. At this point there is not a single realisation of what the other feels or wants. Nine-month old babies already develop associative connections between the words they hear and the things that surround them. They use the words of their parents to sort out the world around them, long before they are capable of understanding or enunciating those words. Understanding language happens later, but before the capacity to speak develops. Children learn more efficiently as parents name more frequently the things around them. Children also show a whole range of different emotions at a very young age. Research on mothers (Johnson *et al.*, 1982) shows that 95% of one-month-old babies showed cheerfulness, 85% anger, 74% surprise, 58% fear, 34% distress and 99% interest. When interacting with their babies, mothers express a range of emotions, which their babies learn this way. It is estimated that babies in the phase from the age of three to six months are exposed to more than 30,000 emotional facial expressions. After four months they can already recognise them. These expressions constitute the first communication between mothers and babies, long before children learn language. Children react during their first year of life to emotional expressions of others, without really being capable of establishing a connection with their own actions. It is the most important phase towards the development of emotional security for the feeling of being loved and having a connection with the parents, and later on with other important people in the child's immediate surroundings.

From ages eighteen months to five years
This phase is characterised by the development of internal mental representations. Children become competent through continuous interaction with stimuli in their surroundings. The first sign of such a development is the appearance of delayed imitation. The child imitates activities that have taken place hours or days ago. It is not capable yet of imagining a multidimensional situation separately and simultaneously, but constantly focuses its attention on one dimension and sets aside other dimensions. The child now learns to use language. The first words it learns are autonomous names for objects with which it has physical contact. Learning verbs is a slower process, because in order to do this, the child must learn to establish connections between things and activities. Children in this age group learn about ten new words per day. The development of communication is only under way by the end of the second year of life. The pleasure of symbolic expression deepens, and the inner repertoire of symbols increases rapidly. When children are two years old, they know 900 words, and by their sixth year they already know about 13,000 (Pinker, 1996). They quickly learn to connect words with the concepts they already know. One exposure to a single word is often sufficient in order to record it in memory. Connecting meanings to a yet unknown word takes

Contd

place after one exposure to the word already, for example within the context of a television programme in which the meaning is depicted. Around the age of two, the attention span has increased sufficiently for them to be able to watch television for longer periods, thus acquiring a great deal of information from it. They also start comparing themselves to age peers in television programmes.

Metaphors and figurative expression are still taken literally by the child during this phase. The child is capable of connecting words to objects, but it cannot reproduce the objects at a symbolic level yet. In this phase children accept everything they perceive as truth, and are not yet capable of distinguishing between the various forms of information. For instance, they believe unconditionally in what television commercials say. However, they do see connections: they develop knowledge on the relationships between people, things and events, and form mental blueprints of cause-and-effect relationships.

During the second year of life, the ability to influence others starts to develop: children start doing things in order to accommodate perceived emotional expressions of, for example, the mother, and also challenge them. They learn to understand someone else's emotions in the light of their objectives. They discover that people get upset when they don't get what they want, and are happy when they do get it. It is assumed that in this phase the rough blueprints are formed in the amygdala, which will determine emotional life later on. By the age of four or five, children begin to understand that emotions are not the result of a correspondence between a desire and a result, but between a desire and the desired result.

From the age of three, the life of a child consists largely of playing. Fantasy is fully released and everything seems possible. Playing with dolls and animal figures takes a particularly important place here. Its function is to start giving expression to identification. The child develops a relationship with toys that represent people or animals and allocates human characteristics to them, either identifying with them or rejecting them. The dolls and animals acquire a symbolic importance. The emphasis lies on the development of the right brain half. The complexity of the neural connections in the brain keeps increasing. Visual images, words, meanings, emotional associations, intentions and desires connect with one another in complex 'memories'. However, children are not capable at this stage of analysing things in a logical manner, and the ability to think in a logical order is not well developed yet. Neither have they developed their own value system, independent from their parents. They generally accept what parents say and interpret it in terms of black-and-white, good-or-bad. They are still blind to nuances.

From ages five to twelve

The first five to six years of life are geared towards developing the basic structures of knowledge of the self, the world and language. Pearce (1992) said that around the sixth year this fundamental world–self–language system is complete and nature focuses on developing its latest addition, the neocortex, with which it leads us into the world of ideas, logic and reason. The six-year-old has a potential neural field capacity greater than the one she previously had or will ever have in the future. Estimates on the number of neurons in our brain are as high as a hundred billion. According to Pearce, it is clear that the brain of a six-year-old contains an immeasurable number of possible neural fields and an unlimited capacity to translate that potential into reality.

Between the fifth and sixth years, children suddenly turn away from the pure fantasy world of toddlers, and grow towards reality. They start dismissing things they see as being 'for babies' or 'for small children'. They are on their way towards a more 'adult' identity and dissociate themselves from being 'a small kid'. Around the seventh year the development of the left brain half takes a central place. Logical reflection in reasoning now starts. When the child is eight she starts integrating information, learning to derive meaning from separate elements. The constructive function of memory starts to develop now. The child is increasingly capable of thinking logically. If A is larger than B and B is larger than C, then A must also be larger than C. The object should tangibly exist and be visually perceptible.

As children become older, they can handle increasingly complex tasks. Automation ensures that the performance of tasks requires cognitive capacities to a lesser extent – in other words, the child uses her capacities more effectively. By the time they are seven, children can describe complex emotions such as pride and jealousy. The ability to speak also develops quickly now. Language, behaviour and communication become increasingly sociable. Between the sixth and seventh year of life a development also takes place of an awareness of what is 'cool' and what is not. Around the age of eight children become aware of moral values and social norms. They learn that taking possession of something one desires does not bring happiness if a social norm is violated, and that forgoing something desired can lead to a good feeling when a moral value compensates for it. Children also become aware of the phenomenon of mixed feelings. They learn to look at possibilities and events from different perspectives, sometimes with conflicting and emotional results. Before children reach the age of eight, they have difficulty distinguishing between

Contd

words and the things they represent. The word 'dog' is their dog (or another specific dog in their surroundings). Around the age of eight the child also develops simple abstraction and recognises natural orders – first this, then that. Only at the age of ten can children describe word meanings. Understanding simple metaphors has already started before children go to school, but the development of symbolic language skills really takes off as they learn to see similarities between different things and events. Using and understanding metaphors implies allocating meanings of familiar concepts to less familiar ones and is an important mechanism for acquiring new knowledge. The development of symbolic skills approaches completion only in late childhood, when the child's conceptual and verbal knowledge starts to resemble that of an adult. The child gradually develops a self-image that consists of images, words and feelings, and learns to establish connections between experiences in the present and the past and in different situations. A 'personal story' emerges and an awareness of a personal way of being, as well as reflecting on one's self. When children reach the age of ten, their own values and aspirations also become part of the self-image. From the ninth year onwards, egocentricity decreases and interest in the world surrounding them grows. The child now shifts her attention to peer groups. What is 'in' and 'cool', and 'looking good' receives attention now. Belonging to the group and being accepted by the children at school are now among the most important things. This expresses itself clearly in conformist consumption behaviour: you've got to have the right clothes. Given the need to be accepted and belong somewhere, all sorts of connections and clubs suddenly become important. Children start forming categories more quickly and reading into the concepts of these categories; they also start seeing the relevant and the irrelevant properties of categories.

From ages twelve to fifteen
The child now discovers that the reality in which he lives is only one of the many imaginable realities. He experiences that the world consists not only of the environment in which he has grown, and can deal with problems from the present, the past and the future. From the age of 12 onwards he develops an adult thought pattern and learns to reflect abstractly, hypothetically and logically, thus allowing for reasoning in a more planned manner. He learns to think in a more advanced form and to see the grey areas between black and white. He analyses problems from different angles, learns to figure out solutions and to examine what works and what does not. He starts understanding the subtleties of irony and sarcasm. The child now starts developing his own identity, which usually means that he

takes a distance from what parents and teachers think. Sometimes this leads to an open 'anti-establishment' attitude and a simplistic fanaticism with a newly acquired idealism. He longs for more complex stimuli and a quick alternation of 'sight bites' and 'sound bites'. The world of the adolescent is larger than that of the peer group. Adolescents become interested in more complex systems such as religion, politics and art. They are able to imagine what life might have to offer them. Friendships deepen, the relationship with the other sex becomes more problematic. During adolescence the thought processes become increasingly flexible and abstract. All the possibilities that a situation offers are now taken into consideration. In contrast to children in the previous phase, who generally could solve problems when the objects were physically present, the adolescent learns to deal with problems concerning objects that are only present in memory, and to survey their possibilities and consequences.

From ages sixteen to nineteen
Around the sixteenth year of life, hormonal development has been completed. The late adolescent leaves childhood behind and starts focusing her attention on the future. She soon becomes aware of the fact that she can stand on her own two feet, becomes an independent person, and develops more adult social relationships. She does not look any more only around herself in order to determine what she should think and do, but develops her own value system and consults herself. She learns to make choices between right and wrong and to put herself in someone else's shoes. During this period the sociological and mental development is concentrated on the prefrontal cortex. The 'executive function' of the brain now develops. The ability to solve problems and make plans for the future increases and the adolescent starts 'thinking over her own thoughts'. Language skills also keep developing further. Research has shown that adolescents know about 60,000 words after secondary school education, and adults with a university education know as many as twice that number. Around the nineteenth year of life the brain is fully developed. The adolescent has become an autonomous person. The world of the school now becomes that of the university or the first job. Distance is taken from the parental home. The young adult now has to learn to confront issues such as independence, intimacy and the need for security, which were previously taken for granted. Around the thirtieth year of life this is all settled: the personality is crystallised and its essence will not change, but the brain keeps developing, and the capacity for reflection and evaluation keeps increasing up to an advanced age (Pinker, 1994).

7.4 Children and brand names

Children come into contact with brands when they are very young. They are particularly confronted with them when watching television. This happens at an age in which they are particularly open to absorption, and learn playfully. Their nerve cells are still extremely elastic; they form connections much faster than neurons of adults. Young brains pick up new things quickly. As we grow, the development of new networks gradually slows down.

Parents take their young children shopping at an early age. The children often sit on the seat of the supermarket trolley. From this spot they have a spacious view of all the products and brands. Experimental research (Hite and Hite, 1995) has shown that children as young as two have already developed preferences for national brands above shop brands, even if the shop brands tasted better. They perceive the brands in their direct surroundings. Their initial appraisal for the brand is based on the example of the parents. When parents repeatedly choose the same brand, the brand becomes familiar and consequently 'good'. And because mother and father know best, the brands they choose must also be the best. This initial preference is developed and strengthened by the television commercials that children see. In the phase in which they still perceive on a primarily visual basis, they are repeatedly exposed to the packages they get to see in the shop, at home and on the television screen, and this is how they become familiar with brands at a very young age. During the second year of life, children begin to ask about specific products. Because they can go more often to the supermarket and can focus better on their surroundings, they learn to know more and more brands. During this phase they base their preferences more on the packages than on visual brand signs or the intrinsic properties of the product. They do not pay attention to verbal information yet. They also use the external visual packaging characteristics to categorise products. Research by Valkenburg (1998) has shown that 40% of two-year-olds recognise products in the shop which have been advertised on television. In three-year-olds the percentage is 60%, and in four-year-olds 84%.

When children are able to walk around by themselves in the supermarket (from the age of three) they themselves begin to take products from the shelves. They start recognising more products in the shop that are used at home and connect them to the commercials they have seen on television. They do not talk any more about dolls and gym shoes, but about 'Barbie' and 'Reebok', and even a Mercedes 'star' on a building is recognised by a three-year-old as an automobile brand (Häberle, 1998). It is only after the fifth year of life, when they have learned to read, that the connection arises between a brand name and the underlying product. One hundred percent of six-year-olds in Germany are familiar with the Coca-Cola logo, and link it to the brown drink (Dammler, 1998). Brand awareness is the strongest in five- and six-year-olds. While 48%

of three- and four-year-olds recognise the McDonald's logo, 94% of five- and six-year-olds do. As children become older, they focus more and more on the functional product brands and start categorising brands on that basis. Research by John and Sujan (1990) has shown that children aged four to five, when categorising breakfast cereals and drinks, base forms and colours of products and packages on a ratio of 2:1 with regard to functional characteristics. In nine- and ten-year-old children, this ratio is the opposite: they use functional characteristics with regard to perceptual ones in a 2:1 ratio. The development of awareness of more symbolic brand meanings begins at a slightly later age, when they start noticing image and user group. Lifestyle associations begin playing a role: 'Can I show up with it, will the other children approve?'

Secondary school-age children attach great value to the right brands, especially for clothing. They do not use brands, as many adults do, to express their individual self-image, but precisely to show that they 'belong'. They are scared to death to wear something that is seen as 'faux' by their environment. Here brands must respond to the ideal image of increasingly narrow age categories. Six- to eight-year-olds tend to get excited about the sweet taste of Coca-Cola. Nine- to eleven-year-olds dismiss younger children with the brown drink. For twelve- to thirteen-year-olds, Coca-Cola is primarily a 'cool' representative of the United States. Something which was an entry product for fourteen- to sixteen-year-olds is now a children's brand for ten- to fourteen-year olds. Kranenburg (1998) says that fifteen years ago, girls played with their Barbies until they were thirteen, and now they stop at ten. Pre-adolescent girls do not focus on playing with toys any more, but on rock idols and Oilily body lotion. Without Carhart overalls, Nike sweaters or Timberland hiking shoes, they cannot show their faces at school any more. Children switch brands at an ever increasing rate – especially if they get the impression that a brand is used by even younger children (Dammler, 1998). On the other hand, brand preference can also increase on a continuous basis. While 41% of six- to nine-year-olds in Germany own an Adidas product, the percentage in fourteen- to sixteen-year-olds is more than 60% (Häberle, 1998).

Around the age of 16–17 a strong urge for individualism develops. Adolescents start choosing brands in order to express their own ideals and to stand apart from others. By the time children finish primary school they start making more independent choices. In the age category of 13 to 17, they do not consult their parents for most of the personal consumption articles they buy. Research by Roper (1996) in the United States gives an overview of this development, which is shown in Table 7.1.

For some products, the emphasis of the choice still very much lies in the properties of the product itself. In other categories, brands already play a primary role, as is the case with toiletries, clothing and even cars. This is where the basis is established for prolonged brand loyalty.

Table 7.1   Percentage of children buying products for themselves.

| | Age category (in years) | | | | | |
| | 6–7 | | 8–12 | | 13–17 | |
	b	g	b	g	b	g
Sweets	36	39	73	63	94	94
Soft drinks	36	28	73	69	92	90
Fast food	31	37	61	53	87	89
Books	19	30	50	50	68	82
Games	19	29	50	39	76	69
Clothing	NA	NA	30	23	71	70
Sports shoes	NA	NA	28	25	68	69
CDs and tapes	4	9	34	26	75	81
Magazines	11	12	32	29	70	79
Jewellery	NA	NA	14	31	40	70
Games	13	11	33	17	66	49
Toiletry articles	NA	NA	11	15	45	59
Films	NA	NA	16	10	53	49
Computer software/CD-ROMs	1	NA	7	3	25	20

b = boys, g = girls, NA = not available
Source: Roper Youth Report, 1996 in Acuff, 1997.

Children develop representations of brands as early as their second year of life. Those early representations are related mainly to external packaging characteristics. Initial brand attitudes are already present during the second year of life. During the third year the child learns brand names. During the fifth year, name and product are connected. Around the ninth year, functional brand meanings are formed. Around the eleventh and twelfth years, symbolic brand meanings arise. Around the age of sixteen to seventeen, brands are used to express personal ideals. By the time they are nineteen, young people's brains are fully developed, having had a 'brand learning period' of fifteen years behind them and having stored an enormous repertoire of brands in their memories; these brand representations take increasingly fixed forms.

Adolescents have a very extensive brand knowledge. The really big brands in the world are those we have grown up with, having found them as children in the families we were part of. By the time we were able to make choice decisions independently, we already had a 'brand learning period' of ten to twenty years behind us. We became familiar with brands as infants, and constantly supplemented our further knowledge of them during our development into adulthood.

The period in which people retain most memories, as well as the strongest and the best ones, is from fifteen to twenty-five. People tend to classify themselves into generations, and these begin when they are fifteen, ending around the twenty-fifth year of life (Zijlmans, 1998). This is because this period is the easiest to delimit: all sorts of important changes take place at this time and act as memory peaks. Older people often recall them and talk about them. This makes it easier for such memories to come to the surface. Throughout their lives people remain enthusiastic about the time when they were young adults – and remember remarkably well things that happened then. According to Zijlmans, it is probably also the most important period for the development of our brand relations.

Around the age of thirty, our personality, elementary knowledge skills and view of the world have taken fairly stable forms. Although learning processes continue throughout our lives, fundamental changes are no longer likely. Our brand knowledge goes on developing during life – new brands come and others gradually fade into oblivion, but the associative networks of the brands that have a significance in our lives remain fairly stable. In particular, the essential meanings that we connect with those brands do not change much. Still, the contents of our memory keep developing every minute, every day. The development of meanings around a phenomenon like a 'personal digital assistant' has, in a manner of speaking, just passed most of us by. The more we are confronted with external stimuli that are connected with such a phenomenon, the more connections arise in our brain. They are initially weak – in fact, they are only *potential* connections. Gradually, as we are exposed more often to the same stimuli, some connections become stronger and can even begin to form part of the meaning core. At the same time, however, there is also an emergence of secondary, tertiary and subsequent connections that are only activated and enter our consciousness under certain conditions. An increasing number of associations become possible. Damasio believes that, depending on the system and the experiences of the organism, the strength of the synapses can also change in the course of time, so the circuit design also changes constantly. The circuits are not only sensitive to the first experience, but remain malleable and keep adjusting themselves as a result of new experiences. Some circuits keep getting a new design through life, depending on the changes the organism goes through. Other circuits remain largely stable and form the core of the picture we have formed of the world around us. The idea that all circuits can be changed is absurd. Such unlimited pliability would make us into individuals unable to recognise each other. It clearly does not work that way. There must be a balance in the brain between circuits that change like mercury and circuits in which change in itself is not impossible, but which do offer more resistance (Damasio, 1995).

What will happen at a certain moment in our memory is unpredictable. There is no little man in our memory (the 'homunculus') that conducts things, as was believed for centuries. It is only our genetic programming and our course through life which influence what takes place in our brain.

Part Two

Brands and Memory

'Brands are not found in the factory or in the studio, the sales channels or the supermarket shelves – not even on the television screen. You only find them in the minds of the consumers.'

(Restall and Gordon, 1984)

Chapter 8

Brands in our Memory

8.1 Introduction

Our memory contains an enormous number of brands – perhaps 10,000. People link information to every brand name stored in their memory. They remember, for instance, sensory experiences with the brand, fragments from advertisements, specific experiences with a user-situation, etc.; in short, anything at all that has to do with the brand. For the owner of a brand it is important to find out what exactly has been stored in people's memories with regard to their brand. This information can help steer the marketing and communication plan, thus increasing chances of a successful strategy. Many producers of branded products and services trade on the basis of unproven assumptions. They may assume, for instance, that most people know which products belong together with a certain brand name, or that consumers who use the brand are extremely extraverted. It is smart – even necessary – to check whether this is really true.

In this part of the book we will attempt to explain how people store information on brands in their memory and which components we can distinguish in the process. It should be mentioned that, in a way, these are artificial distinctions between the various components. Globally speaking, everything is related to everything else, directly as well as indirectly, strongly or perhaps very weakly, and a brand is in fact a holistic complex. Which components enter our consciousness depends on the moment and the situation in which, and the cue with which, we are confronted.

In Part One of this book we gave an extensive explanation of how memory works, and it became clear that the brain is in fact a collection of neurons that pass information between themselves in the form of neurotransmitters. Sensory information that gets attention and is found interesting enough by an observer is converted into information units. Information units are collections of neurons and are also known as nodes. When a person reflects on a node in relation to another node, e.g. 'lollipop' and 'children's party', an associative connection is created between these two nodes (many lollipops are eaten at children's parties). A node used recently or frequently is stored in memory in a unique and striking manner. Such a node involves many associative connections, accesses the person's consciousness easily and quickly, and is often used to evaluate new information. When this junction is called upon, information with which it is connected is also invoked (Van Knippenberg *et al.*, 1991). Brands also function in people's memory as junctions. The information on brands is stored in clusters or chunks in memory, and the brand name itself acts as a trigger for all this information (De Chernatony and McDonald, 1992).

Every neuron is directly or indirectly connected with a large number of other neurons, and these neurons pass signals to each other in the form of neurotransmitters (chemical brain fluids). When an individual is stimulated by her surroundings – she burns her fingers or sees a beautiful flower – an electrical process is initiated in a number of neurons (the sodium/potassium ratio changes). This results in 'a door opening' and a chemical process beginning: the neurotransmitter can flow out of the neuron. This neurotransmitter arrives at a synapse and another neuron soaks it up from there (Kalat, 1995). This continuous flow of fluids between neurons causes an enormous network of information in our head to be created. All types of information is stored in this network: emotional, sensory and cognitive experiences, important and less important information, and so on. Neurobiological research has taught us that all these types of information are processed throughout various areas in our brain and are stored in different places.

8.2 The influence of various elements of memory on brand choice

It is difficult to make well grounded statements on what is the influence of the various elements of memory on brand choice. When an individual is confronted with a problem, a need or a want related to consumption, he will look in his memory or in his surroundings for brands that may solve the problem or fill his need. Normally, he will address, consciously or otherwise, his 'consideration set', i.e. the brands that he considers during his purchase decision process. Very few decisions are taken on the basis of information offered on an exclusively external basis, such as publicity. In most purchasing decisions, brands that are already present in memory play a large role, and decision making may even take place on that basis alone.

Many of the semi-scientific models that describe the choice behaviour of consumers are based on choice processes that take place under high involvement. This derives partially from the fact that choice processes are not observable. They take place inside a person's brain. The researcher can only observe the stimuli given to the individual and the forms of behaviour the individual shows afterwards. These forms of behaviour are most clear and unequivocal when a consumer feels very involved with the purchase or brand, and when the brand has been used in the past as a basis for the development of a model. One of the most well known and most frequently cited models was

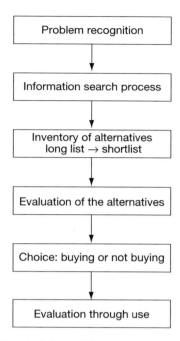

Figure 8.1 The phases of the decision-making process.

developed by Engel, Blackwell and Miniard. Figure 8.1 shows an adjusted version of this model.

Despite the fact that the model has become famous all over the world, there are quite a few disadvantages to it. First of all, consumer decisions do not often happen so straightforwardly in reality. Solving problems comes about through several mutual interactions between cognitive and emotional processes of consumers, their behaviours, and aspects of the physical and social environment (Boom and Weber, 1994). Secondly, the model is geared mainly towards purchases the consumer is very involved with. In a great many purchases the consumer is not that involved and just follows a fixed routine. If consumers think they know enough about a certain product category, they are not motivated to look for new information. Their purchasing behaviour is therefore based on a learned behavioural pattern and they limit their choice to the brands that are already stored in their memory and that they buy regularly – we say that these brands are in their 'purchasing repertoire'.

In a lot of purchasing behaviour, the consumer is not very involved – he follows a learned habit.

Buying behaviour: rational or automatic (Weilbacher, 1993)

Consumers do not think through every brand choice, nor are they mostly loyal to a single brand as a result of such thought processes. They are perfectly satisfied with any of the brands from their acceptable set that happen to be available when the purchase is made. This tendency to systematise relatively trivial, continuous decisions in brand purchases as well as in other daily activities is, as Sir Alfred North Whitehead reminds us, one of the hallmarks of our civilisation: 'Civilisation advances by extending the number of operations which we can perform without thinking about them'. But this alternative point of view about the processes through which consumers make brand purchase decisions is not widely held by marketing practitioners. They believe that brand loyalty develops almost as a consequence of the rational way in which consumers choose among brands. It is not by chance that so much consumer advertising for brands depends upon rational argument. But if one accepts the alternative, non-rational explanation of consumer brand choice, marketing should be at least as concerned with making brands acceptable – helping brands thus to gain entry into every consumer's set of acceptable brands – as in making the final conclusive, clinching sales argument that will win the consumer's loyalty forever (...).

Marketers believe that brand loyalty exists and believe that they are in the exacting business of creating it. This belief has been strengthened by the view widely held by academics that consumer brand choice is based on a rational process, and that the end product of such rational decision making is brand loyalty. A few academics are less certain that consumers care enough about brands to consciously and continuously analyse the differences among them or go to the trouble of becoming loyal to them. Marketers tend to ignore academic views unless the academics agree with them. Thus, there has been little enthusiasm in the marketing community for any argument that brand loyalty is tenuous or even that it does not exist. And since the academic community has almost nothing to do with the day-to-day marketing of brands, what they think about how consumers make brand choices, rationally or otherwise, is, in any event, irrelevant to the practice of marketing.

In other words, marketers of established brands with a large market share must ensure that their brand stays in the purchasing repertoire of important consumers. Marketers of new brands or brands with a low market share must somehow break through the automatic problem solution. They want to ensure that consumers do not think automatically about Pampers when they need nappies, or Macleans when they are out of toothpaste. They also want consumers to take their brands into consideration in their decision-making processes. They can develop strategies to introduce noticeable stimuli in the surroundings, such as large displays at stores, packaging that stands out on the shelves, free samples or sales promotions (two for the price of one), and eye-catching advertising campaigns. Such strategies are supposed to grab the attention of consumers and break with the routine choice behaviour. The objective is to steer consumers temporarily towards a more conscious and controlled level of limited decision making and ensure that they are willing to involve external information in the choice process (Peter and Olson, 1993) (Figure 8.2).

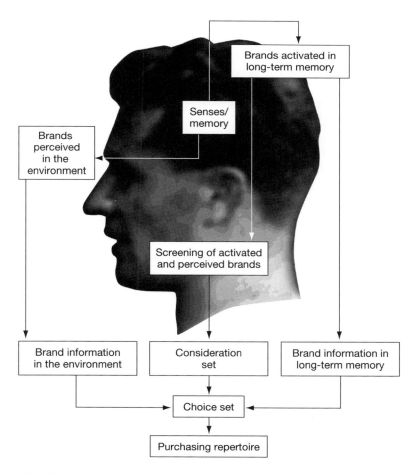

Figure 8.2   The interaction of internal and external information in the choice process.

Disruption! (Dru, 1996)

In 1996, Jean-Marie Dru, chairman of the BDDP group, published a book called *Disruption* which put forward a similar vision as the one described above. He posited that if we look at the advertising landscape across the world, we will notice that substantial ruptures with the prevailing trends rarely take place. A large number of advertising campaigns are predictable: these are oriented towards a standard and, in a more or less creative manner, send out a message whose contents can hardly be called original. Discontinuity in advertising campaigns only happens when the strategy as well as the execution breaks with previous activities, whenever the planner and the creatives reject the usual approach. But this is certainly not the rule. There is a general impression as to this happening only now and then – in fact, it happens very rarely. It is hard to say when and why, and it seems that it usually happens by coincidence.

Dru developed the disruption method in order to make this rupture happen intentionally. He states that disruption involves finding the strategic idea with which the conventions of the market can be broken and knocked down, and with which new insights can be obtained or existing visions can acquire a new content. The disruption method consists of three steps:

(1) Identify the convention
(2) Break through the convention (disruption)
(3) Formulate the brand vision (and remain loyal to it).

New brands or brands with a relatively low market share have to be put in the picture for consumers. One way brands can achieve this is by breaking with conventions in advertising. Things that have been the same for years seem so self-evident that they are hardly noticed. What's more, great creative and strategic talent is needed to break with these conventions in a logical and relevant manner and, at the same time, keep the brand vision central. And then the question remains as to how large the role of external information (such as advertising) is when a purchasing decision is being made.

8.2.1 *Evocation and evaluation*

Every individual perceives all sorts of brands throughout her life. Information on brands that make enough of an impression on the individual or that is repeated often enough is stored in long-term memory. In choice decisions, this long-term memory serves as an important source of information. Choices can come about during simple routine choice processes, merely on the basis of this memory information. Choices in which the perceived risks are greater and for which memory does not have sufficient information about the alternatives available increase the chances of external information being gathered and processed.

Two different phases can be distinguished in the choice process:

(1) *The evocation phase*, in which the available alternatives from which a choice is made are reduced to a limited number from which the ultimate choice is made. This (small) group of brands is called the 'consideration set'.
(2) *The evaluation phase*, in which the choice of (or preference for) one (or more) of the alternatives within the consideration set is made. This results in a 'choice set': a smaller group of brands to which a certain degree of preference is given.

In the historical models of consumer behaviour, the emphasis lay very much on the evaluation of choice alternatives with regard to one another, on the basis of certain choice criteria and interrelated 'decision rules' (see box overleaf). How the selection of brands from which a choice was made came about remained largely unexplained. In the last decade people have become more aware of the significant importance of the emergence of consideration sets.

In scientific research, the emphasis has been primarily on investigating the processing of (new) offered information and its influence on decision making and behaviour. Alba *et al.* did a thorough analysis of the literature in 1991, arriving at the conclusion that there are only a handful of publications that explicitly deal with the role of memory in choice processes. The questions of which of the brands on offer are taken into consideration and why such information is processed, as well as why and how past experiences stored in long-term memory influence these processes, have hardly been looked at. The influence of memory is certainly recognised, but memory itself has not often been the subject of focused scientific research. What is known about it comes mainly from practical research done by market research agencies.

On the basis of the two phases in the choice process (evocation and evaluation) and the two information sources (internal and external), we can now describe two different routes along which a choice comes about. We distinguish:

(1) *Choices made merely on the basis of memory information* – no information from the outside is processed during the choice process.
   • Choices made on the basis of saliency:[3] the choice is predominantly influenced by the position of the brand in the evocation phase. The

---

3   The concept of saliency is discussed in Chapter 16. In short, it is related to the intensity of the memory representation. Salient brands have a prominent place in memory.

Decision rules (Boom and Weber, 1994)

Various basic rules can be distinguished when making purchasing decisions. These rules indicate how the consumer uses the information on various brand attributes in order to arrive at a choice. Decision rules are also known as combination rules, because the consumer can combine the information on the attributes (traits) with each other in different ways. Decision rules vary from very simple to quite complex. They can also take place automatically or be considered intentionally. A distinction is usually made between *compensatory* and *non-compensatory* rules.

Compensatory rules

Compensatory rules are formalised rules that the consumer applies when he wants to make a well balanced choice from the brands in the evoked set. The consumer arrives at a choice by evaluating the brands on the basis of several criteria. The unfavourable evaluation of an attribute of a specific brand can be compensated for with a favourable evaluation of one or several other attributes. The final evaluation is based on the result of all the criteria together. Table 8.1 shows an example (the scores are random):

Table 8.1 Example of compensatory rule.

Attribute	Weight*	Volkswagen	Opel	Fiat
Status value	1	8	8	6
Comfort	3	6	8	6
Attraction	2	6	5	8
Costs per km	4	8	8	6

* The higher the number, the more important the attribute and the higher the attribute is valued for the brand.

The end scores are calculated as follows (for each attribute, score per attribute multiplied by the weight of the attribute):

$$\text{Volkswagen} = (1 \times 8) + (3 \times 6) + (2 \times 6) + (4 \times 8) = 70$$
$$\text{Opel} = (1 \times 8) + (3 \times 8) + (2 \times 5) + (4 \times 8) = 74$$
$$\text{Fiat} = (1 \times 6) + (3 \times 6) + (2 \times 8) + (4 \times 6) = 64$$

When applying the compensatory rules, the choice is an Opel.

Contd

saliency of the brand representation is determinant. There is hardly any evaluation – or none at all – of the attributes. A person wants healthy margarine and takes Flora from the supermarket shelf without thinking.

Non-compensatory decision rules

Applying non-compensatory rules entails that a less favourably evaluated attribute can lead to rejecting the alternative in question. The favourable value of a different trait does not compensate for this. The following non-compensatory rules are usually distinguished:

(1) *The conjunctive decision rule*. The consumer sets minimum requirements or minimum scores for all the attributes he uses when evaluating the alternatives. If one alternative does not comply with the minimal requirements, it is eliminated. If several acceptable brands remain, a different decision rule will be needed in order to choose the best alternative.

(2) *The disjunctive decision rule*. Minimum requirements for the attributes are also set in the disjunctive rule. These requirements are often higher than those of the conjunctive rule. In the disjunctive rule, each brand that scores above the minimum is chosen.

(3) *The lexicographic decision rule*. In this case, the consumer orders the attributes according to their importance. The alternatives are first compared to the most important attribute. If one alternative scores highest, it is chosen.

(4) *Sequential elimination*. In sequential elimination, just as in the conjunctive rule, minimum boundaries are set for each attribute. The alternatives are now eliminated sequentially on the basis of insufficient attribute value. The attributes are used in a random order.

- Choices made on the basis of an evaluation of associations: in the evocation phase the choice is limited to a consideration set. This is followed by the emergence of a more 'definitive' choice within a process of a more extended evaluation of the memory representations of the considered brands in relation to one another. A person is expecting visitors and wants to have a special beer at home. After some inner deliberation he takes home some Stella Artois.

The popularity of a brand, in the sense of a perceived number of people in the social environment of someone that uses it, is an important heuristic within the choice process.

(2) *Choices made on the basis of external information*
- Choices made on the basis of popularity: the choice is primarily based on the frequency and conspicuousness with which a brand is perceived in the surroundings. The consumer tends to conform to the perceived behaviour of others. A younger person sees that almost everyone around him drinks Guinness and he adopts the habit.
- Choices made on the basis of the evaluation of attributes: the choice is limited to those alternatives that present themselves in the surroundings with sufficient strength. A 'definitive' choice comes about subsequently on the basis of a more extensive processing and consideration of external information. The possible initial memory representation plays no role in the decision-making process. For instance, someone decides to buy a fax machine. She collects a lot of information and asks store personnel for advice. She finally goes home with a Brother.

(3) *Choices made on the basis of a combination of memory information and external information*
- Memory representation encourages choice: the presence of a brand in memory encourages its inclusion in the consideration set and the choice set. External information is filtered through this tentative preference. The consumer shows the tendency to absorb mainly new information which corresponds with the brand representation present (selective perception). For instance, a person is about to buy a new car. He only considers German or Scandinavian brands in a more expensive price range. He reads the latest news in all sorts of car magazines and finally decides to buy an Audi A6.
- External information encourages choice: both the inclusion of a brand in the consideration set and the choice decision is predominantly influenced by external information. The resulting tendency towards preference is supported by the memory representation. A 'selective activation' starts working: people remember mainly positive things about the brands that they tend to choose. For instance, someone wants to buy a new bicycle. He is familiar with all sorts of brands but has no clear ideas on them. He collects brochures, buys the magazine *Cycling* and asks the opinions of others. Gradually he starts going for a certain type of Giant. He now remembers having read a good report on it some time ago; in fact, it is a particularly good brand. He takes the plunge and buys a Giant.

In the evocation phase, brands are activated in memory on the basis of the strength of the connections between the brand and the nodes that represent the

The bandwagon effect: indicators of the norm (Sutherland, 1993)

Conformity – being with the in group, not being out of step – is a powerful human motivator. It can make the crucial difference in many brand choice decisions. When there is no real difference between brands or when the choice is not really important to a person, it takes much less than full consensus to influence their judgement. People will go with what they think the majority of other people perceive: the popular view. This is known as the 'bandwagon effect'. It occurs in situations as diverse as voting in elections and backing favourites in horseraces. Canned laughter, opinion polls and the Billboard Top 100 are all indicators of the norm. They tell us how others are reacting and thereby influence how we are likely to react. They provide signals about what to laugh at, what to think about and what to listen to (...). People seem to have a natural aversion to being seen to be out of step with others or different from the norm. This often leads us to take the safe route. We try to anticipate what others would do and then do the same. This can spare us embarrassment and it can sometimes save us from thinking too hard (...).

How popular a brand is thought to be, or how familiar a company is thought to be, is an important dimension of image. Popularity is the magnet. It attracts. And advertising can enhance its power to attract. Try to think of a single product of which the most popular brand is not advertised. I can't. Does this mean, though, that advertising causes popularity? Not exactly. Advertising makes the brand appear popular. It influences its perceived popularity. The more a brand is advertised, the more popular and familiar it is perceived to be (...). Perceived popularity is not always positive. When too many people use a brand, it risks becoming perceived as common. It is not just a case of familiarity breeds contempt. Overpopularity can degrade the currency. Peter de Vries, an American novelist, once said in another context: 'Everyone hates me because I am so universally liked.' Astute advertisers have learnt to guard against this type of reversal. They know that simply giving a brand as much 'hype' as possible in as short a time as possible is not necessarily a good idea. Instead, they try to manage the perceived popularity of the brand as part of a long-term process of image development and ensure that they consolidate a lasting market share.

objectives of the consumer. These can be generic product nodes ('margarine') as well as more situation-dependent nodes, like product applications ('baking and frying'), or specifically desired attributes ('healthy').

> In the evocation phase of the thought process, the accessibility of a brand representation (the saliency of the brand in memory) is probably the most important variable. This is related to the intensity of the association with primary choice cues.

In a choice process in which external information is also processed, the brands perceived in the surroundings can be included in the consideration set. Woodside and Trappey (1992) have shown that the 'top-of-mind associations' of a brand with the product category plus some core meanings largely explain purchasing behaviour. Holden (1993) also found that the inclusion of a brand in a consideration set is strongly correlated with the response time after giving a relevant cue. Consequently, there are strong indications that the 'bare' accessibility of a brand in memory exercises a large influence on brand choice, independently from the more processed contents of the brand representation (Menon and Wänke, 1998). An automatic activation of brands takes place in the very first stage of brand choice, as described in section 3.8.

In two experiments, Nedungadi (1990) showed that influencing the consideration set has a considerable influence on the brand choice, especially when the choice is made predominantly on the basis of memory representations. Strengthening the associations of a brand with the primary choice cues (product category, subcategory, attribute, application, etc.) leads to a larger share in the ultimate choice, even when the brand meanings are not influenced during the evaluation phase. This emphasises the predominant importance that researchers like Ehrenberg also allocate to the saliency of brands, especially in low involvement products (Ehrenberg *et al.*, 1997). However, in brand choices in which processing external information is important, the *a priori* strength of the association of the brand with primary choice cues also has a large influence on its inclusion in the consideration set.

There is probably hardly any evaluation, if any at all, in low involvement products. They develop purchasing tendencies or habits that are closely related to the saliency of associations of a brand with one or several goal-dependent cues. This leads to unconscious, automated choice processes. Increasing the chances of a brand being chosen would therefore be the result of the strengthening of its association with these consideration cues.

There are, of course, product categories in which the evaluation phase plays a larger role in the ultimate choice. In shops we take time to choose from the many French cheeses, or ice creams for dessert. However, here the consideration set also limits the number of alternatives from which a choice is made. And here as well, the encouragement of inclusion of a brand in the consideration set by means of strengthening the brand saliency is probably the most effective persuasion strategy.

When a choice becomes important because of, for instance, a larger perceived risk, uncertainty over the priorities or insufficient familiarity with the available options, external information will play a larger role. However, Beach (1993) emphasises that there are also two different processes here – screening and choice – in his terminology. He posits that screening is not a mere preliminary stage of choice, but a *different* process from choice. Screening dictates what is available for choice: the consideration set comes into being in a different way from the ultimate choice in the choice phase. It does *not* depend on complying with choice criteria, as is usually assumed. This is about pre-choice information. The saliency of a brand and of a limited set of associations has a dominant influence here. For the ultimate choice, brands within the consideration set are evaluated against more developed choice criteria, so that we could in fact speak of 'post-consideration' information. This could include other association categories, like very specific product attributes ('four-wheel drive'), their provenance or the perceived price–value ratio of brands.

Holden (1993) thinks that brand communication should focus mainly on strengthening the chances of a brand being included in the consideration set, i.e. during the evocation phase. After all, without evocation the chances of purchase are nil. This leads to a formation of communication with a high brand saliency content and a strengthening of only some core associations that can be joined with the primary choice cues. Identifying the right cues is crucial here.

When it comes to frequently purchased products, consumers allow their choice behaviour to be primarily led by information that is stored in their memory. Research has shown that they involve only a reduced number of alternatives in the choice process, usually not more than three to five. There are a number of reasons for this. In the first place, convenience, loyalty or experience with certain alternatives make people involve fewer brands in their choice. A second reason lies in the increasingly complex surroundings in which buying takes place. The number of different items ('stock-keeping units') offered in a large supermarket has increased from 10,000 to an overwhelming 20,000-plus in just one decade. A third cause is the ever increasing pressure of time to which people are exposed. Modern society presents us with so many tasks and challenges that we are left with less and less time for each individual activity or action. Just the total amount of information being offered (press, television, radio, internet) is estimated to have multiplied by forty between 1960 and 2000! A fourth cause is a decrease in risk perceptions. In an increasing number of product fields, the consumer cannot actually make any 'wrong' choices. All the well known brands comply with higher quality standards, and all the well known shops, which are in themselves also brands, exercise a certain amount of control over this.

The consideration set in automobiles (Censydiam, 1998)

Censydiam (1998) looked at how many different brands were considered by automobile buyers in Belgium. The average was 2.45. Their spread is as follows:

1 brand	42%
2 brands	22%
3 brands	19%
4 brands	16%

Based on the frequency with which various brands appear together in a shortlist, cluster analysis can be used to develop a 'dendrogram' which shows the relationship between brands. The dendrogram shown in Figure 8.3, based on Censydiam's study, indicates to what degree brands are taken as an alternative with regard to one another.

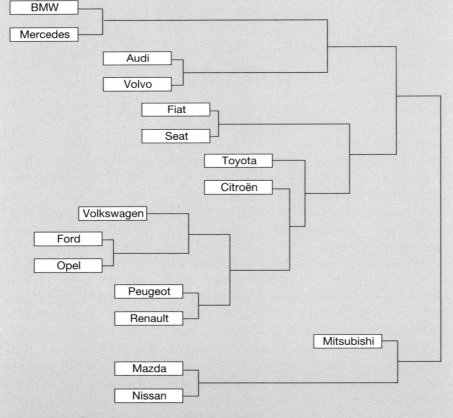

Figure 8.3   Dendrogram of automobile brands.

Which alternatives get weighed up? (Sutherland, 1993)

What determines the alternatives that are actually considered?

Think about a consumer decision that you probably make every day. It's getting on for noon, you are feeling hungry and you ask yourself: 'What am I going to have for lunch today?' Your mind starts to generate alternatives and to evaluate each alternative as you think of it. The process goes something like this:

'Will I have a pie?'

'No, I had a pie yesterday.'

'A sandwich?'

'No, the sandwich shop is too far away and besides, it's raining.'

'I could drive to McDonald's.'

'Yes ... I'll do that.'

There are two things to note here. First, what the mind does is produce alternatives, one at a time. This 'mental agenda' of alternatives is ordered like this:

(1) Pie
(2) Sandwich
(3) McDonald's
(4) Counter lunch at the club
(5) Pizza Hut.

Second, the order in which the alternatives are arranged is the order in which they are elicited by the mind. This order can influence your final choice. You may enjoy Pizza Hut more than McDonald's. But in the example, you didn't go to Pizza Hut, you went to McDonald's. Had you continued your thought process instead of stopping at the third alternative (McDonald's), you would probably have gone to Pizza Hut. But if Pizza Hut is only fifth on your mental agenda of lunch alternatives, it is unlikely to get much of your business. You didn't get to Pizza Hut because you didn't think of it before you hit on a satisfactory solution – McDonald's. You didn't get there physically because you never got there mentally. Even if we like or prefer something, if it is not reasonably high on our mental agenda, it is likely to miss out.

The limited extent of consideration sets results in a small number of brands being responsible for a high percentage of sales in many markets. An analysis by Nielsen (Van der Ouderaa, 1994) shows that in the Netherlands, after measuring over 90 products, the three largest brands represent about 60% of the cash returns. This analysis included food, non-food, drinks, small household articles and do-it-yourself products. The mutual relations between the return shares of these three brands, measured over all categories, are globally 4 : 2 : 1. There is, thus, a pattern, in which should be noticed that the exact ratios depend on the degree of product differentiation and market segmentation. The pattern manifests itself in different countries (including the United States, England and the Netherlands) and presents itself in many different product categories. The average on the 90 analysed categories in the Netherlands was 4.1 : 1.9 : 1.0 (the average shares of the numbers 1, 2 and 3 are 35.1%, 16.3% and 8.6% respectively). These ratios show a large consistency over time. By manipulating external variables (temporary offers, measures changing shelf positioning), suppliers can bring about some temporary changes, but we know from experience that the initial situation is almost always restored after a short period of time. People go back to their routine purchasing habits. Structural changes are in fact only possible when the representation of a brand in the memory of consumers changes in relation to the other choice alternatives. The relative saliency of the brand has to increase and must become part of their consideration set.

Consumers choose from 'consolidation sets' a small number (three to five) alternatives, which are present in their minds and with which they are usually familiar. These consideration sets are relatively stable in time. This is expressed, among other things, in the consistency of relative market shares of the three largest brands in a market.

8.3 The brand as an associative network

'Laura Ashley, Marlboro and Mercedes. Three brand names, each of which evoke a world – rich brands, filled with associations. The raw materials of a product as we perceive them, as we see them in the grocery store, or as they lie on the shelves, are water and hops, textiles, ground beans, metal and wood, dried tobacco leaves. The raw materials of a brand article are much richer than that. The raw materials of brand articles consist of associations. Brand articles are made of feelings, ideas and memories. Brand articles are, in fact, intangible. What is tangible is the physical product, the metal, the wood, the ground beans. A brand article can only be perceived very partially with the senses. The essential part of a brand article, its most important part, is fleeting and exists in the cognitive system of the consumer. It is not the 'brand maker' who 'makes' a brand article – it is actually the consumer who gives shape to a brand article, largely on the basis of what the 'brand manufacturer' offers: a tangible product, advertising. The brand article is much more complex than the tangible product, it is made up of emotions, associations and a fleeting whole that can nonetheless live on for a long time.' (Franzen and Holzhauer, 1987)

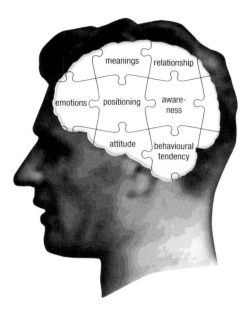

Figure 8.4   Brands in our memory.

Neurobiologists have concluded that the best way we can imagine human memory is as an associative network, with everything being related to everything else. The proof lies in daily as well as scientific practice. If, for instance, you try to remember someone's name and you concentrate on certain attributes or on the person's appearance, chances are you will stumble across the name. Knowledge on brands is stored in memory the same way, in the form of an associative network.

Based on theoretical models of associative memory, we can imagine the brand as a spherical space in which different components are localised. Each component represents a mental brand response and the core is formed by the brand name and related distinguishing marks such as colour, logo, spelling or design. Figure 8.4 shows the brand first, followed by a description of the separate components. For the totality of the brand components, Franzen and Holzhauer introduced in 1987 the name 'psychological product'. In the following text we will use the term 'mental brand response', which refers to the totality of associations, meanings, emotions, attitudes and behavioural tendencies that a brand name evokes in an individual.

The mental brand response is part of the Advertising Response Matrix, developed by Franzen *et al*. All the effects that can appear during or after confrontation with one or several advertisements or advertising campaigns are described in this matrix (Franzen, 1998). The purpose of this matrix is not without controversy. Nowadays when we are warned repeatedly to think more with our 'right brain half' and pay attention to 'the whole', it may not seem so logical to dissect the influence of advertisements and separate it into components. However, the great value of this matrix lies in the fact that it provides an insight into the various roles that brands and advertising have in the lives of people, and which aspects consumers use as 'decisive arguments' when choosing to buy something. Here is a description of the seven mental brand responses.

8.3.1 *The components of the mental brand response*

We distinguish the following as main components of a brand:

(1) *Brand awareness:* the presence of a brand name and the other related identification marks in long-term memory, and the ability to bring this information back to the working memory.
(2) *Brand meanings:* the mental linkage of a brand name to cognitions in long-term memory.
(3) *Brand emotions:* the mental linkage of a brand name to emotions, which can be distinguished on the basis of their nature and intensity.
(4) *Brand positioning:* classifying a brand in a group or subgroup of other brands on the basis of the most typical common attributes, and distinguishing a brand from other brands within the group or subgroup on the basis of its most typical differences.
(5) *Brand attitude:* the durable evaluation with regard to a brand, based on the consideration of positive and negative characteristics of a brand and which has implications for the behaviour related to the brand.
(6) *Brand behaviour tendency:* the tendency anchored in memory to keep buying a brand (the learned purchasing behaviour).
(7) *Brand relationship:* the two-sided connection between a consumer and a brand, consisting of the interaction, communication, reciprocity and continuity components.

It should be noticed that some of these concepts are allocated quite different meanings in the literature. Although this lack of clarity is inconvenient and regularly leads to misunderstandings, it is not a crucial problem. The most important thing is to have concordance on the nature and contents of the information that people store in their memory with relation to a brand.

8.3.2 *The interrelatedness of the responses*

The strength with which a brand representation is present in memory and the conspicuousness of one brand in comparison with another brand name (the brand saliency; an extensive description is given in Chapter 16) is the result of

Connection between brand use and spontaneous awareness

With fast moving consumer goods, the percentage of the population that is spontaneously familiar with a brand has a high correlation with the percentage that uses it. The percentage that does not know the brand spontaneously is closely related with the percentage that does not use these goods. Figure 8.5 shows this connection for toothpaste brands in the Netherlands in 1989 (Van Westendorp, 1996). The columns in the figure show the spontaneous awareness and the lowest line shows the 'prediction' of penetration based on spontaneous awareness.

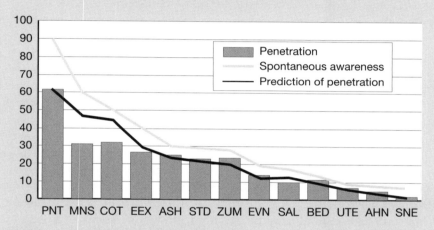

Figure 8.5   Penetration of toothpaste brands.

Ehrenberg (1969) established that this connection can be expressed in the formula

$$\log (1 - A) = Q\log (1 - V)$$

Q is a constant for the different brands in a product category. With this formula the spontaneous awareness of a brand could be predicted on the basis of penetration. See the following example (Ehrenberg, 1969):

Percentage of people who knew the brand 'spontaneously'	Brand						Average
	I	II	III	IV	V	VI	
Observed 100A	48	48	18	12	10	8	24
Theoretical 100A	48	48	17	10	9	10	24
Difference	0	0	1	2	1	−2	0

all the exposures an individual has had to the brand in her life. The most intense exposures come about during the use of the brand, but exposures to other stimuli such as advertisements have an influence on the brand awareness and on all other market responses. In short, all mental brand responses are interrelated – it is not without reason that we speak of an associative network. A brand attitude is influenced, for instance, by the brand emotions and brand meanings; the brand attitude will in turn be connected with the behavioural tendency ... and we could go on and on.

In the last few years much research has been done in trying to understand the connections between a number of these responses. In a great deal of this research, a connection was found between spontaneous brand awareness and brand use (see e.g. Van Westendorp, 1996). A connection thus seems to exist between the order in which brands are spontaneously mentioned and the frequency with which these brands are bought (see Table 8.2). Ehrenberg (1974) and Van Westendorp (1996) found independently of one another that there is a relationship between the brand behaviour tendency and the brand attitude: the brand someone most frequently buys within a category is usually also the brand about which the person has the most positive attitude. Ehrenberg also showed in earlier research that experiences during the use of a brand lead to the formation and strengthening of functional as well as symbolic associations (Ehrenberg, 1974; Franzen, 1992), and consequently also established a connection between brand meanings and brand use.

Research keeps showing that the users of a brand form a much richer associative network around that brand than non-users. The phenomenon of selective perception (and selective retention) results in users perceiving more communication from the brands that they themselves use, and processing these messages more thoroughly. This creates associations that we do not find, or find to a much lesser degree, in non-users.

> The various components of the mental brand response are closely interrelated. This is how the spontaneous awareness and perceived attributes of a brand are strongly correlated with their purchasing frequency.

There are tensions between the holistic and reductionistic approaches of brand representations. All brand responses are highly interrelated. They form one associative network per person, a network in which awareness, associations, emotions, attitude and behavioural tendency are different facets of the total representation of the brand in their memory. We can never activate and make this whole representation visible simultaneously. Research into this can be likened to using a pocket torch in a dark room. We see only that which falls within the beam of light. When we point the torch elsewhere, we see a different part of the contents of the dark room. If we want to get a picture of all the contents, we will have to illuminate the room bit by bit with the beam,

Connection between brand use and brand associations (Castleberry and Ehrenberg, 1990)

Ehrenberg studied the connection between brand use and the perceived brand attributes ('beliefs') for a large number of markets. For many brands in the following markets he showed that the percentage of the category users that have a certain 'belief' with regard to each of the brands is strongly related to its user frequency.

Table 8.2 Percentage of buyers believing perceived brand attributes according to purchase frequency.

	% buyers holding the 'belief'[a]			
	Buying frequency[b]			
Products or services	Regular	Occasional	Infrequent	Never
Breakfast cereals	38	30	21	14
Laundry detergents	58	33	25	17
Fast food chains	55	47	36	30
TV news programmes	56	47	35	28
Average	47	39	29	22

[a]The average across brands and attributes
[b]Frequency of buying, using, or watching the item:
Regular = once a month or more often
Occasional = about every 3, 6, or 12 months, grouped.
Infrequent = less than once a year
Never = never tried

attempting to construct a picture of the whole room from the successively lighted sections. Statistic analysis techniques such as factor analysis help establish relationships between different variables and combine scores on different variables.

8.3.3 *The dual structure of associations*

Associations have a direction. This means that they are not necessarily reciprocal. On the basis of our current insights into the structure of memory, this is also understandable. The association 'Kylian → beer' probably uses different synaptic connections from the association 'beer → Kylian'. Perhaps both associations are present, but there is a large difference in their strength. In this context we speak of a dual association structure. This is also an important difference. In market research, it is mostly only the associations from the brand to the associated product category that are being measured.

However, the choice behaviour of people usually begins with a product need, after which the connections with brands are then activated from the product or from the usage situation. The association 'coffee → Carte Noir' is therefore more important than the association 'Carte Noir → coffee'.

> Associations have a direction. They are connections from a brand to a meaning, but also from a meaning to a brand. This is called the 'dual structure' of an associative network.

In the stage of evocation, associations from the associated product to the brands play the most important role (Holden and Lutz, 1992). Which brands do we think of when we buy a certain product? Which do we think of when we are searching for a specific product attribute? Which do we think of for a specific application or user situation? In the stage of evaluation the emphasis lies on the associations from the brands towards the associated product. What other attributes does the brand have? What kind of people use it? Is it also suitable for other applications? The relative importance of the associations in the two phases of the choice process can therefore be very different.

Figure 8.6 gives a schematic representation of the dual structure of brand associations. The importance of the two association categories differs from product to product. With relatively risk-free consumer articles, we tend to go just by the information that is in our memory, as a result of which it is the associations towards the brand that probably have the largest influence on brand choice. It is precisely in purchases characterised by an extensive external search process and 'online' processing of information that the associations from a brand to attributes and applications can play an important role.

The meaning of the awareness of a brand itself is at any rate relative. What is important is what the brand is connected with in our memory. Many producers of overly well known brands sometimes miss this. When Philips first

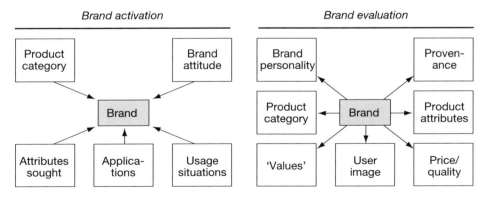

Figure 8.6 The dual structure of brand associations.

introduces electrical toothbrushes into the market and puts its name to them, we are not yet dealing with a strong brand article. Only when electrical toothbrushes make us think of Philips in the first place may this be the case.

Based on the relative strength of these two association directions, we can classify brands into a matrix. Brands with a strong product/brand association (top of mind awareness, or TOMA) generally have a greater chance of being chosen than brands with a weak product/brand association. The latter category has a good chance of being chosen only when there is no other brand with a strong product/brand association. Brands for which both associations are weak have little chance of being chosen on the basis of brand representation (sales of such brands will depend mainly on other marketing factors). The dual structure appears, of course, not only in the connection between product and brand, but in all association categories. The associations between a brand and desired product attributes (or its implications; the pros and cons) and between a brand and usage situations or applications play an important role in the inclusion of a brand in the consideration set. For the segment in which the 'clean' aspect is the determinant for the choice of a laundry detergent, the association 'clean' → Persil has a large influence on the brand choice.

The associations belonging to a brand play a large role in the evaluation phase, during which a deliberation takes place as to whether the symbolic meaning it is connected with fits one's personal value system, and what is the price/quality ratio with regard to the other brands in the consideration set.

8.3.4 *The strength of associations*

Ever since the ground-breaking theory of Hebb (1949), it has been known that connections between neurons are characterised by a strength/weakness dimension (a value or load). In psychological terms, this could be considered as the saliency of associations. They indicate, among others things, the speed with which an association is activated in one person and the total frequency with which this happens within one random check. We ask people things like 'Which brands do you think of when you wash windows?' or 'Which brands of toothpaste do you think of when you think of fighting plaque?'. We measure the time that elapses between posing the questions and the response, and keep track of the order of the answers. Both are indications of the relative strength of the associations (Figure 8.7).

The association from the product, or from the product attribute, towards the brand can be so strong that the brand monopolises this association. The brand enters our consciousness immediately when we think of the product. When the brand itself is given as a cue, the product association is one of the first to be activated. A brand that somehow carries such an association is called a 'master brand'. Just think of blue-jeans by Levi's, soft drinks by Coca-Cola,

Association from brand to product

	High (spontaneous)	Low (aided)
High (spontaneous)	XXXX	XXX
Low (aided)	XX	X

Association from product to brand

The number of crosses represents the influence on the brand behaviour

Figure 8.7 Direction and intensity of brand associations.

coffee by Maxwell House, beer by Guinness, etc. Strong brands are characterised by the direct access to the brand name in memory. Relevant cues, such as the product category, desired or preferred attributes and applications, are connected directly with the brand name in memory. The consumer quickly recalls these brands when she thinks of 'Wild Havanas', 'white teeth' or 'a clean wash'. Weak brands are characterised by weak representations, indirect connections and the lesser strength of these connections. Relevant cues do not give direct access to the brand, but the association has to come about via a detour. The distance that has to be covered before the brand is reached leads to a decrease in the activation. When the connections are also weak, chances are the brand might not be reached.

> The association from a product or product attribute towards a brand can be so strong that the brand has, as it were, a mental monopoly.

8.3.5 *The core of an associative network*

We can classify the associations of brands on the basis of their strength. Associations that are activated spontaneously when we think of a brand are called primary associations. Associations that enter our consciousness after some free 'further association' are secondary associations. Associations that are only activated with the help of specific stimuli from the outside are the weaker, context-dependent associations. There can also be 'induced associations' – meanings that are not connected with the brand in long-term memory, but that are connected with it only in the working memory as a result of, for example, a question in a market survey.

We can imagine a brand to be a spherical space at the centre of which the core associations are localised, and having associations with decreasing intensity surrounding it. The core generally contains the brand name, often also the established external identifying marks of the brand (for example a certain colour, logo, spelling and a specific packaging image) and the main primary associations, such as a product and a dominant attribute, an application, or an image of the users ('young people'). The exact contents of the core are determined individually and differ from brand to brand. The brand core is comparable to the principle of the epicentre postulated by Greenfield (see section 3.7). It is that which immediately enters our consciousness when the brand is activated in our memory. From this core all other sorts of associations can become active, depending on the stimuli that reach us. These can be, for instance, focused questions in an interview situation.

The specific questions that are asked stimulate those interviewed to activate certain associations – associations that may be weak and that they may not become aware of in a process of autonomous or 'free' association. The danger here is that something may be measured which is not part of the 'real' associative network of the brand. Those interviewed establish new connections on the spot: no 'existing', but only 'induced' associations are measured.

We assume that giving meaning to and the attitude development with regard to a brand are largely determined by the core associations. This seems to be even more the case when we deal with simple choice processes in which the alternatives are evaluated on the basis of only one or a few attributes. It is not useful to carry out extensive association tests for Duracell if we know that people who buy batteries are only interested in the lifespan of the brands. Duracell is a master brand in many countries because it is a brand with a small but extremely strong association core. Duracell is intensely linked with the product group of 'alkaline batteries', which 'lasts for a long time' as an attribute, with the quality-suggesting colours of black and gold, and with the sound of a heavy closing door. For more than thirty years these core associations were developed in the memories of more new generations of battery users and constantly strengthened by those who already knew the brand. By no means do all brands have an association core that is so strong, simple, easy to understand and unique.

An associative network has a core – those associations that are spontaneously activated when we think of a brand. This brand core has a large influence on the giving of meaning to and the attitude development with regard to a brand.

8.3.6   *The (multi)dimensionality of an associative network*

Associative networks can be very monodimensional. For instance, the brand makes people think of only one product and a limited number of attributes – and probably a single application. Brinta (a Dutch RTE-cereal brand for kids) is an example of this. Every Dutch person knows exactly what it is, what it's like and what it's for. It leaves absolutely no room for uncertainty. Probably the same applies to Weetabix in the UK. Philips, on the contrary, is an explicitly complex multidimensional brand. People can usually name a large number of products they associate with the brand. That is no wonder, since Philips has given its brand to about 30,000 different products. Depending on the personal relationship through which people associate with Philips, it produces completely different individual associative networks. In the collective portion, products such as lighting and television sets probably constitute the primary associations.

What are the implications of a complex associative network? Associative networks act as internal sources of information. When 'searching' for information during choice processes, we use this internal information as well as that of external sources to different degrees. As our 'knowledge' of a product category increases and our uncertainty becomes correspondingly smaller, we increasingly choose exclusively on the basis of the information that is stored in our memory in the form of networks. Brand associations begin exercising a relatively large influence on our purchasing actions. What is important is that the information that is stored in the associative network be clear and simple, so that we can 'sufficiently' assess/evaluate a product on the basis of that as well.

As the complexity of the associative network increases, the individual associations become less accessible. This causes their significance as an information source for the individual product choice to decrease. On the basis of the strength of the individual associations, the extent of the associative network and its multidimensionality, we could build a matrix in which we classify brands according to these characteristics. In Figure 8.8 we suggest such a matrix, and brands are placed on the basis of our personal assessments.

As the complexity of an associative network increases, the individual associations become less accessible. Therefore, complex brands act less well as a source of information than do 'simple' brands with few but more accessible associations.

8.3.7   *Evaluative and differentiative associations*

'The number of consumers who have a "belief" about a brand is closely related to the number of people who buy or use the brand. However, in a number of "belief"/ brand combinations, the behaviour of consumers strongly deviates from this pattern' (Castleberry and Ehrenberg, 1990).

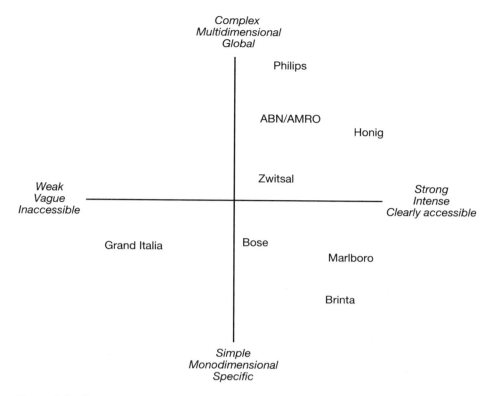

Figure 8.8 Brands classified by the degree of multidimensionality and strength of individual associations.

Researchers investigate very regularly how several competing brands score on certain attributes. The purpose of such research is generally to develop a good positioning strategy or to expose relevant attributes that could be used in advertisements. Andrew Ehrenberg, a marketing professor, regularly expresses his surprise in various publications that researchers do not relate the scores of brands to usage figures (Ehrenberg, 1990). In this section we will explain why it is indeed useful, if not necessary, to do this.

Consumers are confronted daily with an enormous amount of brands within most product categories. The fact that consumers regularly choose certain brands over others already shows us what they think about the other brands in the product category and predicts how they will react in surveys to all sorts of questions on the chosen brand. They are on many counts more positive about the chosen brand than the non-chosen brands. On the one hand this is because, to a greater or lesser degree, they have consciously decided that that one brand fulfils their wishes more than other brands. On the other hand, people generally tend to justify their choices afterwards, and start talking and thinking extremely positively about their choice (Festinger and Carlsmith,

1959). They do this because they may not want to regret their choice. A condition for this is that people should believe that the behaviour was completely voluntary (otherwise they could blame the salesperson for their bad choice). Another condition is that they could have foreseen the negative implications of the undesirable behaviour beforehand (a person who chooses Gerbers baby food and hears later in the news that there are glass splinters in the jar can hardly blame himself: he could not have foreseen it). Research by Festinger (1957) has also shown that, once they have made their choice, people look for information that justifies it. Information that could cast doubts on their choice is ignored. This is how a very positive associative network around the brand name gradually emerges in the memory of the users of a specific brand.

To summarise, we can now posit that the percentage of brands that score high on a number of positive attributes is strongly related to the market shares of these brands. Castleberry and Ehrenberg give an example with various brands of cereals. Table 8.3 clearly shows that the scores of the first two attributes (the first two columns) are strongly correlated (0.9 and 0.8) with the percentage of people that indicated they 'used the brand regularly' (the last column, which in fact shows the market share). The other two attributes (the third and fourth columns) have a low correlation, or none, with the market share (0.3 and −0.4).

The findings that were reported in Table 8.3 are no exceptions. According to Castleberry and Ehrenberg (1990), a table can be made for all brands in every product category which shows that the scores for some attributes are almost identical to the market shares, while the scores for other attributes show no connection whatsoever with them, so it depends very much on the nature of the attributes. This connection is very pronounced for more or less 'generic' attributes of a product category, e.g. 'good taste' for all sorts of food products, drinks and snacks. These are, in a way, evaluative associations. Their average attribute score is always considerably higher for users than for non-users (Castleberry and Ehrenberg, 1990). The more users a brand has, the more people will say that it has certain good attributes. Some associations ('it tastes good') are in fact just other ways of saying 'I love this brand' and 'I use this brand'.

Evaluative associations are closely related to the market share of a brand. This applies especially to the generic attributes of a category.

When a brand has a physical attribute or performance that clearly deviates from the competing brands, this is reflected by the associations. These differentiated associations can also arise from claims that have been consistently linked to the brand by advertising, throughout the years. The product-related associations in users of the various brands tend not to show

Table 8.3 Views of consumers on the attributes of various brands of breakfast cereals.

Brand	Opinion about the brand				
	Popular with the whole family	Good quality	Low in sugar	Fun for children	Percentage of regular buyers
Kellogg's Raisin Bran	37	29	12	7	32
Cheerios	35	39	43	28	31
Kellogg's Corn Flakes	35	54	43	28	27
Kellogg's Sugar Frosted Flakes	31	13	0	37	18
All Bran	8	20	60	1	16
Honey-Nut Cheerios	22	12	2	26	15
Fruit Loops	18	7	0	80	15
Rice Chex	18	23	47	6	9
Crispy Wheats N'Raisins	11	10	8	4	8
Coco-Puffs	5	7	1	54	5
Boo Berry	3	6	1	55	1
Correlation with regular buyers	0.9	0.8	0.3	−0.4	−

Source: Castleberry and Ehrenberg, 1990.

much of a difference between them for brands that are not very differentiated at a product level. In other words, the product-related associations of Heineken for a Heineken drinker, Amstel for an Amstel drinker and Guinness for a Guinness drinker show a high degree of correspondence. However, these associations also show a large difference per brand between its own users and the users of competing brands. Generic product associations cannot be 'claimed' by brands for themselves. They are very much related to the product scheme in memory. A brand that presents itself as a good example of a product category ('Stella Artois is a good brand of beer') gets allocated the defining (generic) attributes of the beer category to the extent that it succeeds in having people also use the brand.

As we saw in the example of the breakfast cereals (see Table 8.3), brands sometimes succeed in developing attribute associations with which they distinguish themselves – sometimes strongly – from other brands in their categories. In this example, for instance, All Bran is strongly associated with 'low in sugar' and Fruit Loops with 'fun for children'. When it comes to associated product attributes, the basis for it must also be in differentiated attributes. To the extent that a product does not distinguish itself from its competitors, it is also practically impossible for a brand to appropriate generic, defining product associations for itself, as countless analyses by Ehrenberg and others have shown. We should mention here that the association measurements on which he bases his observations largely regard product attributes and general attitude questions. In his publications we have hardly encountered any

What makes a brand distinctive? (Donius, 1984)

James F. Donius (1994) carried out a study in the United States into the meanings of three top brands in seven categories. The item battery that respondents used for evaluation was based on a conceptual associative model in which five levels of meaning were distinguished as shown in Figure 8.9 (the items in parenthesis are examples):

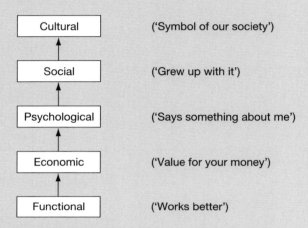

Figure 8.9 Conceptual associative model (Donius, 1994).

The desirability for each product category was researched for each association item. Statistical analysis led to a perceptual map on which brands from various product categories could be placed. Based on this, a brand typology was developed:

Contd

examples of more symbolic brand associations, such as perceived users and brand personality associations. In a situation of a product that does not distinguish itself effectively, attribute associations have the character of mere boundary conditions. This is not a basis on which a brand can effectively distinguish itself perceptually. Differentiation must therefore be sought in the development of differentiated symbolic associations. We will discuss this further in section 10.6.

Differentiating associations emanate from unique product attributes, or are the result of symbolic meanings that advertising has added to the brand.

- Old-fashioned brands (Maxwell House, Campbell's)
- Contemporary brands (Coors, Sprint)
- Stylish/exciting brands (Hilton, Marriott)
- Warm, friendly and reliable brands (Folgers, United, Miller)
- Real leading, winning brands (McDonald's, Budweiser, AT&T)
- Hollow and boring brands (Continental, Taste's Choice, Progress)
- Practical, goal-oriented brands (Holiday Inn, Lipton, Burger King, Wendy's).

Regression analysis, with desired associations per category and brand preference as dependent variables, shows that functional and economic meanings were evaluated as the most desirable, but that cultural, social and psychological meanings were the most explanatory for the brand preference. Based on this, Donius proposes a hierarchy of meaning in which the functional and economic associations act as boundary conditions, but in which the cultural, social and psychological meanings are the main brand differentiators (Figure 8.10).

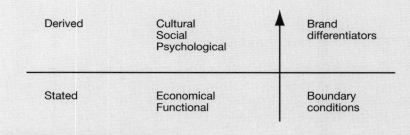

Figure 8.10   Hierarchy of meaning.

Determinant associations

Nowadays people have an awful lot on their minds and are confronted with an avalanche of information and entertainment. As a result, they are putting less cognitive energy into each individual activity or action. A visit to the supermarket should not last longer than about twenty minutes. 'Choosing' a package of coffee or a crate of beer must be done within a few seconds. This raises the question of how much information processing goes on in these regularly recurring choice processes. Which part of an associative network is activated? Which associations are determinant in the choice?

As has already been shown in Part One of this book, automatic (unconscious) activation of parts of a network play a larger role as the involvement decreases. There are very strong indications that only a minimal number of associations play a determinant role in choice decisions. Tigert (1983) and Alpert (1971) call them 'hot buttons' and 'determinant attributes' respectively (Woodside and Trappey, 1992). They are extremely accessible parts of an associative network, like the brand product association, the perceived quality, the brand emotion and the brand attitude. They are automatically activated when a product choice has to be made at the supermarket shelf. Measured in marketing research, they explain a substantial part, around 80%, of the market share.

Research into the connection between supermarket associations and supermarket choice in a town in the South of the United States showed that the accessibility of the store, 'lowest prices', the perceived quality of the meat, the perceived quality of the vegetables and the perceived quality of the cashier handling the transaction largely explain the primary choice of the various supermarkets. During the research the respondents were asked questions such as which stores they thought of first when it comes to a certain evaluative property, and which properties people considered important (as an open question). The answers to the first question gave, according to the researchers, a reliable picture of the automatic cognitive process (Woodside and Trappey, 1992).

8.3.8 *Relevance and brand ideal*

People have an enormous number of associations in their memory with large well known brands they use regularly. Seen from the perspective of the suppliers of those brands, probably only a small part of it is relevant, in the sense that they exercise an influence on the choice behaviour of consumers. The associations must be relevant to their needs and desires with regard to the product category and the values they aim for in life. Establishing this relevance is easy to express as a principle, but in research practice it is often extremely difficult to do. As a result, this is omitted in a lot of image research, which is what Part Three of this book explores. Differences in images between brands are measured, but no details are explored concerning what these differences mean for the brand choice and purchasing behaviour. Still, a certain image clearly does not automatically lead to a choice. For the supplier of a brand, it is necessary to have an insight into the relative importance of a certain association or image component for the consumer. For this reason, in image research, measurements of attitudes and behaviour must always be done simultaneously, examining later which image components are connected to behaviour.

Sometimes establishing the 'brand ideal' can give insight into this: the same measuring instrument used to research associations and images of individual brands is used to find out what the 'ideal brand' looks like in the eyes of the consumer. When brand associations correspond with the brand ideal, we speak of positive associations. When a brand is evaluated in a better light than its competitors on the basis of these dimensions, we speak of 'advantages'. By no means all brand associations are important when it comes to the brand choice process, and distinguishing associations certainly do not always constitute advantages.

8.3.9 *Uniqueness of associations*

Associations that are predominantly connected to one specific brand are called 'unique associations'. To the extent that they are related to product characteristics, they almost always emanate from actual distinguishing product attributes. These are associations that are not part of the generic 'product concept'. When they answer to choice criteria, they can exercise an important influence on the choice process. It is almost self-evident that they are not common in the competitive society we live in. Still, some brands are perceived as 'unique'. This has more to do with the specific combination of associations than with one attribute with which a brand distinguishes itself in a unique manner.

8.3.10 *Strong, positive and unique associations*

As will become clear in Chapter 10 (Brand Meanings), brands can be connected with a large number of different meanings. Not all of them are relevant when it comes to brand choice. A 'strong' brand distinguishes itself in the first place by the relative strength of the associations (their saliency), then to the degree in which it is positively evaluated by consumers on the basis of choice criteria, and finally by its uniqueness. Keller (1998) believes that this order is important. In other words, he thinks it is not important how unique an association is, unless it is relevant. It matters even less how relevant an association is, unless it is so strongly connected to a brand that consumers remember it spontaneously. The opposite also applies: it does not matter how strong an association is, unless it is relevant, and it does not matter how relevant an association is, unless the brand distinguishes itself sufficiently from competing brands. Whether Keller's views are true remains difficult to determine.

According to Keller, the influence of a brand association on the choice process of consumers is determined by:
(1)   Its strength,
(2)   Its relevance, and
(3)   Its uniqueness, in this order.

8.3.11 *The congruence of associations*

People strive towards eliminating contradictions in their knowledge and views. New information that is consistent with existing associations is more easily learned and remembered than information that conflicts with it. Congruence of the meanings of brand associations within a network influences the clarity of the brand and the ease with which it is 'understood'. A brand that is unambiguous and consistent in itself is more easily recalled and facilitates the absorption of new information related to already existing brand meanings. Manufacturers who know how to work with this avoid dissonant information and strive towards an optimal clarity of the associative network. Especially when the brand spreads into other product categories, one should ask what the degree of correspondence is of the new product with the core meanings of the brand. A brand that is connected to several product categories which, in the perception of the consumers, have little or no mutual correspondence irrevocably becomes an incoherent brand itself. The consumer no longer knows what the essence of the brand stands for. A brand that is associated with bread toasters is probably not a very suitable brand for mobile phones.

8.4 Associations and brand functions

Brands are need-satisfiers. They are sold or used because they possess characteristics that are experienced as relevant by a group of consumers. The characteristics can be of a functional nature (people buy Persil because they want a clean wash), or symbolic (people buy a BMW because they want to impress) or emotional (people seek comfort in a box of Merci chocolates). In other words, brands can fulfil various needs. These needs emanate from the nature of the characteristics that consumers associate with the brand name in their memory.

Researchers should take the functions that a brand has for the consumer as a point of departure. If they know that Persil is bought mainly for purposes of functional certainty ('washes clean'), associations connected to this function should be examined, and it might be less useful to measure the user associations. However, when it comes to brands that consumers choose primarily in order to support their self-image, such as Rolex, user associations are probably the most important ones. For consumers, these 'values' represent traits of entities they evaluate positively and that are instrumental in them reaching their goals. Four important groups of 'brand values' can be distinguished:

(1) Values that emanate from the products to which the brand is connected
(2) Symbolic meanings that are 'added' to the product by the brand

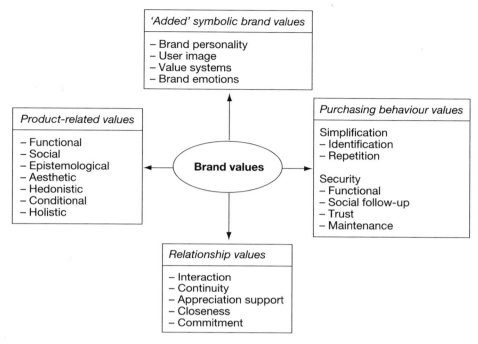

Figure 8.11   Four important groups of 'brand values'.

(3) 'Purchasing behaviour values', meaning the functions of brands in the purchasing behaviour itself

(4) 'Relationship values': the values that are connected with having lengthy relationships (Figure 8.11).

8.4.1   *Product-related values*

Over the years consumer behaviour researchers have been busy categorising the functions that products can have in the lives of people. This is not a simple task. The most well known classification was suggested in 1991 by Sheth under the title 'Why we buy what we buy'. He distinguishes five basic categories of product values. Lai (1995) added three more later on.

(1) *Functional values:* the ability of products to perform instrumental, utilitarian or physical functions. These values emanate from the concrete, tangible attributes of the product as an 'instrument', for instance to prevent or solve problems or to improve material conditions, e.g. laundry detergents, medicines, insurance, means of transportation, kitchen appliances, etc.

(2) *Social values:* the cultural meanings that the use of the product represents, particularly its associations with social groups. These are symbolic meanings that are associated with a product in a specific culture, e.g. wearing blue jeans at the office, smoking 'roll your own' tobacco during meetings, etc.

(3) *Emotional values:* the ability of products to activate emotions and influence moods, e.g. video cameras, drinks, some food products, feature films.

(4) *Epistemological values:* the role that products play in knowledge development and intellectual stimulation: arousing curiosity, acquiring new experiences and broadening knowledge, through e.g. books, newspapers, magazines, certain television programmes, internet, vacations in distant destinations, CD-ROMs, etc.

(5) *Aesthetic values:* the ability of a product to satisfy our feelings for beauty and style preferences. These values emanate from the design and style characteristics of products, e.g. clothing, decoration products, jewellery, watches.

(6) *Hedonistic values:* the ability of products to provide sensory enjoyment, give pleasure or evoke a feeling of comfort; e.g. enjoyment means such as cigarettes and drinks, food products, going to restaurants, certain hotels, night clubs.

(7) *Situational values:* the contribution of products in connection to specific usage situations. The ability to colour the experiencing of this situation. Products used at feasts, e.g. champagne.

(8) *Holistic values:* the appreciation of the harmony of the product in all its aspects. The 'coolness of the whole'. The ideal combination of the preceding values as they take shape in the total product constellation, e.g. large user-friendliness combined with design (Apple's iMAC).

Products can of course include several value categories that go together. Brands are associated with the values of the products they are connected with. They influence their perception and affect the appreciation of the corresponding product performances.

8.4.2 *Symbolic brand values*

The second group of brand values is formed through the symbolic meaning to which brands are connected in a specific culture. They have emerged mainly within a process of interaction between members of a culture or subculture in which (mass) communication plays a part.

Consumers see how brands manifest themselves, how others react to them, and derive symbolic meanings from that. The following symbolic meaning categories can be distinguished:

- *Brand personality:* human personality traits that are attributed to a brand.
- *User image:* perceived social–economic attributes and personality traits of the stereotype users of a brand.
- *Brand emotions:* the cognitive association of brands with specific emotions, or more holistic affect (positive, negative).
- *Brand values:* the associations of a brand with abstract meaning (e.g. 'individualistic' versus 'bringing together'). We will discuss this extensively in section 10.6.3.

Brands can have a symbolic function for the consumer in different ways. We can distinguish three variants (Franzen and Hoogerbrugge, 1996):

(1) The expressive function
(2) The social adaptive function
(3) The impressive function.

(1) *Expressive function*
    People often use brands to show others which values they consider important. Brands offer the consumer the possibility of controlling certain messages about themselves. This is known as the expressive function of a brand:

- The brand shows others who you are
- The brand shows what you stand for
- The brand shows what you consider important
- The brand shows what you consider to be worthy of pursuing or rejecting.

Brands are considered to be the extension of someone's personality. In some circles it makes a big difference whether you drive a BMW or a Nissan, or whether you wear Burberry's raincoats or Levi's blue jeans. The brand is then chosen if it fits the personal image that someone wants to show the world.

For some brands, the symbolic function is the most important one for the consumer. In some product categories the differences between products have become so minimal that the choices are made exclusively on the basis of the symbolic meanings. The functional attributes are then considered to be self-evident, or derived from the symbolic meanings. Cigarette and beer brands are examples of this; the competing brands distinguish themselves mainly on the basis of symbolic meanings.

(2) *Social adaptive function*

People like to look at other people out of curiosity, but also by doing so to find out more about their own position. In this game of perception, positioning and evaluation, brands can play a role. Brands and products often function as symbols for *conforming* to the demands a subculture makes.

Using the same symbols can even be a way to be *accepted* by that specific social group. Brands can help individuals to be included more easily in new groups. A classic example is the acceptance of a classmate on the basis of his Nike Airs.

Brands enable the consumer to *imitate*. By borrowing symbols that are important in a specific culture or subculture, a person can assume the desired identity and thus adapt herself to the standards of the social group in question.

(3) *Impressive function*

In addition to an expressive function, a brand can also have an impressive function for the consumer. The impressive function is about the feelings of contentment, self-satisfaction or self-confidence that emanate from the possession or use of a brand. The meaning of the brand has come about within the cultural context, but the feelings that its use or possession evoke are individual. When going to a job interview, people pay extra attention to the way they look. The right clothes and make-up give a person a feeling of security, but wearing Calvin Klein underwear can increase someone's self-confidence as well.

Choosing a brand on the basis of social values can also be categorised under the impressive function. Here we are referring to issues such as care for the environment or the welfare of fellow human beings. For instance, the consumer can express his involvement with schools by buying the United Biscuits brand McVities, which contains a token that schools can redeem to acquire maths equipment. You should notice, though, that although this is about a social ideal, getting a good feeling about the choice we make is the most important function for ourselves.

The impressive function is about satisfying the private self. Sensory and intellectual satisfaction are also examples of the impressive function. A brand can be pleasing because of its design, colour, taste or smell.

8.4.3 *Purchasing behaviour values*

The third group of values that brands 'provide' is formed by the functions they fulfil in the purchasing behaviour as such, for example its facilitation and risk-reduction. Here we are talking about the 'primal functions' of brands. When we see purchasing behaviour (running errands, shopping, etc.) as an important human activity, we can also distinguish values connected with it. The most important 'purchasing behaviour values' that brands provide are:

(1) *Simplification*
   - *Identification:* the brand name is a container of meanings which facilitates identification. We can illustrate this with a metaphor: in the purchasing environment they act as the signposts of the Automobile Club. Brands tell us where something is (the laundry detergent aisle), what something is (a laundry detergent for delicate fabrics), what it is like (protects colours), and who makes it (Henkel), how good it is (high quality). It enables us to choose the best in an instant, or to make a good price/value trade-off.
   - *Repetition:* brands make it possible to repeat a previous purchase without having to process a lot of information all over again. This can even result in an 'automation' of the purchasing behaviour. This saves consumers a lot of time.

(2) *Security*
   - *Functional security:* a brand provides security because of the continuity of the supply; the composition is constant, the quality is constant, and the user experience is constant. A consumer knows exactly what he is getting from a brand.
   - *Social security:* a brand does not just offer security in a functional sense, but also on a social level. A brand offers security about its approval by colleagues or its being valued by friends. The brand reduces the social risk of the purchase because it has meaning within a group.

(3) *Follow-up*
   - *Trust in the manufacturer:* important and more expensive one-off purchases give consumers a feeling of risk. The awareness of a manufacturer who inspires trust ('AEG will not walk out on you') can reduce or even eliminate the perceived risk.
   - *Maintenance:* the consumer assumes that when he is not happy with the functioning of a product he can contact the manufacturer, and he will help him. Especially when this involves products that require maintenance (means of transportation, some household appliances), he trusts that replacement parts will be immediately available and that quick service will be offered. When dealing with products in which information, education or even training are necessary, the brand is expected to provide this satisfactorily.

Four types of brands (DMB&B, 1994)

The advertising agency DMB&B undertook qualitative and quantitative market research into leading brands in the USA, the UK and Europe (DMB&B, 1994). Their consumer research identified four categories of brands, defined by the type of relationship the brand leader had established with its consumers. The four categories are:

(1) *Power brands*, inspiring rational trust through excellence in product and service performance
(2) *Identity brands*, facilitating character recognition, through associations with the brand's personality
(3) *Explorer brands* enabling consumers to develop personally through challenging them and suggesting possibilities
(4) *Icon brands* are the myths that consumers dream about sharing.

This categorisation enables the competitive nature of brands in a market-place to be identified. For example, extrapolating from their work, airline brands could be categorised as:

- Lufthansa (power brand)
- Virgin (identity brand)
- Qantas (explorer brand – particularly a few years ago)
- BA (icon brand)

It also enables a firm to understand better its portfolio of brands. So for British Airways the following could be suggested:

- BA First Class (power brands)
- BA Club World (identity brand)
- BA World Traveller (explorer brand)
- BA Concorde (icon brand).

Power brands, for example Fairy Liquid and Duracell, need continual R and D investment and high quality standards to ensure they are always at the forefront in delivering the required benefit. Communications campaigns centre on the 'product as hero', dramatically demonstrating how superior the brand is at satisfying consumers' rationally evaluated, functional needs [...].

Identity brands, such as Tango, grow through well established brand personalities. They rapidly overcome consumers' choice dilemmas between functionally similar brands, by enabling consumers to recognise, 'This is who I am: I feel much more comfortable with this brand'. American

Contd

Express, with their campaign 'It says a lot about the real me', is an identity brand. These brands thrive when their personalities are subtly updated to reflect societal changes [...].

Explorer brands strive to be at the edge of social (Nike) and technological (Microsoft and Apple) advances. They are agents of change, supported by very flexible organisational structures that rapidly respond to indicators of new trends (e.g. Swatch). They appeal to early innovators who are attracted by advertising showing how they can personally develop with these brands.

Icon brands have grown through tying themselves to a particular dream. This could be nostalgia (Hovis), culture (e.g. Southern Comfort and Americana), fantasy (e.g. Martini) or moral ideals (e.g. ethical investments at Co-op Bank).

8.4.4 *Relationship values*

A brand relationship is the relationship between a consumer and a brand, and will be discussed in Chapter 15. It can consist of the following components:

• Interaction (e.g. practical, emotional and social experiences in usage)
• Communication (e.g. publicity, reactions of consumers to messages of the brand)
• Reciprocity: the partners mutually influence one another
• Continuity: there is a past, present and expectations regarding the future.

Having good relationships can imply a number of values, which we shall now go on to distinguish.

Interaction

Fournier (1994) defines a relationship between a person and a brand as 'a voluntary or imposed mutual dependence of a person and a brand, characterised by a unique history of interactions and the anticipation of joint events in the future, with the goal of helping achieve instrumental and/or social–psychological aims of the partners, and characterised by a strengthening emotional bond'. These goals are closely related to the previously described brand functions, but the relationship adds to it certain dimensions.

Continuity in life

This is the first dimension. Consumers have respect for those brands that are able to stay around for years and that everyone seems to know. They trust the 'old time favourites' but also go out looking for 'rising stars'. Langer (1997) claims that in today's uncertain world, brands can even bring an element of continuity into their lives.

Fournier believes that some product categories have more of a person/brand relationship than others. Her research shows that there is a great need for the comfort and reassurance of a (long-term) relationship when the consumer experiences great insecurity. The risk feeling plays an important role here, in a financial, functional and social sense (Fournier, 1994).

Appreciation support

The relationship is based on the perceived attitude of the brand by the consumer: does the brand do what I can expect of it? Will it disappoint me? Is it making an effort to give meaning to the relationship and maintain it? Meertens and Grumkow call this 'appreciation support', i.e. others' recognition and appreciation.

Psychological closeness (intimacy and love)

How close is the brand to the consumer? Does the brand understand what I need, does it have an understanding of my views on life, does it value my loyalty, does it respect me? The brand gives the consumer the feeling that it is totally made for him. Fournier speaks of intimacy when the consumer knows a brand very well or is very familiar with it, and of love when there is a great affinity with and positive feelings are experienced towards the brand.

Involvement and commitment

Involvement is the importance that someone attaches to the brand. There is attachment when internal powers that bind the consumer to a brand are present, expressing themselves, for instance, in a willingness to invest in the relationship. The higher the commitment of both partners, the greater the chances are of maintaining the relationship for a long time. Some brands give consumers the feeling that they are irreplaceable, and that they could not live without them. In a way, they have become dependent on them – perhaps even addicted.

Chapter 9

Brand Awareness

9.1 Brands in memory

Brand awareness is a precondition for the existence of brands. A name that is not present in memory is not a brand. We speak of awareness when we can retrieve the name from memory on the basis of a cue. This is easiest when the brand name itself functions as a cue, and what we do is recognise the brand. In research jargon this is called 'aided brand awareness'.

As we saw in Part One, we can recognise at a later time an infinite number of stimuli we have perceived in the course of our lives. Aided brand awareness has only a marginal influence on the choice behaviour of consumers. It is only in situations in which none of the choice alternatives is well represented in our memory that brand familiarity ('that brand does seem familiar') can be determinant in the choice process. In purchases in which the consumer regularly has to choose (and re-choose) merely on the basis of the knowledge that is stored in her memory, aided brand awareness (i.e. brand recognition) has hardly any significance. This applies especially to all purchases that are made in self-service circumstances.

When we are able to retrieve a brand from memory on the basis of other cues, we speak of a 'spontaneous brand awareness' (Figure 9.1). Spontaneous brand awareness is usually researched by using a product category as a cue,

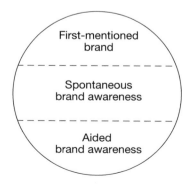

Figure 9.1 Brand awareness.

e.g. 'name all the brands of toothpaste you know'. We activate the toothpaste 'node' and determine towards which brands this activation spreads. We have already seen that the activation chooses the strongest connection, that is, the brand name that is most strongly associated with the product category cue. We can also activate brands whose connection to the product category is weaker. Consequently, the order in which brands are spontaneously named on the basis of a cue that is related to the product category gives an impression of the relative strength of the associations between this product category and various brands.

Figure 9.2 is a representation of the responses of one person in the United States to the question of naming all the brands for treating the common cold. During the course of five minutes, twenty-two brands were spontaneously named (Alba and Hutchinson, 1987). Not only is the large time difference between the first and last named brand striking, but also the clustering in which brands were retrieved from memory by the respondent: groups of brands which have common characteristics were constantly mentioned together. The positioning of the brands, which we will analyse further in Chapter 12, works here as an inner cue to activate brands that somehow belong together.

A great deal of research has shown that there is a strong connection between buying and using brands and the relative spontaneous awareness of these brands. People activate most quickly the names of the brands they themselves use, or those brands they have used in the recent past. They usually name first the brand they consider as 'their' brand. A 'real' Heineken drinker will activate Heineken immediately upon being asked to name all the beer brands he knows. Naming a brand first after a cue that is related to the product category is known as 'top-of-mind awareness'.

However, many markets do not experience such pronounced brand preference as the beer market: consumers often choose from a limited repertoire of several brands, all of which they find acceptable and which they also buy. The relationship between purchasing behaviour and top-of-mind awareness is less pronounced here. Establishing 'naked' spontaneous brand awareness of brands in a product category can be registered by examining the order in which brand names are named and the time that elapses between giving a cue and naming the brand name.

9.2 Extent, intensity and breadth of the brand awareness

Three important aspects are distinguished when it comes to brand awareness:

(1) The total extent of the brand awareness
(2) The intensity of the brand awareness
(3) The breadth of the brand awareness.

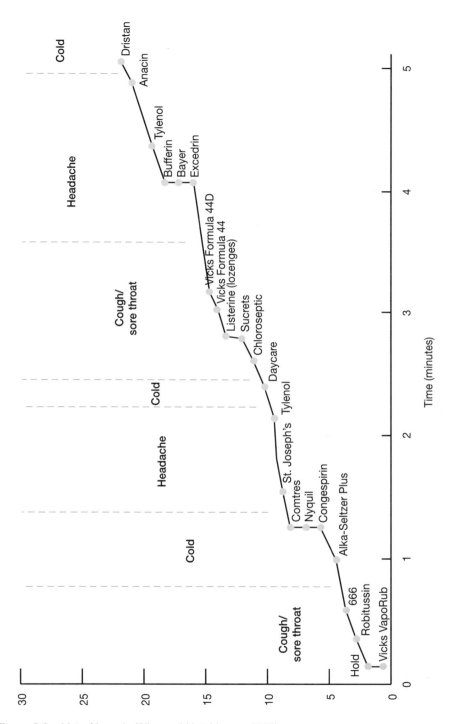

Figure 9.2 List of brands (Alba and Hutchinson, 1987).

The *total extent* entails all the people that know the brand one way or another: the sum of its spontaneous recollection and aided recollection (brand recollection). The *intensity* is related to the strength with which the brand is present in memory. This is expressed in the time elapsed between the beginning of the activation and its entrance into consciousness. In the ordinal number, it is the place within a series of activated brands. Finally, the *breadth* refers to the series of product categories or subcategories with which a brand is connected in memory. Some brands do have a very narrow awareness, being connected to only one category or subcategory. The Dutch beer brand Wieckse Witte is only associated with white beer, and 'Buckler' only with low alcohol light beer. Bavaria is associated with both beer and alcohol-free beer (Malt). Amstel is connected with lager, light beer, malt, old brown and bock beer. Nivea is associated with a large number of different toiletry articles, while Fa is only associated with bath and shower products and Right Guard only with deodorant articles. Philips is associated with a large number of electronic and electrotechnical appliances (I once heard a respondent say 'Philips stands for anything that has a plug on it') – it is a brand with a very 'broad' awareness. The breadth of the brand awareness, combined with the depth per product category, has a large influence on the choice behaviour of consumers.

There is a large amount of marketing literature that suggests that well known brands have various advantages over those that are less well known. They achieve higher levels of appreciation and preference by consumers and retailers alike. This connection between awareness and attitude is one of the most robust empirical generalisations within marketing science. Three plausible theoretical explanations are given for this (Rindfleisch and Inman, 1998):

(1) The 'mere exposure' hypothesis: repeated exposure to a stimulus leads to an increase of positive affect.
(2) 'Accessibility of information' hypothesis: less well known brands are usually connected to fewer meanings as well, due to which they have shortcomings as sources of inner information.
(3) The 'social desirability' hypothesis: most people tend to behave according to the expectations of their social environment, even when it goes against their own opinion. Because of this, many people have a tendency to buy the large, well known brands, especially when the brand is socially visible.

Of these three hypotheses, that of social desirability seems to provide the strongest theoretical explanation for the relationship between brand awareness and brand attitude (Rindfleisch and Inman, 1998).

Brand awareness also functions as a heuristic, especially with consumers who have little or no experience with a product category and who do not have relevant product schemes (Hoyer and Brown, 1990). They tend to choose a brand that they know, involving no or fewer 'unknown' brands in their choice process. The presence of a brand name in long-term memory therefore has an important influence on the structure of the consideration set.

The strength of the association of a product category with a brand has a large influence on the brand choice of consumers. The strength is expressed in the speed with which a brand is activated when the product category is given as a cue and placed within a series of activated brands (the ordinal number).

Chapter 10
Brand Meanings

10.1 Introduction

In section 5.1 we explained that three forms of cognitions can be distinguished in memory representations. Applied to brands, these are:

(1) *Direct (analogous) representations of sensory 'sensations'*: what does a brand look like, what does it sound like, how does it smell, how does it feel? This also includes representations of, e.g. packaging, advertisements, the products people encounter and the sensory perceptions of those products, places where people have encountered those brands, people who saw others use the brand, and so on.

(2) *Propositional representations*: the abstract meanings of a brand, i.e. the non-sensory perceptible meanings that are derived from the sensory experiences. These are meanings constructed by the human mind on the basis of perceptions – they are interpretations.

(3) *Language:* words, sentences and stories used to express the experiences with and the meanings of a brand. Language associated with a brand can be an analogous representation: when we perceive the KLM brand frequently together with the word 'reliable', a connection can emerge between these two which has an analogous character. Language will usually have the function of only expressing meanings that are present in our memory on an analogous or propositional basis.

One of the biggest problems anyone who is professionally involved with brands (researchers, manufacturers, advertising agencies, etc.) is confronted with is that brand meanings (images) are almost exclusively described in words – while they probably are present in our memories on a primarily visual, auditive and symbolic basis. The authors of this book have not been able to avoid this problem. We do make a referral to Hirschman's *cri de coeur* (1998) (see page 180). It distinguishes idiosyncratic images that are determined individually from cultural as well as subcultural associations that are shared by the members of a subculture. Sikkel (1999) believes in the existence of proper

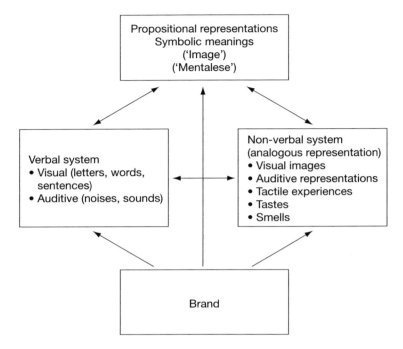

Figure 10.1 The three forms of cognitions applied to brands.

descriptions in language to this end. There needs to be a constant awareness of this problem (Figure 10.1).

All kinds of things are associated with brands in our memory. Brand associations are mental links between the brand name and the analogous representation and symbolic meanings in the memory of the consumer, and which are made with the brands on the basis of direct or indirect experiences. Sometimes these are direct associations, like Shredded Wheat → breakfast cereal. Sometimes it involves associations that are connected with a brand in chains, like Perrier → mineral water → France → stylish. These are network-like connections whose individual elements can be activated by the brand or by each other, depending on the stimuli we receive. An example of such a network is that of the brand 7-Up in Figure 10.2. This example was elaborated in the Netherlands on the basis of a limited number of interviews in which no other stimuli than the brand name itself were used. We have attempted to represent the strength of the associations with the thickness of the lines. Each associative network consists of a link of sub-networks. A brand is therefore usually associatively connected to one or more products, which in turn are represented in our memory in the form of associative networks.

Connections with images, sounds, tastes and smells ensure that a brand name gets 'meaning': what a brand stands for becomes clear to people. For

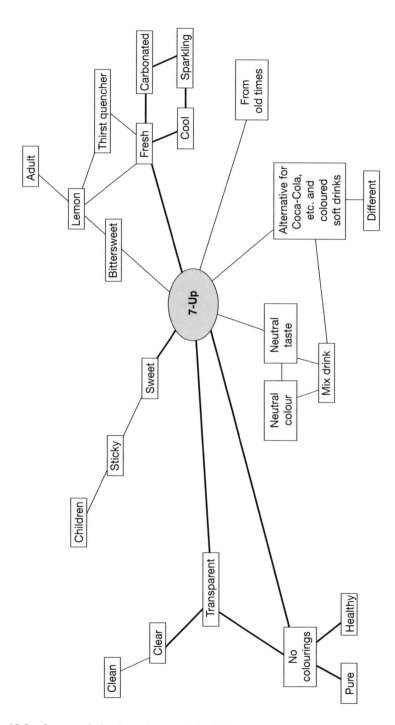

Figure 10.2 An associative brand network for 7-Up.

There is more to meaning than words (Hirschman, 1998)

My reflections on representation have been in process for almost twenty years, ever since I first started thinking about symbolism, images, and meaning as research topics. In one of my earliest efforts, I speculated that all tangible objects are capable of carrying at least four layers of meaning:

(1) *Direct sensory or iconic impressions*, such as colour, shape, texture, size, weight, sound, taste and so forth, which I felt would be invariable across all humans.

(2) *Idiosyncratic meanings*, which are associations due to unique, personal experiences with the object and which vary completely across people. For example, I associate the soupy song 'Love is blue' with a certain boy I was dating at a certain place during a particular time in my life. Whenever I hear the song (fortunately, not often) I think of that boy, that place and that time – what cognitive psychologists would term autobiographical or episodic memory.

(3) *Subcultural associations*, which are thoughts and images that are usually connected to an object by members of a given subculture. For example, growing up as a girl in the southern United States, I have associations with the confederate flag and with the song 'Dixie' that are probably quite different from those of a black girl growing up in the same place.

(4) *Cultural associations*, which are thoughts and images associated with an object by most members of a given culture. For example, most Americans probably look upon Santa Claus, Mickey Mouse and Big Bird with affection (...).

I believe that we have become too enamoured of and dependent on words – verbal or written text – in the research we conduct on meaning, symbolism and imagery, and in the representation of our findings. With

Contd

example, Volvo stands for safety and Volkswagen for reliability. The meanings that people allocate to a brand can be of different natures and levels. Sometimes the meaning of a brand can emanate directly from the functional product, and at other times an abstract or symbolic meaning is linked to the brand with the help of communication. In general, people find the meanings that brands disseminate so important that they link them associatively to the brand name in their memory. With BMW, for example, they immediately think of status, and with Douwe Egberts, the biggest fmcg brand in the Netherlands, it is togetherness. Below we have classified the brand meanings into ten groups.

very few exceptions (and one of the major ones is the work of Linda Scott (1994) on visual rhetoric), we shy away from dealing with non-written texts. As an example, let's consider my own procedure. If I conduct in-depth interviews with twenty consumers on a given topic, I take the interview tapes to be typed and work from the typed transcriptions to do my analysis. I don't ask these consumers to express their ideas by drawing a picture or singing a song or making a meal or playing music or dancing. Nor do I as a researcher contemplate doing any of the above as a journal submission. I simply rely on their words and represent my own account in words, which limits both me and them tremendously (...). Our translation capabilities suggest, to me at least, that we just cannot represent all of the meaning in a visual (or other sensory) image simply by using words to describe it. Our vocabulary for scent is especially impoverished. Further, a given internal of external sensory image – say a song or a whiff of perfume – may trigger related symbolic associations that evoke other sensory images, as well as verbal and cognitive associations (...). Many days I feel that I am less sure of things now than I was back in 1980 when I first proposed the multilayered model of meaning. That model, born as it was during the reign of cognitive theory, very much reflected the hegemonic bias in favour of verbal conceptual associations – little sentences or phrases that were mentally stored as linkages to a central concept.

Since then, I've come to recognise in my own head what was formerly invisible in my theoretical formulations. That is, for me, much of meaning is composed of visual and auditory images, wordless pictures and sounds that for many of life's most important objects and events are the key symbolic elements. I wish I knew some way to project these images outward so that they would be accessible to others. I wish I knew some way that the people I've spoken to as informants could project their inner images outward to me so that I could fully comprehend the meaning that they are trying to communicate with their words. I wish I knew some way to represent all of these inner images so that others could see what we mean.

Each categorisation contains debatable decisions. Still, an overview makes sense, if for no other reason than to remind us that research usually exposes only part of these associations. This may result in a conviction that the measured associations are the most important, seen from the choice processes of the consumer. However, it is certainly not impossible to overlook certain association categories.

Language is merely a way of giving expression to brand meanings that are present in memory on a visual, auditive and symbolic basis. The capacity for language to do this properly is limited.

Categories of brand meanings

(1) *Brand signs:* the visual, auditive, smell, tactile and taste traits of the brand, such as:
 - Logo, brand image, spelling
 - Colour
 - Design, form
 - Sound (music, voice)
 - Smell

(2) *Sub-brands* (e.g. the influence of the sub-brand Volkswagen Golf on the brand Volkswagen, or of the sub-brand Pickwick Country Garden on the brand Pickwick).

(3) *Provenance/history*
 - Country/region/place of provenance (Limburger beer, Italian cars, Swedish furniture)
 - The history of the brand (age, development)
 - Authenticity
 - Image of the company behind the brand
   - general company traits
   - capabilities of the company
   - economic traits
   - product-related company associations
   - cultural aspects
   - brands and relationships

(4) *Product-related brand meanings*
 - Products (washing machines, biscuits)
   - product categories (chips, underwear, sweets)
   - product variants (biscuits with chocolate, waterbeds)
 - Product exterior
   - form
   - colour
   - material
 - Product attributes, traits and performance
   - composition, ingredients (natural smell and taste substances)
   - method of use
   - usage characteristics (durability)
   - experimental attributes (taste, smell, sound, softness, firmness, flexibility)
   - usage effects (effects, advantages, disadvantages)

- Applications (microwaveable)
- Services (warranty, delivery)

(5) *Situational meanings (situations)*
- Usage moments
  - moments of the day (only in the evenings or only in the mornings)
  - day of the week (or at the weekend)
  - season
  - special days (Christmas)
- Usage situations
  - social context (alone or with others)
  - physical situation (on the terrace, at the locker room of the sports club, camping)

(6) *Symbolic meanings (symbols)*
- User types (stereotypes)
  - age
  - gender
  - appearance
  - social class, middle class
  - occupation, education (construction workers, housewives, students)
  - personality (caring, macho, dominant)
  - lifestyle (yuppie, DINK)
- Brand personality
- Value systems
  - impressive values
  - expressive values
  - personal end values
  - societal values

(7) *Perceived quality*
- Objective and relative

(8) *Perceived price*
- Absolute and relative
- Price/value ratio

(9) *Presentation*
- Shops, branches
- Package (appearance, variations, style)

Contd

(10) *Advertising and other communication means*
- Style
- Contents
- Slogan/payoff
- Place
- Time (when was the communication observed?)
- Attitude with regard to advertising
- Persons (real or animation) who keep returning in brand advertisements

It is important to determine which categories of brand meanings are present in memory for individual brands, and which role they play in the development of the other components of the mental brand response and in the ultimate purchase. To get more of an insight into this, we will continue to elaborate on the association categories in the following sections.

A brand is a central node within an associative network, in which it is directly or indirectly connected to a multitude of associations. We can distinguish ten different categories of brand meanings.

10.2   Brand signs

Brand signs are all the visual, auditive, smell, tactile and taste signs of the brand that people link associatively to the brand; but which sign constitutes the central representation of a brand? When we invoke a brand spontaneously in our memory, what is it that enters our consciousness first? The packaging? The name? The way in which the name is usually represented? The central representation is associatively connected directly with other distinguishing marks that we have frequently perceived in the past, like a logo or a certain colour. When we perceive these distinguishing marks again, they activate the central node in the associative network and we become aware of the brand name. Although this is in fact about associations of the brand's distinguishing marks with the brand name, in our schematic representation of the mental brand response we include the distinguishing marks in the central component, which represents the awareness and saliency of the brand as such.

The brand name is the most unchangeable component of the brand. All other components can gradually be adapted to changing circumstances as years go by, but a name is 'holy'. Changes (Raider → Twix) are not impossible, but they are usually extremely expensive.

By brand signs we mean not only the name itself, but also the following elements which are part of it:

- Visual style characteristics (spelling of a name, graphic design, brand image/logo, colour)
- Auditive characteristics (music, voice)
- Olfactory characteristics (smell)
- Taste characteristics (sweet, salty, bitter, sour)
- Tactile characteristics (solid, soft).

The basic function of brand signs is brand identification. For the brand it is essential to be recognised as quickly as possible – certainly when choice decisions are based purely on memory representations. Consistently linking the name to the other distinguishing marks in expressions of the brand is important not only to allocate those expressions to the correct brand during the perception, but mainly to establish the brand and the distinguishing marks as strongly as possible in memory. Every brand expression should contribute to the strengthening of the representation of the brand name and the recognition signs in memory.

Research has shown that a stimulus is recognised more quickly if it consists of elements that are strongly interrelated. This integration can be based on extremely superficial characteristics. If we have always perceived KLM together with a specific shade of blue, this will eventually facilitate the identification, although the name and the colour had no initial connection to one another. The integration can also be based on shared meanings in which name and signs point to each other's contents. The word 'Milka', in its unique spelling, together with the picture of a cow, facilitates brand recognition. Also, if both the cow and the packaging of Milka are always lilac, an integrated sign network is created in our memory, allowing Milka to be recognised in the supermarket in a fraction of a second.

When developing brand signs, attempts are sometimes made to create images with a meaning that is not intrinsically connected to the name, but which is extrinsically added to it. Sometimes it is clear to almost everyone, without any need for explanation, which meaning is being alluded to (a tree stands for growth). Quite often it is most clear from the beginning which meaning is being alluded to, and a lot has to be invested in making the meaning of the sign clear to the mass public. Even if one initially succeeds in making a meaning clear, it usually gets relegated to the background in the course of time. What ultimately remains are a word and an image that, in time, only connect to one another associatively through frequent joint perception. Although a brand logo whose content is not integrated into the sign system of a brand can also contribute to brand identification, one could ask whether an efficient solution has been chosen. This applies ever more strongly to loose, pure graphic forms that do not represent any meaning at all. Many brands show that a unique typography or spelling of the brand name itself, processed into a characteristic form using special colours, can form a very effective identification network.

A sign system with integrated content leads to quicker brand recognition than brand signs that have no content-related relationship between them.

10.3   The origin of the brand and sub-brands

The origins and history of a brand can hold an important position within the associative network. Some brands make people spontaneously think of a country or region, or of a company behind the brand. We can hereby distinguish the following association categories:

(1)   Country/region/place of provenance
(2)   Company/manufacturer of the brand
(3)   History of the brand
(4)   Authenticity of the brand.

We will go on to elaborate on the first two categories.

Country of origin

Consumers can have stereotypical associations with products that come from various countries. These associations can play an important role in their evaluation of those products. It is important to find out to what degree a country is associated with a specific product category, like Switzerland with watches, France with wine and Italy with pasta. These products are part of the specific scheme with which the country is represented in our memory. When a brand is associatively connected to such a country, it can result in these associations being linked to the brand in question. For example, when it comes to cars and airlines, the country of origin belongs to the very first associations that are activated when a brand enters consciousness.

Research by Roth and Romeo (1992) has pointed out that consumers are more willing to buy a brand that comes from countries with a good reputation in the corresponding categories than from countries that are not associated with those categories at all. Particularly consumers with little or no product experience tend to base their evaluations largely on the country of origin. A good country reputation in the product group is a condition for them to include the brand in the consideration set. As people acquire more product

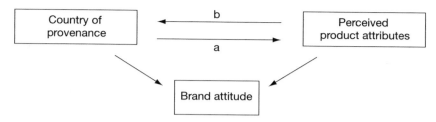

Figure 10.3 Relationship between country of provenance and brand evaluation.

experience, the direct influence of the origin on the evaluation decreases, although it still remains influential on the associations that people have with brands from various countries. Han (1989) observed that experts in a product field are also prone to connect the country of origin with brand evaluations. He suggests that the country of origin functions as a summarising construct for experts: they do not derive brand attributes from it – what they do is summarise them (direction 'b' in Figure 10.3 compared with direction 'a' for consumers with little or no product experience).

In addition to the product-related country reputation, more general country images can also have an influence on brands. Consumers all over the world expect German cars to be reliable and structurally excellent, Swedish cars to be safe and environmentally friendly, French cars to provide comfort and design, Italian cars to be sporty and rusty, English cars to have leather and wood, and Japanese cars to be economical and durable. Here we are not just seeing the automobile reputations of these countries, but also an echo of their more general characteristics. Research by Anholt (1998) into these general country images is summarised overleaf.

The country of origin can play an important role when evaluating brands. This happens especially when the country has a strong reputation in a product category, or precisely when this reputation is missing. The country image can influence the brand evaluation.

Company/manufacturer

The degree to which brands are associated with the company that brings them into the market varies strongly from category to category and from brand to brand. Here we can distinguish various levels:

(1) Individual brands: the company behind the brand is anonymous, or is not associated with the brand (Bounty, Jif, Aquafresh).
(2) Individual brands whose manufacturer is known but remains completely in the background (Marlboro, Flora, Ariel).

Country images

Anholt (1998) asked sixty respondents in six cities (Hong Kong, Colombo, London, Copenhagen, São Paulo and Boston) to indicate which two characteristics from a series of fourteen could be associated with twelve countries. The fourteen characteristics were: arrogance, humility, efficiency, inefficiency, energy, laziness, wealth, poverty, cleanliness, misery, order, modernity, tradition and style. The following country profiles were derived from it. Each of the reported characteristics per country was mentioned by at least 30% of the respondents:

France	•	unclear
Germany	•	arrogance, order
Sweden	•	efficiency, modernity
Great Britain	•	arrogance, tradition
Brazil	•	style, misery
Italy	•	style, laziness
Spain	•	inefficiency, laziness
Switzerland	•	wealth, order
Belgium	•	unclear
The Netherlands	•	modernity, arrogance
Portugal	•	poverty, backwardness
Denmark	•	cleanliness, modernity

(3) The individual brand is associated with a company, but individual brand associations dominate (PG Tips of Brooke Bond, Nescafé of Nestlé, Kellogg's Corn Flakes, KitKat of Nestlé). The company's brand functions as an endorser of the individual brand.

(4) The company brand is perceived primarily, the individual brand is differentiated ('sub-brand') from the company's brand (Philishave, Saab 900, Apple Macintosh, Shell-Helix, Gillette Sensor).

(5) The company brand is the only brand to be perceived (Michelin, Digital, Wedgwood, Visa, Nikon).

Two developments can be seen within this context. First, companies behind individual brands are coming out of anonymity, and are increasingly attempting to establish a relationship between their brands and their company. In addition, companies which in the past brought all products and services into the market under the company brand are doing more 'sub-branding' of their individual products or product categories. There are good reasons for both strategies.

The 7500 brands of Nestlé and their origin: an interview with Peter Brabeck-Lemathe, CEO Nestlé (Parsons, 1996)

(...) 'Nestlé' has 10 worldwide corporate strategic brands, including Nestlé itself, Nescafé, Maggi, Friskies, Buitoni and Carnation. Additionally, we have 45 different strategic worldwide product brands, among them KitKat, Coffeemate, and Crunch. Then there are 25 regional corporate strategic brands, such as Perugina, Findus and Stouffer's together with about 100 regional product brands – Eskimo, Taster's Choice, Go-Cat and so on. Each corporate brand has its own 'territory' into which the local brands will fall. We also have some 700 local strategic brands that are important to particular countries, like Brigadeiro in Brazil.

Then there are 7500 purely local brands (...). Our first principle is to consolidate all our resources behind the key corporate strategic brands. Whatever the product brand or range brand, it has to be supported by one of our corporate brands. Let me give you an example. Rowntree had a 'one product, one brand' policy: KitKat, Smarties, Rolo, After Eight. No mention of Rowntree. When we acquired the company, we applied our system, and KitKat became Nestlé KitKat (...). Nestlé is a brand in its own right. For consumers, relevance of Nestlé as a company comes first of all through contact with products that are branded Nestlé. If we want to be perceived as the world's leading food company, we have to offer consumers an increasing amount of products that they can identify as Nestlé. The choice of products that we will put together under the Nestlé brand depends on the way these products enhance the Nestlé image – not on what Nestlé brings to their products. Therefore each of these products has to have deep roots. Take infant cereals, for example. This is the only product that has an automatic right to the Nestlé brand because it is with infant cereals that Nestlé began. Next come baby food and infant formula, powdered, condensed, and refrigerated milk products, chocolate, confectionery, breakfast cereals, and ice-cream. All are basic Nestlé territory positioned under nourishment and enjoyment. They have earned the Nestlé brand too.

Today, about 40% of total turnover is from products covered by the Nestlé corporate brand, which makes our company very relevant to consumers. Every day, they are in contact with Nestlé-branded products (...). For products that don't carry the Nestlé brand, we have been creating a Nestlé Seal of Guarantee to put on the back, and linked to Nestlé by a short note like: 'All Maggi products benefit from Nestlé experience in producing quality foods all over the world'. But we have to strike a

Contd

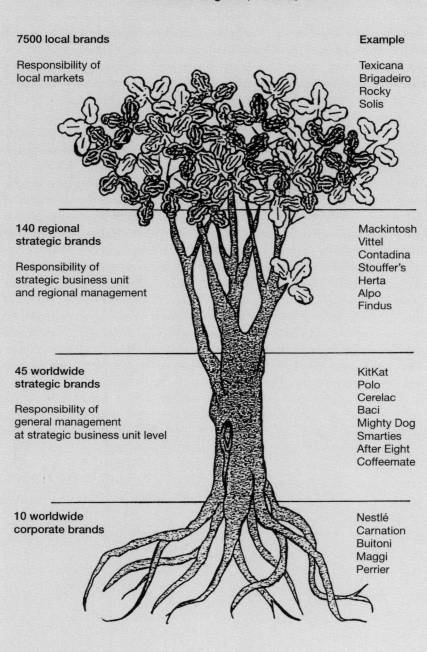

Nestlé Branding Tree, Parsons, 1996

7500 local brands

Responsibility of
local markets

**140 regional
strategic brands**

Responsibility of
strategic business unit
and regional management

**45 worldwide
strategic brands**

Responsibility of
general management
at strategic business unit level

**10 worldwide
corporate brands**

Example

Texicana
Brigadeiro
Rocky
Solis

Mackintosh
Vittel
Contadina
Stouffer's
Herta
Alpo
Findus

KitKat
Polo
Cerelac
Baci
Mighty Dog
Smarties
After Eight
Coffeemate

Nestlé
Carnation
Buitoni
Maggi
Perrier

balance between making purchasers aware of Nestlé and preserving the distinct personalities of our other strategic corporate brands. Where we have a relevant core competence combined with a specific brand territory, as we do with Maggi and Buitoni for example, it is better to keep a separate brand identity. We do not combine Nestlé/Buitoni, because Buitoni is more than a product: it represents the authentic Italian lifestyle. Nor do we have Nestlé/Maggi. Maggi offers local recipes to suit local tastes, even though it belongs to a multinational. A Maggi bouillon in China tastes different from one in Chile.

There are a few exceptions to our brand strategy, for instance pet food. For many reasons, including cultural aspects, we are not using our Nestlé Seal of Guarantee on products destined for animal consumption. We also decided to drop the Nestlé symbol from mineral water. We felt that people buying water are looking for the purity of the source, whereas our seal is that of a manufacturer. So we set up a special institute, Perrier-Vittel, which puts its own guarantee on mineral water (...). If one day we take frozen food into Eastern Europe, I'm sure we will use Maggi, not Findus. In Germany, Maggi is a powerhouse. When we launched under Maggi, we got a unanimous reaction from the trade that finally we understood branding.

Chambourcy is another example. It covers all our white refrigerated products in Europe – more than a billion dollars. From an image point of view, it is perhaps the most advanced, nutritional, and 'cool' of all our brands. But it did nothing to build the overall Nestlé identity. So we are dropping the Chambourcy corporate strategic brand altogether and using Nestlé instead.

The first development, involving companies dropping their anonymity, assumes that the associations that consumers form with the name of the whole company (e.g. Nestlé) can strengthen the perception of the individual brands that this company is launching (e.g. KitKat and Rolo). This is especially important for individual brands that are not yet strong enough, as is the case during the introductory and development phases. The name of the company serves to reduce consumer insecurity. In individual brands that are able to stand on their own two feet, the company brand can make consumers start associating the individual brands with quality and prestige traits and positive feelings that already fit the company as a whole. Confidence in the brand is thus increased. Although the stronger emphasis of the company behind the brand is also visible in low involvement products, the endorsement function of the company brand is expressed most strongly through products with which consumers perceive a greater risk and which they cannot evaluate properly (durable consumer goods), or at all (complex services), before the purchase.

'Driver brands' and 'endorsement brands' (Aaker, 1996)

David Aaker (1996) made a distinction between 'driver brands' and 'endorsement brands'. By 'driver brands' he understood those brands that represent in the first instance what the buyer expects to get. These brands represent the collection of attributes he looks for and the user experiences he expects. The 'endorsement brands' add to this the credibility of and the confidence in the company. The endorsement brand reassures the consumer that the driver brand will fulfil its promises. We think this dichotomy is too simple. There is often a double unity of consumer brand (VW) and individual brand (Golf), both of whose relative influence on the choice can hardly be isolated. The individual brand tends to be characterised primarily by associations with products and product attributes and with stereotyping of its users. With company brands we usually also see organisational associations: associations with the scope of the organisation, its value system, persons who come to the foreground, its degree of openness/closedness, its social orientation, and its success or failure.

Image from the 1996 Formula Shell campaign, in which the provenance of Formula is emphasised. The campaign chose communication on a high distinguishing abstract level in which Shell is positioned as a leading provider.

The question as to how 'broad' the endorsement of a corporate brand can be depends mainly on the perceived competence area of the company. Linking a company brand (Cadbury) to categories that do not correspond with its core expertise in chocolate (mashed potatoes and synthetic meat products) results in damage to the perceived expertise and a loss of identity. For this reason, when facing contradictions in their portfolios (e.g. food products, laundry detergents and cosmetics), companies tend to waive the use of the 'official' company name (e.g. Unilever) as an endorsement brand. Instead, they support their individual brands with strategic corporate brands (see the previous box with the 7500 brands of Nestlé).

When the company name is associated strongly with one specific product category (Carlsberg, Coca Cola), it is generally not used when supporting other brands of the same category (Tuborg, Fanta).

The association of an independent brand with the name of the company behind it can reduce the consumer's insecurity and add quality and prestige associations of the company name to the brand.

The increasing tendency towards 'sub-branding', especially in companies who traditionally brought out all their different products under one name (the company name), stems from the need to strengthen the associations between a brand and a specific product category. The associations with the sub-brand help consumers identify and understand the product. In addition, it is sometimes desirable to give each individual product or product group its own set of associations. Especially when entering new markets in which consumers search for very specific product attributes, it sometimes seems necessary to add a sub-brand to the main brand, and to then link this sub-brand associatively to the desired attributes. Associative research by Whan Park *et al.* (1996) shows that in a combination of two brands (corporate brand and product brand, main brand and sub-brand, or two brands independent of one another), the specific contribution of each brand influences the evaluation of the combination. When the associations of the component brands are mutually complementary, it results in a stronger positive effect on consumer choice than when dealing with two brands that are positively evaluated by themselves, but which do not complement each other associatively. The order in which the two brands are perceived influences the associations that are activated by the combination. In other words, the name 'Golf' (of Volkswagen) invokes a different association profile than 'Volkswagen-Golf'.

The addition of a sub-brand, with its own set of product-related meanings, to a company brand can support the positioning in the category or subcategory and can make a relevant difference to them.

The associations that people make with the company behind the brand are different from those that people make towards a product-related brand or sub-brand. In principle, scores of corporate associations can be distinguished. They can usually be classified into six categories:

(1) General characteristics
(2) Capacities
(3) Economic characteristics
(4) Product-related company associations
(5) Cultural aspects
(6) People and relationships.

Here is an overview of specific associations within each of the six categories:

(1) *General company characteristics*
   • Nationality (home front)
   • Internationality (European, global)
   • Familiarity
   • History (age)
   • Image of branches and locations.

(2) *Capacities of the company*
   • Competence/expertise
   • Scope of activities
   • Innovation potential (trying to stay up to date)
   • Leadership/following potential.

(3) *Economic characteristics*
   • Size/turnover
   • Financial strength and profitability
   • General success (growth, stagnation, decline).

(4) *Product-related company associations*
   • Specific categories in which the company is active
   • Reputation (credibility) at product or product category level
   • Quality of the products/services
   • Style/design of the products
   • Service orientation (good service delivery).

(5) *Cultural aspects of the company*
- Values
- Ethics
- Competitiveness
- Openness/closedness (towards personnel and customers)
- Honesty/reliability (e.g. with regard to distribution of profits)
- Dynamics
- Progressiveness/conservatism
- Freedom/bureaucracy
- Care for the surroundings (the environment)
- Social responsibility (showing respect for others)
- Attitude and behaviour towards personnel (e.g. in relation to health and safety).

(6) *People and relationships*
- Founders, leaders
- Contact with personnel (e.g. the contact that consumers have with people behind the counter)
- Attitude with regard to consumers (customer focus)
- Responsiveness.

Needless to say, the influence of the 'corporate image' on the choice behaviour of consumers is determined to a large extent by the role that is allocated to the company brand: does it function as a main brand (Philips, IBM, Virgin), or does it just have an endorsement function behind other main brands (KitKat of Nestlé)?

In the first case, the company associations can be a sizeable and important part of the brand associative network and exert a large influence on the evaluation of products and services. Research has shown that this can have positive and negative implications. In most cases there seems to be a positive relationship between the knowledge a consumer has about a company and his relationship to the brand in question. However, a contrast effect can also appear when there is a gap between the corporate associations and the product-related associations. This happens when a company with a weak reputation brings out a strong product or vice-versa (Brown, 1998), and when a company brings out products that are not in keeping with the perceived competencies (leather accessories by Wedgwood). Many companies are afraid of this contrast effect, and ensure that the company is perceived as little as possible (Procter and Gamble). Brown and Dacin (1997) observed that the contrast effect appears especially when the corporate associations are relevant to product evaluation.

The importance of organisational associations (Maathuis, 1999)

In an extensive experimental study into the value of company brands (in this case, Philips, KPN (Dutch telephone company), Compaq and Samsung), Maathuis (1999) researched the influence of corporate brands on the choice of consumers. This study focused on the choice of two new products: a 'webmaster' and an electronic 'safety set'. These were thus choice situations that were characterised by a higher risk perception and a lack of product experience. Maathuis distinguished two categories of company associations:

(1) Product-related associations
(2) Organisational associations: facts related to the organisation, the financial performance of the company, people and culture, and country of provenance.

The research showed that:

• Organisational associations influence the evaluation of the company brand positively.
• Organisational associations have a larger influence on minimal product knowledge and large risks, compensating for feelings of ignorance and insecurity.
• The influence of organisational associations decreases as the consumer has more product knowledge at her disposal.
• Company traits strongly vary in the degree to which they invoke organisational associations. In this respect, national brands score considerably better than brands from other countries.
• Organisational associations are more abstract than product associations.
• Organisational associations have a more positive influence on the fit between the company brand and new products, thus facilitating extensions of company brands.
• When there is a weak fit between company brand and extension, organisational associations compensate for a weak brand/product evaluation.
• The evaluation of product/brand combinations depends on the consumer's product knowledge and risk perceptions, which strongly vary.

The support function of a company brand behind other main brands is usually expressed in the composition of new brands. Consumers who do not yet have a good image of such a new brand can still form a positive expectation of the product on the basis of what they know about the producer. A strong company reputation can reduce the perceived risk. The influence of corporate associations on product evaluation is the greatest when the perceived risks are large, the product knowledge is minimal and memory cannot fall back on previous experiences. Research by Brown and Dacin (1997) indicates that the perception of the capabilities of a company exerts a particularly large influence on its overall evaluation as well as on the perception of product attributes. The capability perceptions function as an evaluation basis wherever product attributes are difficult to evaluate. They also play a role when introducing new products and new brands. At the same time, the results of this research show that the perceived social responsibility of the company also influences the attitude of consumers with regard to the products, although to a lesser degree than the capability associations. 'Doing good things' and 'being seen as a good guy' influence the overall attitudes with regard to the company, and consequently – indirectly – the evaluation of its products.

Consumers more and more want not only a 'good product', they also want it to be produced by a 'good company'.

10.4 Product-related brand meanings

10.4.1 *Associations between the brand name and the product category*

The first associations that come into consciousness when activating a brand name are almost always associations with products or product categories. It is so self-evident that we tend not to give it another thought. This is certainly the case when it comes to 'mono brands', in which the brand is linked to only one product. Foster's is lager and After Eight is mint-chocolate. When it comes to an umbrella or a company brand, things get more complicated. What is Nivea and what is Philips? With this type of brand we see that the brand's association strength with the individual product categories in which one is operating can strongly vary. This has an influence on the purchasing behaviour and on the degree to which the brand is included in the various categories of the consideration set. A brand that is strong in a specific product category is not automatically strong in another. The market share for 1986 of some brands of toiletry articles in different product groups in former West Germany varies as

Table 10.1   Market shares for 1986 of various brands of toiletries in different product groups in former West Germany (G&I panel in Hätty, 1989).

	Nivea	Fa	Bac	Palmolive
Cream	*26.3*	0.8	–	1.0
Lotion	18.7	1.5	–	1.1
Soap	5.4	*7.2*	0.4	5.0
Shower gel	3.6	6.5	2.2	–
Bubble bath	7.8	7.5	–	–
Deodorant stick	–	3.6	*32.4*	–
Facial tonic	13.1	–	–	–
Cleansing milk	11.2	–	–	–
Shaving cream	2.7	–	–	*33.4*
Aftershave	3.0	–	–	–
Shampoo	5.4	0.4	–	–
Cream rinse	5.6	0.8	–	–
Suntan cream	16.7	–	–	–

shown in Table 10.1 (the product categories the brands were originally linked with are italicised).

If a brand is to be included in the consideration set of a category or subcategory, it is necessary for it to be firmly linked to that category in memory. In umbrella and company brands it makes sense to follow the development of these associations and to determine the relative strength of the associations with regard to the other brands within each category. Associations from the brand to product categories as well as from product categories to the various brands can give an idea of this. It is often assumed that a good product plus a well known brand are sufficient conditions for success. Nothing could be further from the truth. A brand can only be a strong brand within a product category when brand and category are firmly linked to one another in memory.

10.4.2   *Associations with product attributes*

Consumers associate most brands they know with physical and/or functional product attributes. This is called the product image. This is frequently also seen as *the* image of a brand, disregarding the more symbolic meaning that brands usually have. The reason is probably that many companies are constantly working towards further improvement of the attributes of their products and services and control of their quality, and this causes them to become a central part in their brand philosophy as well.

We generally see a strong connection between the associations with product attributes, the brand attitude and the purchasing behaviour with regard to a brand. Respondents generally evaluate the product attributes of brands with a large market share more positively than would be expected merely on the basis of 'blind' evaluations of products themselves.

Table 10.2 Belief scores for users and non-users of breakfast cereals in 1973 (Castleberry and Ehrenberg, 1990).

	Corn Flakes	Weetabix	Rice Crispies	Shredded Wheat	Sugar Puffs	Frosties	Special K	All brands	Average brand
% who buy regularly	48	29	13	12	10	9	7	7	17
% 'liked by the family':									
– users	83	70	65	67	51	54	43	34	55
– non-users	40	14	13	6	11	7	4	3	8

Associations of users and non-users of a brand

Because users of a brand are confronted with the brand and find out more about it (through selective perception) in all kinds of situations, an increasingly extensive and more intense associative network comes into being. According to Castleberry and Ehrenberg (1990), even general product traits are increasingly linked by users to their own brand. Table 10.2 shows how this works with breakfast cereals in England. The scores for 'liked by the family' vary for users and non-users: of all cereal users, 15% say that Sugar Puffs is liked by the whole family, while Sugar Puffs users score 51% and non-users only 11%. The scores come from research done by BMRB in 1964 and 1984 and Field Control in 1973 and 1974.

Positive associations and attitudes arise mainly due to user experiences. Consumers always believe that the brands they use are in most ways better than those they do not use. They adjust their attitudes to their behaviour. Differences between the functional product associations of brands that we determine in market research are often more a reflection of their relative market shares, and therefore of the number of users, than of real product differences.

Positive associations and attitudes arise mainly because of user experiences, so users of a brand show a richer and more positive association network than non-users.

Service associations

Functional brand associations also include the perceptions of the service. For service organisations, these can be part of the core associations, and in brands linked to durable or semi-durable products they can be important supportive associations. Also, service associations often have a superficial and generic character, such as helpful, friendly, expert and efficient. But when it comes to brands with which people have developed a more intense relationship, the associations can acquire a much deeper emotional load. This can involve the experiencing of personal attention and care and of a real involvement of the brand in the ups and downs of the client. We will discuss this again in Chapter 15 when looking at brand relationships.

10.5 Situational meanings

Associations with the moments and situations in which consumers use a brand can be important components of the associative network. They can form ideal representations and be linked to moods that represent values to the consumers. When a person thinks of a certain brand of beer and imagines idyllic surroundings in which he is completely alone and can enjoy his beer at leisure, this points to a value such as 'individual enjoyment'.

Situational associations can be related to memories of precious moments in life. This goes further than associations with mornings and breakfast and evenings after dinner. Situations have meaning mainly due to the social context in which the brand is used. What does it mean to use the brand in the private context of the bathroom or in the social context of a pub? Which social setting is a brand associated with: family life, the inner circle of friends, or the external circle of business relationships? Which feelings are these situations associated with, and how are those feelings valued? Perceptions of the use of a brand by others or the representation of user situations in advertisements also lead to situational associations. The use of After Eight following what is clearly a festive dinner with family and friends is probably one of the strongest associations with that brand, as a result of an advertising campaign that was kept up for years.

10.6 Symbolic meanings

Consumers allocate human attributes to brands. The representations of brands in memory often resemble representations that people make of others in their memory. Here we can distinguish the following association categories:

- Representations of the users of the brand: the 'user image'
- Personality traits of the brand itself: the 'brand personality'
- Symbolic meanings: 'values'.

10.6.1 *User associations*

Consumers have an image of the type of person that uses a brand. If they think of the brand John Lewis, they see in front of them a stereotypical visitor to the department store, and when they think of Waterstone's they think of a stereotypical reader. In research situations, respondents are sometimes asked to describe the stereotypical users of a brand with the help of human personality traits.

It is important to make a distinction between user associations and the brand personality, which will be described in the following sections: in user associations a set of human personality traits is associated with the stereotypical user of a brand, and in brand personality a set of human personality traits is directly associated with a brand. Both concepts are thus described in terms of personality traits, and this regularly results in a lack of clarity. Another source of confusion is that in some situations the brand personality emanates from the user associations: people project the attributes of a stereotypical user of a brand onto the brand itself.

10.6.2 *Brand personality*

'Vodka is cool, KLM is reliable, Grolsch is individualistic, ABN/AMRO is businesslike.'

People use such terms when they talk about brands. They are the same terms they use when talking about people in their surroundings. Allocating personal traits to a brand is also called brand personification. The development of a brand personality grows as the behaviour of a brand becomes more 'personalised'. That can be the case because the brand manifests itself through people, for instance in the form of people who appear in advertisements.

Consumers must see the brand 'doing things', as it were, on the basis of which they can form an image of the 'brand as a person'. All activities from the marketing mix can be perceived and interpreted by consumers as forms of behaviour of a brand, on the basis of which personality traits are attributed to brands. Especially in qualitative research, respondents are often asked to imagine a brand as if it were a person and to then describe the traits of this person. The researcher stimulates the respondents until she has an idea of the demographic and socioeconomic traits of the brand as a person and of the personality traits as they are found in personality studies.

To research these traits, respondents are confronted with lists of characteristics that are usually derived from the 'Big Five' personality traits, a well known list from personality studies. These Big Five consist of the features of openness, conscientiousness, extraversion, agreeability and neuroticism (a mnemonic device: the first letters of the Big Five form the word 'ocean') (Engler, 1995). In qualitative research, respondents are asked to describe the person (by asking, for example, what hobbies the person has, whether he is successful, has many friends, etc.). The researcher has to watch out that the respondents do not confuse the brand personality with the personality of a prototypical user.

Jennifer Aaker (1996), a researcher at the University of California in Los Angeles, did an extensive study on brand personality with the goal of developing a valid and reliable measuring instrument to map out the brand personality. The study, which has a qualitative as well as a quantitative part, is based on the Big Five personality traits and resulted in a new Big Five which is applicable to brands. On the basis of these new Big Five, Aaker developed a research instrument called the 'Brand Personality Scale' (see Figure 10.4). An extensive description of the instrument can be found in Part Three of this book.

Research into the brand personality has advantages and disadvantages. An advantage is that it is a creative form of research. Respondents are asked to think of the brand differently through personality traits. The easiest way is to assume that the personality is something that directs behaviour in the individual. Conversely, we can also conclude that someone's 'inner traits' can be derived from their behaviour. A person who goes to many parties, has many social contacts, etc. may be described as an extravert. A disadvantage is that the concept of personality is more complicated than most researchers think. A journey among a number of authorities in the field of personality studies seems endless and chaotic. The journey goes from Freud's ideas about unconscious motivation and development phases, via Jung's collective unconscious and Skinner's behaviourism, to Kelly's idea of the personality being a system of cognitive constructs. The theories and ideas on personality that have been formulated since Aristotle can be classified into eight basic movements: psychoanalysis, the neo-psychological approach, modern psychoanalysis, behaviour and learning theories, dispositional theories, humanistic and existential theories, cognitive theories and the non-western approach (Nawas, 1986; Scroggs, 1994; Engler, 1995; Scroggs, 1996). The lists of personality traits that are used in research on brand personality almost always come from the movement that deals with dispositional theory. Not many researchers take into consideration the fact that there are several movements and that a different movement will have a different list (which can probably be applicable in a certain situation). Another problem with research into brand personality is whether people in daily life really describe the brands around them as persons (which is very debatable), or whether this only happens in research situations. There is no doubt that people can experience Absolut Vodka as a 'hip' brand, but whether people spontaneously

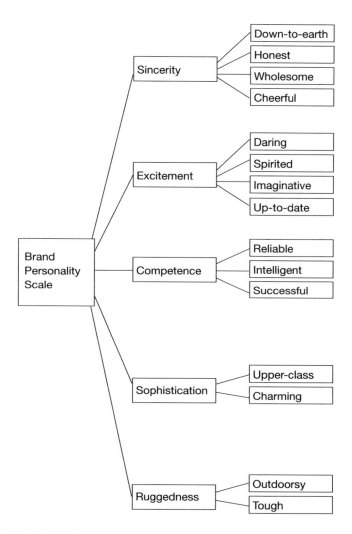

Figure 10.4 The Brand Personality Scale (Aaker, 1996).

describe Campbell's Soup as 'Mrs Campbell, a rosy-cheeked and plump grandmother who lives in a warm, cosy house and wears an apron as she cooks wonderful things for her grandchildren', as Jennifer Aaker (1997) claims, is questionable. If allocating personality traits to brands really takes place exclusively or primarily during research, that does not mean that research into brand personality is useless, but it does mean we have to use the term more carefully.

Brand personality is the description of a brand in terms of personality traits. Brand personality is not the same as 'user associations'. User associations are about a set of human personality traits associated with the stereotypical user of a brand, and brand personality is about a set of personality traits associated exclusively with the brand.

10.6.3 *Value systems*

Every individual has value systems, a durable collection of beliefs or views about which behaviours and lifestyles are desirable or good (Rokeach, 1973). At the same time, large differences and similarities can be seen for individuals within this value system. For some people, individual freedom is very important, and for others it is harmony within the community (Zimbardo and Leippe, 1991). Everyone considers honesty and health as important values, but not everyone places them at the top of their list.

People's value system has a large influence on the way they see themselves in relation to the world around them. We can even say that all the choices people make in their lives are based to a greater or lesser degree on the basic values that are stored in their self-concept. If a person feels very strongly about the value of authenticity, when looking at the pasta shelves in the supermarket she will automatically look for grains in the package. If the person loves renewal or innovation, she will immediately notice a name or package she had not seen before or, at any rate, one that looks different.

It was not until 1973 that a study into values was published that was of any use to marketing and communication science. This study into values, carried out by the American Rokeach, produced eighteen terminal values and eighteen instrumental values. Terminal values are those things towards which you strive in life, and instrumental values are, in Rokeach's perspective, personal characteristics that help people materialise those terminal values. Thanks to many marketing researchers, the results of this study became axioms: to them, the thirty-six Rokeach values are the absolute dimensions of human aspirations that deserve a place of honour in any questionnaire as the ultimate clarifying variables of consumer behaviour (Sikkel and Oppenhuisen, 1998). The research of Rokeach, which on the one hand can be considered as pioneering, is also susceptible to a great deal of criticism. The assumed universality of these values can be called into question. It is possible that the values that Rokeach found are only applicable to the middle of the United States in the early 1970s. A more important point of criticism – the limited empirical substantiation – was recognised by Rokeach himself. There are quite a few snags in the method Rokeach used to arrive at his inventory (Vyncke, 1992).

Sikkel and Oppenhuisen made an inventory that fits the Dutch population of 1997. The research towards arriving at this inventory was carried out by means of qualitative interviews with twenty respondents. The interviews lasted three hours; the starting points of the talks were twenty-two pictures of photo collages which, together, illuminate many aspects of life (birth, friendship, death, career, etc.). The texts of the interviews were screened for anything that could contain a value. This was followed by a quantitative part in which 2432 respondents helped find out to what degree there are dimensions and clusters within the values (Sikkel and Oppenhuisen, 1998).

On the 160 definitive values that came forth from the study, a factor analysis was performed. The basis of this factor analysis was quantitative research in which respondents were asked to indicate the distances between the various values. An outline of the results is given in Table 10.3 (Sikkel and Oppenhuisen, 1998).

The first two factors have also been found in many other studies. In various studies (see, for example, the descriptions of Market Structure Research and

Table 10.3 Interpretation of the factors 1 to 6 (italicised) with their most characteristic values.

Factor	1	2	3
Binding	*Relationships* moving atmosphere cosiness love	*Geared towards others* listening to someone understanding being helpful being responsible	*Society* love for one's country being solemn proud being tough
Freedom	*Career* climbing the ladder being passionate power perseverance	*Geared towards the self* relaxing being healthy staying/being young having no worries	*Having your own fun* being active relaxing doing something having time
Factor	4	5	6
Binding	*Security* safety rest luxury having your own place	*Family life* being a mother having children hugging taking care	*Making yourself* *attractive* looking well-groomed being distinguished cleanliness having prestige
Freedom	*Challenge* being provocative being spontaneous expanding your boundaries being exciting being a hero	*Freedom* being satisfied having no worries rest freedom	*Going your own way* going your own way believing being rebellious love for your country being idealistic

Source: Sikkel and Oppenhuisen, 1998.

IMPMAP in Part Three) the results are indicated in a coordinate system with a vertical coordinate that can be described as 'expressing' versus 'repressing' (or extraversion versus introversion) and a horizontal coordinate with 'ego-oriented' (also described as 'masculine') and 'geared towards others' (feminine) as its extremes. We will look at this again in Chapters 12 and 16 when discussing brand positioning and brand representations.

Many researchers conclude that three levels can be distinguished within the value system of consumers: general values, domain-specific values and product attributes as values. General values can influence or even determine a person's whole life. These values are so strong that they can influence domain-specific and product-related values. Domain-specific values are only related to a specific consumption domain and are also described in terms of this domain. A general value like 'ambition' could be translated in the automobile market as 'imposing' and then into concrete product attributes like 'large', 'luxurious', etc. Vinson *et al.* (1977) describe them as views that are important for economic, social, religious and other actions. According to these authors, people develop values through the experiences they acquire in specific situations or domains, and this behaviour can only be understood or explained within the context of this situation or domain (Vinson *et al.*, 1977). Product attributes are related only to the consumption aspect and are mainly visible in the form of expectations that the consumer has about certain attributes of products that may be for sale (Franzen and Holzhauer, 1987). Vinson *et al.* describe them as evaluative views on product attributes (such as views that are applied in expected-value research). Product attributes are less abstract than general and domain-specific values, and consist of descriptive as well as evaluative beliefs. These beliefs play a large role in the purchasing decisions of consumers and can vary strongly among consumers.

On the basis of inventories by Rokeach (1973), Vinson *et al.* (1977) and Vyncke (1992), Franzen made a distinction between instrumental or functional values, symbolic values, and social values. Instrumental values are about preferred capacities, attributes and performance of the product itself. In daily advertising practice they are generally called 'product benefits' (Franzen, 1992). Symbolic values can be classified into three different categories: expressive values, impressive values and terminal values. Expressive values are about our relationship to others and how we want to be seen by others. Impressive values are geared towards our self-perception (having a good feeling about yourself, inner harmony, being frugal, etc.). Terminal values are ideal representations about life as we would ultimately prefer it to be. They are, as it were, the highest ideals towards which we strive in life. Finally, there is a group of social values. They are the ideals we cherish with regard to our living environment and the society as a whole (e.g. peace in the world, preserving nature and national freedom).

A categorisation of values inevitably leads to discussions. Even when it comes to a relatively simple classification into two groups, as was proposed by Rokeach, people never run out of things to say. As early as 1970, Gorsuch had already remarked that a general categorisation into the two groups 'instrumental' and 'terminal', as proposed by Rokeach, was not tenable. 'Instrumental' values and 'end' values are determined individually and situationally. Heath and Fogel (1978) also arrived at the conclusion that Rokeach's classification was not valid. Instead of two categories they proposed a classification into eight dimensions of interrelated values. Sikkel and Oppenhuisen (1998) seem to have arrived at a similar solution for their classification of Dutch values: they established six dimensions with opposite value clusters. They believe that, to a large degree, values are determined individually, and that the interrelatedness, as Rokeach posits it, does not apply on a general level. A value called 'instrumental' by Rokeach can very well be a terminal value for consumers. Every person is characterised by what the 'instrumental' and 'end' values are for himself.

For people who are involved in market research, classifying the positioning of brands and brand extensions can be very enlightening. The insight that some brands distinguish themselves on the basis of ideology, others on the basis of unique product attributes, and yet others by their 'style' offers points of connection for doing proper and useful research. Moreover, the strength of a brand is also determined by the degree to which it represents values that the consumer looks for in the product or products in question. This is essentially a different combination of values at various levels for each product.

Value diffuseness and value conflict undermine a brand. That can happen if there is no congruence between products a brand is connected with and the values it represents, or if the values are unclear or mutually conflicting.

Brand meanings as 'values'

'Values' as previously described are attributes of people. Each individual has her own value system. In the marketing and market research practice the concept of 'brand values' is also used. The term refers to brand meanings which may or may not correspond with the values of individuals and groups. A meaning that coincides with a value for one person can be irreconcilable with the value system for someone else. Thus the same meaning can therefore represent a value as well as an anti-value. It would therefore be better to use the concept of 'symbolic brand meanings'.

Brand meanings that correspond with the ideals of individuals or groups are brand values. For others, however, the same meanings can constitute anti-values.

The hierarchical structure of brand meanings

We have been emphasising that a brand is an associative network in which everything is interrelated. Depending on the situation and the cue one is confronted with, certain parts of this network can be activated and enter our working memory. Some scientists believe that the knowledge that is stored in our memory is organised in a certain way so that we can have easier access to it. Various models have been developed to describe those 'structures of meaning' in our memory (Pieters, 1989). These models have different levels, almost without exception, that are ordered in a continuum from concrete to abstract. The lowest level consists of the most concrete, the 'analogue' representations of our sensory perceptions of the objects themselves. This is about the superficial characteristics of the things in our life. The highest level consists of our central value orientations, for instance our striving towards harmony or power. The emphasis in these models lies on instrumentality: to what extent do 'lower' meanings contribute to 'higher' ones? Which meanings are instrumental in the realisation of our higher goals and values? For this reason these structures are designated with the term 'means–end chains'.

Three main levels are generally distinguished:

(1) The level of physical and sensory attributes
(2) The level of the direct functional implications of these traits and their advantages and disadvantages
(3) The level of the symbolic meanings (values) with which these, in turn, are connected.

Within each of the three main levels, sub-levels can also be distinguished, thus creating a means–end hierarchy that consists of the following elements:

Level 1
- The brand signs: name, spelling, colour, image (logo), sound, visual style.
- The products, product variants and product categories the brand is associated with.
- The concrete product attributes: the visible, palpable, taste and smell attributes of the products.
- The abstract product attributes: the summing-up of the product attributes in umbrella meanings. For example, cars may be categorised as 'family cars', 'space cars', etc.

Level 2
- The functional implications: the perceptible direct implications of the use of the product for the consumer. For instance, 'fast', 'strong', 'easy', 'durable'.

Level 3

- The psychosocial implications: the feelings that the brand or product invokes during its use: these are also known as 'impressive values', like 'cosy', 'intimate', 'happy'.
- The expressive values: the personality traits with which the brand is associated, like young, individualistic, no-nonsense.
- The terminal values: the ideal representations of personal life, such as freedom and independence, health and wisdom, with which the brand is connected.
- The social values: the ideal representations of the society in which we live, with which we associate the brand: peace in the world, a better environment, an 'honest' society, etc.

Structures of meaning are more complex than the hierarchical order that has been previously suggested. In research they are seldom ordered so neatly. We generally encounter groupings that emanate from the order of the questions, or which are afterwards brought in by the researcher. For this reason, a fixed classification for all consumers makes less sense.

The research into means–end hierarchies usually takes place with what is known as laddering techniques. Their essence is that people keep being asked why they find an attribute allocated to a brand to be important and why they consider their chosen answer to be important, and so on until the person cannot give any more answers to the 'why' questions. This leads the association process to increasingly higher and more abstract levels of meaning. Some comments should be made at this point. The laddering method exposes the connection between brand meanings on the one hand and the value system of the consumer on the other. This is often a useful thing to do. At the same time, one has to face the question of which levels of meaning in long-term memory are really connected to the brand and which connections are only established in the working memory as a result of the questions. It is sometimes too easily assumed that all levels of meaning are connected hierarchically with the brand. A second comment is related to the fact that consumers cannot easily place a brand in their own 'means–end chain' when the brand meanings do not correspond with their personal values. A third comment has to do with the obfuscation of the core meanings of a brand as a result of the research method used. It is mostly on the basis of these core meanings that consumers classify brands into categories and distinguish them from other brands within these categories. The core meanings also constitute the basis of a 'brand concept', which is discussed in the chapter on positioning. In most laddering research we know, no distinction is made on the 'importance of the distinguished meanings'.

Table 10.4 shows the levels of meaning of the VW Polo and the Renault Twingo with the help of a laddering technique. In this small-scale study

(Beekman, 1995) it seems that only the owners of a certain brand are capable of formulating a value ladder for that brand. A Polo driver can formulate a ladder for a Polo, but not for a Twingo. People are probably only capable of relating a self-chosen brand to their personal values, but they cannot put themselves in the situation of someone with a different value system, and cannot relate the associations of a brand they themselves reject to other values because they do not have those values. It also seems that people are incapable of relating the brand attributes to the terminal values. Even if we accept the hypothesis of the hierarchical structure of brand meanings, we have to ask ourselves at which level the hierarchy stops. Certainly not all brands and products are connected with the most central terminal value – happiness. With relation to this, the question remains current: what are the boundaries of an associative network of a brand? When are these boundaries crossed? That is probably difficult to determine, but the function of products and brands in our lives should at least be taken into account. It is not very useful to find out through which intermediate levels a brand – whose basic function is mere identification (of product and attributes), linked to a product of marginal meaning (liquorice sweet) – is associated with our life happiness. In the

Table 10.4 Hierarchical levels of meaning of VW Polo and Renault Twingo, based on Beekman, 1995.

	Terminal values	• safety • security • having a career • active life	• love for children • pleasure in life • personal lifestyle • youthful
Level 3	Expressive values	• ambitious • tough • sporty • representative	• sporty • 'different' • happy • vital
	Psychosocial implications	• businesslike • 'confidence' • vital	• awake • helpful • comfortable
Level 2	Functional implications	• fast • reliable • efficient	• seems bigger • easy for transporting children and things • French
Level 1	Abstract attributes	• German • solid	• sporty • 'space' car image
	Concrete attributes	• cage construction • fast motor ('small Golf')	• space in the car • comfortable seats
	Brand signs	VW Polo	Renault Twingo

mentioned Twingo study it appeared that the owners of the brand had difficulty with the recurring 'why' question. The answer usually came after a lot of thinking. This shows that the associative network of the brand and the value system are two separate systems in the memory of the consumer, without there having to be an automatic link between one system and the other.

Laddering research provides hierarchical brand meaning structures. This helps establish a link between brand associations and value systems, or the medium goal chain. It is important to find out where the associative network turns into the values of the brand users.

Research into the spontaneous associations of the brands Heineken and Grolsch shows that the representations of sensory perceptions are at any rate more accessible than those of more abstract 'higher order' meanings (Timmerman, 1998). Of all the 'free' associations, 52% consisted of product, advertising and user associations. Only 8% (Heineken) and 11% (Grolsch) of the free associations were related to more psychological/symbolic meanings. Respondents also failed to report many symbolic meanings when associations were directed with the help of cards ('package', 'advertisement', 'average user', 'brand personality', etc.). This may be the result of the research method followed, but it can only point to the possibility of these high abstract meanings being less present in long-term memory or of them only being achieved with the help of special projective techniques. It may also be the case that many people find it harder to express high abstract meanings.

Representations of sensory perceptions seem more accessible than the abstract higher order meanings.

10.7 Perceived quality

Consumers form an image of the quality of a brand. They perceive it as perhaps 'very good' or even 'bad'. This 'perceived quality' is mono-dimensional, an abstraction of a higher order. It consists of a continuum rather than a dichotomous judgement. The quality perception is a direct association from the brand.

When forming a quality image, consumers allow themselves to be led by external cues such as packaging and price, and by their own usage experiences. Users of a brand form an impression of the degree to which the brand responds to their expectations in usage. The cues play a large role when there are not enough user experiences or when it is difficult to establish the quality of use. The expectations can be varied. For instance, in service brands they can be related to the attributes of the service itself, the physical conditions in which the service takes place, the reliability of the service, the helpfulness, promptness and empathy of the service provider, the securities that are given, etc. Consumers integrate their evaluation of separate functional and symbolic attributes of a brand into one total evaluation. 'Perceived quality' is a summary, a global whole. It is also a relativistic concept: the quality perception of individual brands comes about within the context of the competition surroundings. The perceived quality of Pepsi-Cola is partially influenced by the perceived quality of Coca-Cola, of B-brands like Herschi and private labels like Real American Cola.

Perceived quality is category-dependent. The quality of a brand can vary from (sub)category to (sub)category: the brand Marlboro can be evaluated differently in the subcategory of 'full flavour' cigarettes than in the subcategory of 'ultra-lights'. This is partly due to the fact that it is compared with other brands in the various subcategories. The perceived quality of brands is also influenced by situational variables – the goal towards which and the physical and social environment in which they are used. The same brand can be evaluated differently in relation to the different usage situations; the question of whether there is individual or social consumption plays a particularly important role. Studies on the connection between performance and the development of brands in the market and variables that lie behind it (like the PIMS database[4]) indicate that the 'perceived quality' is the single most important variable that exerts an influence on the profitability of companies, an influence that is even greater than that of the market share or the scope of the marketing efforts. High perceived quality of a brand leads to the willingness of consumers to pay more for it, to a greater satisfaction, to a higher degree of brand confidence and a reduced sensitivity to price reductions of competing brands.

'Perceived quality' is monodimensional and an abstraction of a higher order. It is the single most important variable that is of influence to the profitability of companies (PIMS).

---

4   The 'Profit Impact of Market Strategy' (PIMS) database was elaborated in 1972 by the Marketing Science Institute in the United States. About 450 companies participate in it, reporting on more than 3000 business units. Each unit periodically reports information on finances, market, clients and quality. The researchers establish the correlations and trend developments. The PIMS database is the only database in the whole world that contains strategic information on a large variety of companies. Various sub-databases are analysed for the effects of all kinds of strategic variables, which include advertising expenditures. Connections are always made with the ultimate financial results, like the profits, the returns on invested capital, and the cash flow. The PIMS database is now maintained by the Strategic Planning Institute.

Perceived quality and market position

Figure 10.5 represents the connection between the market position of brands and scores for perceived quality, borrowed from the analyses of the PIMS database (Buzzel and Gale, 1987). On the horizontal coordinate the relative quality is expressed in five evaluation classes, from low to high. The vertical coordinate shows the profits in gross margins (return on sales, or ROS) and the returns on invested capital (return on investment, or ROI).

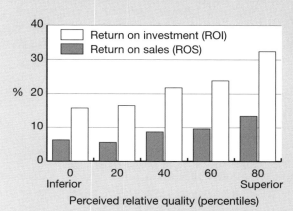

Figure 10.5 Connection between market position of brands and perceived quality.

An important connection was also established between the perceived quality and the relative market position of the brands. Market leaders reach considerably higher scores on perceived quality than the numbers two and three in the market. As the position of the market leaders becomes more dominant, the difference in perceived quality also increases. What we have here is probably an interaction between the two variables.

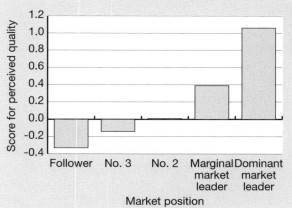

Figure 10.6 Connection between relative market position of brands and perceived quality.

10.8   Perceived (relative) price

Consumers usually do not know exactly how much a brand costs, but they have an idea whether a brand is more expensive or cheaper than its competitors. This 'perceived relative price' is an important brand association because consumers often base their perceptual structure of a category (the categorisation of brands, which is discussed in section 12.2) on it. They classify brands into a number of successive price brackets, from 'very cheap' to 'very expensive'. In some product categories as many as five different price brackets can be distinguished. The classification of a brand into one of these brackets influences the consideration set as well as its possible inclusion in it. Hotels in the United States are classified into the following six categories on the basis of their perceived relative price (Aaker, 1991):

(1) Budget   Motel 6, Me sleep
(2) Economy   Days Inn, Comfort
(3) Mid-range   Holiday Inn, Ramada
(4) Luxury   Marriott, Clarion
(5) Super luxury   Hyatt Regency
(6) Luxury suites   Embassy, Guest Quarters

If a consumer cannot compare brands with each other very easily, for example because of lack of experience, the perceived relative price of a brand often functions as a signal for estimating the relative quality. This is the case for infrequently purchased articles (like photography equipment) and products whose intrinsic attributes are difficult to evaluate (like many cosmetic products). Price perceptions also act as quality signals for products such as wine and perfume, in which large price differences are the case, and personal taste (smell) is not trusted sufficiently.

10.8.1   *Perceived value*

Consumers combine quality and price perceptions in one value perception. A user who evaluates a brand as superior and the price as not being too high allocates the brand a high value. If someone sees the quality as only average and the price as relatively high, the brand is being given a low value perception. A study of Total Research in the United States (Alleborn, 1994) shows that the influence of perceived quality on the perceived value is considerably larger than that of the perceived price. The conclusion is that the perceived quality explains an average of 80% of the variance in perceived value. Fornell *et al.* (1996) also established that the satisfaction of users with their brands is more strongly influenced by the quality perceptions than by the price. Research by the advertising agency Y and R (Aaker, 1996) suggests that 'perceived quality' and 'value' should be seen more as two different dimensions. In this study, perceived quality seems to be strongly related to the prestige that is allocated to a brand, while value is mainly related to the brand's functional performance.

Quality perceptions play the most important role in the perceived value of a brand. Perceived price exerts a subordinate influence on it.

10.9   Presentation

The external appearance of a brand is an important association category. We are talking here about the total image of packaging and branches. These play a particularly important role in the identification of brands during the purchasing process. The visual images with which a brand is associated in memory can help find a brand article among the enormous amounts of other articles in the supermarket or locate a bank more easily in overcrowded shopping centres. This is therefore not only about the brand's unique colour or the specific logo, as important as that is, but primarily about the unique way these are integrated into the total presentation of the brand article or the company branch.

Consistency of the core identity throughout time can be an important contribution to the speed at which a brand is identified. The history of the Douwe Egberts coffee package goes back to 1898, when the Frisian woman pouring coffee was introduced. The package as we know it now dates back to the beginning of the twentieth century. In 1925 the DE stamp was added to the package. The most significant change after that took place in 1983, when the words 'Douwe' and 'Egberts' were placed on top of each other instead of next to each other – with the purpose of strengthening the brand signal on the supermarket shelves. Douwe Egberts coffee is the largest brand article in Dutch groceries.

Changing the basic elements of a package often leads to an immediate decline of the sales of the brand in question: what is on the shelf no longer corresponds with what is in the memory, and the consumer becomes immediately insecure. The motto is: do it step by step so no one notices.

10.10   Associations in advertising

Many brands manifest themselves mostly through their advertising activities. They appear weekly on television or in the printed media. Consumers store their perceptions of them as 'advertising associations'. All kinds of advertising can become associated with a brand. These can be content-related messages ('dry buttocks'), the way in which an expression is processed, the persons that appear in it, the media in which those expressions are perceived, or even the moment at which and the situation in which that perception took place. The goal of advertisers is usually to influence the associative network of the advertised brand. However, messages and presentation characteristics are very often stored as advertising associations without being directly linked to the brand. Advertising associations can be very distinctive, influence the saliency of a brand and thus influence the purchasing behaviour. But when the goal is to develop specific brand associations, it is necessary to find out whether this has really taken place.

In a study in which respondents were asked to freely associate the brands of Heineken and Grolsch, advertising associations appeared almost as frequently as product-related associations and prior to other association categories. In a method in which the association process was steered with the help of 35 different association category cues ('average user', 'price', 'origin', 'slogan', etc.), the advertising associations for Heineken were the ones that appeared most frequently. That the brands are mainly perceived as 'advertising' applies here to a significant degree (Timmerman, 1998).

Advertisements that people perceive are often stored as advertising associations. They do not automatically lead to 'more direct' brand perceptions.

Chapter 11

Brand Emotions

11.1 Introduction

'People sometimes say that the human being is free. People sometimes say that the essence of human consciousness is freedom: the freedom to choose, the freedom to feel, the freedom to determine one's own destiny to the extent that the outside world allows it. The freedom of a person manifests itself most strongly where and to the extent to which that person can dedicate himself to his individual way of experiencing. Whoever gets closer to his feelings gets closer to his own being, from which he determines, to the extent that it is possible, his destiny. Feeling is the expression of our most individual self, that nothing and no one imposes on us. Feeling is a hallmark of the individual and the core of freedom... Or isn't it?' (Frijda, 1993).

We encounter 'pieces of wisdom' from psychology in an increasing number of fields. The same goes for advertising and marketing. These profundities are regularly used inappropriately or dubious conclusions are drawn from them. For instance, the anatomical difference between our left and right brain (and its implications) is almost always exaggerated. Another example is that the term 'attitude' is usually incorrectly used in texts on advertising and marketing, and excessively high expectations of consumer behaviour are linked to it. A last example – and that is what this chapter is about – is that the terms 'emotion' and 'feeling' are interchanged quite often. This chapter will show that emotions are inner processes over which the individual has little influence and which can manifest themselves in four ways. Feelings are only one of these manifestations; they are the conscious experiences of an emotion. From the description given by advertisers and market researchers of the concept of emotion and the way it is translated in research, it seems that not everyone has knowledge of the most recent findings from psychological research. These findings are summarised in this chapter and are linked to brands.

11.2 Emotions

11.2.1 *Emotions according to Frijda*

Everyone knows emotions and feelings from their own personal life. We know them so well that they apparently have no secrets for us. We know exactly what it is to be angry or scared, and we possess an extended vocabulary to be able to express all sorts of primary emotions and more shaded emotional situations.

Among scientists there is quite a lot of discrepancy about the definition of emotions, partly because there are so many scientists studying emotions. This is largely due to the fact that there are so many different emotions and that all those different emotions manifest themselves differently. Emotions such as disgust, anger and surprise show characteristic facial expressions. Cognitive evaluation of the event plays a minimal role in the emotion of fright (Fischer, 1991), and the emotion of fear can be best described through all kinds of physiological changes (like shaking and sweating). Because of all these differences, some scientists have put physical excitement as central to their definition, while others have done the same for subjective experiences and for the motor expression of emotions. Yet another group of scientists have chosen the safe way by positing that emotions are multi-component processes in which all these manifestations come together (Averill, 1982; Scherer, 1984; Frijda, 1991).

This book is based on the definition that the Dutch psychologist Frijda gave on the concept of emotions. He described emotions as inner processes that are stirred by an event that is important to the individual in question and that can reveal themselves in four ways – feelings, expressive behaviour, motivated behaviour and physiological changes (Frijda, 1991). Various other psychologists also posit such a definition in which the emotional reaction is separated into various components. Scherer (1996) says that people are agreeing more and more that the concept of emotion should not be used as a synonym for feeling. Feeling is generally considered to be one of the many components of the concept of emotion. Other components are neurophysical response patterns (in the central and autonomous nervous system) and motor expressions (in the face, voice and gestures). According to Scherer, social psychologists often point towards these three components – feelings, physical reactions and expression – as the emotional reaction triangle. In this chapter we will discuss the various manifestations more extensively.

Emotions are not the same as feelings. Emotions are inner processes that are stirred by an event that is important to the individual in question. Emotions can reveal themselves in four ways: feelings, expressive behaviour, motivated behaviour and physiological changes. Feelings are therefore only one of four manifestations of an emotion.

According to Frijda, three aspects are of crucial importance in the inner emotional process: the degree of involvement of a person in what happens, the cognitive evaluation of an event (appraisal) and the change in behavioural tendencies (action readiness) (Frijda, 1986, 1991; Fischer, 1991). In a nutshell, Frijda claims that an emotion comes about when someone is touched personally by something: an event is evaluated by the individual as being of personal interest.

Interests are a type of motive or goal and they can be of a very varied nature (Fischer, 1991): 'I don't want to die', 'I want new shoes', 'I want a child', 'I want a fair share'. Cognitive appraisal is necessary to be able to estimate whether an interest is at issue. The appraisal often takes place unconsciously and can also have a biological or evolutionary origin. For instance, almost everyone is scared of unexpected things, due to a survival instinct. If people consider an event to be important, an impulse to act follows (action readiness). People stiffen when they are scared of something, they shake or hide if they are scared, laugh when they hear a good joke or if they want to appear friendly. During the inner emotion process it is possible for the person to be confronted with a feeling or affect and for all kinds of physiological changes to appear (palpitations or sweating). The emotion process is shown graphically in Figure 11.1.

An important concept from Figure 11.1, regulation, has not been explained up to now. People regulate their emotions constantly, often because they have learned from their parents or other members of their culture to do so (Frijda, 1986). Frijda says that two simultaneous processes occur in every emotional experience:

(1) Having an emotion
(2) Regulating the emotion.

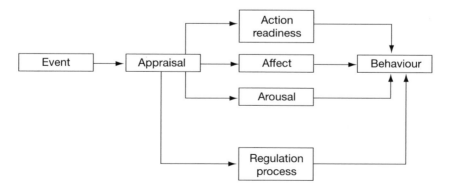

Figure 11.1 The emotional process according to Frijda.

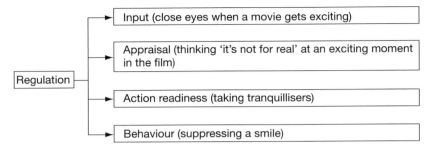

Figure 11.2   The role of regulation in the emotional process.

The regulation can take place in each phase of the process (see Figure 11.2).

The regulation of emotions is necessary in a society in which many people live together. When you get a present you show gladness; at a funeral you show sorrow. In scientific research as well as in daily life, it seems that people have a lot of trouble regulating their emotions. Frijda claims that this is the result of the passionate character of emotions: emotions occur automatically. 'We feel according to steady patterns. We are subject to the laws of feeling' (Frijda, 1993). In other words, emotions follow a process-like course (Frijda, 1986). Certain events lead time and again, anywhere in the world, to the same 'action readiness', and without regulation they would lead to the same behaviour.

People are constantly 'forced' to regulate their emotions by the culture in which they live. This uses up a lot of energy because emotions occur automatically.

11.2.2   *The reasonableness of an emotion*

LeDoux (1996) describes in a simple manner why he thinks that cognition is not necessary in order to experience an emotion. As he puts it, if you walk through the woods and see a twig that looks like a snake, you are overcome with fear, your heart rate will increase, etc. Afterwards you will see it is a twig and will go on walking. The process of being scared, experiencing heightened adrenaline, is caused by the amygdala. The identification of the twig is done because the neocortex becomes active and tries to determine the nature of what you saw. The amygdala made a quick scan of the sensory perception. The identification of the product was wrong, but seen from a survival perspective it is more important to mistake a twig for a snake than to find out later that the twig was a snake.

From this, LeDoux derives that the sensory experience goes directly to the amygdala and that the person experiences an emotion without cognitive processing. Despite the fact that LeDoux is one of the great physiologists of our times, many psychologists question this way of thinking. They claim that every sensory experience needs a form of interpretation. Otherwise we would be scared of any arbitrary thing and go shivering and quivering through life. The fact that the person in the previous description mistakes a twig for a snake already implies an interpretation. Frijda claims that the interpretation (which he calls 'appraisal') is necessary to the conscious or unconscious experiencing of an emotion, and that interpretation requires cognitive processing.

11.2.3 *Emotions as agents*

Why do people do the things they do? Why do they make, consciously or unconsciously, certain choices? Part of the answer to these questions lies locked up in our genes. The other part is explained by the way in which our society is set up and how we are brought up in this society. The question as to where the dividing line is between 'genes' and 'society' is enormously complicated. In order to make scientific statements about this, a lot of research would be necessary in which identical twins are separated immediately after birth and brought up in different (sub)cultures. Philosophising extensively on this subject is far beyond the scope of this book. Part One of this book deals with our brain and how this brain develops during our life. To what extent this development comes from the genes or is caused by society is a question we have set aside.

All kinds of things are stored in our memory: explicit information (factual and conscious information like the capital of Spain, German grammatical cases, the main actors of the movie Titanic) and implicit information (automatic information that ensures we can walk, breathe, etc., and information we are not aware of). There is a cluster of implicit and explicit information around the things people consider important in life. When you think of your mother, you think automatically of her laughter, her perfume, her face, things you have learned from her, her most typical remarks, her favourite television programme, and so on.

11.2.4 *Basic emotions*

Almost all emotion theoreticians have formulated a list of what are known as basic emotions, which (according to these scientists) are more important than all other emotions. Some scientists claim this because they can prove that the basic emotions have a biological origin and other emotions do not. Others believe that all emotions are mixtures of a small number of basic emotions (e.g. Plutchik, 1962; Tomkins, 1962, 1963; Izard, 1971; Tomkins, 1984; Oatley and Johnson-Laird, 1987). Table 11.1 gives a summary of the basic emotions postulated by just a few important psychologists.

What can be noticed immediately is that these lists do not resemble each other at all. Apparently, it is difficult for researchers to find a criterion on the

Table 11.1 Basic emotions distinguished by psychologists (Ortony and Turner, 1990).

Psychologist	Basic emotions	Reasons to name the basic emotions
James (1884)	fear, sadness, love, fury	involvement of the body
McDougall (1926)	anger, disgust, delight, fear, subjugation, tenderness, admiration	related to instincts
Watson (1930)	fear, love, fury	'hardwired'
Mowrer (1960)	pain, pleasure	not acquired
Izard (1971)	anger, contempt, disgust, suffering, fear, guilt, interest, joy, shame, surprise	'hardwired'
Arnold (1980)	anger, aversion, courage, separation, yearning, desperation, fear, hate, hope, love, sorrow	imply a behavioural tendency
Plutchik (1980)	acceptance, anger, anticipation, disgust, joy, fear, sorrow, surprise	related to adaptive body processes (based on the evolution theory)
Ekman *et al.* (1982)	anger, disgust, fear, joy, sorrow, surprise	have a universal facial expression
Gray (1982)	fury and terror, worry, joy	'hardwired'
Panksepp (1982)	expectation, fear, fury, panic	'hardwired'
Tomkins (1984)	anger, interest, contempt, disgust, fear, joy, shame, surprise	tightness of the firing of neurons
Weiner and Graham (1984)	happiness, sorrow	independent of attributes
Frijda (1986)	yearning, happiness, interest, surprise, admiration, grief	cause various forms of action willingness
Oatley and Johnson-Laird (1987)	anger, disgust, worry, happiness, sorrow	require a propositional content

basis of which they can assess whether there is an emotion or not. An even greater problem emerges when researchers react to each other's lists: the basic emotion that one researcher distinguishes may not even be called an emotion by another researcher! So the question 'What are the basic emotions?' is one that cannot be answered yet. Therefore, when researching emotions we do not recommend taking just any list with basic emotions as a point of departure and have respondents react to it. In the next section we will explain a better way of researching emotions.

The great scientists still do not agree on whether basic emotions exist and, if they do, what they are. For this reason, when researching emotions we do not recommend taking just any list with basic emotions as a point of departure and asking respondents to react to it.

11.2.5 *Research into emotions*

Measuring emotions involves doing research into their nature and quality as well as their intensity and strength. 'What emotion are we dealing with and how strongly is it present?' As has been said earlier, emotions are inner processes that reveal themselves to the outside world in four ways (feelings, expressive behaviour, motivated behaviour and physiological reactions). We depend on these manifestations to evaluate or measure emotions. When we evaluate other people's emotional reactions in daily life, we watch their facial expressions, the trembling in their voice, drops of sweat in their forehead, etc. The manifestations are also used in scientific research. According to Frijda (1991), it is wrong to equate feelings with emotions and to use these feelings exclusively to measure emotions. None of the manifestations provides the only or best measure of emotions. It is better to quantify as many manifestations as possible and combine the scores. Proper and thorough research into emotions implies face-to-face research. Having respondents fill in questionnaires reporting on their emotions and feelings does not seem to be as reliable. It is much better to combine such questionnaires with observations of, say, facial expressions.

Feelings

Feelings are conscious sensations of emotions and can be measured with checklists and evaluation scales or by registering the reactions that respondents give to words or pictures. Respondents are asked to say which of a number of feelings is or was present during a specific episode (sometimes they have to name it themselves and sometimes they can point to it on a picture or a list with words), or to indicate the intensity of these feelings on a scale of three or more (seven to ten). The reliability of the research into feelings can be increased by using a number of different scales that measure a certain feeling or a certain aspect of a feeling and combining the scores.

Many researchers place feelings in a coordinate system with pleasant/unpleasant (positive/negative) and high/low activation (active/passive) as coordinates, or by constructing circle-formed or circumplex models on the basis of these dimensions (Plutchik, 1980; Russell, 1980, 1983; Larsen and Diener, 1992; Scherer, 1996). Figure 11.3 shows two examples.

Such models are much used in practice for research into emotions and feelings that advertising and brands invoke (see e.g. Zeitlin and Westwood, 1986; Pieters and Van Raay 1992). Conceptual and methodological criticism can also be given to models (Scherer, 1996). In the first place, it is too simple a representation of reality; according to Scherer (1996), the enormous number of verbal expression possibilities for emotions – especially for subjective feelings – which appear in almost all languages show that very subtle variations in emotional processes are possible. Secondly, conclusions are being linked to the positions of feelings in the models without there being empirical proof for it. For instance, it is wrong to assume that one must always strive towards an association with feelings in the positive–active quadrant. Feelings that have to do with 'love' do not provide such a strong activation, but can provide a life-long relationship and, in some cases, it is very good to confront people with negative feelings in order to convey a message.

Expressive behaviour

Facial expressions are the quickest accessible indices of emotions. Several methods have been developed to classify and quantitatively measure facial expressions of people in pictures. The most objective and extensive method is FACS (Facial Action Coding System), developed by Ekman and Friesen (see the description in the box on page 226). Researchers are currently trying to develop instruments with which the intonation and trembling in the voice as well as paralinguistic aspects of speech (hesitations, etc.) can be measured. Up to now, none of these methods has reached the status of standardised measuring instrument, and we are left only with FACS for purposes of measuring expressive behaviour. The same goes for research into body posture, body movement, general movement traits and graphic expression forms (such as handwriting).

Motivated behaviour

As was explained earlier in this chapter, emotional behaviour can be described as 'passionate' (a passion is an urge that a person cannot resist, and which has to be realised). People are 'overcome' by an emotion and nature determines which behaviour the emotion elicits. By means of regulation processes people are sometimes capable of hiding undesirable or improper behaviour or of showing it in a different way. In many situations, a specific emotional stimulus

**The circumplex model
of Larsen and Deiner (1992)**

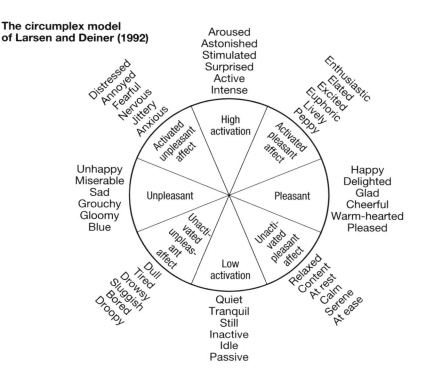

Types of emotional responses
(BBDO Worldwide, unpublished)

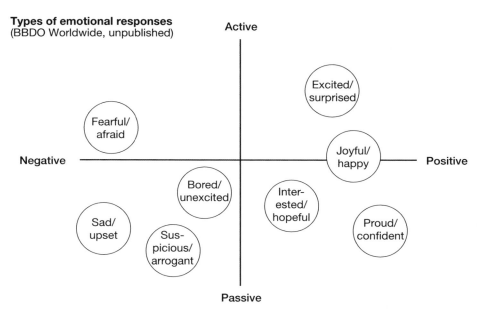

Figure 11.3 Two examples of models with the dimensions 'active–passive' and 'positive–negative'.

What is FACS? (Ekman *et al.*, 1980)

Spontaneous facial expressions were found to provide accurate information about more specific aspects of emotional experience than just the pleasant versus unpleasant distinction. Videotape recordings were gathered while subjects viewed motion picture films and then reported on their subjective experience. A new technique for measuring facial movement isolated a particular type of smile that was related to differences in reported happiness between those who showed this action and those who did not, to the intensity of happiness, and to which of two happy experiences was reported as happier. Those who showed a set of facial actions hypothesised to be signs of various negative affects reported experiencing more negative emotions than those who did not show these actions. How much these facial expressions were shown was related to the reported intensity of negative affect. Specific facial actions associated with the experience of disgust were identified (Ekman *et al.*, 1980).

From this quote it becomes very clear what the authors believe is the relevance of measuring facial expressions and how these measurements can be combined with 'self-report' questionnaires. FACS, the Facial Action Coding System, was developed in the 1970s by Paul Ekman and Wallace Friesen, two scientists of the University of California at Berkeley. The development of the instrument brought Ekman and Friesen much renown and they are still doing research to improve the instrument and to prove its validity and reliability. FACS is an instrument with which *all* the facial expressions of people are registered (not only those expressions which are assumed to be related to emotions). The facial expressions are subdivided into minimal parts which are then coded according to a detailed coding scheme. FACS distinguishes forty-four expression units, which includes the smallest units that can be anatomically distinguished and visually perceived (Ekman and Friesen, 1976; 1978). Every movement in the face

Contd

brings about the same behaviour in different people – within this context, the psychologist Fridlund (1991) speaks of 'prototypical behaviour' – and emotions can thus be used as predictors of behaviour.

Analysis of the emotional behaviour of adults is done with self-report questionnaires which ask about behaviour shown previously or previous interests; none of these questionnaires is standardised so that they can be used as an accepted scale to measure emotions. A researcher can also use lists with categories to observe and evaluate motivated behaviour in a systematic manner. In psychology this is done with children who are not capable of reporting on their own.

can be described in terms of the combination of expression units shown by a respondent. Through the detailed description of the expression units, an indication can also be given of when a movement begins and when it ends (e.g. when anger turns into disappointment).

FACS is used in research as follows: respondents are received individually and upon entering have to fill in a questionnaire, on which they can indicate 'how they feel at that moment' on a 9-point scale. There are separate scales for interest, anger, disgust, fear, happiness, pain, sorrow, surprise and excitement. The respondent is asked to give per feeling the number of times it was experienced (frequency), how long the feeling was experienced (duration), and how intense or extreme the feeling was (intensity). Respondents are then confronted with the emotional stimulus (usually a film of a positive or a negative event). After confrontation with the stimulus, they are asked again to fill in a questionnaire with the same structure as the previous one. At the end of the study, the respondent is told that he was filmed and he can indicate whether he has any objections to the pictures being used for further research. The pictures are analysed with the FACS described above. The researcher can combine the results of the FACS with the answers that respondents have indicated on the questionnaire. This is how studies can be done on the degree to which a certain form of laughter goes together with a feeling of happiness and with a certain intensity of happiness. It is also possible to find out whether perceiving an emotional stimulus influences the feeling of happiness (and its intensity), or whether this is expressed with a longer or different type of laughter.

Ekman and his followers give courses around the world in how to use FACS. After the course, participants obtain an official diploma and they can be hired in all kinds of situations to analyse facial expressions with the FACS method. For more information you can contact the University of California at Berkeley.

Physiological reactions

Various physiological reactions can appear under emotional circumstances. There are strong individual and situational differences with regard to the 'baseline' of psychological parameters; for this reason, emotional reactions are usually measured with the help of scores that deviate from the baseline. Heart rate and electrodermal activity are used a lot as indicators of emotions in experimental research. As a result of the relatively low correlations between the various physiological reactions, what constitutes the best indicator is not clear yet.

> In an ideal piece of research on emotions, several manifestations are measured. The scores for these manifestations are then combined.

11.3 Brand emotions

In recent years, specialised publications have paid increasing attention to the phenomenon that emotions that are shown in advertisements or invoked in the recipients are linked to the advertised brand through classical conditioning. The brand responses that arise this way are also called 'brand feelings' or 'brand emotions' in practice (Franzen, 1998; Keller, 1998). A widely used example within this context is Douwe Egberts: for years, Douwe Egberts has been linking the emotions 'cosiness' and 'togetherness' to its name. Several marketing managers suspect that in many markets (such as the beer market) emotions are the decisive factor in the ultimate brand choice. This is why these brand emotions are used in a lot of brand research. How this happens exactly will be discussed later. For now, let us take another look at brand emotions.

The authors of this book wonder whether the processes described in the preceding sections occur when people are confronted with a brand. For instance, this confrontation should lead to at least one of the four manifestations that were described in section 11.2.5. That certain affective reactions are important or even decisive for the brand choice is evident. However, one can wonder whether these reactions go much further than positive sensations such as 'appealing', 'likeable' or 'pleasurable', and whether these sensations may be called emotions.

> Brands invoke affective reactions in people. However, one can wonder whether these reactions go much further than positive sensations such as 'appealing', 'likeable' or 'pleasurable', and whether these sensations may be called emotions.

Emotions can be used in several ways as a marketing instrument. An emotion can be linked to the brand as a sort of 'benefit'. 'Cosiness' and 'togetherness' are the attributes of the brand Douwe Egberts, just as 'care' is an attribute of Blue Band and 'sensuality' of Häagen Dazs. This is not so much about the experiencing of the emotion, but about the cognitive recognition by consumers that a certain emotion belongs with a brand. It is of course necessary for the emotion to have some relevance for consumers. If emotions are used as 'emotional benefits', we also speak of the strategic use of emotions. Brands that succeed in strategically linking emotions to them are generally connected to products that have something to do with these emotions. Brands of ice-cream, cocktail snacks and beer can be connected in a logical manner to fun and pleasure.

Emotions can also be used to evoke attention (in this case we speak of the tactical use of emotions). The Dutch campaign 'Even Apeldoorn bellen' is a good example of the use of emotions (pleasure) in a tactical way. The Netherlands took great pleasure in seeing the films of Centraal Beheer, and research data showed that the commercials made people laugh a lot. People evaluated the commercials of Centraal Beheer as fun and funny. These associations were actually not brought about with the brand Centraal Beheer: people thought the insurance company was not funny at all – it was, at most, 'likeable'. Other examples of the use of emotions in a tactical way are expressions that attempt to invoke fear in consumers in order to get attention for an important message ('drinking destroys more than you'd want'; 'you aren't very smart if you play with fireworks'). These examples clearly show that the emotions that fulfil a tactical function are related to the communication of a brand and not to the brand itself. Since this book is about brands and not about commercials, we will not elaborate further on the tactical function of emotions and the related research. For more information, see Franzen (1998).

Two types of 'emotional' response are possible:
(1) The confrontation with the brand invokes an affective response. Affective responses are not the same as emotions. The affective responses are not specific. At most, people experience brands as pleasurable or non-pleasurable. In addition, the question remains as to whether the affective relationship that dominates everything is not a feeling of familiarity. Many people experience familiarity as something positive. They buy Douwe Egberts because of this familiarity and not because of the cosiness and togetherness.
(2) The emotion is used as a 'benefit'. Emotions are strategically linked to the brand name. Consumers recognise that a certain emotion belongs with a brand, but do not experience the emotion.

11.3.1   *Research into brand emotions*

The previous section has clearly shown that the confrontation with a brand can bring about two types of emotional reactions. The affective reactions to brands are too weak to be registered with standard instruments for measuring emotions; FACS, for instance, would produce nothing. In quantitative research the affective reactions can be measured with semantic differentials. The semantic differential was developed by Osgood *et al.* (1957) and, according to Eagly and Chaiken (1993), is the most popular way of measuring attitudes. The scale is also suitable for research into the affective responses to brands. There is a technically based assumption about a hypothetically semantic space

ABN/AMRO is:

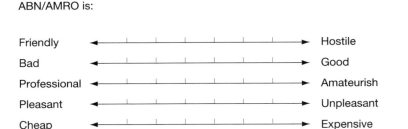

Figure 11.4 An example of the semantic differential.

of an unknown number of dimensions in which the meaning of every word and concept can be represented with a point. Respondents are asked to evaluate a specific concept on a set of semantic scales. These scales are defined by verbal contradictions with a neutral centre. They generally consist of seven differentiated steps. Figure 11.4 shows an example of a semantic differential. The technique will be discussed in more detail in Part Three of this book.

The 'emotion as benefit' can be researched in all sorts of ways. The goal of the study is to find out which emotion consumers associate with a brand, and the intensity with which they do this. The techniques that are suitable for doing this will be described in detail in Part Three.

Chapter 12

Brand Positioning

12.1   Introduction

Brands do not exist by themselves: some way or other they hold a relation to competing brands. In the eyes of many consumers, Volvo is safer than Alfa Romeo, Pepsi-Cola sweeter than Coca-Cola, and Benetton more expensive than H&M. Consumers constantly choose between brands which, at first sight, can resemble each other a lot and promise the same things. By positioning brands well, marketers can ensure that a brand gets a unique and favourable position in the brain of consumers. If this is kept up consistently, the position can become the imaginary property of the brand. This is how Volvo has become owner of the brain position that stands for safety. Ries and Ries (1998) claim that a brand does not enter the brain unless it stands for something. However, as soon as the brand has finally got a place in the brain, the manufacturer is usually planning something new. Markets may change, but brands cannot change, ever. At most, they may go through slight changes, but their essential characteristics may not be altered, according to Ries and Ries. When bringing what is known as brand extensions into the market, a greedy use is made of the brain positions that brands have already attained. In section 12.4.2, which deals with brand extensions, it will become clear how it is that many companies have the tendency to expand the product assortment under their brand. A good current example of this is Virgin. Richard Branson seems to possess the talent of linking to the brand various product categories, all of which are related to the brand concept (some more than others). Due to the initial success of Virgin, a real hype has emerged around the subject of 'brand extensions from the brand concept'. This is apparent from the large number of books and articles that have appeared on the subject.

Although Virgin is a model to many people, it is only a test case at the moment. There is no doubt about the fact that various products are doing well (Virgin Atlantic, Virgin Music), but other products still have to prove prolonged success. Virgin Vodka does not seem to be a success and Virgin Cola is also leading an existence in the shadow of Coke and Pepsi. Seven of the eleven highest profile Virgin companies were losing money in 1999 (Wells,

2000). It should also be noted that the brand Virgin is not representative of all brands around the globe. Other markets have different laws and principles, and that is what this chapter is about.

The positioning of brands is very difficult: in the first place, because markets are overfull, and in the second place because we are dealing with the memory and the experiences of people. It is necessary to get an insight into the way people store information in memory, which positions certain brands take, and which traits they are associated with. Why do consumers ultimately choose one brand and not another?

As was described in sections 5.6 and 6.1, network models assume that units of information are embedded in an organised structure and in meaningful mutual connections. People create order out of the chaos that surrounds them by placing in a group in their memory objects with common characteristics and giving a label to this group (word, image, description), and allocating meanings to this label – meanings that apply to the individual units within the group. Such a group of objects with common characteristics is also called a category. Within a category there is homogeneity, and between categories there is heterogeneity. The individual determines for herself which objects she wants to place in a category and why. Research has shown that the categories used by people within a specific culture strongly resemble one another (Leyens and Dardenne, 1996). To categorise objects they have to interpret them, and to this end they use concepts. In Part One (sections 5.2 and 5.5) we saw how a concept is an abstract representation of a collection of characteristics that are most defining to an object category.

12.2 Categorisation

12.2.1 *Classical categorisation theories*

Within 'classical' categorisation theories it has been accepted that all our 'concepts' are organised into 'hierarchies' in long-term memory. The assumed hierarchical structures have a horizontal and a vertical dimension. Within the vertical dimension various levels can be distinguished, from the very general to the very specific, from abstract to concrete. The horizontal dimension represents the characteristics differences between groups at the same level. The top of the hierarchy is formed by an extreme abstract representation of the categorised phenomenon. This is not very informative. As we go further down the hierarchy, an increasing number of attributes are added and the concepts become more concrete. A category or subcategory, or sub-subcategory (and so on) is a grouping of products and/or brands in which the internal correspondence between the characteristics has been maximised with regard to the other categories at the same level.

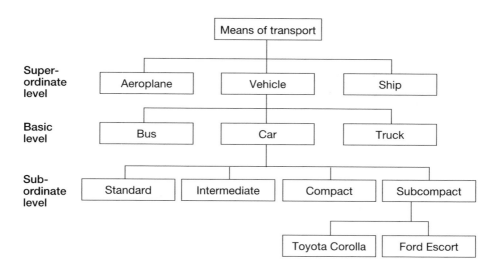

Figure 12.1   Hierarchical structure of means of transport.

A medium level functions as a 'basic level'. Experiences with the 'natural grouping' research method also point to this. This basic level optimises the balance between the richness of the representation and the extent to which it is differentiated from other categories at the same level. The basic level represents in the simplest way how we perceive a phenomenon and contains most of the information on all the entities that fall under it. All the characteristics of the upper, more abstract categories are therefore applicable to all the lower categories. This hierarchical structure of transportation means is represented in Figure 12.1.

Consumers establish relationships between various brands. On the basis of mutual agreements, they place brands in a common category or subcategory. This will often happen on the basis of products or product variants with which brands are associated, but other association types can also form the basis for the categorisation.

12.2.2 *The prototype approach*

The assumption of a strict hierarchical structure of our knowledge in long-term memory has now been abandoned. People are confronted on a daily basis with a bombardment of stimuli, and memory is set up in such a way that it is capable of interpreting these stimuli quickly and properly. Scientists have introduced the 'prototype' approach, which seems to have become widely accepted now in psychology. According to this approach, one entity in each category serves as a prototype – the archetype, the most original and most representative example for the objects in the corresponding category. In marketing practice, a category often emerges from a specific brand – the first brand to become linked with certain new or different meanings and which then starts acting as a prototype for brands with similar attributes that appear in its wake. In many product fields we encounter such prototypical brands. Their emergence often goes back decades or even generations. Kleenex, the world's first facial tissue introduced in 1924, is a prototype in the tissue market; Persil, launched in 1909, is a prototypical detergent. These prototypical brands are generally market leaders in their category and subcategory and are perceived as the most authentic or even 'the only real ones' ('Coca-Cola: the real thing'; 'Budweiser: the king of beers'). In the Dutch beer market we can see how certain subcategories are dominated by one specific brand which, as it were, was the first of its type – Bavaria Malt for alcohol-free beer, Palm for amber-coloured beer, Hoegaarden for white beer, Lingens Blond for light beer. These probably function as prototypes – the most characteristic brands in the corresponding subcategories. These prototypes make it possible to compare a new (later) brand and classify it into a category or subcategory.

> Some brands start functioning as prototypes for their category. They act as reference frameworks for the interpretation of other brands. They are often market leaders and are seen as 'the only real ones'.

As was seen in section 5.5, there is no concordance among scientists over the nature of the prototype. One theory says that this is an abstraction (a combination of abstract meanings), another that concepts are represented by concrete samples (Medin and Schaffer, 1978), and a third posits that it is a mixture of abstract and concrete representations (Cantor and Kihlstrom, 1987). According to this last view, consumers have an abstract representation of a typical member of a category, but will associate it with a concrete brand. When classifying a new brand into a category it is not necessary for this brand to share all of its traits with all the other members of the category. This is the phenomenon of 'family kinship'.

The more traits a member has in common with other members of a category, the more characteristic this member is of the category and the easier it is to interpret and categorise the brand (Rosch and Mervis, 1975 in Bousch, 1993). The more atypical a brand is, the longer it takes before we know what it is exactly. According to Miller (1981), the human brain is continuously trying to discover analogies by relating new experiences to something that is already known. Categorisation is therefore not only a means to give brands a place in our memory, thanks to which we can retrieve them more easily, but it also helps consumers understand a brand. By placing the brand in a product category or subcategory, it automatically acquires the meanings of that category or subcategory. Small differences are solved by giving a 'tag' to a brand, a mental note that says 'this brand does belong in the group, but also deviates slightly from it in a certain way'. With larger differences a new category or subcategory is 'formed', or the whole category structure is adjusted. Boundaries between categories usually cannot be drawn too sharply and are subject to constant change.

Brands can be combined for all sorts of reasons. Mervis and Rosch (in Bousch, 1993) posit that a category exists when two or more objects are treated as equivalents. This can take any arbitrary number of forms, such as giving them the same name or dealing with them in the same way. Equivalence can be related to all the components of the mental brand response (and the corresponding sub-components) that were discussed previously:

(1) Brand familiarity   Brand I know well
(2) Brand meanings   Provenance (brands from Japan), user
                                   image (brands for the *nouveau riche* or
                                   for 'Bill and Jane')
(3) Brand emotions   Brands that touch me (youth
                                   sentimentality)
(4) Brand attitude   Brands that are 'OK' and with which
                                   I can show up
(5) Brand behavioural tendency   Brands I would never buy; brands I
                                   always buy
(6) Brand relationship   Brands I love

Research shows that consumers within certain markets hold the same principles. For instance, the categorisation in the automobile market almost always takes place on the basis of the country of provenance (Japanese, French, German or Italian cars) and on the basis of class (high, middle and low).

A certain degree of equivalence is a basic condition for categorisation; it ensures homogeneity within a group. At the same time, differences within a group become clear. How these processes occur simultaneously can be seen in the following descriptions and differentiating characteristics.

Characteristic traits

Brands within a subcategory always have some common characteristic traits. The degree to which a brand possesses these traits determines the degree to which it is seen as a more or less suitable representative of the subcategory.

When it has these traits to an insufficient degree, it will probably fall through the choice process and will not be included in the consideration set. The characteristic traits function as border conditions for considering the brand as a choice alternative. When the characteristic traits of a subcategory have a high degree of association with the brand, it will be evaluated as 'better' and will have more of a chance of being chosen. Brands in a category can therefore be arranged according to a grading structure, going from most representative to least representative for the category. An analysis of the composition of consideration sets can clarify the question of which brands are seen as alternatives to each other, and are thus classified into the same subcategory.

Brands in a category are arranged by the degree to which they are seen as representative for that category.

Differentiating traits

Differentiation is the degree of distinctiveness of a brand: how different it is from its competitors. According to Aaker (1996), differentiation is a bottom-line characteristic of a brand. When a brand is not seen 'differently' to a certain degree, it is difficult for the consumer to determine his choice on that basis, and certainly to have extra money for it. In the 'BrandAsset Valuator' research model of Y&R, differentiation is also the first criterion a successful brand has to comply with. It gives indications that relatively successful new brands often get high differentiation scores, and that older brands run a particular risk of losing their distinctiveness. This could be a sign of weakening of long existing brands that do not invest enough in relationships and communication of brand differentiating attributes. This does not have to be exclusively limited to product attributes, as is shown by a brand like Coca-Cola, which does not really distinguish itself at a product level but is still perceived as highly distinctive (Agres and Dubitsky, 1996).

When a categorisation is based on perceived common product traits, more symbolic associations form the basis of perceived differences between the members of a category or subcategory. Establishing the perceived similarities and differences between brands is essential to understanding and influencing brand choice behaviour. In Part Three of this book we will give an overview of the research methods and techniques that could be used to bring these to the surface. Some techniques are based on the degree of perceived similarities ('natural grouping' and 'MSA'), others look explicitly to the degree to which brands differ from each other. The perceived relationships between brands can then be graphically shown in the form of a perceptual map, through statistical analyses like multidimensional scaling and correspondence analysis.

Less filling, yet great taste (Keller, 1998)

'Often, the key to positioning is not so much in achieving a point of difference as in achieving necessary or competitive points of parity! For example, consider the introduction of Miller Lite beer. When Philip Morris bought Miller Brewing, its flagship High Life brand was not competing particularly well, leading the company to decide to introduce a light beer. The initial advertising strategy for Miller Lite was to assure parity with a necessary and important consideration in the category by stating that it 'tastes great' while at the same time creating a point of difference with the fact that it contained one-third fewer calories (96 calories vs. 150 calories for conventional 12-ounce full-strength beer) and was thus 'less filling'. As is often the case, the point of parity and point of difference were somewhat conflicting, as consumers tend to equate taste with calories. To overcome potential consumer resistance to this notion, Miller employed credible spokespeople, primarily popular former professional athletes who would presumably not drink a beer unless it tasted good. These ex-jocks were placed in amusing situations in ads where they debated the merits of Miller Lite as to which of the two product benefits – 'tastes great' or 'less filling' – was more descriptive of the beer. The ads ended with the clever tagline, 'Everything you've always wanted in a beer ... and less'.

Figure 12.7 gives an example of such a map, based on evaluations of Dutch insurance companies. The distances between the brands correspond as closely as possible with the original evaluations.

Symbolic associations are often the basis for differentiation of brands within a category.

So far it has become clear that categories are flexible and have vague boundaries. There are no laws that determine in which categories people have to place objects. From their self-concept and value system they form their own individual rules and principles. Still, market research shows that the categories of members of the same culture or subculture (e.g. consumers from Western Europe) resemble one another very closely. These categories are stored permanently in the memory of large groups of consumers. Next to the permanent categories, depending on the situation, consumers form what is known as *ad hoc* categories. Someone who is on a diet can form a category of 'light' products, and someone who is expecting a baby forms an 'everything for the baby' category. Such *ad hoc* categories can also arise in a research situation: specific brand meanings are activated by the question asked by the researcher, thanks to which brands that are connected to very different products can still be placed in a common category. It remains to be seen whether the categories that arise this way also play a role in the purchasing behaviour of consumers.

12.3   Brand positioning

The principle that consumers can classify a brand in a group or subgroup of other brands on the basis of the most characteristic common attributes and differentiate the brand from other brands within the group or subgroup on the basis of its most characteristic differences is called 'brand positioning'. The preceding sections have shown that there are many ways of forming groups, and that differentiation can also be made between permanent and ad-hoc categories.

Several articles and books have appeared lately which postulate that products no longer form the basis for brand positioning. Mosmans and van der Vorst (1997) posit that brands are organising principles that do not so much take the company's own possibilities as a point of departure ('making shoes', 'taking care of banking business') as make the relationship between supply and demand a central one. 'A brand as a strategic instrument takes the relationship between the company and the surroundings as a point of departure [...]. Brands as strategic points of reference assume that the core of strategic development lies in the building and expansion of all the relationships that the suppliers maintain with their surroundings [...]. Brands create a context. They offer a framework for interpretation in which the production and acquisition of a product or service acquires a meaning in its most fundamental form' (Mosmans and van der Vorst, 1998). Rijkenberg (1998) suggests roughly the same: 'Concepting brings a value, a vision, a new concept into the market and adds afterwards, depending on that vision, products that belong there, easily exchanging them for others if it is convenient. The manifestation form of the product or the assortment by itself is communication, it radiates the values of the concept [...]. Concepting departs from the fight to death that is fought in saturated, tightly defined markets and target groups on the basis of product propositions. Nike is not a thing for you, Nike means something to you. Ikea is not a furniture store, Ikea's vision on contemporary shopping and living (the fun is yours!) means something for a large group of people. A target group is not formulated too tightly beforehand in terms of purchasing behaviour or social–demographic factors. After all, a new concept releases precisely a new type of purchasing behaviour, and the 'follow-up' group emerges as the

Levi's as a brand concept (Gilmore, 1997)

Businesses that have a well known and successful brand at their disposal tend to expand their product assortment under that brand. Philips is the ultimate example of this. Originally a brand of light bulbs, in the early 1990s Philips encompassed about 110 product groups, under which 30,000 different products were brought into the market. The assortment went from toilet seats (ended in 1997) to personal computers and from citrus presses to MRI scanners. 'Perhaps the most common mistake when you become successful is to try to stamp your brand on everything (...). It often takes a calamity to focus a company's collective mind. When you're doing very well the temptation is to keep adding bits here and there. Ultimately you risk losing your core consumer', says Robert Holloway, global marketing vice-president of Levi Strauss (Gilmore, 1997).

In the early 1970s Levi Strauss, which had produced only denim clothing for over 100 years, began to introduce a broad series of products under the brand Levi's into the market. An assortment of baby clothes, classic men's suits and women's clothing were successively launched under the Levi's brand. This undermined the brand to the point that the company was in the red. In the mid 1980s the mistake was recognised and a decision was made to return to the roots of the Levi's brand: denim, jeans, youth, sex, rebellion and valour. All future innovations would be 'Levi-like'. The European marketing manager put up all the core values of Levi's on a wall in his office. From that moment on, all new product ideas were tested on this wall according to the core values of Levi's. 'During the history of Levi Strauss we have learned that with an already strong brand, equity is linked to a complex list of associations in the minds of consumers. The moment you produce something that disturbs that set of associations – the soul of the brand – you're in trouble. One can only wonder about the future of brands that forget that simple fact.'

'adherents' join with the brand [...]. Concept brands assume the character of a movement (new religions?) because there is a large identification of the adherents with the brand. Buyers and brands strengthen and validate each other. There is a great feeling of mutual interconnectedness. Concept brands distinguish themselves from classical 'product brands' because they do not claim any intrinsic qualities, improvements, apparent improvements or added value, but bring a body of thoughts, a vision, a world into the market.'

These quotes show that there is an assumption within the 'concept trend' that brands are no longer characterised primarily on the basis of the products or product variants they are associatively connected to. The authors believe that concept thinking is very important (even though we use a different definition, as will become clear in the next section), but the association between product and brand (especially in this direction) should not be underestimated. The intensity of this association (the saliency of the product–brand association) and the degree to which the brand is seen as a good representative of the category or subcategory influence, in turn, the inclusion or exclusion of the brand in the consideration set. In particular when it comes to brand extensions – linking a brand to a new product category – this can lead to problems. Sometimes it is too easily assumed that 'well known brand' plus 'good product' are sufficient conditions for acceptance by the market. In a market in which other brands are intensely associated with the (sub)category, such brand extensions usually have a hard time acquiring a position of any significance.

Every brand has core meanings that are most characteristic for a brand (unique position). If a brand has always been connected with only one product category, this brand–product association will probably constitute the basis for the categorisation: the brand will be classified in long-term memory with the product category, subcategory or sub-subcategory it shares these core meanings with. In a product category we usually find subcategories that add a specific meaning to the upper level. This meaning defines the subcategory. This is how private cars are first defined on the basis of their class and then on the basis of their provenance. Figure 12.2 shows a categorisation of private cars in Belgium for 1992. The brand Toyota is categorised with four other Japanese middle-class automobile brands. There we also find a group of brands from France and a group from Germany. We see that some brands are categorised on the basis of three core meanings: product category (cars), class (high, middle, low), and provenance (Japan, Germany, etc.). Each of these three meaning categories predominantly defines the individual brands. It would be interesting to determine by which other core meanings the individual brands within a subcategory are defined: are for example Toyota and Nissan each a subcategory, and if they are, by which core meaning are these subcategories defined?

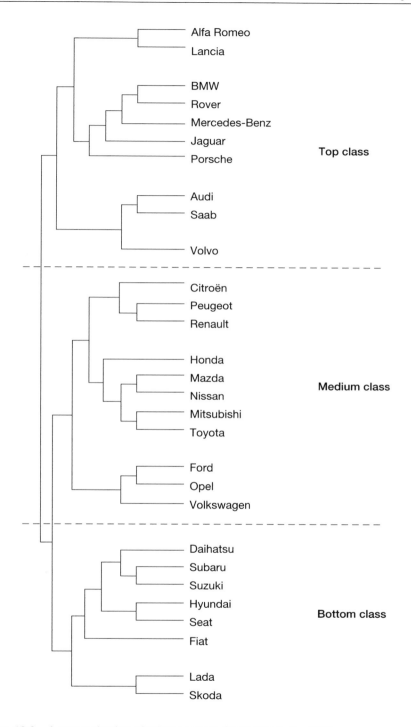

Figure 12.2   A categorisation of private cars in Great Britain for 1992.

The 'Brandscape'

Alexander Biel, one of the great brand gurus, postulated the idea of a 'brandscape'. People often choose brands from a self-image or self-ideal they strive towards. By looking at the brands that an individual uses, others can develop a 'mental print' of the person (Biel, 1991). Thus brands from different product categories start belonging together. A businessman who likes to show off drives a Jaguar, wears a Rolex and drinks Glen Livet. A not-so-original young man wears Nike sports shoes and Levi's 501, watches MTV and drinks Pepsi. There could also be categories which include 'all show-off brands' or 'all brands for young men'.

In an extension of the theories of Alexander Biel, the advertising agency Young and Rubicam (Y&R) developed a standard measuring instrument for image and attitude research, the BrandAsset Valuator, which is applied to a large number of brands that are linked to a great variety of products (an extensive description can be found in Part Three of this book). On the basis of the associations found, the agency combines *post hoc* brands from very different product groups into 'categories' of 'corresponding' brands. Although it can be useful for a policy maker to establish similarities between brands in very different product fields, this does not mean that consumers also categorise brands in a similar way. The question for the time being is whether a consumer does form a brandscape and, if so, whether that is the case in long-term memory or in a short-lived (research) situation. We are not aware of any essential research in which respondents spontaneously establish a relationship between, for example, Rolex and Jaguar. That these brands can form, together with other brands, the brandscape of a person who is status oriented is still uncertain.

12.4 Brand concepts

In the previous section we gave a definition of brand positioning. On what basis does brand positioning take place? The basis of each categorisation forms the brand concept: the abstract representation of the most defining associations of a brand. The products sold under that brand name are the category. Historically speaking, within the theory of consumer behaviour, products and product attributes have been taken as a basis for categorisation characteristics in consumers. At the time these were mostly mono-brands: each brand stood for a unique product with unique product attributes. In the early 1990s, when a more central importance began to be allocated to brands, people also began envisioning the possibility that brands themselves could form the basis of certain categorisations (Bousch, 1993). This involves brands that are linked to a series of different products: line brands (Grolsch pilsner, Grolsch special malt, Grolsch winter frost, Grolsch 2.5, etc.), umbrella brands (Nivea cream, Nivea visage, Nivea shampoo, Nivea deodorant, Nivea Baby, etc.), and company brands, in which all the products of one company get the same brand (Philips, chronologically, for light bulbs, audio and video equipment, domestic appliances, mobile telephones, etc.).

Here we can also ask ourselves which of the characteristic traits belong to the brand and to what extent these are shared by the various products/services in the brand category. Johnson's baby cream is a good example of the category. Johnson's Q-tips is a less typifying example. The products within a brand category must somehow, and to some extent, be equivalent to each other, because the association with the brand name suggests it. When people come across a Philips mobile telephone, they are essentially being told that this telephone is a member of a brand category, 'products made by Philips', and therefore has certain traits that typify the concept 'Philips products' (such as average quality, solid but not exceptional, reliable, mass brand, etc.). Individual products and services are more or less good representatives of a brand concept. Certain products can be prototypical for a brand, meaning that other products are related to it in order to determine to what degree they possess the characteristics of the brand. The contrast theory implies that some products cannot be included in the brand category because they have one or more characteristics that deviate significantly from those that determine the brand concept. Zwitsal's[5] laundry detergent for baby clothes was once a flop because Zwitsal essentially meant baby skincare, and consumers could not place a detergent into the 'Zwitsal concept'.

Brands themselves can also constitute the basis for categorisation. The underlying products are more or less suitable examples of the brand category.

Brands almost always arise on the basis of a specific product or product category. Many brands are thus primarily defined and categorised from the original product or brand association – as was the case in the preceding example of cars and in the later example of laundry detergents in Figure 12.4. Brands can also have other core meanings, for instance through specific attributes of the products they are or have been connected with. Becel (the Dutch version of Flora) was originally connected only with 'margarine' and with 'cholesterol-lowering'. In the associative network of Becel, cholesterol-lowering has become a core meaning that has made it possible to connect the brand to other product categories within which the meaning of 'cholesterol-lowering' is a relevant attribute. The 'brand concept' can thus arise,

---

5   Zwitsal is a Dutch brand of baby products equivalent to Johnson's.

categorising the various Becel products (margarine, frying fat, dressings, coffee milk and cheese) that it contains.

Companies have the tendency to link their brands to an increasing number of products. The brand 'Virgin', which originally was only linked to a chain of record stores (Virgin Megastore) with its characteristics 'low cost, no frills, good quality, anti-establishment', was given afterwards to an airline Virgin Atlantic, a soft drink, a vodka, a ginger beer, a financial services company (Virgin Direct), cosmetics (Virgin Vie), a railway company (Virgin Trains), a wedding store (Virgin Bride), while the introduction of Virgin cinemas, a Virgin Stores periodical and Virgin-net (e-commerce) is in preparation. Richard Branson himself, Virgin's founding father, does not even know how many companies he owns. 'May be 250?' he says. 'More like 150', one of his right hand men says. Not a single relationship can be pointed at a product level. Most of the companies operated at a loss in 1999 (Wells, 2000) 'He should get out of the businesses that don't fit the Virgin/Branson personality, such as beverages, cosmetics, financial services, and build on its image of irreverence in a few key-areas – airlines, cell phones, music, the internet, maybe even trains' says Allen Adamson (Landor Associates) in Wells (2000).

It remains to be seen whether consumers will also place such different products in a common category merely on the basis of a common brand. Virgin is a test case for brand policy.

12.4.1 *Basic concepts*

Consumers develop a brand concept on the basis of core meanings of a brand. Whatever is in the 'core of the brand' differs from brand to brand. Essentially, brand concepts can be based on all the association categories described in Chapter 10. A number of basic brand concepts can be distinguished, though. Without pretending to be all-encompassing, in this section we will describe the most common. Needless to say, we will also encounter mixed forms in practice. These are the basic brand concepts we distinguish:

- Brand = one product
- Brand = one product category
- Brand = product attribute
- Brand = domain
- Brand = provenance
- Brand = people
- Brand = design
- Brand = emotion
- Brand = personality
- Brand = value system
- Brand = ideology

- Brand = low price
- Brand = luxury
- Brand = organisation.

The brand as one product

The brand only represents one product with one composition. It is the name of one object. The brand can have a variety of associations at different levels of meaning, but the brand/product association is central to it. The brand immediately invokes the product it is linked to. Dettol is a bactericide, Weetabix is a breakfast cereal, Alka-Seltzer is an antacid for digestion problems, Chiquita are bananas, After Eight is chocolate filled with peppermint. Brands like these do not raise any questions as to what is in the packet. The brand tells exactly what we can expect. Some brands fall together with such a specific product that the brand name has gone on to function as a product indication. There is no generic product name for 'Post-it'. 'Post-its' are post-its. A 'Mars' is a mars, 'Tia Maria' is tia maria, 'Marmite' is marmite.

The brand as product category

The brand is connected to one product category, but within this category it offers various product variants. Del Monte is fruit; it encompasses canned fruit, juices and syrups, and it includes a large variety of different fruits, such as apricots, pears, peaches, oranges, grapefruit, apple and passionfruit. A category brand is usually associated primarily with its basic category; with Del Monte this is canned pineapple; with Grolsch, it is lager. This often makes it difficult to position the brand properly in the subcategories as well, especially when another 'special brand' functions as a prototype within such a subcategory. Category branding is widely applied because it strikes a balance between the concreteness but also narrowness of product brands, and the width but also abstractness of corporate brands. Examples of successful category brands are: Cadbury (chocolate), Dulux (paint), Duracell (batteries), Schweppes (soft drinks) and McVities (biscuits).

The brand as product attribute

The brand is strongly associated with a special product attribute or with a consumer benefit. It encompasses various product categories in which consumers experience this attribute as relevant. The letters in the product Becel (the continental version of Flora) stand for 'blood cholesterol lowering' and, in fact, this indicates exactly what Becel stands for: Becel has 'unsaturated fatty acids' as an attribute and 'cholesterol-lowering' as a consumer advantage. This type of brand usually arises as a basic product in which the attribute is central

Image from a television commercial from 1998 in which the main target group is shown (busy, active middle-aged men) and linked to the core meaning of Becel: margarine with a high content of unsaturated fatty acids that help keep the blood's cholesterol content under control.

and is then linked to other product categories. Becel started with margarine, followed by Becel oil, Becel dressing, Becel coffee milk and Becel cheese. The expansion of the brand is limited by the extent to which the attribute is desired in other products. Becel cheese seems to be a less successful 'brand extension'.

The brand as a domain

The brand is primarily associated with a certain 'domain', a space over which it possesses specific expertise. A domain can be tightly delimited or very broadly defined. It usually involves a categorisation at a higher abstract level than the product category. For instance, that of 'financial services' as a domain under which categories such as 'financing', 'investing', 'saving', 'insuring' and 'money transfers' fall. Large general banks such as Abbey National are examples of such domain brands. Domains can be very broadly defined. A common definition is based on common applications and complementariness. Gillette means 'shaving' in the broadest sense of the word; it includes all the equipment and toiletry articles that are used in the process. Gillette tries to develop its brand into an even higher level of abstraction: 'everything a man needs in a bathroom' (thus including fragrances and shower gels as well).

Nivea (from 'Neveus' or 'snow-white') started in 1912 as a product brand, a basic face cream in a blue tin, to which Nivea talcum powder and Nivea hair lotion were quickly added. In the 1970s a new 'brand extension strategy' was formulated, leading to the introduction of a large number of body care products for all kinds of target groups. In addition to the association with 'body care', the core meanings of Nivea are 'caring', 'protective', natural', 'fresh', 'uncomplicated', 'relatively cheap'. Nivea has extensive expertise, but it is limited to a few tightly described characteristics. In 1997 Beiersdorf announced the introduction of a cosmetics line under the brand Nivea Make-Up. Would Hollaway's remarks (see box on page 240) be applicable here? Other examples include Lego (educational toys) Seven Seas (health supplements), Kiwi (shoe care), Vaseline (skin care).

The brand as provenance

Provenance, a place of origin, is an important association for many brands. With automobile brands, for instance, it is a primary categorisation variable. For some brands, the country or region of origin forms the most important association, and is the core of the brand concept. Singapore Airlines is intensely associated with stewardesses of the Singaporean nationality, their appearance and character attributes. Grand Italia, a Dutch pasta brand, represents 'eating Italian style' with an emphasis on pasta dishes. Perrier is mineral water from France. Royal Doulton is quintessentially English.

The brand as people

In the first place, the brand represents a person or a combination of several people. In its purest form, the brand is the name of someone known by many for her extraordinary performance in a specific field: artists, musicians, and television and sports personalities. When the activities take the form of an enterprise ('Borg' fashion), the brand represents primarily the still-living founders. This is especially the case in the initial phase of all kinds of consultancy firms such as advertising agencies, law firms and organisational consultancy agencies. When the organisations become older and the founders are no longer in the foreground or have stepped down, these brands usually develop into a different concept type. However, by keeping their founder's legend alive, these 'brand people' can maintain their original core for a long time: Disney and Chanel are good examples of it. Virgin's image is inseparable from Richard Branson.

The brand as design

The brand is no longer connected to a specific product category or a specific domain, but is perceived as an authority in the field of design. It is known for its taste and design capacities. The most well known example is Swatch, originally connected only to watches, but with 'design' as its core meaning. 'We offer the consumer not only a watch, this is not merely about the mechanical side of the product, but the message behind it: high quality, low cost, provocative, joy of life, and personal culture' (Taylor, 1993). Besides watches there are now Swatch telephones and Swatch skis. Other typical style brands are Laura Ashley and Alessi.

The brand as emotion

The brand is intensively connected with certain emotions and invokes feelings that go together with them. The Dutch coffee brand Douwe Egberts is primarily associated with situations in which people take care of their dear ones and the feelings they have: togetherness and care. Walkers is fun, Save the Children is warm, Persil is caring and family, Andrex is heartwarming.

The brand as personality

The brand is no longer a representative of products, but the products are now expressions of the abstract inner 'characteristics of the brand'. Although most brands are associated with certain person-related traits, this is about brands that are primarily defined by these traits. The brand personality of Marlboro is characterised by features such as 'masculinity', 'independence', 'sense of adventure'; as well as cigarettes, clothes collections and trips that are in concordance with the brand are sold under its name. Whiskey drinkers drink to the 'American way of life', to the good old times, honesty and naturalness with 'Jack Daniels'. Häagen Dazs is hip, cool and sensual.

The brand as value system

The core of this type of brand is formed by a set of values that is intensely experienced by the people who are directly connected to the brand, and who exert a power of attraction in broader circles. This happens in political parties, religious denominations and charity institutions. Brands in the consumption sphere can also be primarily defined by a set of values: Chivas Regal means status, Chanel is timeless simplicity, Whiskas means caring, Schweppes contemporary adultness.

The brand as ideology

The brand is a representation of a social ideal, of a vision of how the world could be improved and a higher quality of life could be achieved. The brand is always aspirational: it purports to contribute to the achievement of a better condition than that of today. Apple is not just a PC – Apple purports to give space to the creativity in people. The Body Shop is not just a shop for toiletry articles, and has absolutely nothing to do with glamour. The Body Shop has to do with togetherness with distant peoples, with 'being good citizens', with an altruistic way of life. The Body Shop does not test products on animals and donates money to Indian tribes that are oppressed. Whoever buys something there is doing a noble deed. Nike is passion for sports. It wants to make the best sports shoes and fitness articles in the world. This means working closely with top athletes and giving them the best that is technologically possible in that field. It means constant innovation. At the same time, Nike stimulates amateur athletes and weekend joggers to expand their boundaries: 'just do it'. Leisure-time shoes do not really fit into that concept: their introduction was indeed a flop.

The brand as a low price

The brand is perceived mainly as the cheap alternative in its category. It is connected to a product or series of products that deliver an adequate performance on the generic functions but usually have no special added attributes. The presentation (package) and the service are generally minimised: examples are easyJet and Aldi.

The brand as luxury

The brand is perceived as the 'luxury variant' in its category. It is connected to a product or series of products of exceptionally high quality. It is also an 'expensive' brand. Research shows that this involves a complex of meanings that are associated with luxury brands to different degrees (Kapferer, 1998). Some important elements are:

- The beauty of the product
- The excellence of the products
- The magic of the brand
- Uniqueness
- Tradition
- Creativity
- Exclusivity
- Avantgardism.

Luxury brands can be classified into four sub-groups on the basis of the scores of each of these elements. We can thus distinguish:

- *Object brands:* luxury brands that are strongly associated with a certain product (Chanel No. 5, Porsche 911, etc.) and in which the beauty and excellence of the product are the most valued attributes of the brand.
- *Creativity brands:* in which it is not so much about excellence but more about sensuality and creativity: examples of this group are Hugo Boss and Gucci.

– *Magical brands:* these are about magical radiation. These brands are 'the great classics'. They are not subject to fashion: examples are Dunhill and Vuiton.
– *Exclusivity brands:* in which the emphasis lies on the small number of people that possess these brands or can afford them. These are brands that function as symbols for the privileged, the really rich people: Mercedes and Chivas are examples of this group.

The brand as organisation

The producing organisation is the central feature in the perception of the customers. This occurs especially with brands of service companies, where the product itself is intangible and often even almost invisible. Consultancies in particular fall into this category, especially when they operate in different markets, as is the case with the broad consultancies that developed out of the traditional accountancies like Anderson, and Ernst & Young. In this type of concept matters like competencies, reliability and authority are at the centre of the brand representation.

Brand concepts arise on the basis of the core meanings of a brand. Several concept types can be distinguished.

12.4.2 *The effects of brand extensions*

Many companies tend to expand the product assortment under their brands. There are often good reasons for this. The most important is that the sales potential of a specific product or product variant is sometimes too minimal to carry the costs of the whole brand operation. By uniting several products under one brand, a flow of income can probably be generated, making this possible. The familiarity and the associative network of a brand with consumers also represent an asset for companies that has to be maximised. By spreading the brand more widely, additional sales and profits can probably be generated. Moreover, the use of established brands may be necessary for the introduction of new products. After all, setting up a new brand is time-consuming and extremely expensive. In 1988 Tauber estimated the necessary investment for a new brand in the United States at a minimum of 150 million dollars. This is reason enough to consider seriously the exploitation of brands. This also means that its implications for the associative network of the brand have to be estimated as accurately as possible.

In view of the enormous variety of brands and brand concepts, no general rules can be applied for this purpose. However, the effects can be classified in a spectrum from positive to negative, from brand-enhancing to brand-

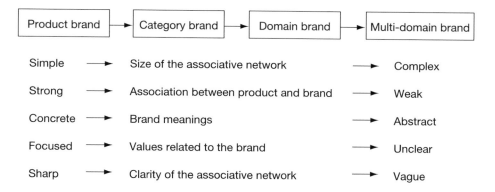

Figure 12.3   The development from product brand into multi-domain brand.

damaging. The desired core meanings of a brand form the point of departure. The first question is whether the meaning of the brand is *relevant* in the new product category. Another question is what effects the connection between the brand and a new product or product variant has somewhere down the line. In a very general way, expansion of the product range under a brand results in the core meanings of a brand developing to a higher abstract level. A product brand quickly becomes a category brand and then a domain brand. Further spreading can result in a situation in which it only represents the origin of the products ('by Philips'). Figure 12.3 summarises the development a brand usually goes through in its life course from product brand to multi-domain brand.

Brands whose meanings are on a higher abstract level from the very beginning (personality brand, value brand, ideology brand, luxury brand) have an easier time with 'extending'. But even with these brands the question arises as to what the essence of the brand is and what effects an extension has on it. The following possibilities can be distinguished:

- *The extension enriches the brand:* the extension adds new meanings to the brand that are in harmony with the existing ones. For example, a category brand (Grolsch) adds a product variant with special attributes (The Cannon, 10% alcohol), thus strengthening the perceived expertise of the brand in the category.
- *The extension strengthens the brand:* the extension corresponds with the core meaning of the brand and strengthens it because it contributes to the awareness of this meaning. For example, a product like Becel salad dressing would contribute to the cholesterol-lowering core association of Becel (the continental equivalent of Flora).

- *The extension is neutral with regard to the brand:* the extension is connected to the core meaning, but has no specific influence on it. This often happens with extensions of a category in which the brand meaning is less relevant or credible. Becel cheese would be an example of it.
- *The extension muddles the brand:* successive extensions towards product categories that have no plausible relation to that with which the brand is associated can lead to a muddling of the core meanings. At some point, the brand Hero in the Netherlands was linked to about 500 different products among which any kinship hardly existed. Once a market leader in the tinned foods market, it slid into an obscure existence. Hero has now redefined its essence as meaning 'fruit'.
- *The extension is in conflict with the brand:* the extension does not correspond with the core meaning of the brand, but its importance is too small to exert any influence (e.g. Philips toilet seats and 'light' versions of brands that are primarily based on taste: 'Camel light' next to 'Camel full flavour').
- *The extension damages the brand:* the extension of the brand is in conflict with its core meaning and gets such attention that it undermines it. Miller Lite beer in the United States led to the decline of the original Miller High Life. Levi's classical men's costumes and ladies' skirts weakened the Levi's jeans brand.

Strong brands are strong because they represent clear meanings by which people know exactly what they can expect of the things on which they encounter those brands. Strong brands have a focus. Just as with microscopes and binoculars, focusing leads to sharp perception of what we are focusing on and everything else around is out of focus. The essential question on brand extension is, what is the focus of the brand? Does the extension connect with it or does it lead to the de-focusing of a brand, through which it loses its core meaning?

When spreading brands into other product categories or domains, brand meanings tend to develop into higher abstract levels, due to which they function less well in choices of individual product categories.

12.5 Research practice

A great deal of research is being done currently into brand positioning. The hierarchical structured concept categories discussed at the beginning of this chapter are often found within market research. This can be due to the research method used, in which a pre-selection of products and brands is offered to respondents from a product-related perspective.

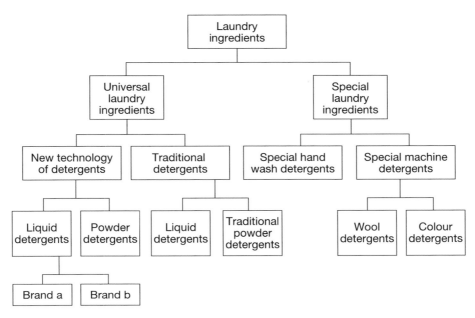

Figure 12.4 Categorisation of laundry detergents by consumers in Austria (BBDO Team, 1993).

Figure 12.4 shows the results of a study into how consumers in Austria categorise laundry detergents. They first make a classification into 'universal' (for the regular wash), and 'special' (for delicate wash). This is the basic distinction that is made. We also call it the basic level. The basic level represents the most important differences that people perceive between laundry detergents. The special laundry detergents are categorised again into detergents for hand wash and detergents for the washing machine. The special laundry detergents for the machine are in turn subclassified into wool detergents and detergents for coloured (fine) wash. The universal laundry detergents are subclassified into 'traditional' and 'new technology' laundry detergents ('with fat solvents'), a distinction that also applies to powders and liquid laundry detergents. Finally, brands are brought into this categorisation, forming the lowest and most specific level.

12.5.1 *Perceptual space*

People are capable of relating the meanings of entities to one another and of expressing the distance between the entities in a linear order on this basis (Glass and Holyoak, 1986). This is how they seem to supply the psychological distance of abstract meanings with a measure. They can give the distance

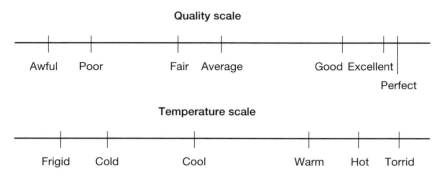

Figure 12.5 A perceptual space (Glass and Holyoak, 1986).

between various values that represent a quality level or with which a temperature is expressed (see Figure 12.5).

How they arrive at this evaluation, and what its underlying neuropsychological basis is, still remains to be answered. Nonetheless, this capacity forms the basis of research into brand positioning. In essence, this study is about determining which associations consumers use when evaluating brands and to what extent they assign these cognitions and feelings to the various brands. The basis of positioning research usually comprises brands and meanings that are defined beforehand and that have been presented to the consumer in verbal and/or visual form; then respondents are asked to evaluate each individual brand on each of the attributes, establishing the similarities and differences afterwards via statistical analyses. Assuming that consumers themselves compare brands with one another, another method is also used in which the researched brands have to be evaluated in relation to one another on an offered attribute: on the basis of an attribute, consumers are asked which of the researched brands are associated with that attribute and to what extent. Again, with the help of correspondence analyses, one or several spatial representations (perceptual maps) are constructed of which researched associations, together with the individual brands, form part. This is how a visual representation of the way in which consumers look at a category arises. The coordinates of such maps are strongly determined by the most distinguishing associations – those attributes in which consumers see large differences between the individual brands. The two dimensions of a perceptual map often explain between 80 and 90% of the data. The coordinates usually provide no neat verbal contradictions, such as modern versus old-fashioned, but subordinate dimensions instead. The interpretation of the perceptual map takes place from the centre. The further removed from the centre brands and associations are, the more distinctive or discriminating they are. The attributes that are least distinctive end up in the middle.

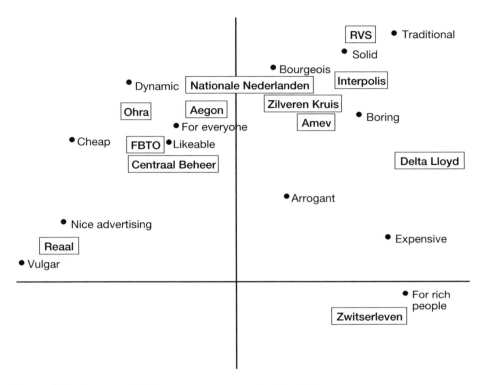

Figure 12.6   Image of Dutch insurance companies for 1996.

Figure 12.6 shows an example for Dutch insurance companies. This perceptual map is based on measurements done with the NIPO Triad question method. Three brands that are familiar to the respondent are presented. The respondent has to indicate which two fit best with one another and which two fit the least. The respondent is then asked to choose from 32 qualifications in order to indicate why this is so (Akerboom and Parker Brady, 1996).

When the measuring instrument consists of product-related as well as symbolic meanings, these are usually represented by the basic dimensions of the perceptual maps. Figure 12.7 shows how brands of toothpaste are positioned against each other in England. 'Macleans' is not a very functional brand that was perceived as 'young and active'. 'Sensodyne' is the most functional brand for tooth protection but has hardly any symbolic meaning.

Brands within a category are related to one another on the basis of the perceived degree to which they differ on relevant dimensions. Spatial representations can be constructed in which the distances between brands and from brands to the meanings are expressed: the 'perceptual maps'.

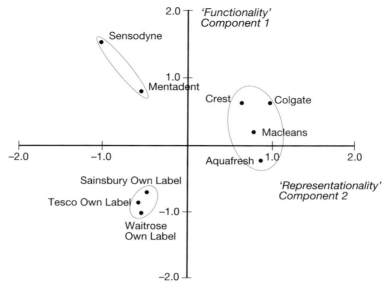

Figure 12.7   Positioning of toothpaste brands in England.

12.5.2   *Basic dimensions*

Positioning research often makes use of standard measuring instruments that are used regardless of the product category to be researched. This poses a risk of product- and brand-specific associations being overlooked and some associations being measured that have little or no relation to the autonomous product and brand perceptions. It is always preferable to make an inventory of the product- and brand-specific associations via qualitative research and to then quantify them via survey research.

Opposite is an example of value positioning for Dutch beer brands. This study used the SWOCC value inventory only. Although various positionings of the individual brands are visible, these perceptual maps only tell part of the story.

It is striking that application of several standard measuring instruments still produces a large degree of correspondence with regard to the perceptual dimensions. The SWOCC value study (Sikkel and Oppenhuisen, 1998) produced six basic dimensions, a number of which correspond with the results of research by Schwarz and Bilsky (1987), the results of Personal Drives Analysis of FHV/BBDO, the semiometric study of Trendbox and the psychometric study of Censydiam and Market Response.[6] The two basic

---

6   Trendbox, Censydiam and Market Response are Dutch market research companies.

The value positioning of Dutch beer brands

The value positioning of Dutch beer brands was researched (Centerdata, 1999) with the help of the SWOCC value measuring instrument developed by Sikkel and Oppenhuisen (1998). For each brand a determination was made of the degree to which they were associated with the six value dimensions that were found in the basic SWOCC study. This produced the mentioned three maps, which together represent the perceptual space (Figure 12.8). These show, for example, that Grolsch distinguishes itself strongly from other brands in the 'unique identity' and 'freedom from concerns' dimension, Amstel is strongly associated with 'family life', and Heineken with 'having a career' and 'being dependent on the opinion of others'. The results only reflect meanings contingent in the measuring instrument – in this case, values. Another measuring instrument might provide a different perceptual space.

Magazine advertisement in which the basic values of Grolsch are supported: self-awareness, independence, individuality and stylishness.

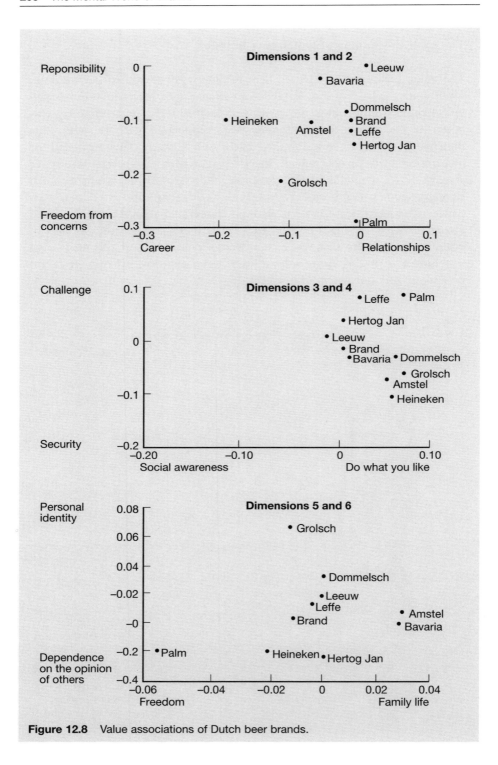

Figure 12.8 Value associations of Dutch beer brands.

dimensions that come forth in all these studies are:

(1) *A social interaction dimension*
    Meanings (values) that go together with the focus on the 'self' (enjoying, being attractive, relaxed, successful, staying young) or 'the other' (being helpful, responsible, understanding, taking the other into consideration). This dimension is also described as masculine ('geared towards the self') or feminine ('geared towards the other'), as well as social recognition ('look at me') versus social integration ('look, I belong') and inner directedness versus outer directedness.
(2) *The dimension of 'expressing' versus 'repressing'*
    Meanings that go together with 'repressing' are control, being composed, looking for safety and functionality, resistance against change, being traditional. Meanings that go together with 'expressing' are emotionality, looking for challenges, spontaneity, mind-broadening, being open to change, being modern. This dimension is also described as 'extraversion' versus 'introversion'.

After comparing eight different European and American research methods to map out values, Hansen (1998) arrives at the same two basic dimensions. The labelling differs somewhat, but the descriptions of the two dimensions show great similarities.

Hansen describes a market segmentation based on the Kompas measuring instrument of Gallup in Scandinavia, which led to eight different value segments situated in relation to the two basic dimensions 'modern versus traditional' and 'social versus individual'. A summary of them is included in Table 12.1 and in the box that follows it.

Table 12.1   Main dimensions from various research methods into values.

	1. Dimension	2. Dimension
VALS	Modern/Traditional	Action-oriented/Principle-oriented
RISC	Openness/Resistance to change	Ethics/Hedonism
CCA	Change/Stability	Material/'Spiritual' works
Grunert/Schwartz	Openness to change/Conservatism	Self-enhancement/Self-transcendence
Valuescope	Change to Modernity/Stability	Pragmatism/Loyalty/Materialism/Humanism
Kompas	Modern/Traditional	Individually oriented/Socially oriented
Danish attitudes	Modern/Traditional	Individuality/Collectivity
Minerva	Modern/Traditional	Social/Individual

Source: Hansen, 1998.

Eight value segments in Scandinavia (Hansen, 1998)

'Kompas' is a value inventory developed by Gallup in Scandinavia, based on 59 different values. Eight value segments of the Scandinavian population were distinguished with this measuring instrument (Hansen, 1998). A ninth segment is characterised by the average score on the 59 values.

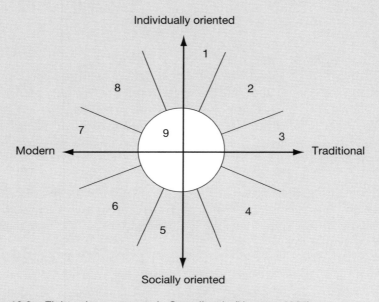

Figure 12.9 Eight value segments in Scandinavia (Hansen, 1998).

(1) The individually oriented
The slightly derogatory term 'bourgeois' is apt here. The individually oriented are frequently mature men. In the household there are two people and they normally own their own home. Only few have a higher education, but many are trade educated. They are married and have an annual household income in the range of DKK 200–400.000. They can afford a car or motorbike, which is used for driving around in Jutland, where half of the individually oriented live. The individually oriented are the kind of people who will only call the plumber if a tornado has passed by. They handle power drills, grinding machines and a wide selection of saws and other tools for indoor and outdoor repairs and maintenance expertly. Some of the tools are not inexpensive. They do the pools, lotto etc. and have a savings account in the bank.

Contd

(2) Traditional/individually oriented

The traditional individually oriented have little economic power and are no longer in the prime of life. Their children have left home. The attitudes and lifestyles of the traditional individually oriented are quite predictable and stable. They spend a lot of money on the pools and lotto. They find that too little is done for the elderly and the weak, and they think that the gap between rich and poor has grown too wide. The government ought to do something for a return to family values. Also, the government ought to keep an eye on the doings of the business community.

(3) The traditionals

There are many elderly people in this segment, and many single-person households. After a long life together, the husband has died, leaving his wife to fend for herself. The home is cosy. In these families cooking and baking are popular activities. For many of the traditionals, there is no lack of free time to pursue these interests: in many cases, one or both household members no longer work. The children have long since moved out.

(4) Traditional/socially oriented

An ageing but also active group of the population. Almost half of the group are sixty years old or more and they have a grade school education behind them, rarely more. They are pensioners or people not in the labour market. There are no or few children. Many are widows or widowers living in apartments in larger cities. They do not have an impressive income, but they have a remarkable ability to get the most out of what is available. One out of four has a cottage, a timeshare apartment or a swimming pool.

(5) The socially oriented

This segment has more women than men. Three or four people live in the house. The children are mostly between 10 and 30 years. The socially oriented are often white-collar workers employed within the public sector. They are active and sociable people. They prioritise closeness, honesty and healthy human relationships. They often live in cities. Politically they are affiliated with the social democrats or the left-of-centre parties. They are 'green' idealistic families where everybody helps with everything. The man in the house knows how to cook, do housework and care for the children. The socially oriented are united by a great interest in aesthetic, artistic, cultural and intellectual activities.

Contd

(6) The modern/socially oriented

Materialism is not exactly 'in' here. It applies to them as people and it applies to their homes. They are, however, well educated and many university graduates are found in this segment. There are two or more adults in the household. The man is employed within the public sector in the higher salary range. The woman is independent or a housewife. Money is not spent in the same way as it is by the moderns. The car is not quite as trendy, the expensive durables are fewer. The modern socially oriented are more idealistic. When they talk about recent developments, it is not so much e-mail or getting on to 'the next new thing' that they are concerned with but rather intellectual and cultural questions, and not least spending time with other people.

(7) The moderns

The moderns are much drawn to all new things. For instance, their homes are veritable showcases for the most recent advances in consumer electronics. To the moderns, the distinction between what is HOT and what is NOT is crucial. In the typical modern family, the male head of the household holds an advanced degree and works as a senior executive, while his wife is self-employed. They have two children, both in their teens. They are pro-NATO, career-oriented and vote Liberal just like mum and dad. Unlike earlier generations of teenagers, the young moderns desperately seek security. Typical representatives of 'the gapless generation', they love advertising and dream about the sixties and seventies. Rebellious behaviour, body piercing and 'the artist formerly known as Prince' are NOT. Morten Korch films (popular Danish comedies from the fifties) and invitations in thick envelopes are HOT. The moderns belong to the affluent part of the population and are great spenders when it comes to durable goods. The most recent acquisition could well be a black Peugeot 406, which looks great in the driveway in the nice neighbourhood where they live. Once inside the house, you are likely to come across an impressive selection of PCs, fax machines, cellular phones and answer machines. All in a home which blends classical modernism with kitsch and a little bit of romance. On the table you will find a quality daily newspaper, professional journals and the Danish equivalent of the *Financial Times*. The CD player plays soft rock and the tickets for next weekend's trip to Prague have just arrived. To the moderns, knowledge and culture is power. They play golf and tennis and participate in other socially acceptable leisure activities such as going to the opera. As with other things, the moderns have an expensive taste in clothes. Their wardrobes feature designer clothes labelled Hugo

Contd

Boss, Calvin Klein, etc. Manufacturers of exclusive personal care items are also well represented in their homes. The nondurable consumer goods include Italian gastronomic specialities, some of which have been bought in Denmark, while others (olive oil and spice) have been brought home from frequent trips abroad. The possession of several credit cards makes it easier for the moderns to act on impulse when they come across something they would like to buy. But then again, expensive habits are not a problem for those who can afford them.

(8) The modern/individually oriented

This is a segment with quite large households. They are more self-confident than most, with a sensible balance between private consumption and a healthy financial situation. The segment comprises many young success-oriented men with good theoretical backgrounds and careers. The housewife is self-employed and there are three or more children in the home, a few of them below 13 years of age. The other children are apprentices or students. For better or worse the modern individually oriented represent the PC boom and are among the 900,000 households that will not accept less than 32 megabyte RAM on their Pentium PC. The printer is the latest model, and many have CD-ROM drives and modems. For shopping the family uses the car, frequently a slightly used one from a classified advertisement in one of the major dailies. The car is also used when some of the family members go to play golf, tennis, badminton or the like. There are no less than 93% of the modern individually oriented who are actively engaged in sports and exercise.

Censydiam (Callebout *et al.*, 1994) points to Adler's motivation theories for the explanation of the basic dimensions. Sikkel and Oppenhuisen (1998) build on the theories of value hierarchies, in which very global values become more specific as the objects they are related to become more concrete. These theories imply that, at a high abstract level, only a limited number of 'essential values' could be distinguished. From this perspective it is understandable that positioning research uses standard inventories of meanings like the SWOCC value inventories. We hereby only expose associations at a high level of abstraction, while the consumer frequently bases the choice process on very concrete product attributes. Perceptual maps only tell part of the story.

There are strong indications that social brand perceptions at a high abstract level fall within an area that is defined by two basic dimensions: a social interaction dimension and an 'expressing' versus 'repressing' dimension.

The positioning of automobile brands in Belgium

Censydiam uses value association batteries to measure the position of brands/models in a market with regard to one another and determines their relationship with motivational segments. The agency uses, among other things, an abstract value battery of person associations and of animal associations. The motivational segmentation is also brought about by having the respondents describe their 'ideal brand' in this association category. Such research, carried out on the associations of automobile brands in Belgium (for 1996 and 1998), has produced the perceptual maps shown below. Seven main categories of cars were distinguished on the basis of the mapping:

- Sporty, energetic, original cars
- Status and superior cars
- Compromise cars: status and functional
- Compromise cars: cheap and functional
- Cheerful, young, spontaneous cars
- Simple, loveable cars
- Rational, low-budget cars.

It is striking that these categories deviate considerably from those which were found with natural grouping in Belgium (see page 241). Here the question remains as to whether categories can be identified *post hoc* or should preferably be indicated directly by the respondents. We have previously established that categories are not fixed, but that various categorisations are possible, depending on the task or goal for which the categorisation is made (Figure 12.10). In this case, the applied research instrument was determinant to the categorisation. The second perceptual map gives the position of the brands with regard to the items in the value battery (Figure 12.11).

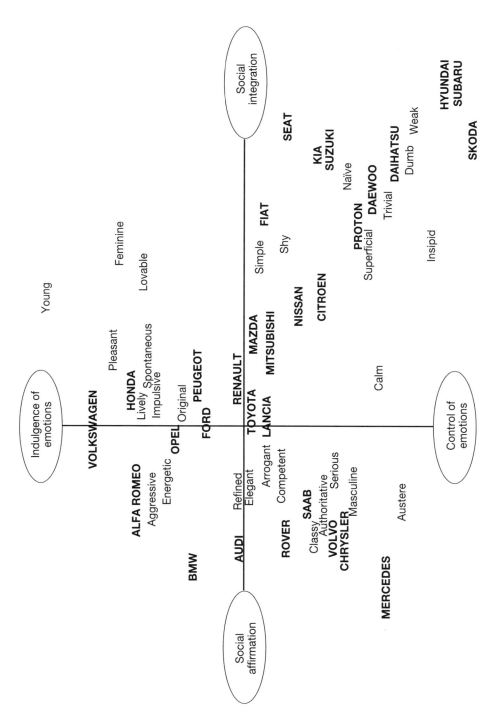

Figure 12.10 Brand positions.

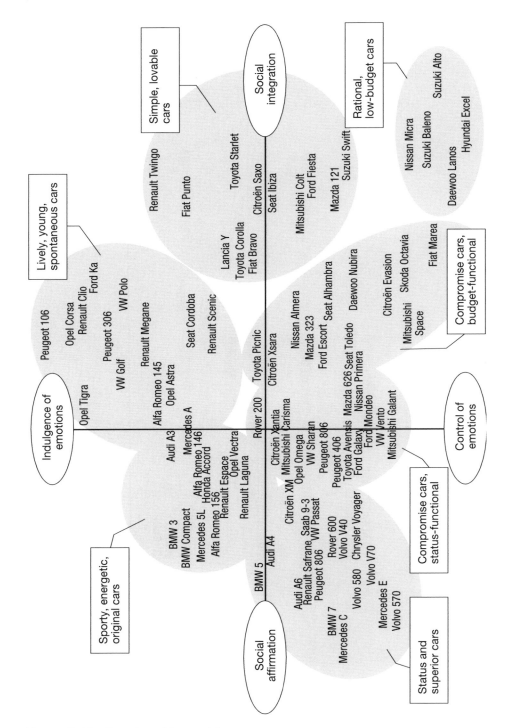

Figure 12.11   Grouping of the models.

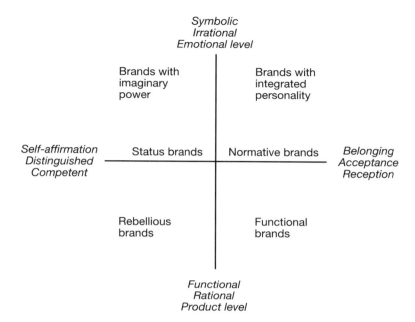

Figure 12.12   A general typology of brands (Moens, 1999).

Based on the results of market research in several markets, Moens (1999) arrives at a general typology of brands from the two basic dimensions (Figure 12.12).

He distinguishes six basic typologies (we will adhere to his terminology):

(1) *Brands with imaginary power and brands with an integrated personality:* these brands have surpassed the product level. They add an emotional and symbolic value to the product.
   • Brands with imaginary power. They create a personal, aspirational world for the consumer. They are associated with self-assuredness without being seen as arrogant. They give their users a feeling of mental freedom and of making an individual choice. Examples are Harley Davidson, Nike, Alfa Romeo and Marlboro.
   • Brands with an integrated personality. With these brands there is a balance between product-related meanings and the brand personality. They radiate warmth, pleasure and involvement and give their users a 'we' feeling. Examples in the Netherlands are Coca-Cola, Heineken and Opel, in the UK Persil, McVities.

(2) *Status and normative brands:* brands in which there is a balance between the perception of the product characteristics and the social values and norms the brand is associated with.

- Norm brands: large, strong brands that give their users a feeling of security and belonging. These brands are associated with quality; they owe their existence partly to the fact that they are large and generally accepted. Examples are Heinz, Cadbury, Persil, Kodak.
- Status brands: these brands owe their position to the fact that they are experienced as distinguished, and users can reaffirm their own personality through them. These are generally luxury brands that radiate class. Examples are Mercedes, Rolex, Gucci, Ben and Jerry, B&O, Dior and Häagen Dazs and Moët et Chandon.

(3) *Rebellious brands and functional brands:* these are brands in which the product-related meanings are central. They are simple and basic and have no strong emotional associations.

- Functional brands. These are brands that are primarily seen as honest, no-nonsense and simple. They are relatively cheap and provide a solution for budget problems. Examples are Zeeuws Meisje, Witte Reus ('White Giant' detergents), Baron hotels and own-brand labels.
- Rebellious brands: brands that are experienced as anti-normative. They are bought by groups who have the urge to resist the established order and who see themselves as intelligent. Examples are Red Bull, Pepsi Max, Saab, Diesel, Absolut, Tommy Hilfiger.

Chapter 13

Brand Attitudes

13.1   Attitudes

'Ask a person what his or her attitude on a topic is, and the person will likely have one. It may be an issue the person has never thought about before and will never think about again, but for that brief moment, he or she may well have an attitude, even an apparently strong one. Clearly, if the attitude is a temporary whim, it will not predict behavior very reliably. This problem – ubiquity of attitudes – has plagued research on attitude–behavior consistency. Attitudes seem to be everywhere, but several factors influence which attitudes matter to a person, and consequently, which predict behavior. Which attitudes are really there and which are not?' (Fiske & Taylor, 1991, p.520)

Just as with so many other concepts from the social sciences, it is difficult to give a generally accepted definition of the concept of attitude. Based on an extensive literature study, Van der Pligt and De Vries have arrived at the conclusion that a number of central components can be derived from the number of definitions that have been given on the concept up to now (Van der Pligt and de Vries, 1991). According to these two authors, an attitude is:

(1)   Geared towards an object, person, instance or event
(2)   Evaluative: favourable or unfavourable, positive or negative
(3)   Partially based on cognitive convictions over the attitude object; in other words, the consideration of positive and negative characteristics of the object leads to an attitude
(4)   Has implications for the behaviour with regard to the attitude object.

Since the 1920s a lot of attention has been paid to measuring attitudes. This has resulted in a vast number of models and methods by which insight into the attitudes of people can be obtained. This interest stems largely from the hope many researchers have of being able to predict people's behaviour based on insights into their attitudes. Can we explain the behaviour of a specific person with regard to a specific object on the basis of knowledge of people's attitudes in general with regard to an object or brand? Definitely. Think, for instance, of someone who likes brown bread: she will buy brown bread more often than white bread; someone who is very positive about the brand Levi's will buy blue jeans of this brand more often than of another brand. But what about the following situations? Imagine that you hate the brand Laura Ashley, and you think all the articles sold under this brand name are hideous. Generally you do not hide this opinion. Your friends know your opinion on Laura Ashley and know exactly how you will react if they show you a picture of a real Laura Ashley couch. In other words, they can predict your reaction. But what if you walk into your mother-in-law's house for the first time and it looks like a Laura Ashley showroom? You may not show your feelings about her things, or you may even tell her without blinking that she has decorated the house very nicely. This is not the expected behaviour. Then imagine that the same mother-in-law invites you to her birthday celebration. You are of course planning to go, and as a present you buy her two Laura Ashley cushions for her couch. The market researcher whom you first told you hate Laura Ashley couches and who then registers that you bought something in a Laura Ashley store, is faced with a contradiction. How is this possible?

A lot can be said about this example. Devotees of qualitative research will claim that in large samples such as the one described above, exceptions are 'neutralised', and that is indeed so. However, social context can exert a large influence on our behaviour. According to the frequently cited model of Fishbein and Ajzen from 1975, which will be extensively described, the social context is as important as the attitude when explaining and predicting behaviour. It is actually strange that this fact is so rarely included in market research, if we see how often the model is quoted in books on marketing and brands. The most recent version of the model (mainly adjusted by Ajzen on the basis of criticism of other scientists and new research findings) is shown in Figure 13.1.

According to this model, behaviour cannot be directly predicted from attitude but from behavioural intention. The relationship between intention and behaviour can be disturbed by barriers to exhibiting behaviour or by deficient skills of the person (the brand is not present in the store or the person cannot reach the store because he is in a wheelchair). The intention can be predicted from four factors: preceding behaviour (or habit),[7] the attitude, the social norm (the opinion of significant others as perceived by the person) and self-efficacy (someone's estimate of the degree to which they are really capable

---

7   It makes a big difference whether people have experience with the 'attitude object'. In the first place, there can be a reversed causality (this means that an attitude is derived from a previous behaviour; I always eat wholewheat bread, so I seem to like it). As regards personal effectiveness, it rests on the results of previous attempts to perform a certain behaviour. A previous experience can also constitute a cause of behavioural advantages and disadvantages and assessing the values of barriers for performing behaviour (Van der Pligt and De Vries , 1991).

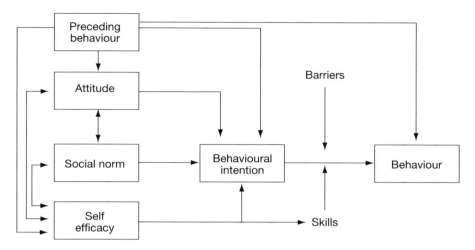

Figure 13.1 A model of behavioural determinants (Van der Pligt and De Vries, 1991).

of showing the desired behaviour).[8] External variables do have an effect on these behavioural determinants, but not directly on the intention or the behaviour itself. Besides having an influence on the self-effectiveness of the intention, this factor also has an influence on behaviour through skills. Previous behaviour influences attitude and also has a direct effect on the intention and the behaviour. Furthermore, the attitude and the social standards are related to self-effectiveness. Finally, previous behaviour, attitude and social norms are interrelated. Thus preceding behaviour (experience) will influence attitude, and the attitudes and social norms will not be completely independent of one another. Despite the apparent completeness, the predictability value of the model is sometimes limited (Van der Pligt and De Vries, 1991). This is caused mainly by the limited relationship between attitude and behaviour (in other words, it remains difficult to establish the relationship between attitude and behaviour).[9]

---

8   The concept of self-efficacy is borrowed from the work of Bandura (1986), but has also been included in a model of behavioural determinants by Ajzen (1988) under the term 'perceived control on behaviour'. The estimate of self-efficacy seems to be the result of four factors: the previous experience with the behaviour, the observation of others, persuasion by others, and the perception of one's own reactions (like insecurity and nervousness). Measuring self-efficacy is done in different ways. As a guideline, Bandura proposes distinguishing three aspects within self-efficacy: experienced difficulty (can the behaviour be performed with difficulty or ease), generalisation potential (does it vary per situation or is it always the same), and certainty (is the person sure of being able to perform the behaviour or are there doubts) (Van der Pligt and De Vries, 1991).

9   In Chapter 14 on brand behavioural tendencies, a study of Baldinger and Rubinson (1996) is described in which a clear connection is shown between attitude and behaviour: purchasing behaviour and attitude mutually influence each another. We do not know anything about the validity of the study: for example, it is not clear how the concept of attitude is operationalised and whether the results apply to the whole population. The study looks promising but it should be repeated so general pronouncements can be made on the relationship between attitude and behaviour.

The fact that various researchers have not succeeded in demonstrating the relationship between attitude and behaviour can be attributed to a methodological mistake on their part. Fishbein and Ajzen (1975; see also Ajzen and Fishbein, 1977) have shown us that that relationship can be established only if attitude and behaviour are defined to an equal degree of specificity (or generalness). They call this 'the principle of correspondence', by which they mean that there is no point in asking someone's attitude towards environmentally friendly skin care products and then to predict that they will buy body lotion at The Body Shop within a certain period of time. According to the principle of correspondence, it is even impossible to ask someone's attitude with regard to The Body Shop and to make predictions on that basis regarding possible purchases at that shop. Fishbein and Ajzen believe that every behaviour consists of a number of components:

(1) Action (what the person does)
(2) Goal (of the action)
(3) Context (in which the action takes place)
(4) Time (in which the action takes place).

The specificity or generalness of attitude and behaviour can be evaluated on the basis of these four components. Most attitude measurements are geared exclusively towards the goal of the behaviour: predictions are made on the chances of someone quitting smoking based on the question of whether a person considers 'healthy living' (a goal) important. A better 'attitude question' for making predictions on the chances of a person quitting smoking would be: 'Do you intend to never again smoke a cigarette starting tomorrow at 9 am?' Of course, in this example there is a large chance of the relationship between attitude and behaviour being inhibited by self-efficacy (after all, smoking is an addiction). In short, an attitude that should predict behaviour is always geared towards the behaviour with regard to the attitude object. It is not enough to only ask about the attitude with regard to the object. The research results that are collected this way look less exciting but have a much larger prediction power.

Research into the relationship between attitude and behaviour must strive towards the 'principle of correspondence'.

A few years before Fishbein and Ajzen published their ideas, a group of scientists at Yale University carried out a pioneering study in the area of attitudes. The theories that resulted from this study have become known as the Yale Reinforcement Perspective. The basic idea behind the Perspective is that people's views and attitudes become habits because the expression of these views and attitudes is followed by a positive ratification or reward (Doob,

1947; Hyovland *et al.*, 1953). If a person experiences that the brand Lessini (artificial lemonade) satisfies her thirst (positive ratification), she will develop a positive attitude towards this brand. A person is faced with this attitude if she is walking down a supermarket aisle and is suddenly facing a bottle of Lessini on a shelf, if she opens her kitchen cabinet and sees the bottle, or if she sees a parasol with the logo. The attitude has become a habit in the sense that she does not have to search her memory each time looking for all sorts of knowledge elements, emotions and experiences related to the brand, and forms an attitude on this basis; the attitude is already there and comes to her immediately. The phenomenon of 'habit' is discussed in section 4.3 and Chapter 14.

If an individual has already formed an attitude, this attitude becomes a 'habit': the individual does not have to construct an attitude again each time she is confronted with the brand. The attitude is already there and comes to her at once.

How easily the attitude 'enters' someone's consciousness depends, of course, on the strength of the attitude. This 'entering' is also called accessibility. An attitude is accessible if the association between the attitude object and the corresponding evaluation is strong. The accessibility of an attitude (and therefore its attitude strength) is determined by confronting respondents with attitude objects and registering how quickly they report an evaluation (Fazio, 1989; Fiske and Taylor, 1991). Fiske and Taylor add to this that the accessibility of an attitude has various practical implications. They claim that accessible attitudes influence the way in which people perceive the attitude object (if people have a positive attitude towards a candidate for a chairperson position and this attitude is also very accessible, they will evaluate the candidate's speech very positively). It also seems that the more accessible an attitude is, the smaller the chances are that someone will allow himself to be influenced by opposite information; accessible attitudes are therefore durable. Finally, it has been shown that accessible attitudes exert an increasing influence on behaviour. An attitude becomes accessible if it is activated frequently or regularly (on a daily basis, Apple's I-Mac has shown its user-friendliness). The liveliness of the information plays an important role here (it is better to experience time and again how fine it is to work with the I-Mac than to hear it through advertising or through others). In addition to frequency and regularity, 'chronicity' has an influence on making an attitude accessible. Everyone knows people who evaluate objects, persons and situations on only one or two dimensions. Frequently used dimensions are 'beautiful' or 'looks expensive'. A person who loves status and showing off will evaluate positively those objects that score highly on these dimensions (Fiske and Taylor, 1991).

Attitudes are usually measured with multi-attribute scales. These scales are described extensively in Part Three of this book. In this chapter it suffices to mention that this is a collective name for a number of statistical procedures. Respondents can indicate on a scale to what degree they think certain attributes fit with a brand (for instance, attributes such as expensive, contemporary, and 'fits me'):

'Heineken is an expensive brand'

agrees completely	agrees	neutral	disagrees	disagrees completely

After all the respondents have filled in the scales, statistical analysis techniques are used to identify a number of dimensions, the least possible, that fit the most with a large amount of data. With multi-attribute scales, the researcher gets information on the nature or content of an attitude as well as on its intensity. If a respondent scores a more extreme scale value, it could be assumed that his attitude is more extreme. Unfortunately, this method of measuring intensity is not quite pure. Research keeps showing that filling in extreme values is a character trait of respondents; extreme scores have been found in all statements or attributes. It is better to use response times as an indicator of the intensity of an attitude. Respondents get to see, for example, the Volvo logo. The researcher then names an attribute and asks whether it fits this brand. The more quickly the respondent says yes, the earlier the association between the attribute and the brand is activated. From theories that have been described earlier in this section we already know that quick activation is an indication of the strength or intensity of an attitude.

13.2   Brand attitudes

Very possibly, nowhere is the need to predict people's behaviour greater than in the advertising and marketing world. This need has probably ensured a lot of discussion about attitudes. A distinction is usually made between attitudes concerning advertising and attitudes concerning brands. The positive attitude with regard to advertising is also called likeability. This concept is further described in section 13.3 when we discuss the influencing of brand attitude. We should remark beforehand that several product categories (especially within fast-moving consumer goods) are not really important to people, and that one can hardly speak of an attitude with respect to the brands within these product categories (the quote on page 269 applies to these categories).

In several books and articles on brands and advertising, brand preference is used as a synonym for brand attitude. We do not quite agree with this. Franzen (1998) described brand preference as the situation in which the consumer gives a degree of preference to a certain brand above other brands in the consideration set. The consideration set includes the brands a consumer considers buying at a certain moment. The preference for brands within the

The consideration set

Brand awareness is a first condition for a brand to be included in the consideration set. As we have seen, brand awareness depends on the cue that brings the brand into consciousness. This can be any cue a brand is associatively connected to. Cues can be the product category or subcategory as well as specific choice criteria that are related to the goal the consumer has in mind, like certain applications, user situations and product attributes. The strength of the associations of a brand with the used cue determines whether a brand enters consciousness and is then included in the consideration set. When the association between a brand and the cues that are determinant to inclusion in the consideration set is not strong enough, the brand runs the risk of not being recognised as an alternative in the shop environment. Consumers only consider those brands they recognise and associate with the attributes sought. In the race towards being accepted as a candidate, two things are important: brand awareness (saliency) and good accessibility of the positioning in memory. The time pressure under which purchasing decisions are taken in shops ensures that brands that are recognised quickly have the advantage. The positioning influences which brands are seen as members of a desired category. Research has shown that, in general, the brand-product category association exerts the greatest influence on the inclusion in the consideration set. Within the hierarchy of categories, it is the basic level that exerts the strongest influence on it. Brands that function as prototypes in a basic category are remembered more often and more quickly, and therefore have a greater chance of forming part of the consideration set. They have, as it were, a memory advantage over their competitors. Atypical brands are at a disadvantage: they are remembered less often and less quickly. When a choice process is focused on a subcategory, the strength of the association of a brand with the subcategory cue is determinant to whether the choice candidate is taken into consideration. Experimental research (Nedungadi, 1990) indicates that the brand preference has a larger effect on brand choice within a subcategory than within basic categories. It seems that, as choice criteria become more specific, the consideration set becomes smaller and the strength of the brand association with the desired attribute exerts a larger influence on the inclusion of the brand in this set. In niche marketing, the chances of a brand being selected are thus strongly determined and limited by the relative saliency of the association that functions primarily as subcategory cue.

consideration set can vary strongly, from a very marked preference of one specific brand to more gradual preference for a number of different alternatives. The number of brands that form part of the consideration set has a large influence on the purchasing behaviour. If this is only one brand, probably all purchases concentrate on that one brand. This happens in products in which there is taste habituation, like cigarettes and roll-your-own tobacco. If the consideration set consists of a larger number of brands, the purchases will be distributed across it, depending on relative preference levels and situational variables. The larger the scope of the consideration set, the smaller the chance the individual brand within this set has of being bought. It is a misconception to think that this consideration set includes all the brands towards which consumers have a positive attitude. People buy products on a daily basis without thinking much about it: this is low involvement (see sections 3.8 and 8.2). The attitudes with regard to the brands in such product categories can be called more neutral than positive. Still, consumers develop a preference for a number of brands. This phenomenon can be explained by the fact that certain brands are larger than others and are thus more prominently present in the surroundings of a consumer. The brand for which someone develops a preference is just the first brand that comes to mind. More research would be necessary in order to make well founded statements on why people develop preferences.

Another reason why it is a misconception to assume that the consideration set only includes brands people have a positive attitude about is that people allow themselves to be influenced in their purchasing decisions by other people in their surroundings (see section 13.1, page 271). This can be seen very clearly in certain consumer groups. For instance, schoolchildren buy brands under pressure from their peers. They buy Palladiums in order to be accepted, even though they think the shoes are ugly and too expensive.

13.3   Influencing the brand attitude

A lot of research has been done into the possibility of influencing attitudes. Classical research on attitude changes has focused mainly on which information message had the greatest chances of changing an attitude. Factors such as the credibility of the source of the message, the clarity of the information and the attention of the recipient to the information have been extensively researched (Van der Pligt and De Vries, 1991). For example, it has been shown that the chances of attitude change are greater when the source comes across as being an expert (e.g. a doctor), if the information is clear, and if there is a successful attempt at attracting the attention of the recipient (e.g. with catchy music). It is also important for the information to be found appealing by the recipient: he should feel involved in the subject. More recent research focuses mainly on the role of information processing in attitude changes. A frequently quoted example of such research is the Elaboration Likelihood Model of Petty and Cacioppo (1986) and the Heuristic–Systematic Model of Chaiken *et al.* (1989) derived from it.

The advertising literature regularly makes a distinction between attitude with regard to advertisements (AAD: 'attitude towards the ad') and attitude with regard to the advertised brand (AB: 'attitude towards the brand'). A positive attitude with regard to an advertisement is also called 'likeability'. It is a reaction towards the contents of an advertisement as well as towards its form and execution. Research has shown that a positive AAD influences advertisement effectiveness in the short as well as the long term. Likeability is not just 'fun'. Usefulness and personal relevance are the most important reasons for likeability. An advertisement is valued if it is informative, credible and convincing, and fits the personal needs and interests of the recipient. The entertainment factor is also important to likeability. Advertisement appreciation seems to be especially important to the advertising reach. There are indications that likeability contributes to influencing the choice, but it is not a strong indication of it (Franzen, 1992; Goessens, 1995). 'Attitude towards the ad' would have an influence on 'attitude towards the brand' via classical conditioning. However, both psychological and market research teach us that user experience is more important: positive user experience leads to a positive attitude towards the brand. The influence of behaviour on the brand attitude will be discussed further in the following chapter, which deals with brand behavioural tendency.

Attitudes with regard to a brand arise mainly from user experience with that brand.

Chapter 14

Brand Behavioural Tendencies

14.1 Habits

A lot of purchasing behaviour, especially for low involvement products, has the character of a habitual action. We go into a supermarket and get all kinds of packages, bottles and tins from the shelves without thinking much about them. This usually involves products that we have already been using for a long time and buy regularly, and brands we have known for a long time. The question is now: to what degree are we still dealing with conscious choice processes or with displayed behaviour which is embedded in our memory as such?

Since Pavlov and Thorndike (Baddeley, 1990) we have been familiar with conditioning mechanisms. Their basic principle is that the association between a stimulus and a response that is followed by a reward is strengthened. This reward can be of a material (money) or a mental (enjoyment) nature. Baddeley (1990) posits that there are at least two types of long-term learning processes. One of them is about processes in which there is conscious reflection, for which information is processed and which are under the influence of free will and choice strategies. The other would be 'implicit', taking place outside our consciousness in a completely automatic mode. The development of habits is a learning process that takes place in a different area of the brain from that in which there is information processing. This takes place outside the hippocampus and the amygdala (Mishkin and Appenzeller, 1987). It is non-cognitive and not based on knowledge or memories, but on the emergence of autonomous connections between a stimulus and a response.

Responses emanate partially from an initial phase in which the behaviour was the result of a conscious choice process. In these earlier phases the alternatives were evaluated in the light of personal goals and choice criteria. Several brands were often tried in this phase. But with the increase in experience the cognitive effort simultaneously decreases, ultimately resulting in a constant repetition of the previous behaviour. We no longer have to think about what to choose: the action has been automated. We can reserve our cognitive capacities for other (more important) issues. Another explanation for the emergence of habits is that they do not emanate from an earlier phase in which information was intently processed, but from a phase in which there was random behaviour. People need something and make an arbitrary choice from the available supply. When the resulting experiences are not negative, the same behaviour is repeated. The exposed repetition, followed by satisfying user experiences, leads to the emergence of a habit.

Habits are autonomous connections between a stimulus (brand) and a behavioural response. They are the result of increasing experience, following which the cognitive effort decreases and the behaviour becomes automated.

The implication of the emergence of a habit is that, after some time, its origin cannot be traced. Many beer drinkers drink the same brand their whole life. If we asked them on their fortieth birthday about their purchasing behaviour and their brand perceptions, in order to trace why they choose that specific brand and not a different one, we would seldom get satisfying results. We are a good twenty years too late with our research! An analysis into the connection between purchasing behaviour and underlying variables for beer brands in the Netherlands led to the conclusion that the brand choice was most frequently explained by these variables:

- I am very loyal to this brand
- This brand satisfies my wishes
- The hierarchy of spontaneous brand awareness.

These associations clearly do not constitute the basis of the behaviour: they emanate from it! They are indicators of the brand choice, but do not explain it.

Van Westendorp (1996) posits that a large part of purchasing behaviour can be attributed to 'habitual behaviour'. This is acquired behaviour within which this learning will usually have no intentional character, but happens via the indicated conditioning processes. Once acquired, and given a certain stimulus situation, the behaviour happens automatically and with a low consciousness level. Wherever habits have emerged via learning processes, the behaviour will emerge as a habit if the perception of the stimulus situation (the supermarket shelf or the consumer's changed motivation) gives no reason to reinterpret the meanings. At any rate, it is possible for habits to have an autonomous motivating meaning. We begin to use brands because they appeal to us in one way or another; this is followed by habit forming, which in turn leads to an appreciation of the brands used.

We can analyse brands in our memory theoretically, but we have to remain aware of the fact that everything is interrelated. Behavioural tendencies, in the sense of acquired purchasing habits, are among the most important

The automaticity of everyday life (Bargh, 1997)

Automaticity pervades everyday life, playing an important role in creating the psychological situation from which subjective experience and subsequent conscious and intentional processes originate. Our perceptions, evaluations, and the goals we pursue can and do come under environmental control. Because these perceptual interpretations, likes and dislikes, and reasons for our behaviour are not consciously experienced, we make sense of them in terms of those aspects of which we are consciously aware, and our theories as to what would have caused us to feel or act that way (...).

Our understandings of what cause us to think, feel, and do are in large part after-the-fact rationalisations. As Gazzaniga argued, consciousness may exist in order for us to make sense and a coherent pattern out of all of it, so that we feel a sense of stability and control. (...).

I emphatically emphasise the point that automatic, nonconscious processes pervade all aspects of mental and social life, in order to overcome what I consider dominant, even implicit, assumptions to the contrary. But in making the case, *pace* Skinner, that even goal-directed, complex social behaviour need not require conscious cognitive choice processes, something must be said about the conditions under which nonconsciousness control is believed to occur, and exactly how unnecessary I am claiming consciousness to be (...).

In my opinion, it was the serial stage model in which conscious judgement and reasoning processes were assumed to follow perception and precede responses to the environment that caused us to overestimate the mediational role of conscious processes. This meta-assumption put conscious recognition and reasoning processes as a causally prior stage, almost as a roadblock in the way of affective reactions and behavioural responses (...).

The most fundamental change in psychology since the 1960s has been a movement away from the serial stage of cognition, in which conscious judgement and reasoning processes were assumed to follow perception and precede affective reactions and behavioural response (...). In the present parallel models there is no theoretical *a priori* requirement for conscious processes to mediate the perceptual, evaluative, or behavioural effect, as there was in the serial stage models of the 1960s (...). We now know that much of attributional judgement is spontaneous, unintended and nonconscious. Whereas evaluative judgements were once thought to be computed consciously based on a consideration of recognised stimulus features, Zajonc (1980) argued, and later research verified, that affective reactions can be prior to, more immediate, and independent of even the most basic conscious processes such as recognition of the stimulus. And now, as research demonstrates, even intentions and goals, and the cognitions and behaviours that are carried out in pursuit of those goals, can become automated and bypass conscious choice and guidance.

components of the total association brand network in our memory. Here we would like to emphasise the difference between behavioural *tendency* and behavioural *intention*. In brand research the question is often asked which brand, or brands, people are planning to buy in the following purchase in a category. The code word for this is 'purchasing intention', but the concept of 'intention' points to a resolution, a mentally taken decision to do something, and that rarely happens. It may happen with important choices that involve larger risks and that entail going through a whole decision process. But, by far, in most purchases we deal with *tendencies*: acquired tendencies to display a repeated behaviour which involve no conscious resolution. Analyses of purchasing *intention* scores in relation to actual purchases indicate that brand choice behaviour is more strongly related to the purchasing behaviour in the past (tendencies) than to 'purchasing' in the future (intentions).

14.2　The brand repertoire

In many markets people alternate between two, three or four brands with a certain regularity. In some markets, the number of brands the consumer uses is even larger, and multiple brand behaviour is the rule. Snacks are an example of a market in which consumers are tuned into trying new possibilities again and again. Trial purchases are easier to realise, but individual brands will always constitute a small part of a consumer's purchases in that category. On the other hand, in other markets consumers gravitate towards one main brand which also constitutes a large part of their individual purchases. Cigarettes, razors and sanitary towels/tampons are examples of this. These are usually products in which a strong sensory habituation (taste, feeling) plays a role. In these markets it is very difficult for new brands to realise trial, because there is a strong preferential relationship between the consumer and his or her current brand. If the marketer knows how to make the consumer try the new brand just once, chances are he will still fall back upon his old brand afterwards. The results of the BASIS research show that, on average, only 50% of first trial buyers make a second purchase, and only 50% of second trial buyers make a third purchase.

In most markets, consumers form what is known as the 'brand repertoire', a collection of brands within a product category over which they spread their purchases over time. A brand repertoire is related to the previously discussed consideration set, but it is not the same thing. The consideration set is a mental response, and the brand repertoire, conversely, points to a behavioural pattern. Jones (1995) gives an overview of the scope of the brand repertoire over several product categories (measured over one year) (Table 14.1).

Table 14.1   Brand repertoire for several product categories (United States, 1991).

Product categories	One brand	Two brands	Three or more brands
Laundry detergents	33	24	43
Bath soap	30	25	45
Shampoo	33	24	43
Tissues	18	16	66
Ice cream	31	28	41
Mayonnaise	55	31	14
Peanut butter	48	30	22
Ground coffee	32	22	46
Breakfast cereals	6	7	87
Pain killers	43	29	28

Source: Jones, 1995.

Measured over these ten categories, 43.5% of consumers alternate their purchasing between three or more brands; 33% buy only one brand. This second group consists of two sub-groups:

(1) Consumers who make very few purchases in the category and have therefore less opportunity to alternate between purchasing several brands
(2) Consumers who have a strong preference for one brand, and who even tend to postpone their purchase when 'their' brand is not available.

The first sub-group, the light buyers in the category, form the largest 'part' of the '100% loyal buyers'. This is illustrated in Table 14.2 for the category of laundry detergents (Jones, 1995).

The 'heavy buyers' in the category of laundry detergents are mainly consumers who alternate between buying six or more brands.

A study by MRCA on 27 product categories showed that the number of brands that is bought in alternating fashion by the medium–heavy and heavy category of buyers averages 3.9, and as many as 5.7 with heavy buyers

Table 14.2   Scope of the repertoire with share in category.

	Share in total buyers (%)	Share in sold category volume (%)
One brand	33	18
Two brands	24	20
Three brands	14	16
Four brands	11	13
Five brands	6	10
Six or more brands	12	23

Source: Jones, 1995

(Hallberg, 1995). This corresponds globally with the analyses of Jones, as the previous laundry detergents example shows.

> The 100% brand-loyal buyers are predominantly light buyers in a category, who therefore have fewer opportunities to alternate between buying several brands. 'Heavy' category buyers usually alternate between buying many brands.

Although the research done by Jones (1995) and Hallberg (1995) has broken new ground, it has an important shortcoming. Their research (as well as that of Ehrenberg, which will be discussed later in this chapter) registers behaviour by household and not by individual consumer. The fact that several brands of shampoo are bought in each household can be explained by the different wishes of the individual family members: father wants Head and Shoulders because he has dandruff, mother wants an expensive brand for her permed hair, and they buy Johnson's for the baby. In the laundry detergents market, buying several brands can even be explained for individual consumers: someone buys Dreft for the delicate wash, Persil Colour for the coloured wash and Ariel for whites.

The share represented by a brand in all the purchases of the individual consumer within a product category during a certain period is called the 'share of customer' or 'share of requirements'. The 'share of customer' can show various gradations. Buyers of a brand can generally be classified into one of three classes on the basis of their 'share of customer':

- The 'low loyals' with a share of customer lower than 20%
- The 'medium loyals' with a share of customer between 20 and 50%
- The 'high loyals' with a share of customer larger than 50%.

In an average brand (within the category of fast moving consumer goods), the share of customer amounts to an average of 25–30%. For heavy buyers in a category in the United States it is only 18% (Hallberg, 1995).

An analysis of sixty brands in the United States (Baldinger and Rubinson, 1996) showed that there is an almost perfect correlation between the percentage of 'high loyals' and the market share of a brand. In larger brands they were responsible for 80% of the volume, in smaller brands 56% (Figure 14.1).

> The 'share of customer' of the average brand in the category of fast moving consumer goods is 25 to 30%.

On the basis of purchasing behaviour research done over a period of more than 30 years in more than 50 different product categories and in several countries, Ehrenberg and Uncles (1995) have shown that the frequency with which people buy a brand appears to be strongly habitual. Table 14.3 gives an

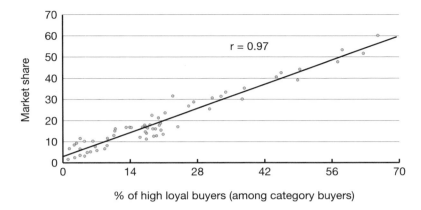

% of high loyal buyers (among category buyers)

Figure 14.1 Market share vs. loyalty (Baldinger and Rubinson, 1996).

overview of a number of average scores (yearly averages over 5–10 largest brands in twelve categories in four countries).

Although these purchasing patterns differ from individual to individual and from household to household, the aggregated behaviour of all buyers together at a market level shows a picture that responds to the same patterns for

Table 14.3 Average score of brands.

Category/country/year	Average penetration (%)	One-time buyers (%)	100%-Brand loyal (%)	Duplicates the brand (% who also bought)		
				Largest (%)	3rd (%)	5th (%)
Toothpaste, Germany, 1990	38	37	16	58	40	19
Gasoline, UK, 1990	34	34	0	62	48	51
Toothpaste, Japan, 1983	28	52	7	67	34	10
Cereals, UK, 1968	27	24	12	74	11	15
Orange juice, USA, 1984	26	49	17	59	35	10
Liquid laundry detergents, Japan, 1983	24	57	15	46	31	28
Paper towels, USA, 1992	23	54	4	55	46	43
Laundry detergents, Germany, 1990	20	48	16	32	27	10
Cleaning products, UK, 1988	14	61	14	44	37	7
Cheese, UK, 1988	12	54	12	42	28	20
Beer for home consumption, UK, 1992	10	56	10	19	13	11
Paper towels, UK, 1988	8	52	19	40	11	12
Average	22	49	12	50	31	20

Source: Ehrenberg and Uncles, 1995.

different products and brands. This applies particularly to markets that are in equilibrium and in which market shares remain stable during approximately one year. It does not just apply to what is known as 'fast moving consumer goods', but also to contrasting categories like medicines, choice of shops, choice of television programmes, petrol and cosmetics. We establish the same patterns even when we analyse the purchasing of automobile brands over longer periods.

The purchasing patterns in all these markets can be described as follows (Ehrenberg and Uncles, 1995; 1999):

(1) The numbers of consumers who buy a certain brand within a certain period, e.g. one year, vary from brand to brand. We can also say that the penetration of various brands varies.
(2) There is a strong correlation between this penetration and the market shares of the brands.
(3) The average frequency with which the various brands are purchased by their buyers is close together. On average, large brands are purchased more frequently than small brands, but the difference is not large (this is the 'double jeopardy' or 'double risk' phenomenon: small brands are bought by fewer people who also buy them less often).
(4) Large brands are thus large because they have many buyers and are, on average, purchased slightly more often by those buyers.
(5) Most buyers of a brand buy it infrequently.
(6) The number of buyers who purchase a brand increases with the length of the period being measured. The penetration therefore depends on the length of time over which measuring is done.
(7) The average number of repeated purchases measured from quarter to quarter is relatively low, but measured from brand to brand is close together.
(8) From a global perspective, repeated purchasing levels are stable through time. This means that individual consumers show stable purchasing patterns.
(9) The average amount spent per purchase does not differ much from brand to brand.

These patterns are illustrated by the example in Table 14.4 from the instant coffee market in the United States (Ehrenberg and Uncles, 1999).

The 'patterns' that emerged from the research of Ehrenberg and Uncles seem to be applicable mainly to short-term market development. They do not explain as yet how it is that, in markets that appear stable in the short term (like the Dutch beer market), the share development over the long term (measured over twenty years) is enormous.

Their proposition of 'brand loyalty' emanating from penetration, with a double-jeopardy correction, is also somewhat controversial. Baldinger and

Table 14.4   The instant coffee market (USA, per year) (1981).

	Market share	Penetration	Average number*		Share per consumer
			Of the brand	Of all brands	
All brands	100%	67%	–	7	–
Maxwell House	19	24	3.6	9	40
Sanka	15	21	3.3	9	37
Tasters Choice	14	22	2.8	9	31
High Point	13	22	2.6	8	32
Folgers	11	18	2.7	9	30
Nescafé	8	13	2.9	11	26
Brim	4	9	2.0	9	22
Maxim	3	6	2.6	11	24
Other brands	13	20	3.0	9	33
Average brand	11	17	2.8	9	31

* per buyer of the brand

Rubinson (1996) establish in an analysis of 117 brands that the penetration of a brand explains about 50–66% of the variance in the share of customer in a product category. This may support the double-jeopardy pattern. At the same time, they conclude that the share of customer contributes independently to the market share and that this contribution increases to the extent the market share is higher (Figure 14.2).

Large brands are large because they have many buyers and they buy more often. The penetration is the most important variable behind the market share. The purchasing frequency plays a subordinate role.

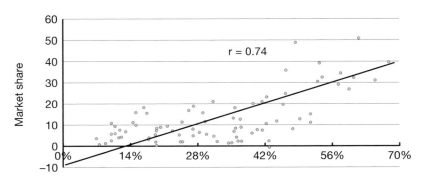

Figure 14.2   Ratio of share of requirements and market share (Baldinger and Rubinson, 1996).

Seen over a longer period, there are not many buyers with 100% brand loyalty. Most buyers of a certain brand tend to buy other brands as well. Seen over several product categories and several brands, these individual purchasing patterns also show great similarities. The degree to which buyers of brand A also buy brand B is a function of the penetration of brand B. Or, since penetration and market share are very much closely linked, of the market share of brand B.

In section 14.3 we give an example of the duplication of brand purchases in the American instant coffee market. We should point out, though, that purchasing behaviour is the result of demand as well as the supply. The degree to which and the quality with which brands are present in the purchasing location (e.g. the height at which they are placed in the shelves) have an equally large influence on the ultimate purchasing behaviour. In marketing slang, we are dealing with a 'push-and-pull' process.

14.3   Duplication of brand purchases

Deviations from the general pattern shown in Table 14.5 reflect the existence of certain specific subcategories. When products are bought for specific purposes (e.g. herbal tea for sleeping goes next to black tea for the daytime), brands in this subcategory can show high duplication levels with the 'large' brands. When brands are hardly differentiated at a product level (Coca-Cola and Pepsi Cola, Amstel beer and Bavaria beer), we also see that the markets are hardly segmented. In other words, there is little difference in the composition of buyers' groups of the different brands. The buyers who are 100% brand-loyal are generally the very light users in the product category.

These general patterns indicate that the performance of a brand in the market in terms of penetration, purchasing frequency, repeated purchases and purchasing duplication with other brands largely reflects the effect of one single factor. Ehrenberg believes that this factor is the market share of a brand. This would make the market share the explanatory factor of all brand performance instead of the result of other marketing factors. It is not surprising that marketing people have great trouble accepting this conclusion. We also believe that the explanation of behavioural patterns should not be sought exclusively in the behaviour itself. After all, the market share is nothing more than a reflection of the aggregated behaviour of all buyers in a category. All 'pull-and-push' variables are reflected in the market share, but at the same time the market share is not everything. Although behaviour can be and is anchored in our memory as such, it is at the same time a component of the total brand associative system, as was previously explained. It is interrelated with all the other components of this system and we think it cannot be seen separately from it. As Ferguson (1989) posited, each variable interacts in a

Table 14.5 Duplication of the American instant coffee market (1981).

Instant coffee	% who also bought							
	Maxwell House	Sanka	Tasters Choice	High Point	Folgers	Nescafé	Brim	Maxim
Buyers of								
Maxwell House	–	32	29	32	38	26	13	13
Sanka	36	–	32	40	25	23	20	11
Tasters Choice	31	32	–	36	28	20	17	14
High Point	34	38	34	–	31	22	18	10
Folgers	51	30	35	40	–	25	15	11
Nescafé	48	39	34	40	34	–	15	8
Brim	33	45	39	44	27	20	–	16
Maxim	52	38	51	39	34	17	25	–
Average	41	36	36	39	31	22	17	12

Source: Ehrenberg and Uncles, 1995

The process theory of brand choice (Stephan and Tannenholz, 1994)

(1) The experience a consumer receives from using a brand solidifies her perceptions of it. These fixed perceptions can rarely be changed through advertising alone.

(2) How a consumer perceives each of the different brands in a category determines which ones are used and which ones are not. The consumer may perceive different brands to be superior on different desirable attributes and this results in her switching around within a set of brands rather than using a single brand.

(3) When a consumer uses a set of brands, her fluctuating wants and desires are what cause her to switch from one brand to another.

(4) In many categories, brand use itself is what causes a consumer's desire to fluctuate. The consumer may temporarily satisfy certain desires by using one brand but deprive herself of other satisfactions she could have received from a competing brand.

(5) As consumers' desires fluctuate relative to their fixed perceptions of brands, a consistent process of brand choice (brand switching) results over time.

Contd

(6) Advertising and promotion intervene in the process of brand choice by temporarily changing the probability of a user purchasing the brand the next time the category is on the shopping list.

- Advertising intervenes by temporarily intensifying the consumer's desire for some benefit the brand is already perceived to provide.
- Price promotion intervenes by temporarily changing the perception of price/value.

(7) New brands, line extensions, product improvements, disequilibrium price changes and restages of existing brands change consumers' perceptions and permanently alter the process of brand choice (the probabilities of brands being selected) for some category users.

(8) It is the fate of most brands that their own advertising will never improve users' perceptions, but instead that new competitors will diminish these perceptions over time.

Currently, an advertising strategy that has successfully positioned a new brand is then expected to improve that position over time. Since this is rarely possible, most advertising for established brands produces relatively low persuasion scores, and the advertising on behalf of one brand tends to be offset by its competitors. New brands quickly settle into a market share pecking order with the competition and rarely move up, as advertising is asked to accomplish the irrelevant goal of improving perceptions. Not only do established brands rarely improve their market share – unless the product is reformulated – the average brand actually loses about a third of a share point each year to new entries. Advertising for an established brand, particularly a well differentiated one, will be much more effective if it exploits the brand's positioning. Specifically, advertising should exploit the important elements of positioning that differentiate the brand from competing brands in a set. For example, if consumers use a brand of toothpaste to prevent decay, and some of these consumers also use other brands for other reasons, advertising alone will not improve perceptions of the brand's decay-fighting ability, but it can and should make decay prevention more important.

The key to more effective advertising is to understand exactly what it is about your brand that is both differentiating and important to current users. Often the driving elements of a brand's positioning are not what marketers assume.

system with the other variables in such a way that cause and effect cannot be separated. A certain variable can simultaneously be cause and effect. Marketing people, and certainly the communication specialists among them, tend to see brand awareness and brand image as the causes of a brand's market position. They have the greatest trouble not thinking in these terms of cause/effect relationships, as well as wanting to see patterns in the displayed purchasing behaviour, as exposed particularly by Ehrenberg, as pure 'habitual actions'. All the same, we cannot ignore these facts. We should not look for the explanatory factor in the market share, as Ehrenberg does on the basis of the purely statistical connections that he found, but in the total representation that the brand has acquired for itself in the course of its history in the memory of its users. There is not a single component that explains the rest. The fact that it is extremely difficult and probably impossible to prove this statistically, e.g. in the form of scores or research questions, is something different altogether. That has to do with the complexity of human memory, which we can approach analytically, but cannot separate and certainly cannot represent with one single factor (the market share).

14.4 Market laws

14.4.1 *The double-jeopardy phenomenon*

Large brands are large because they have more buyers who also purchase the brand slightly more often. Small brands are small because they have fewer buyers who also purchase the brand less often. The theoretical explanation for preventing this double-jeopardy phenomenon is the asymmetry in the awareness of or the exposure to issues (such as products and brands) that are equal, but that differ in popularity. The following example will clarify this. Imagine there are two restaurants in the village. One restaurant, A, is well known and the second restaurant, B, is only known by some of the villagers. When people ask the inhabitants of the village which restaurant they prefer, most inhabitants who know A but not B will name A as their favourite. Those who also know B but think A and B are equally good will distribute their preference evenly. This will result in a greater popularity of A and a lesser popularity of B: double-jeopardy – the small restaurant is less well known and gets relatively fewer preferential votes.

This phenomenon happens in all brands in all product categories. Brand articles in a stabilised market hardly differ from each other on a functional basis. Only connoisseurs will taste the difference between, for example, Heineken and Carlsberg beers, between Coca-Cola and Pepsi, between Spa and Perrier, and between a cup of Douwe Egberts and a cup of Maxwell House. Still, there are differences in sales and it is assumed that some brands are stronger than others. Ehrenberg thinks that this is not the case. Some brands are just popular and have a large market share. Brands are mainly large and small, and as a result of this double-jeopardy effect the large brands register a little more success in measurements on purchasing behaviour, brand loyalty and attitude than the small brands.

14.4.2 *The Dirichlet formula*

The systematic connection between penetration, purchasing frequency, duplication with purchasing of other brands and market share is expressed in what is known as the Dirichlet formula. This is a mathematical formula with which predictions can be made on the average purchasing frequency of a brand and the duplication with other brands on the basis of that brand's market share. Next to knowledge of the market share, numerical data are needed for:

- The number of households that bought the product type in a year
- The average purchasing frequency of the product type
- The number of brands that is bought on average per household.

There seems to be a correlation larger than 0.9 between the predicted purchasing frequency of a brand and the purchasing frequency observed in the market.

The predominant importance of penetration

The Dirichlet formula shows that, given the market share of a brand, reliable predictions can be made on the penetration and purchasing frequency of that brand. As a result, the sales of a brand depend largely on the penetration of the brand. There is a brand-loyal purchasing behaviour, but it also shows the 'double-jeopardy' traits: the purchasing frequency in large brands is slightly higher than in smaller brands. There are exceptions to this (see e.g. Dowling and Uncles, 1997), but they really are exceptions (Figure 14.3). These are:

(1) *Super-loyalty brands:* some large brands that have more highly loyal users than predicted by Dirichlet
(2) *Niche brands:* brands that answer to very specific expectations of smaller buyer segments and realise higher purchasing frequencies in them
(3) *Variation brands:* brands that are bought for specific situations or moments, like alcohol-free beer. They show a much lower purchasing frequency than that predicted by Dirichlet.

These three types of brands appear a lot less frequently than the 'regular' large and small brands, which do respond to the Dirichlet patterns. An increase in the penetration is the most effective way of allowing a brand to grow. The

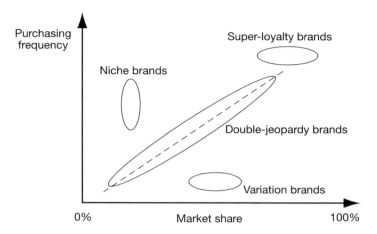

Figure 14.3 Double-jeopardy and brand loyalty (Dowling and Uncles, 1997).

connection between penetration and market share is shown in Figure 14.4, based on an analysis by Jones (1995) of the sale of 142 brands in the United States over a period of one year. Penetration and market share increase together, the connection becoming stronger as the penetration grows. This is the result of the double-jeopardy phenomenon, in which higher penetration is also linked to a higher purchasing frequency.

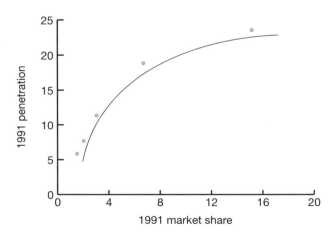

Figure 14.4 The connection between market share and penetration (Jones, 1995).

14.5 The connection between brand attitude and brand loyalty

The concept of brand loyalty can lead to misunderstandings because of the mental state and the type of behaviour it involves. The Van Dale Dutch dictionary gives the following definition of 'loyal' (the Dutch word is 'trouw'): 'keeping to an existing moral, personal bond, a joined pact, and not yielding in it'. Webster defines it as 'faithful and devoted to a person or a cause to whom fidelity is held to be due', and 'unswerving in allegiance'. Its mental component is synonymous with commitment – the state or an instance of being obligated or emotionally impelled.

The question many people have is to what degree repeated purchases of brands can be traced back to an underlying bonding, or whether they are pure habitual actions. In other words: to what degree is there a 'real brand loyalty'? And to the degree that it exists, how durable is the behavioural component? How steadfast are consumers with regard to their loyalty to brands? And can brand loyalty be predicted from the brand attitude?

Baldinger and Rubinson (1996) have done research in order to be able to give an answer to the last question. We should say beforehand that they are not clear about how they operationalise the brand attitude. In order to make well founded statements about the relationship between brand attitude and brand loyalty, panel research is needed in which all brand purchases in a category are recorded over a reasonably long period of time (at least one year), performing periodical attitude measurements with the same sample.[10] This leads to a matrix in which buyers of a brand are segmented into both traits. Baldinger and Rubinson report on such a panel research and its corresponding analysis, carried out in the United States for 27 brands of fast-moving consumer goods. The buyers were classified into three classes according to behaviour (low, medium and high loyals) and attitude (strong, medium and weak). This resulted in a 3 × 3 matrix with nine segments (see Figure 14.5).

This shows a strong correlation between behaviour and attitude: of the buyers with a weak attitude (74%), only 1% showed a high brand loyalty. Of the buyers with a strong attitude (12%), three-quarters (9%) showed a high brand loyalty. At the same time, it seems that 85% of the buyers of the average brand had a weak or medium attitude towards the brand and low-to-medium brand loyalty purchasing behaviour!

The durability of the brand loyalty did not prove to be very high either. The next matrix (Figure 14.6) gives the percentage of buyers in each of the segments who are still in the same segment after one year. Of all the buyers

---

10 If you want to have data on purchasing behaviour, it is better to record this than to ask respondents about it. Respondents in a research situation regularly say they buy certain brands, when in reality they do not. This may have to do with the fact that they do not know exactly which brands they buy, or because the researcher asks leading questions.

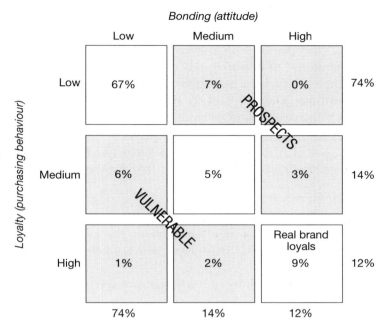

Figure 14.5 Relationship between attitude and loyalty.

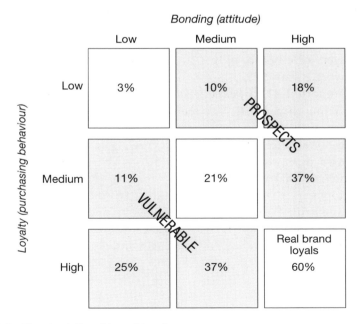

Figure 14.6 The durability of brand loyalty.

with a high brand loyalty, only 53% repeatedly showed a share of customer larger than 50% after one year. Only 60% of the 'real loyals' (strong bonding with a brand in combination with a share of customer larger than 50%) in the first year appeared still to belong to this category in the second year; in 40% of this group there was a reduction either in the strength of the bonding or in the share of customer. Only 37% of the high loyals (share of customer larger than 50%) with an average attitude were still high loyals in the second year.

Only 9% of users of an average brand have a high bonding that goes together with high brand loyalty purchasing behaviour. This situation is not very stable over time.

Finally, the study attempted to discover to what degree developments in attitudes were predictors for developments in the market shares of the researched brands. To this end, two subgroups were followed:

(1) Prospects: the buyers whose attitude was stronger than the behavioural loyalty
(2) Vulnerable: the buyers whose attitude was weaker than the purchasing loyalty.

The range of both groups seemed to be 10–11%. The ratio between these two groups appeared to correspond with the development of the market share in two-thirds of the researched brands. When looking at this as a whole, the main conclusions are that:

• Of all buyers of a brand, only a small proportion (12%) show a share of customer larger than 50%
• A small proportion (12%) experience a high commitment to the brand
• A strong connection exists between the following: three-quarters (9%) of these buyers seem to be truly 'brand loyal', at least at the time the research was being done. After all, of all the 'high loyals', only 53% showed after a year a share of customer larger than 50%! The durability of the brand loyalty thus proved to be relative
• The development in the attitude in two thirds of the brands correlated with the development of the purchasing behaviour and, as a result of it, the market share as well. There is a two-sided causal relationship between them: purchasing behaviour and attitude mutually influence one another.

Chapter 15
Brand Relationships

15.1   Introduction

'Relationships' seems to be the magic word of recent years. One cannot open a marketing book or attend a congress without there being a discussion on relationship management or relationships that should arise between consumer and brand. One regularly hears and reads about agencies being started that specialise in relationship marketing and organising 'brand events'. There is also a group of publicists who use the laws of quantum physics to explain that our whole existence is the sum of a countless number of relationships. They even go so far as to posit that people do not exist without relationships: 'in relationships we define our personality and our identity' (Geursen, 1998). In a comparable manner, a brand would only exist thanks to its relationships (Geursen, 1994, 1998).

This chapter will focus on the phenomenon of relationships. Most knowledge on relationships comes from psychology and natural sciences. In the next two sections we will describe relationships from the perspective of these two disciplines, after which we will go back to brands.

15.2   The psychology of a relationship

> I am cast upon a horrible, desolate island; void of all hope of recovery. I am singled out and separated, as it were, from all the world, to be miserable. I am divided from mankind, a solitary; one banished from human society. I have no soul to speak to or to relieve me. (Daniel Defoe, 1908, in *Robinson Crusoe*)

Many psychology books on relationships begin with this quote from Robinson Crusoe (e.g. Hinde, 1997, Forsyth, 1990). Apparently, man is a social animal who depends on other people to satisfy many of his most basic needs in the area of survival (babies need other people to get food), psychology (people need contact and love), information (they need others to learn how they should behave in certain situations), interpersonal goals (people need each other's support) and common goals (people need each other when they want to accomplish a 'large' goal) (Forsyth, 1990). In other words, people enter relationships for all kinds of reasons. But what is a relationship? People do not seem to be able to agree on one definition. Participants in a relationship experience and interpret a relationship differently from outsiders (Hinde, 1997). And then there is the problem of the boundaries of a relationship; do we have a relationship with, say, the people we run into at the bus stop daily? Do we have a relationship with people we know from television? According to Hinde, every relationship consists of the following components – interaction, communication, reciprocity and continuity.

15.2.1 *Interaction*

Hinde believes a relationship is a series of interactions between two individuals who know each other and in which each interaction from the series can be influenced by previous interactions between the participants and by expectations over the interactions in the future. It is important that the interactions really take place in the past or future, but equally important are the feelings and emotions that these interactions invoke and the meaning given to them. Hinde also believes that, because of the constant reciprocity of various interactions within one relationship and the influence of all these interactions on each other and therefore the nature of the relationship, we cannot interpret a relationship as a static entity but as a process. In interactions a distinction can be made between nature and quality. The nature of interactions can be used to distinguish various types of relationships and say something about the strength of a relationship. Solid relationships are characterised by a large diversity of interactions through which more aspects of the participants are revealed. The quality of the interaction depends on the perceptions of the relationship partners. Verbal expression and non-verbal signals are the most important indicators of this quality.

15.2.2 *Communication (dominance and affinity)*

Relationships cannot exist without communication. As soon as at least two people are connected and a message is sent from one to the other, there is communication. Whether this message is intentional or not is not important (Drost, 1996). There are three communication channels: the verbal, the non-verbal and the paralingual. The verbal channel is used to send messages. Paralingual messages, such as sentence intonation, pitch and hesitation, are produced with the organs of speech, but are not verbal. Non-verbal messages are actually the most interesting, not only because of the nature of the messages, which are mainly related to interpersonal emotions and values, but also and especially because they form a leakage channel. The non-verbal channel is the one we are least in control of, thanks to which a lot escapes the sender's attention. In an interaction situation, people constantly send communication messages. Some of these messages are content-related in their nature and point to the outside world. The outside world consists of objects and issues that are not related to the relationship between those interacting. The messages that do relate to them are the relational ones. Content-related messages may or may not be sent at will, but relational messages are always sent out, willingly or not, thus making it impossible not to communicate. Simply said, there are two types of relational messages: messages to negotiate over power relationships and messages to indicate whether you like or dislike someone.

Negotiating power relationships

An essential need of people is to have a certain degree of control over the world around them (and the objects, events and persons in this world), thanks to which it becomes more orderly and predictable. For this reason, the relationship messages between two interaction partners indicate the control they want to have over their interaction partner. Examples of relationship messages are 'Open the window!', 'Can I be of any assistance?', 'Get lost!', 'Do you mind if I sit next to you?', 'Do you want to marry me?'. The relationship proposal can only be understood by interpreting it as a whole and not as a sum of loose elements, since it involves a combination of communication channels.

Power relationships are complementary: if one person is the boss, his interaction partner will be the subordinate. Because one person's increase of control irrevocably leads to loss of control for the other, this forms a solid basis for conflicts (Drost, 1996). The way in which people deal with conflicts can vary strongly; some people always remain loyal to their partner, others tend to break the relationship or talk about the problem. A conflict does not necessarily have to be bad for a relationship; it is often even necessary to renegotiate on power relationships.

Affinity

As a comparison to the relational messages concerning the distribution of control, we can look at what sent messages have to say about the emotions of the sender with regard to the other and the relationship – the affinity. Affinity is the generic term for emotions that are related to the 'other'. Affinity can be interpreted as a dimension with a positive and a negative pole. On the positive side there are behaviours that show the person likes the other, is oriented towards the other, has warm feelings and the like. On the other side there are expressions of disapproval, rejection and aggression. As with the need for control, the need for positive affinity is universal and deeply embedded. It is essential for people to be accepted and to be liked. However, sometimes people are threatened and negative affinity is needed as a defence. Unlike the messages related to power relationships, the affinity messages are not of a complementary but of a symmetrical nature. Friendly behaviour incites friendly behaviour and hostile behaviour incites hostile behaviour. Here we can also speak of a negotiation process that precedes the stable condition – a process in which the parties have to arrive at an agreement on whether and how people like each other (Drost, 1996).

Solid relationships in which the partners trust each other sufficiently go together with self-disclosure. Trust can be gained by being perceived as someone who is motivated to put her own interests aside in order to comply with the wishes of the other. By exposing oneself, partners in a relationship build on knowledge about each other and learn to construct a total picture of the other person. This knowledge reaches much further than the common interactions and has the potential of changing future interactions in a fundamental way. Self-disclosure can vary in its breadth and depth. As a relationship develops, each individual reveals more areas to the other and penetration in these areas deepens.

The interaction circle

The dominance and affinity dimensions are united in the interaction circle. The circle is divided equally into eight parts, each with a different combination of dominance and affinity. The intensity of dominance and affinity is expressed by the distance to the middle point. Every relationship message can be placed in the circle (Figure 15.1). The mechanism of complementary and symmetrical forces makes it possible to predict the course of the relationship (Drost, 1996).

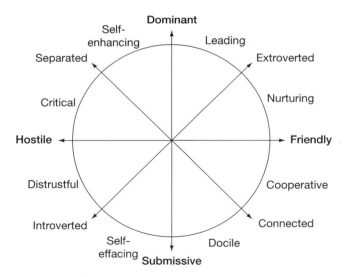

Figure 15.1 The interpersonal circle (Hinde, 1997).

15.2.3 *Reciprocity*

An important characteristic of every relationship is that partners influence each other mutually. On the basis of previous interactions and communication, partners develop an image of each other. This image is connected to feelings and cognitions and makes it possible for expectations to arise about future relationships. The reciprocity manifests itself very clearly in solid relationships. One of the most important aspects of a solid relationship is the degree to which a person is committed to his interaction partner in the relationship. The commitment of one participant in a relationship is largely influenced by his perception of the partner's commitment. Commitment is probably the greatest when an individual is satisfied with the relationship, if he is more dependent on the relationship, if he has made great investments in it, and if the relationship is central to the individual's life (Hinde, 1997).

15.2.4 *Continuity*

Continuity means that a relationship goes further than an isolated meeting or interaction. There is a concatenation of interactions over a longer period of time. Previous interactions influence future interactions and thus the nature and intensity of the relationship.

Every relationship gives expressions to the components: interaction, communication, reciprocity and continuity.

15.3 Quantum theory

The ideas described in this section could be of consequence to the whole book, and even to its existence: followers of quantum theory consider a book too linear. We have chosen to write our book in the 'old style' but, obviously, a chapter on relationships is not complete without a description of quantum theory.

Under the effects of the ideas of Isaac Newton, the seventeenth century saw an end to the matter-of-course power of magic and the Church for explanations on phenomena. Until the Renaissance, the worldview of Western man was determined by Christian belief and Aristotelian philosophy. Newton's thoughts and assertions led to a scientific revolution which naturally resulted in a conflict with the Church. Newton taught us that everything around us goes through mechanical processes. Reality can be described according to these processes and can thus be mastered, controlled and predicted. Newton was not the only one to change the worldview of his times; also in the seventeenth

The apple of Newton (Van Ginneken, 1999)

Just as many other great innovators, Newton was sometimes aware of the limitations of his thinking, but it was mainly his adherents and followers who gradually spread a simplified version of it. According to the simplified version, the universe consists of no more and no less than a collection of bodies between which a few simple forces act. More complicated objects are formed in 'building stones': the whole is no more than the sum of the parts. The building stones or bricks can be imagined as 'things' that have a durable specific form and content, a specific quantity (measurements) and quality (substance). Changes in it are linear: the causes are proportional to the effects. Reciprocity is simple: in principle it is measurable, predictable and controllable. It is the world of cuckoo clocks, steam engines and factories – the world of the early industrial revolution.

century René Descartes published his *Discourse on Method* in which he explained that mathematics can serve as an example of all acquisition of knowledge. Newton adds to this the 'empirical thought': on the basis of mathematics (the rationalistic method) we arrive at hypotheses and these can be tested through careful observation. A belief in objective truth and in the objectivity of science arose thanks to these views. A strict division came about between mind (the observer) and matter (what is observed). The new worldview brought about much progress: it brought us the advantages of medical discoveries, healthy nutrition for everyone in the West, means of transportation and telecommunications equipment (Geursen, 1994).

Around 1900 came a new revolution in the way people looked at the world. Science became increasingly professional, researchers acquired more experience, there was better equipment, and around the middle of the twentieth century, the computer came into the picture. These possibilities, which provided the means of giving better answers to research questions, led to the insight that the world was less predictable than had been thought since the seventeenth century. Great scientists like Einstein, Bohr and Heisenberg taught us, among other things, that the world is different from how we perceive it, and that science is not as objective as it seems. The observer (and thus also the scientific researcher) influences the system she observes as well as her own research results. Mind and matter seem not to be separated at all. The time was ripe for new views and quantum theory was introduced (Bor, Petersma and Kingma, 1995; Wolinsky, 1993).

According to Wolinsky, who wrote a book titled *Quantum Consciousness*, the basis of quantum is formed by two important principles or theories:

(1) *The uncertainty principle of Heisenberg.* In the middle of the 1920s, Heisenberg succeeded in showing that the observer influences the results of a natural experiment because of the choices he makes. The observer observes not only a world 'outside', as Newtonian physicists claimed, but he changes, influences and, according to some physicists, also creates what he sees by means of his observation. In other words, all of reality is created by the observer.

(2) *Einstein's theory of relativity.* Space and time lose their absolute character. Wolinsky (1993) explains that space is not absolute, by saying that everything consists of emptiness, and form is closed emptiness. In other words, everything (the universe and everything in it) is made of the same substance at a micro-level. We observe forms (objects and persons) because the particles this substance consists of are closer together in some places than in others. This is how we perceive people, chairs, water, and so on.

In Part One we saw that a memory of an object, a person or a situation is constantly remade and adapted to new experiences with the object, person or situation. From this we can conclude that the past does not exist: we create the past here and now. This fact has important implications for carrying out and interpreting research: a respondent creates a memory in a research situation (see page 66). The same way, people create their future in the here and now. The future is what you make of it. You have an influence on it. And if you think about the future and report on it, there is a perception that has been constructed here and now. In a similar way, Einstein explains that time has lost its absolute character: there is only present time, while we create the future and the past at this moment.

The idea that time and space lose their absolute character was a great source of inspiration for the artist Piet Mondriaan (Figure 15.2). At the beginning of the twentieth century, the classical, static worldview was gradually pushed aside by the worldview of modern physics. In modern art there was a parallel development: people experienced reality in a completely different way. Mondriaan went so far as to want to 'destroy' three-dimensional space and switch off time (Bor *et al.*, 1995).

The basis of quantum theory is formed by the uncertainty principle of Heisenberg and Einstein's theory of relativity.

Quantum theory and its consequences point us towards the relativity of everything, the influence of the researcher as a participant of that which is being researched, and the sensitivity of mutual connections in large and complex systems. The quantum world teaches us that no previously determined, fixed descriptions can be given of directions in processes. Instead

Figure 15.2 Piet Mondriaan: composition with red, black, blue, yellow and grey.
Source: edition and colour-correction Stedelijk Museum Amsterdam 8 P. Mondriaan 1920 c/o Beeldrecht Amsterdam.

we should speak of potentials or opportunities that can develop into actual ideas, depending on who discovers them and what they want to discover (Geursen, 1994). That the 'world of quantum' cannot be ruled by the daily laws of cause and effect but by probabilities and correlations is made clear below.

Quantum theory has important implications for brands and marketing. Geursen (1998) claims that the way we work and live together is increasingly taking the form of a network society: 'a system full of organisms, mutually connected and evaluating together, in permanent movement, closely interwoven, full of surprises and without a centre or visible outside boundaries [...]. Systems form themselves because the separate components come into contact within a large interactivity, just as people come into contact with each other for various reasons. Because without relationships we do not exist. In relationships we define our personality and identity. In relationships we find

Lorenz's butterfly (Van Ginneken, 1999)

The American Edward Lorenz made a computer model for the weather development of the northern hemisphere. He made a matrix of points, named some values for each of the points (temperature, wind directions, humidity, solar radiation, etc.) and tried to predict how the weather would develop. That was fairly successful, until something went wrong. He had to enter the same data again, but to his surprise the final weather forecast was completely different. Only then did he realise that the second time, because of annoyance and impatience, he had entered a single decimal after the point. These minuscule differences now seemed to lead to radically different results. In a scientific article he compared this with the flapping of the wings of a seagull in one place, which could lead to the unleashing of a storm in a different place. That image caught on, especially when he replaced it in a subsequent lecture by a title with the even more provoking question, 'Can the flapping of the wings of a butterfly in Brazil unchain a tornado in Texas?' The answer was affirmative. The lecture was held at the yearly congress of the American Association for the Advancement of Science, which always gets a lot of publicity. A colleague had already proposed the name 'chaos theory', and the name was a hit. The principle that very small causes can sometimes have very large consequences seemed to be applicable to all kinds of other areas as well, and gradually appeared to be following a very un-Newtonian logic in all kinds of ways.

energy and ideas. We define our lives in the relationships between ourselves and others and between ourselves and the various environments in which we function. We do not end at our bodies – we are our relationships. In a comparable way, a brand also exists only by virtue of its relationships.' A brand is nothing more than something made by the producer, but which forms a network of and for consumers who share a certain interest, problem, challenge, image or dream. The brand becomes a creator of conditions: it creates possibilities for contact. Section 15.4.2 on relationships through brands is all about the brand as creator of conditions for contact opportunities.

A brand becomes a creator of conditions under the influence of quantum philosophy: it creates possibilities for contact between consumers with shared interests, problems, challenges, images or dreams.

15.4 Brand relationships

15.4.1 *Relationships with brands*

A brand relationship is the relationship between a consumer and a brand, and consists of the following components:

(1) Interaction (e.g. practical, emotional and social experiences of use).
(2) Communication (e.g. advertising, consumer reactions to messages of the brands, the communication showing the balance of power – 'who is the expert?' – and how the affinity is understood).
(3) Reciprocity.
(4) Continuity.

Question marks are regularly placed over the existence of relationships between consumers and brands. Experts ask themselves whether such relationships really exist and, if they do, whether they are also present in less prestigious product groups. Langer (1997) carried out extensive research into answering these questions. She came to the conclusion that consumers are less cynical about brands than they appear to be. They respect brands that are able to stay in the market for years and that everyone knows. They trust the 'old time favourites' but also go out looking for 'rising stars'. According to Langer, in the uncertain world of today, brands can even bring an element of continuity into people's lives.

Various researchers believe, just like Langer, that people develop relationships with brands that surround them. Susan Fournier (1994) was one of the first to carry out fundamental research into the question of whether the relationships between person and brand can be defined in the same way as the relationships between two people. Fournier defines a relationship between person and brand as a voluntary or imposed mutual dependency of a person and a brand that is characterised by a unique history of interactions and the anticipation of common events in the future, which has as its goals helping to reach the instrumental and/or social–psychological goals of the partners, and which is characterised by a strengthening emotional bond. Fournier's research shows that the responses of consumers about certain brands show large similarities with what is known from the theories of relationships between people. Acceptance of the concept of relationship within a brand context helps us understand better what brands can mean to consumers. She posits that a brand can become a partner in a relationship, and this implies that it should be possible to personify the brand. A relationship is, in fact, a two-sided connection. The person in the person/brand relationship should be able to imagine that the brand knows him and knows what his wishes and feelings are. The principle of personification was discussed in section 10.6.

Fournier believes that certain product categories show more of a person/brand relationship than others. Her research has shown that there is a stronger need for the comfort and reassurance of a long-term relationship when the consumer experiences great insecurity. The risk feeling plays an important role in its financial, functional and social meaning. She thinks consumers are not so interested in a relationship with brands in a product category such as peas. A small-scale study by Bremer (1996) among clients of Robeco Funds confirmed Fournier's claim that the risk feeling plays an important role in the emergence of relationships. These can be functional and financial risks as well as self-image risks. The larger people perceive the risks to be, the stronger the need for comfort and reassurance that a long-term relationship with a brand can entail. Langer's research (1997) showed that relationships with consumers are not only to be made for the top brands that stand as icons in society and radiate superiority (e.g. Rolex, BMW, Mercedes Benz and Giorgio Armani). Relationships can also emerge between consumers and 'regular' brands like Heinz and Persil. According to Langer, this can be explained by the fact that having a relationship can serve various important intentions for consumers:

- *Practical role:* always returning to the same brand can be a question of habit and convenience.
- *Emotional role:* consumers identify with brands and use them for self-expression and as links to the past.
- *Social role:* of course, brands also make it possible to show others who you are and what you stand for: they are a shorthand communication of who you are.

Customer service, in the broadest sense of the word, can play a crucial role in the decision of consumers to go into a relationship or break it off. Brands can win back unsatisfied consumers, they can extenuate complaints by expressing their apologies, etc. On the other hand, indifferent or irresponsible customer service can ensure that clients will leave and stay away forever. This also risks the development of a negative word-of-mouth campaign (Langer, 1997).

Much research has still to be done into the relationship between consumer and brand. A very good first step was made by Langer (1997) and Fournier (1994). In the extension of her project on relationships between brand and consumer, Fournier developed a research instrument to map out this relationship. This technique, called Brand Relationship Quality, will be discussed in Part Three.

Exploration of brand–person relationships (Fournier, 1995)

Analysis of the brand stories of three in-depth interviews demonstrates how multi-layered, elaborate knowledge structures can develop around a brand, with deeper and richer layers of meaning reflecting stronger, more durable relationship ties. The varieties of information stored in the brand schema are depicted in Figure 15.3.

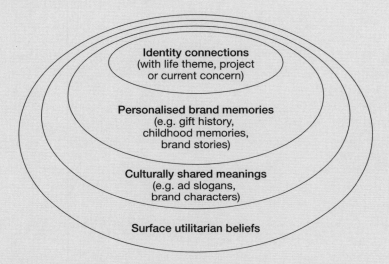

Figure 15.3 Levels of meaning in the brand relationship schema (note: meaning levels deepen in moving towards the centre.

(...) A brand's meaning is also embellished through advertising, particularly the use of slogans and brand characters or personalities (e.g. 'Cereal? I use Tony the Tiger ... Cleanser and stuff like that? Umm, the Dow Scrubbing Bubbles clean my tub.') These devices give consumers a 'tag' to attach to the brand, an alternative label to use in conversing and thinking about the brand. Referenced in this way, the label acts as a nickname that demonstrates close friendship between the person and the brand, deepening feelings of intimacy and attachment. Feelings of intimate knowledge regarding the brand were also enriched through public relations activities in which details about brand history and management decisions were revealed. The sharing of intimate knowledge about a brand culminates in deeper relationship ties. More elaborate brand schemas also exist in the form of connections established between the brand and the user's sense of self. The phenomenon of a personal brand memory comprising noteworthy

Contd

brand-related experiences also deserves mention. Often the brand has acquired a personal history through gift-giving episodes or strong affiliations with loved ones (e.g. 'that perfume will always make me think of him'). The brand is also frequently remembered as a prop in a salient past event. These memories fuse the brand with happy past experiences and respected others, embellishing the brand schema beyond the utilitarian core.

The relationship stability is related to the degree to which the meaning of the brand is elaborated beyond its stable core, linking consumption of the brand to important events, activities, people, or identity themes. The net effect of the enhanced meaning system is to personalise the brand – a process that heightens judgements of product uniqueness and reduces the temptation to try competing brands. In elaborating the brand schema, feelings of familiarity and intimacy are also enhanced, further deepening the relationship bond.

Enduring relationships also benefit from a rich affective grounding reminiscent of concepts of passionate love in the interpersonal domain. The effect of supporting relationship endurance was much greater than that implied in notions of simple preference or liking. Those in stable relationships felt that 'something was missing' when they hadn't used their brands for a while. They tended to characterise their brands as irreplaceable and unique, and anticipated a great sense of loss if the brand was removed from the market. They felt that their brands were truly 'meant for them' and suggested feelings of dependency and addictive, selfish attachment. These strong affective ties protected the relationship from transgressions and intrusions, again encouraging stability and endurance over time.

On the behavioural side, consumption rituals (Rook, 1985) emerged as a central process through which brand relationships were maintained. Behavioural interdependencies formed through routinised, frequent, strong, or diverse interactions with the brand served to solidify relationship ties, encouraging endurance, stability, and tolerance. In several cases, behavioural interdependence developed to a point of near addiction in which no substitutes were entertained or tolerated. Strong levels of dependency often sustained relationship ties despite affective involvements, intimacy levels, or identity ties.

High levels of commitment (the intention to behave in a manner supportive of relationship longevity) also characterised successful brand relationships. It was not uncommon for informants to openly profess commitment to a brand (e.g. 'I am very loyal to a brand; I would not use any other'). These stated pledges encouraged relationship stability by reinforcing maintenance-enhancing behaviours and implicating the self in relationship outcomes.

15.4.2 *Relationships through brands*

Geursen (1994) wrote that marketing becomes the achievement of meeting points and of experiences with people. In an article in *Source* he explained again what he meant by this: 'a brand can form a network of and for people who share a certain interest, problem, challenge, image or dream. The only thing the producer can 'own' is the capacity of making a physical environment and physical products (preferably made-to-measure) and of creating ideas for meetings. The shared experiences is what it's all about. The brand is a creator of conditions: it creates possibilities for contact' (Geursen, 1998). Langer (1997) also concluded on the basis of her research that there are meeting points in many places around the world which are steered by brands: she calls these 'brand clubs'. By means of these clubs connections are created between the brand and users and between users. Some brands have official clubs. For instance, Swatch and Harley Davidson each has an official club where collectors/drivers meet; meetings are regularly organised for and by owners of a Rolex. The membership of a brand club is usually less formal than in the examples described above. Informal brand clubs emerge as owners of the same brand of cars talk to each other at a party; they compliment one another on their good taste, and feel validated in their choices (Langer, 1997). Or they can, for instance, flash their headlights on the highway when they see someone else driving a Volkswagen Beetle.

A distinction can be made between relationships that consumers enter with brands and relationships they enter through brands.

Chapter 16

The Brand Representation

16.1   Introduction

In Part One we saw that our brain consists of a large number of neurons and that there are synaptic connections between these neurons: each neuron can make direct or indirect contact with 50,000 others to send and receive messages and thus develop enormous networks during the course of our lives. An important point of departure that social psychologists have borrowed from neuropsychology is that memory can be compared to a network of units that have mutual associative connections between them. Although this formulation seems to point to neurological science (as was described in Part One), it is important to realise that the associative network is only a metaphor (Van Knippenberg *et al.*, 1991). On the basis of studies in which respondents were asked to think out loud while they are solving a problem, we can draw the following conclusion about people's memory (Howes, 1990; Anderson, 1995; Damasio, 1995; Pinker, 1997):

(1)   Representations are not stored as exact reproductions of objects or events, or words or sentences (see section 3.9 on page 65). According to Damasio, the brain does not collect Polaroid photos of people, objects or landscapes and does not store sound tapes with music or voices either. Given the enormous quantity of knowledge that we collect during our lives, storage of any kind of reproduction could present us with insurmountable capacity problems. We know from personal experience that our memory of a specific object, face or scene is not an exact reproduction but an interpretation, a newly constructed version of the original (Damasio, 1995). The brain tries to arrive at a reproduction but this is almost always impossible. It does not go further than a reconstruction.

(2)   People create order in their memory by categorising objects with common characteristics. More on the subject can be found in sections 5.6 and 12.2.

(3) Connections arise between information units and between categories. These connections come about through the simultaneous perception of elements or because elements resemble one another (for detailed information see section 3.6). Connections that are repeated often, that are lively or that have come about recently are the strongest.

Earlier in Part Two, we saw that connections also arise between the information units that people store in their memory with regard to a brand. We have tried to classify the varied collection of information that can be found in this 'associative brand network' into seven logical groups. We want to point out once again that a brand has a holistic structure and that each subdivision into components is artificial. In this chapter the various components from the mental brand response come together again into one brand representation in memory. The authors see the mental brand response (see section 8.3) as a synonym of brand representation. The brand name functions as the label of the representation. Additionally, this chapter establishes connections between the brand representation and important concepts such as brand equity and brand image. When describing these concepts it will become clear that the authors do not see memory as a two-dimensional space. Some information in memory is more elementary. The elementary information units sometimes serve as building blocks for other information: for instance, brand attitude is constructed from knowledge, emotions and experiences. The information in memory also differs in its degree of abstractness: some information is more abstract and lies, as it were, at another level. For instance, the concept of brand image is described in this book as the 'global total impression of the information that is stored in memory with regard to a brand and which is shared by the members of a culture or subculture'. The authors do not equate the image with the sum of the separate components of the mental brand responses. In section 16.3 it will become clear that not all market researchers and marketing managers use this definition.

> The brand representation is equal to the mental brand response. The brand name functions as a label for the representation.

16.2   The development stages of a brand representation

In 1999 the brand name Ben was launched in the Netherlands for a mobile phone network. A conscious choice was made for a name without telecommunications associations, but for the name of a person that made a human approach to communications possible (KesselsKramer, 1999). This section will show that a lot of energy and money is needed to make a success of a new brand. Different examples and percentages are given of brands from the groceries branch which unfortunately died an early death. In a short period of time, the name Ben has built up a large following (Trendbox, 1999). Time will tell whether consumers are also going to love the brand and will become loyal users.

Brands that people buy regularly, about which they know a lot and which they would rather not see disappear from the stores were at one time completely unknown phenomena for the same people. This still applies to many other brands they encounter, for example in foreign supermarkets while on vacation. The development of an unknown name and the corresponding symbols (like the logo) into a popular brand goes through a number of stages. The first stage, getting to know the brand name and thus the development of the very first associations, is completed with some brands in early childhood (as was described in section 7.4). These are generally 'old' brands that have been around for a long time and with which new generations are still growing up. Their origin sometimes lies in the nineteenth century, in the industrial revolution (Heinz goes back to 1860; Johnson's set up business in 1885 and Robert McVitie began baking biscuits in 1830). Every year new brands are launched that meet a 'blank' population and are confronted with the task of developing their position in memory from nothing. Many entrepreneurs underestimate the enormous efforts that are needed to make a new brand successful, for instance by having it penetrate into one of the three top positions in a category.

Golder (2000) executed an historical analysis on a scientific basis of the stability of 650 brands in 100 product categories in the USA, over a period of 75 years (1923–1997). He found that 23% of the market leaders in 1923 were still also market leaders in 1997. Another 25% of the original market leaders were still in the top five in 1997 (Table 16.1).

The stability of fmcg brands was much greater than that of durable brands. Within the fashion categories not one brand maintained its leadership position. These results demonstrate the effects of automated buying behaviour in the

Table 16.1   The stability of 650 brands in the USA (1923–1997).

Starting position 1923	Sample	Position in 1997			
		Number 1 (%)	Number 2 (%)	Number 3 (%)	4 + 5 (%)
Number 1 brand	97	23	8	9	8
Number 2 brand	70	11	9	3	4
Number 3 brand	43	5	7	2	5
Number 4 brand	26	4	4	4	4
Number 5 brand	12	0	0	25	0

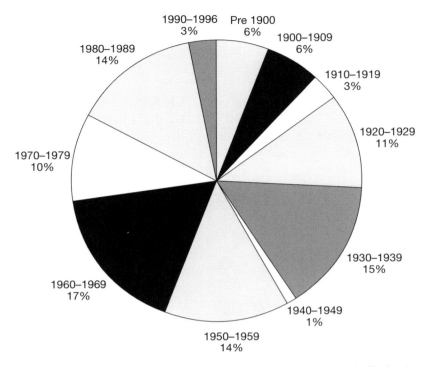

Figure 16.1 Launch dates of the top 100 brands in the grocery branch in England (Oxford Corporate Consultants, AC Nielsen).

fmcg markets and of more wilful and elaborated choice processes in the fashion industries.

In 1996 AC Nielsen looked at the age of the top 100 brands in the groceries branch in England (see Figure 16.1). Of these brands, 41% were launched before 1940. Almost every living resident of England has grown up with them. However, at the same time 17% of these top brands appeared on the scene after 1980; they succeeded in winning for themselves a large number of the English consumers in a relatively short time. 'Short time' usually means a decade, allowing for exceptions. Every year, only one brand enters the top 100, and one drops out. The underestimation of the necessary effort is the main reason why most brands undergo a premature burial: 80% of introductions regularly fail.

The development of the market position of a brand is a reflection of the development that a brand goes through in the memories and behaviour of all categories of buyers. Using purchasing behaviour as a point of departure, we can distinguish five stages (see Figure 16.2).

Successful new brands (AC Nielsen, 1999)

The market research agency AC Nielsen put together an overview of brands that were not in the Dutch market in 1990 but were now part of it. This overview only includes completely new brands or already existing brands that were introduced in a totally new product category (i.e. no line extensions). These are also brands, food and non-food, that are sold through grocery channels and that have succeeded in winning a steady place and a reasonably good sales volume. It turned out that only 22 new brands had made it in this period.

Lingen's Blond	Chicken Tonight
Palm	Magnum
Coolbest	Aardappel Anders
DubbelFrisss	Lipton
Xylifresh	Always
Nescafé	Kleenex toilet paper
Yakult	Pantene
Mona Goede Morgen	Ambi Pur Flush
Vifit	Sanex
Fysiq	Dove
Wake-Up	Dreft

The average market share of these brands in their product category in 1998 amounted to 15%. The total sales of these brands amounted to 650 million Dutch guilders in 1998, with which they represent together 6% of the total sales of brand articles in this sales channel. This means that about three introductions per year seem to be successful in the long term. Together they have succeeded in taking a good 1% of brand articles sales in the foodstuffs channel per year! Part of these sales also include those of extensions of brands that have been around for a long time, like Nescafé, Kleenex, Dreft and Pantene.

These behavioural stages also reflect the development of the mental brand representation – the 'stages of mind' the brand is in. The development of mental representation as well as of the purchasing behaviour can be globally described as in Figure 16.3. For this figure we should remark that the development does not always follow such a neatly structured path.

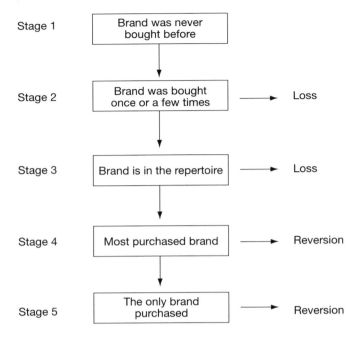

Figure 16.2 The development of the market position of a brand.

In the scheme we have departed from the current insights on the development of person/brand relationships. The most important are:

(1) Mental brand representations and brand purchasing behaviour develop in a mutual interaction.
(2) Minimal familiarity with a brand article is necessary before it is bought for the first time. This familiarity concerns the brand name (and brand signs) as well as the core meanings of the brand.
(3) An implicit evaluation takes place of these initial brand meanings from goals and values of the individual: 'Could the brand possibly be relevant for me?'. If answered affirmatively, the brand is included in the consideration set.
(4) This can lead to the first trial purchase and eventually to one or several subsequent purchases in order to evaluate the brand further. This leads to a strengthening of the brand familiarity and an expansion of the associative network with which it is connected. What arises is an image of the performance of the brand in comparison with the competition.

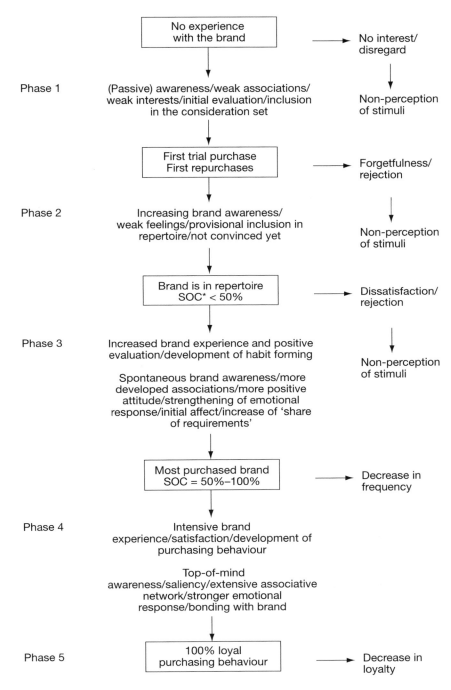

*Share of customer (the share of the brand in the total purchases of a customer)

Figure 16.3 The development of the mental representation in purchasing behaviour.

(5) Association development is strongly influenced by purchase and use behaviour. Consumers who use a brand have a larger number of associations with it, and those associations are also more accessible than they are for non-users. People start seeing more differences with competing brands.

(6) Attitude development also goes together with use behaviour. They influence each other mutually. Ehrenberg (1997) says that, although argument over causal connections is often complex and contradictory, empirical data indicate that behavioural changes usually precede attitude changes.

(7) Initial experiences can lead to an inclusion of the brand in the brand repertoire. Consumers develop a 'purchasing probability' which usually remains fairly stable during longer periods of time (one or two years). This purchasing probability can also increase or decrease gradually.

(8) The emotional response to the brand is also strengthened by brand experiences in their broadest sense (use and information processing). The saliency of a brand increases.

(9) The gradual strengthening of the emotional response can lead to such a commitment that the brand is the only one accepted in its category, but this does not occur often.

When describing these development stages, one should always keep in mind the possibility of weakening and decline of a brand. An analysis of 1251 brands in the United States concerning the degree to which the growth of market shares can be converted into growth of penetration or purchasing frequency showed that 60% (!) of the brands did not demonstrate any growth at all – instead, they showed regression. In addition, 2% remained stable and only 38% showed a sales growth (Sylvester *et al.*, 1994).

> The mental brand representation and the brand purchasing behaviour develop in interaction with one another. The associative network increases mainly in scope and strength as a result of user experience.

The development stages as described previously can form the basis for segmentation of the category buyers from the position of the individual brand. The next box shows a classification into development stages based on a measuring instrument of Millward Brown. We can see, for example, that the largest brands distinguish themselves mainly through high scores for 'advantage' (uniqueness, supremacy) and 'bonding' (commitment). It is also noticeable how minimal the differences in familiarity are between the leading brands and dying brands. Large strong brands distinguish themselves mainly through the emotions they invoke in their buyers.

The 'Brand Dynamic Pyramid' of Millward Brown

Millward Brown constructed a measuring instrument of the mental brand response called the 'Consumer Value Model'. On the basis of this instrument a response hierarchy was constructed, the 'Brand Dynamics Pyramid', which consists of five levels (Dyson *et al.*, 1996):

(1) *Presence:* a factor constructed on the basis of spontaneous awareness, remembered trial use and active understanding of the brand promise.
(2) *Relevance:* an evaluation of the degree to which the brand responds to the core criteria of the consumer (functional and/or symbolic), and to what degree its price is acceptable.
(3) *Performance:* an evaluation of the performance of the product compared with the competition.
(4) *Advantage:* an evaluation of the degree to which a brand represents a unique proposition in a functional and symbolic sense, in combination with direct questions related to uniqueness, supremacy and enthusiasm.
(5) *Bonding:* the brand is the only one accepted by the consumer.

Figure 16.4 shows the average scores for all the brands already studied with this instrument in different product categories. The scores for individual brands can of course deviate from these. In addition to the average scores for the mental brand response, the financial 'share of customer' that corresponds with it has been depicted (the behavioural component of brand loyalty).

Contd

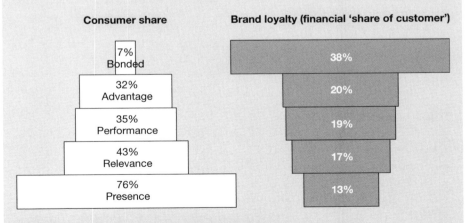

Figure 16.4   Consumer share and brand loyalty (Dyson *et al.*, 1996).

Millward Brown measured the average scores for the mental brand response for three different categories of brands, parting from the Brand Dynamics Pyramid (Dyson *et al.*, 1996). This was done for market leaders, so-called 'premium brands' (brands whose price is at least 50% higher than the average of the category) and dying brands. A comparison between market leaders and dying brands shows that the scores for 'presence', 'relevance' and 'performance' hardly differ from each other (Figure 16.5). The big difference arises in the two highest levels of the pyramid:

- *'Advantage'*: 53% for the market leaders compared with 35% for the dying brands, and
- *'Bonding'*: 26% compared with 4%. Strong brands are strong thanks to the distinguishing meanings they are connected to and the emotional bond consumers have with them.

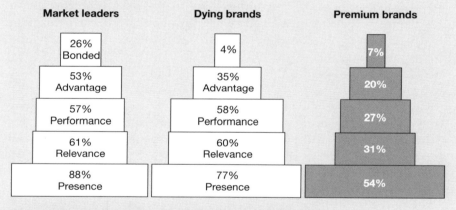

Figure 16.5   The Brand Dynamics Pyramid for market leaders, premium brands and dying brands (Dyson *et al.*, 1996).

BRANDZ: eight brand types

Based on the Brand Dynamics Model, Millward Brown researched 3500 brands in seven countries (United States, Brazil, France, Germany, China, Japan and Great Britain) for WPP in the 'BRANDZ project'. An analysis of brands into the flow of consumers from a preceding to the following level resulted in an identification of underlying patterns on the basis of which a classification of eight different brand types could be made (Farr, 1999). To this end, the scores were combined in two factors:

Contd

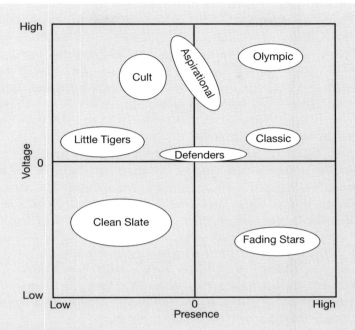

Figure 16.6 BRANDZ map

(1) *Presence:* represents the awareness of the brand.
(2) *Voltage:* represents the scores at the levels of 'advantage' and 'bonding'.

On the basis of these two factors a map was constructed in which each of the eight brand types could be placed (Figure 16.6). The eight brand types are shown in Table 16.2.

Little tigers (e.g. First Direct) These are brands with low presence, but the few who know about them clearly feel they deliver exactly what is wanted, so they have high conversions to advantage and bonding. The challenge is to expand the knowledge without diluting the appeal.

Contd

Table 16.2 The eight brand types according to Farr (1999).

Type	Share in sample (%)
1 Little tigers	15
2 Cult	3
3 Aspirational	12
4 Olympic	2
5 Classic	11
6 Defender	28
7 Fading stars	12
8 Clean slates	17
Total	100

Cult brands (e.g. Clinique)
These brands are not familiar to all, and have a low conversion to relevance, as they are not appealing to everyone, but the high conversion to bonding demonstrates a committed and sometimes fanatical following. The key challenge is: can they become better known without losing their power and ability to deliver strongly to consumers?

Aspirational brands (e.g. Armani)
These are relatively well known but not brands suitable for a mass audience, hence the low relevance. They are often too expensive for most consumers. It is difficult for these brands to extend their franchise without alienating their core users. They need to maintain their mystique in order to maintain their premium.

Olympic brands (e.g. Pedigree Chum)
These are well known, well loved with a large core following. These brands have both high presence and more than their fair share of bonding. They are likely to be talked about in everyday life and are part of the cultural fabric of the country.

Classic brands (e.g. Tesco)
Classic brands are usually brand leaders. They have high presence and then score well at all levels up to bonding, but they only have their fair share. They are in a strong position in the market, but are far from invulnerable.

Defenders (e.g. Littlewoods)
These brands have a good balance between product performance and price, but no real product-based or emotionally rooted advantages. They sit uneasily on a borderline between maintaining and losing loyalty.

Fading stars (e.g. Channel 4)
These are brands that are well known, but now lack real unique advantages. Hence they convert less than their fair share to advantage and bonding. It is likely that they will be relying strongly on pricing and promotions to maintain share. To turn the tide for these brands a concerted effort at redefining their appeal will be required. The first issue to address might well be the product itself, and there may well be a targeting issue to consider: only then is it probably worth advertising.

Clean slates (e.g. West Cigarettes)
These brands are little known and without strengths for the few who may be aware of them. In other words they are a blank canvas to be painted on.

16.3   Interconnectedness between the elements of the brand representation

As early as 1958, March and Simon wrote that the contents of human memory can be described at any moment as subdivided into two parts: one part that exerts an important influence on behaviour at that moment and a much larger part that does hardly anything or nothing at all. They called the part that influences behaviour the 'evoked set' (in Laroche *et al.*, 1986, p. 10). In 1969 Howard and Seth (1969) added the concept of 'evoked set' to the theories on consumer behaviour, positing that the number of brands that are considered a possibility by the buyer in a 'choice' situation is usually reduced, and the collective name of 'evoked set' is given to those brands the buyer considers as acceptable for his next purchase. Later, Howard (1977) made a distinction between the evoked set and the consideration set. He described the consideration set as the subgroup of brands that a consumer considers buying from the group of brands that he knows in a specific product class.

By then Ehrenberg (1974) had pointed out the routine and stable purchasing behaviour of people and its connection with awareness and earlier trial purchases (Awareness → Trial → Reinforcement). He focused on the existence of a 'brand repertoire': small sets of brands that consumers buy with alternating frequency, showing a certain 'purchasing probability' for each brand. In the 1980s the 'share of customer' concept developed from here, as the share of the brand in the category consumption of an individual or a household.

All these concepts have been discussed in the preceding chapters. It has also become clear that, at an individual level, the issue is about connections within an associative network. The positions that brands take in this network are summarised in Figure 16.7.

In this diagram, mental positions and purchasing behaviour are connected because, as was previously described, purchasing habits as such form part of the associative brand network. A categorisation of brands into mental positions cannot end with an attitude position, as was the case until recently.

Research like that of Millward Brown (see page 319) indicates that, in essence, there is probably a hierarchical connection between the different components of the mental brand responses. Brand awareness functions as a basis, and brand relationship, in the form of a strong connectedness with the brand, as its strongest manifestation. This hierarchical connection occurs mainly when people consider buying a certain brand for the first time. Not all the stages of the hierarchy are covered when buying well known or frequently purchased brands. For instance, in the chapter on brand attitude we explained that once a consumer has formed an attitude towards a brand, she does not have to search in her memory each time for all sorts of core meanings, emotions and experiences related to the brand in order to construct an attitude on that basis – the attitude is there and comes to her at once when she is confronted with the brand. The ground structure of the hierarchy is shown in Figure 16.8.

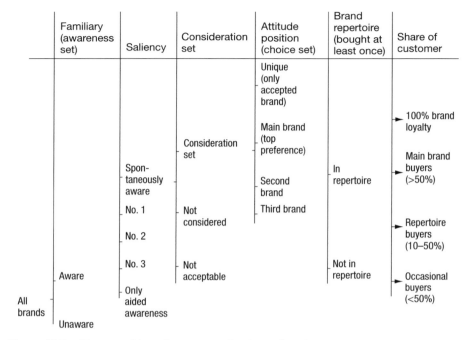

Familiary (awareness set)	Saliency	Consideration set	Attitude position (choice set)	Brand repertoire (bought at least once)	Share of customer
			Unique (only accepted brand)		100% brand loyalty
		Consideration set	Main brand (top preference)		Main brand buyers (>50%)
	Spon-taneously aware		Second brand	In repertoire	
	No. 1	Not considered	Third brand		Repertoire buyers (10–50%)
	No. 2				
	No. 3	Not acceptable		Not in repertoire	Occasional buyers (<50%)
Aware	Only aided awareness				
All brands					
Unaware					

Figure 16.7 Diagram of brand awareness to share of customer.

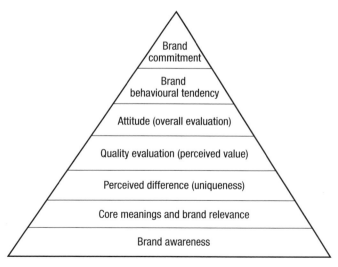

Figure 16.8 Hierarchical connection between the components of the mental brand response.

16.4   The saliency of a brand representation

Some brand representations have a more dominant positioning in our memory than others. They are represented more strongly and we have a larger involvement with them. The psychological term for this is saliency. Sutherland (1993) defines saliency as the probability of a brand entering our consciousness at any given moment. Saliency is the intensity of the brand representation, the prominence with which the brand name and the corresponding associative network are represented in our memory. With 'prominence' we are referring to the probability of the brand entering our consciousness spontaneously and before other names when we are confronted with certain cues. This is an effect of the relative strength of the synaptic connection between cues and brands. The cues consist of various associations with which the brand is connected: products and product attributes, applications, situations, moments and symbolic associations. The cues can be given to us internally and externally: for instance, we feel like (internal cue) having a beer and at the same time think of Guinness, or we walk along piles of beer crates in a supermarket (external cue) and, of all the brands that are there, our attention immediately goes to the spot where the Guinness is.

Brand saliency exerts a large influence on our perception and purchasing behaviour. The extent to which this happens depends partly on the nature of the choice process. In an uncertain situation, many people tend to choose brands they are familiar with. In a supermarket we take a large number of decisions within a short period of time, basing them almost completely on the knowledge embedded in our memory. We do not read the information on the packaging and rarely ask personnel for advice. The concept of self-service is even based on people not needing any additional information than the brand on the packaging. Brand awareness and the way the brand is represented in memory play the main role here. Sutherland (1993) believes he can prove this with a study. He posits that brands in a supermarket that have equal prominence on the shelves do not have an equal chance of being perceived. After observing clients in a supermarket, it appeared that 56% of the purchases were about 'localising behaviour'. Clients screened the brands on the shelves, only to identify the brand they bought the last time and place it automatically in their shopping cart, without giving conscious attention to the alternatives. Here we are dealing with a process of scanning and focusing in which attention is only concentrated on the salient brand. The simple fact that a brand is present on the shelf does not necessarily mean that it is consciously perceived. Research in the United States into the behaviour of buyers also shows an extremely limited evaluation (Hoyer, 1984; Dickson and Sawyer, 1986). Buyers of margarine, coffee, toothpaste, laundry detergents and breakfast cereals stayed an average of 12 seconds in front of the corresponding shelves before taking a brand and placing it in their shopping carts. They gave only limited attention to an average of 1.2 brands. At best, all the other brands were scanned.

An eye fixation study of shopping behaviour (Russo and Leclerc, 1994) revealed that consumers allocated an average of 3.44 seconds to the initial 'screening' phase of the in-store choice process for a product category that contained 16 packages. This suggests that each package was allocated approximately two-tenths of a second for scanning.

A comparable study in the Netherlands produced even shorter search times (Brouwer and Van der Weijde, 1998). The time between the moment a consumer starts looking at or considering brands on the shelf and the moment that an article is taken from the shelf averages 5.2 seconds for coffee, 3.4 seconds for beer, 3.0 seconds for butter and only 1.2 seconds for milk. The search time depends, among other things, on the scope of the consideration set and the brand loyalty. However, a spread of the search times seemed relatively minimal for these categories. Brand-loyal buyers only needed 1.6 seconds for beer, while switchers took 6.9 seconds.

Some researchers, based on this scanning and focusing behaviour in shops and the corresponding automatic purchasing behaviour in low involvement products (as is the case with most daily consumption goods), posit that pure saliency is the most important choice-influencing variable. This ignores the fact that brand saliency has been preceded by a comparison and consideration process, and that it can emanate from specific brand associations. In other words, saliency can be the result of the development of a choice process in time, in which the choice is narrowed to one or a few alternatives on the basis of experiences and perceptions. In this process, the saliency of a brand increases gradually: it comes to the forefront of our memory and other brands are either pushed to the back or even not activated or perceived at all.

When acquiring things that are purchased less frequently, in product categories we know less about and with which we experience greater risks, we tend to have less pronounced brand preferences. Newly acquired information (e.g. a salesperson's argument) can strongly influence the choice. However, in such a situation, a brand that is spontaneously familiar and saliently represented in our memory reduces the risks we perceive in the purchase.

16.5 The brand image

16.5.1 *The image concept from a historical perspective*

Sigmund Freud was one of the first to use the concept of image. The described image is a representation of another person in the subconscious. For Freud this is usually one of the parents. Such an image is formed in early childhood and is usually an idealised representation and not necessarily a true portrait of the person (Reber, 1997). The images from Freud's time, in which the unconscious is central, have reigned supreme recently. In all kinds of marketing and brand research, respondents are put under hypnosis or spurred into 'free expression'; with coloured paper or a chunk of clay, respondents are asked to represent the image of a brand. After Freud, the concept was not used very much, but between the two world wars it suddenly came into frequent use, especially in the United States, when building the reputations of film stars and politicians.

In the 1950s, David Ogilvy introduced the concept of image in marketing and advertising literature. Those years also saw the emergence of the term 'brand personality' – the analogy between the image of a brand and the human personality. The literature of this period stated that a brand also has a character or a personality, although how they come about and function is not dealt with. In the 1980s this way of looking at images re-emerged. The images from the 1950s were adopted by the major brand gurus without much criticism.

In the 1960s a systematic comparison was made between the concepts of image and stereotype. It was assumed that all brands can be evaluated on a number of standard dimensions (like young/old, old-fashioned/modern). The world is seen as a great axis on which brands can take different positions. The sometimes unpleasant consequences of such an approach can be found in much of current quantitative image research. A large number of brands have to be evaluated by the respondent on a fixed number of dimensions, using a 5-point scale. The problem is that such research never helps find out what the specific image aspects of the brand are, aspects in which it distinguishes itself from competitors in positive and negative ways. The saliency of association elements remains concealed (Asselbergs, 1987). Sometimes compensation is sought by doing a qualitative study beforehand. The results of such studies are often extremely outdated (e.g. in tracking). Questionnaires are based on qualitative research of many years back. Another problem is the interpretation. Advertisers and advertising professionals are terrified of a brand scoring high on the 'old-fashioned' dimension: a brand has to be young. They often forget that old-fashioned is positive in the eyes of consumers, and is translated into 'old and trusted'. They also forget that there is no way that a brand that has been fifty years on the market will be considered young by consumers. In the 1970s systematic attention was paid for the first time to the influence of images on the behaviour of consumers. The psychologists Fishbein and Ajzen (1975) published their 'theory of reasoned behaviour', which became legendary in some circles. They posited that the consumer associates positive and negative experiences with a brand and allows himself to be led in his future behaviour by the positive or negative image that has thus emerged of a brand. It is not difficult to see that this is an oversimplified representation of reality (Asselbergs, 1997). Many people think positively about the brand Ferrari, but only a few have at their disposal the financial means to buy one.

In the 1970s there was a sort of hype around the concept of image, both in serious and in popular literature. In this period there was a new movement of researchers who first of all linked the image to the concept of attitude and then later on even equated them with each other. By equating both concepts with each other, researchers avoided the need to define the image theoretically while, at the same time, they had a large arsenal of proven measuring techniques at their disposal. There is a lot of criticism on the use of those techniques. People cannot quite accept using an attitude measurement to measure images. The main criticism is the same as that given for quantitative image research: too few dimensions are used and the interpretation is unsatisfactory.

In the 1980s, interest in the phenomenon of image took on alarming proportions. Products started resembling one another increasingly, and the differentiation had to come from an 'added value' at the level of the brand image. Maybe it also has to do with the lack of inventiveness on the producer's part. Apparently it is difficult to make real improvements in a product and to keep up that differentiation in the long term, and thus people resort to marketing tricks. An increasing emphasis was given to the subjective and unique character of an image. People were supposed to have a unique memory content, and each individual formed her own images and representations of brands.

This train of thought has been studied by various disciplines in recent years. In the next section we provide a description of the current views on brand image and attempt to give some theoretical foundation to the concept.

16.5.2 *The brand image now*

Peter Georgescu (long-time chairman of the international Y&R group) described at a Y&R congress an experiment in which the value or influence of a brand image was shown. This experiment was carried out several years earlier and described in a 'respected British medical journal'. It was shown that women who were unwell felt better after taking brand aspirin than after taking generic aspirin. This in itself is not so impressive, but what was also shown was that some women received brand placebos and others got generic placebos. The conclusion of Georgescu was that branding had an analgesic effect. Therefore brands really have a meaning for consumers (Adformatie, 1996).

Both in the literature on brands and advertising and in practice there is a lot of discord and lack of clarity on the concept of brand image. In the first place, different concepts are used, all of which describe approximately the same thing (brand personality, brand identity, soul, image and brand image). Secondly, almost everyone has their own definition of the concept of image. According to Sutherland (1993), an image is 'a function of the attributes that are associated with it, the degree of those attributes it is perceived to have and how important that attribute dimension is in people's minds when they make a decision'. Kapferer (1996) claims that an image is the way in which a certain public imagines a product, brand, political figure, country, etc.; the way in which such a public decodes the signals the brand sends out via its products, services and communication programme.

The Dutch economic psychologist Poiesz constructed a continuum to order all the definitions of image that have ever been developed. He arrived at the conclusion that three groups can be distinguished (Poiesz, 1989):

(1) The definitions in the first group assume that an image only arises after an individual processes thoroughly and extensively the information he is offered on an object or something which is already present in his memory. According to this reasoning, a brand image is equivalent to an associative network and the mental brand response, or is very strongly derived from it.

(2) The definitions in group two are based on a different principle. The image is considered as the theoretical and operational equivalent of attitude, as defined earlier by Fishbein (1967) as an acquired tendency to consistently evaluate an object or a person positively or negatively. Fishbein claims that an attitude is made up of 'beliefs' – associations between the objects and various attributes (Eagly and Chaiken, 1993). An attitude is the multiplication of behavioural beliefs (the perceived consequences of behaviour) and the valuation of these consequences (the value that is allocated to the consequences). In other words, a brand image is the tendency an individual has of evaluating a brand positively at first sight ('let's try it – why not?') or negatively ('you think "bah" and turn away'). This tendency is always formed out of associations related to a brand that an individual has stored. According to this hypothesis, the best way to measure a brand image is with attitude scales.

(3) The definitions that Poiesz collected in group three describe the image as a simple and global total impression of the memory contents. Images are diffuse and not necessarily substantiated with views on the image object. What is central here is the place that the object takes in relation to its competitors (Verhallen, 1988; Poiesz, 1989).

A small-scale study among experts (see Appendix, page 437) made it clear that there is a fourth group that can be added: various market researchers and strategists of advertising agencies equate the brand image with the symbolic meanings of a brand (thus everything that is not factual/instrumental).

The definitions of the concept of brand image can be subdivided into four groups:
(1)   The brand image is equal to the associative brand network.
(2)   The brand image is equal to the brand attitude.
(3)   The brand image is a global total impression of memory.
(4)   The brand image is equal to the symbolic meanings of a brand.

Writers of books and articles on brands and brand images are at pains to make us aware of the fact that a brand image is different from the brand identity. In the most ideal case, a company's marketing department formulates an identity for its brand, probably in cooperation with an advertising agency. The product composition and design, the way the brand is sold (in which stores and for what price), the form and contents of the advertisements and the packaging are all subordinate to this identity. Based on all the impressions and experiences that a consumer has with a brand, he forms an 'image'. In this context, image is seen as a 'picture', but that word is also difficult to define. The term 'image' comes from contemporary psychology, in which an image is seen as, crudely described, 'a picture in the mind'. According to Reber (1997) this rather common description indicates fairly well the essence of the term in both daily and scientific usage. However, three restrictions should be mentioned (after Reber, 1997):

(1) The image is not necessarily limited to visual representation. If you think of a bicycle you probably also hear the sound of a bicycle bell. And if you think of your mother, you might also recall the smell of her perfume.
(2) An image is not necessarily seen as a reproduction of a previous event, but instead as a reconstruction, a synthesis.
(3) The image in the mind seems capable of 'adjusting' mentally to new and old information. If you think of your mother you do not remember the very first image you ever stored of her. You keep adjusting this image so that it adapts to new information. When people think of Heineken, chances are they are not remembering the very first commercial they saw of that brand. People adapt the image of Heineken so that it fits new information.

Gestalt psychologists have shown that people have an innate tendency to perceive the world around them as a whole. All kinds of things in our surroundings are integrated in a logical way into a comprehensive total package. Brand articles can also be seen as 'Gestalts', they are wholes made up of many elements. In the perception they come across as one whole with their own characteristic colour (Campari), form (Volkswagen Beetle), smell (Chanel No. 5, Maja) or style (Dunhill) (Franzen and Holzhauer, 1987). Splitting up a brand into loose elements, as happens in the mental brand response of Franzen *et al.* (1998), does not indicate how people perceive in reality, but it can provide points of connection for research and strategy development. How people interpret the meaning of brands is partially stored in the brand itself (the brand identity). The individual himself also determines partially how he interprets a brand and the meanings he ascribes to it. Thus each individual has his own unique experiences and develops unique memory contents. Research by Bruner (1990) has shown that people seem to become collectively programmed by the culture in which they live. The meanings that members of a culture ascribe to a brand resemble one another strongly and, for that reason, can function as symbols. If you wear an Aussi, you're a chum; if you drive a BMW you're a show-off! We define the brand image on the basis of the theories of gestalt psychology and Bruner's research as 'the global total impression of the information related to the brand that is stored in memory and which is shared by the members of a culture or subculture'.

In this book the concept of brand image is defined as the global total impression of the information related to the brand that is stored in memory and which is shared by the members of a culture or subculture.

16.6   Brand equity

As was seen in section 8.2 (page 135), brands exert an enormous influence on the choice and purchasing behaviour of consumers. In the groceries sector in the Netherlands, national brands reaped 80% of the sales in 1998. The remaining 20% was shared between generic products ('no names'), products with a 'fantasy name' without any familiarity ('labels'), and the shops' own brand labels. These own brand labels are increasingly acquiring 'brand status' in the sense that they are well known and have an associative network and buyers' group.

It has also become clear that the three largest brands in a category earn together an average of 60% of the sales, in an average ratio of $4:2:1$. Consumers are also prepared to pay a higher price for brands they have a relationship with. A British analysis showed that, measured over a large number of product categories, a 40% higher price was paid for market leaders in comparison to own brand labels (Yasin, 1996). Finally, the brand positions of already established brands seem to be very stable. Provided they are well managed, they are able to maintain their market share over the years. They form a future guarantee of sales for their products.

The stability of established brands is demonstrated by the fact that market shares in a specific year are largely predictable on the basis of shares from the preceding year. Figure 16.9 shows the almost perfect correlation between the market shares in two consecutive years, measured over 71 brands (Farr, 1998). For 40 of the 71 brands the market share remained stable, changing by less than 0.5%. While 31 brands showed a change of more than 0.5%, only four changed by significantly more than 1% (Figure 16.10).

An analysis of the Dutch beer market shows that, over a five-year period, the market share of the average brand changed only 0.1% per year (Table 16.3)!

A meta-analysis of 419 cases from the period 1975–1994 (Dekimpe and Hassens, 1995) also showed that the large majority (78%) of the market shares

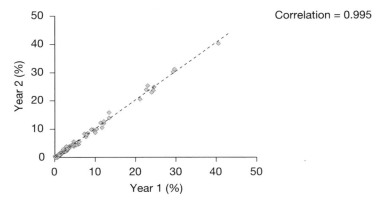

Figure 16.9   Development of market share – shares in year 2 versus year 1.

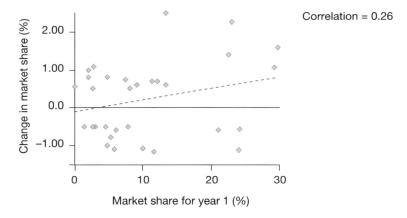

Figure 16.10   Change in the market share versus the market share in year 1.

Table 16.3   Analysis of the Dutch beer market (1995–1999)

Brand	1995	1996	1997	1998	1999
A	100	97	97	96	96
B	100	100	99	96	95
C	100	100	98	98	102
D	100	101	112	115	107
E	100	101	93	95	97
F	100	96	91	93	94
G	100	85	67	52	53
H	100	97	94	92	91
Other brands	100	107	107	111	111

are stable. Unless the scope of the market itself evolves, the marketing efforts for the various brands tend to neutralise one another. This is the case for durable products as well as fast moving consumer products.

Although these changes from year to year are important to the producers involved, the prevailing impression is still one of a very high degree of stability.

Market shares of 'established brands' are highly stable. For most brands, the share in a specific year is nearly the same as in the preceding year. A minority of brands show a growth or decline in market share of about 1% per year. In the long term, such a development can have major implications for the market position of brands.

The concept of 'brand equity' emerged in the 1980s as a label for this capacity of brands to influence purchasing behaviour and generate stable sales. Equity is borrowed from accountancy, where it means 'net worth', or assets after deduction of liabilities. It is clear that the concept functions as a metaphor when it comes to brands. What it means exactly has been a subject of discussion since its introduction.

In countless definitions of the phenomenon of brand equity formulated by various researchers, four components can be distinguished (Franzen, 1998):

(1) The presence of a brand in the psyche of consumers.
(2) Its influence on their purchasing behaviour.
(3) Its effects on the market positions and financial results of a brand.
(4) The financial value of a brand as an important asset of a company, which can be included in the balance and is expressed in a sale of the company (or of the brand itself).

We can thus gradually see a differentiation of the concept of brand equity taking shape. The components under 1 and 2 are increasingly designated the term 'consumer equity', component 3 'financial equity', and component 4 'brand value'. Following on the above-mentioned components, Franzen (1998) distinguishes two basic levels: 'consumer equity' and 'financial–economic brand equity'. Consumer equity is subdivided into 'mental brand equity' and 'behavioural brand equity'. The various components of the equity concept can be defined as follows:

(1) *Consumer equity:*
 • Mental brand equity: the inclusion of a brand in the consideration set of consumers, or the conscious and active preference for it, based on their perceptions and feelings.
 • Behavioural equity: the habit-related or conscious loyal purchase of a brand by consumers to supply an important part of their category needs.

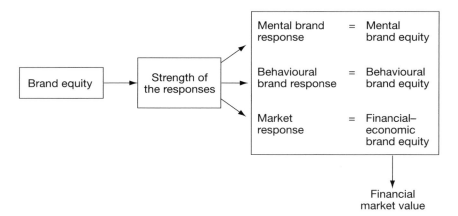

Figure 16.11 The concept of brand equity.

(2) *Financial–economic brand equity:* the influence of consumer equity on the financial–economic performance of the brand in the market, expressed by the degree of distribution, sales, market share, price-premium, margin and profits that it realises.

Here the concept of equity represents the quantitative component – that is, the degree to which a brand succeeds in accomplishing positive consumer and market responses. We could also call it the strength of a brand. Strong brands have a high equity, weak brands a low equity. The three components of brand equity are represented in Figure 16.11.

What characterises a strong brand? (Franzen, 1998)

Mental brand equity
- *High saliency:* the brand has a strong presence in memory (high 'share of mind'). It scores high on spontaneous awareness (TOMA) and on emotional closeness. Consumers have the feeling they know the brand very well.
- *Clear product meanings:* consumers know what the brand essentially means and where it distinguishes itself functionally. It has a strong associative connection with the underlying product categories. It has a high saliency in relation to relevant product attributes that are sought in this category by consumers.
- *Distinguishing symbolic meanings:* the brand has a clear individual personality, with which it distinguishes itself from competing brands in the category. The symbolic meanings represent important values to the users (connecting interest).

Contd

- *High perceived quality:* the quality of the brand within the underlying product categories is evaluated as relatively high in comparison with the competing brands. Consumers evaluate the performance of the brand positively and see it as a leader in this category. They have a high esteem for and confidence in the brand.
- *Anchored users:* a relatively large part of the brand users are loyalists: anchored users who have a high degree of bonding with the brand and do not show much of an urge to switch.
- *Attractive for non-users:* the brand is seen by non-users as an acceptable alternative for the brands they now use: it is part of their consideration set. There are more 'prospects' than 'potential deserters'.

Behavioural brand equity
- *High degree of penetration:* the brand has many users in comparison with other brands (the penetration increases).
- *Good intake:* the brand is bought by a relatively large number of new category users, especially the new generations.
- *Few deserters:* the brand has a stable user group throughout the years, and few deserters in comparison with competing brands (switching in).
- *High degree of brand loyalty:* the brand has a relatively high 'share of requirements' within the categories or subcategories, especially with the heavy buyers.
- *Good premium:* consumers are prepared to pay a good premium for the brand in comparison with competing brands and are relatively less sensitive to price discounts from competitors.

Financial–economic brand equity
- *Good level of distribution:* the brand has a high weighted distribution within the relevant sales channels for the categories and target groups.
- *Relatively high market share:* in measurements of market share within the category or subcategory, the brand is one of the largest two.
- *Relatively high price:* the brand realises a relatively high price premium with regard to the competing brands.
- *Low price elasticity:* the brand is less sensitive than competing brands to changes in the price distance from competing brands.
- *High financial market share:* the brand has a higher share in the market on the basis of sales value than on the basis of the sold volume.
- *High net profits/ROI:* the brand produces a high net profit and high returns on investment (ROI).

The questions researchers currently face are: 'How does brand equity arise?', 'How can I measure it?', 'How can I influence it?'. In short: 'How can I manage a brand so that its position is protected and strengthened as much as possible?'

In the preceding chapters we have shown how complicated the representation of brands in memory can be. In Part Three we will give an overview of research methods and techniques that are available to entrepreneurs to give an impression of the way their brand is represented in the relevant population. But what is it that the ultimate power of a brand determines? Which components of the brand representation contribute to it or take away from it, and to what degree? What is the causal connection between familiarity, image, commitment and purchasing behaviour? These are questions that can only be partially answered at present.

In Part Three the authors suggest a means by which the answers could conceivably be found. Current research practice keeps investing in separately measuring the individual components of the associative brand network. We have familiarity, image, attitude and behavioural research in all types and sizes, but their mutual interconnectedness is seldom or never established, and nobody talks about cause-and-effect relationships. Still, it is obvious that the issue ultimately revolves around these questions.

What should be determined is what the brand choice actually controls in terms of purchasing behaviour in a specific market (product category). In order to say something about this, a model is needed to represent the effects of a specific market. This subject does not belong in this book, but we recommend the chapter on 'Market stimulation' by Schuring and Vogel in Franzen *et al.* (1998).

To understand why people buy certain brands, insight is necessary into what drives consumers to buy a certain type of product and which attributes they look for in it, given the application or user situation. How is the market structured and which subcategories have to be distinguished? Which core attributes are desirable in a category or subcategory? The authors firmly believe that there are almost always a limited number of determinant attributes. Brands are activated in memory from these attributes, or external brand information is looked for and processed. The authors are also convinced that the brand representations present in memory exert the most important influence here – allowing for exceptions, of course.

The strength of a brand lies primarily in the strength of the association from 'goal cues' towards the brand. Goal cues consist of general category cues (people need biscuits), attribute cues (people want 'healthy' margarine), application cues (hiking shoes), situation cues (Sunday night drink). The saliency of the associations from these cues towards brands has a determinant influence on the brand choice in many categories. We saw, for example, the strong connection between brand awareness and brand use. Brand awareness is in fact the strength of the association of a product category towards a brand.

In categories where the perceived risks are greater, the choice is more 'ego involved', the supply renews itself constantly, or the memory information is inadequate, a more extensive evaluation process then takes place in which all sorts of associations of the brand (image) have a larger influence on the ultimate choice decisions. Even then, what is mostly looked at is the consideration set of a limited number of brands (or shops) that comes about on the basis of the strength or saliency of associations from some goal cues towards the brands.

In order to determine which components of the mental brand response have which influence on the choice behaviour, research is needed in which that choice behaviour is thoroughly examined (e.g. using the constant sum method; see page 398), all relevant association categories are included, and the influence of association components on the brand choice is determined with regression analyses. Experimental research by Franzen *et al.* (1998) into the brand equity of beer and margarine brands in the Netherlands has shown that a limited set of five to six association components (factors) explains about 50% of the variance in choice behaviour.

Part Three

Research

'The more we know and the better we are able to map out things, the more we find out that we actually understand very little.'

Chapter 17

Visions on Brand Research

Both in their private and professional lives, people are looking for explanations for the phenomena in the world. Until the Middle Ages, the Church provided answers to people's questions. This changed in the seventeenth century. Great men of learning such as Newton and Descartes put forward the view that everything in the world undergoes mechanical processes. Reality could be described through these processes and thus mastered, controlled and predicted. People in those times had a sacred belief in the objectivity of science; mind (the observer) and matter (what is observed) were strictly separated (Van der Ploeg, 1992; Bor, Petersma and Kingma, 1995). In section 15.3 we explained that a new worldview emerged in the twentieth century with the development of Einstein's theory of relativity and the uncertainty principle of Heisenberg. People were shown the relativity of everything, the influence of the researcher as a participant in the researched object, and the sensitivity of mutual connections in large and complex systems. No predetermined, fixed descriptions could be given on the course and results of processes. The world was not ruled by the laws of cause and effect, but by probabilities and correlations. With this new worldview many certainties fell away. People could not hold on to the Church or to regular patterns any more.

Any attempt to sum up post-modern thought briefly and concisely will irrevocably end up causing problems. Pluriformity seems to be one of the core concepts of today's thinking: many styles of thinking and many 'truths' are used next to each other. This pluriformity is particularly visible when studying visions on brands. Some researchers see the brands as an associative network; they claim to be able to trace the essence of a brand by measuring all its components and combining the scores. Another group of researchers sees the brand as a holistic concept; the brand is more than a sum of the components in the associative network. Yet other researchers are unsatisfied with the individualistic (or American?) character of theories on brands and look for their answers to scientists like Moscovici (1981) and Bruner (1990), who ascribe an important role to social interaction and the culture people live in when meaning is given to objects (and brands). A difference can also be distinguished in perspective: the brand is seen from the consumer's perspective (social–psychological), from the producer's perspective (economic) or as it manifests itself in society (a semiotic perspective).

In other words, different visions on brands can be distinguished and all these visions are true. Trying to arrive at a unanimous definition that the world can agree with seems as pointless as fighting a war over religion. In the following chapters we will give an overview of all the techniques that are presently available in the Netherlands to measure brand representations. We are striving towards completeness, but some instruments may still be missing from the list. This could be the result of the fear some research agencies have of giving out their 'secrets'. The techniques that will be described have emerged from the visions on brands described above. Comparing techniques without looking at the visions behind them is the same as comparing apples and pears. The ideal method does not exist and, within one vision, many roads lead to Rome. In the next chapter we will use a scheme for the ideal research to explain how things can go wrong when carrying out research, especially when interpreting results. It is important to examine this, because without proper analysis research creates pseudo-realities.

There are different visions on brands, which produce different research techniques. Comparing the techniques without looking at the visions behind them is like comparing apples and pears.

Chapter 18

Research into Brand Representation

18.1 Research practice

'Many research agencies use a coordinate system. A growing number of them applies it blindly and dogmatically. This is why we keep encountering them – two-dimensional planes like a pond or three-dimensional cubes in which brands have to find their positions. Primitive coordinates such as cheap/expensive or young/old used to be sufficient. But the urge towards sophistication has also hit the research market. Dimensions become spiritualised and depth increases. What do you think of introvert/extravert, ego-oriented/socially oriented, thinking, feeling, intuitive, sensory [...]? All Great Truths, since they come from equally great thinkers like Jung, Adler and the old Greeks. It cannot be more fundamental. All those types are recognisable: you recognise your neighbour and your colleagues in it. [...] But now comes the bad news: [...] all those visions are true. I mean, all those dimensions of all those researchers together are true. The problem is that the individual researcher chooses one, two or three dimensions himself and uses them as spectacles (read: dogma) to look at the world. Everything seen through the same spectacles: "Look, there goes an upper left type. And there is a clear lower right case." Every person gets a place in that cross. No one looks at which of the dimensions are suitable for the market in question, no, just join my cross.' (Geursen, 1994)

The number of techniques for measuring brand representations is growing disproportionately. An increasing number of advertisers want to find out about the 'image' consumers have of their brand, the way their brand is perceived and experienced, and the associations the brand invokes in consumers. This urge emanates particularly from the awareness of the fact that the consumer is an active recipient, with her own opinion and her own experiences. The brand identity that advertisers want to convey to their target group through communication is not always the same as the image that this target group develops of the brand.

In practice, people speak more about image research than about research into brand representation. In section 16.5 we saw that there is a lot of discord on what an image is. The authors define brand image as 'the total global impression of the information that is stored in memory with regard to a brand

and which is shared by the members of a culture or subculture' (see section 16.5.2). In subsequent chapters we will show that some techniques are suitable for mapping out the total impression. This does not mean that the other techniques that are described are less interesting: insight into these components of the mental brand response is essential to the ability to understand and direct a brand. In the previous chapter we claimed that it is not necessary to formulate a unanimous definition for the concept of a brand, although it is, of course, important for an advertiser and the research agency involved to look at the brand from the same perspective, in order to avoid a Babel-like confusion.

Things can often go wrong in research into brand representation. Too often, standard instruments are used for all brands in all product categories. It remains to be seen whether an instrument that provides insight into fast moving consumer goods can also be used for something like financial services. Besides, the analysis of research results does not always work correctly. These results are seldom corrected for the double jeopardy effect, and the relationship with purchasing behaviour is left out. In the next section we make a recommendation for ideal research into brand representation.

18.2 The ideal research

In research into brand representation or brand image it is important for the researcher and advertiser to essentially agree on a definition of the concept of representation. Do they see a brand representation as a sum of a number of components or as a holistic whole? Another important question is the degree to which they already have information on the brand in question: is there a need for input research or output research? In input research the advertiser is involved in sounding out and developing a brand representation. In output research he wants to measure which components consumers associate with the brand name, or the influence of sales promotion on the image of a brand (Asselbergs, 1997; Bronner, 1997).

If the budget and the available time allow it, it is highly recommended to go back as often as possible to the imaginary zero situation, in which no knowledge exists on the brand yet. Advertisers and researchers often think, wrongfully, that they have an insight into the brand representation, and immediately start doing output research. A researcher should also realise that society changes constantly and so does the way people look at brands and the meanings these brands propagate (for instance, certain statements become less important/relevant over the years). In research into brand representation it is useful to go through a number of phases.

Phase 1

The first phase is a reconnaissance phase. You should do proper preliminary research into choice variables. Which attributes of the product or the brand are considered important by consumers? Find out the usage context of the brand (when, why, how and what is it used for?). Try to find out as well how it is that relevant concrete attributes are connected with 'values' at a higher abstract level. Reflect on which respondents are involved in the research. Is there a need for a representative sample? In almost every study it is interesting to interview users and non-users of the researched brand. The users group also tends to fall into various more or less homogeneous subgroups. For example, a distinction can be made between young people who are going to buy a laundry detergent for the first time and older people who have been loyal to a certain brand for years. These groups of people probably look for different aspects of laundry detergent brands. In such cases it can be useful to take a stratified sample. In a stratified sample the population is first subdivided into a number of more or less homogeneous target groups or 'strata', after which a sample is taken from every 'stratum'. This method of sampling is chosen when researchers want to be sure that certain groups of people are considerably well represented in the final sample (Reber, 1997; Swanborn, 1987). The research results have to be linked back to the data on the respondents. For instance, users of a brand report differently on their brand than do non-users: they are more positive and, in general, know more about the brand.

Phase 2

Write down the spontaneous reactions of some respondents on a brand. The difference drawn in section 8.2 between the evocation and evaluation phases in the choice process of consumers is important within this context. In the evocation phase the total number of choice alternatives is reduced to a limited group (the consideration set) from which the ultimate choice emerges. In the evaluation phase the brands that have made it into this consideration set are weighed against each other. In the evocation state the associations *towards* the brand are measured (Holden and Lutz, 1992). Which brands do respondents think of when they are planning to buy a certain product? Which brands do they think of when they look for a certain attribute? The researcher tries to find out, for example, which brand is named first when she gives cues such as 'environmentally conscious' or 'electrical toothbrush'. When the associations are collected it is important that the researcher determine their strength: in which order were the brands named, and how much time was there between the cue and the naming of the brands (the response time)? In the evaluation stage, what is asked is mainly the associations *from* the brand. What associations does the brand name invoke in respondents? What stereotypes of users does the respondent think of when hearing the brand name (see 'Categories of brand meanings' at the beginning of Chapter 10)? The strength of the associations also has to be determined after collecting the associations (order and response times).

In phase 2 it is important to give the respondents as few cues/stimuli as possible so that they are not 'steered'. The research is intended to provide insight into traits that people immediately think of when reflecting on a brand. At this stage it is not yet necessary to guarantee representativeness, for which reason experts (e.g. marketing or product managers of a brand, or strategists from advertising agencies) can also be involved. However, one should take into consideration the fact that the traits that are mentioned first are not necessarily the traits that a consumer finds most important and on the basis of which she arrives at a purchasing choice. Two small-scale studies have shown that spontaneous reactions are particularly related to sensory perceptions or concrete traits of a brand (for instance, Heineken has a green label) (De Vries, 1997; Timmerman, 1998). It is very possible for a brand to possess traits that the consumer does not name spontaneously, but on the basis of which she does arrive at the final purchasing decision.

Projective techniques and stimulus material are necessary to bring out the more abstract reactions. Besides the brand name, respondents are also shown things such as a picture of the packaging or cards with words to which they are asked to respond. For example, in a study on Heineken respondents were shown cards with 'Holland', 'outdoor cafe', 'luxury', 'normal', 'herring' and 'Christmas'. For each card they were asked to say whether they thought it fits with Heineken and why. Instead of cards with words, the researcher can use photographs or pictures of animals on the cards: in short, based on budget and taste he can choose from the projective techniques described in section 18.4.3. It is also possible to ask the respondents to collect pictures themselves or to take pictures that they think fit with the brand and bring them to the research session. It is very important that the words or images that are used in the research are properly validated beforehand.

In the 'projective techniques toolkit', the most contrasting instruments are described, and sometimes (for instance, in 'planet description') it is reasonable to wonder what the added value of a technique is over the more standardised techniques. By using a 'wilder' technique, a researcher makes it very difficult for himself to interpret the results afterwards and validity can suffer. Respondents may start becoming creative, independently of the actual assignment (draw a planet that fits brand X to the best of your ability). Up to now, essential research has not asked which added value different projective techniques have in relation to one another. On the basis of the categorisation of brand associations for each association category, an abstract (verbal) cue can be given and the respondent asked to give his thoughts on the brand the cue invokes. This can continue until nothing more comes up. It is then necessary to find out the relevance of the associations.

Phase 3

On the basis of the results from phases 1 and 2, the researcher already has quite a good image of the components of the brand representation that are considered important by some respondents. This image is not standardised and, because of the qualitative character of the methods, not representative of a large population either. Many advertisers need a representative image of the brand representation or the brand image. They do not want to know what has been said in a certain group discussion by some respondents about their brand – they want to know what *people* think of the brand. Quantitative research is necessary to find that out. It is of course very difficult to throw abstract concepts such as brand representation and brand image into a quantitative questionnaire. Only with the help of good qualitative preliminary research is it possible to arrive at statements and questions that are relevant in the eyes of a consumer (for a brand like Coca Cola it is certainly possible to ask for 'authenticity'; for a brand like Harpic it seems less important). To arrive at a good quantitative questionnaire from phases 1 and 2, an intermediary step is necessary; the contours that have already become visible have to be built with standardised quantitative research. Based on the results from the preceding phases, in this phase the researcher has to construct tailor-made measuring instruments with which the degree of frequency in a large sample is measured. It is sometimes difficult to introduce parts of already existing standardised measuring instruments. Examples of such standardised research are IMPMAP of Infratest Burke, Brand Fitness of BBDO and the Zaltman Metaphor Elicitation Technique, which will be discussed further on. Unfortunately, there is no answer to the question of which technique is the most suitable in a certain situation. Research of the literature provided no data on the validity of the techniques.

Phase 4

The results from phases 1 to 3 can provide a basis for a quantitative question-naire that can be used in a tracking instrument and/or to determine the relationship between the brand representation and consumer behaviour. Research by Baldinger and Rubinson (1996), Schuring and Vogel (1997) and Marder (1997) has shown that 'modelling' and the 'constant sum method' are particularly suited to making predictions on future behaviour. It is therefore better to use cognitive response analysis and questionnaires with scales when you want to test your findings from qualitative research in a large group of respondents, and the constant sum method and modelling when you want to make predictions of behaviour. The research has to be carried out in a repre-sentative sample, and good analysis techniques are necessary (correspondence analysis, principal component analysis, factor analysis, etc.) to determine the

Table 18.1   Scores of different automobile brands on several brand meanings.

	Brand A	Brand B	Brand C	Brand D	Total per row
Driving comfort	50	52	83	70	255 (30.6%)
Status	20	18	70	60	168 (20.1%)
Economical	9	2	2	20	33 (3.9%)
Safe	39	28	68	78	213 (25.5%)
Beautiful	13	50	59	44	166 (19.9%)
Total per column	131 (15.7%)	150 (27.9%)	282 (33.8%)	272 (32.6%)	835 (100%)

mutual connections between different variables, and between different variables and purchasing behaviour.

In this phase it is essential to protect the results against the double-jeopardy effect (we provide an extensive description of this effect in sections 14.2 and 14.4.1). As a result of this double-jeopardy effect, respondents regularly make associations with large brands in research (the market leaders). If there are fans (frequent users) of a large brand among the respondents, this effect will be additionally strengthened. If the researcher only looks at the number of associations, he is in fact measuring the size of the brands and that is not the intention. He will have to correct his results. There are different methods for doing this. The simplest one is to compare the expected and actual scores per cell. A fictional example will help clarify this (see Table 18.1).

Bronner (1993) proposes a number of steps to correct the results of the double-jeopardy effect in Table 18.1:[11]

- The totals are calculated per row and per column.
- The totals per row and per column are added up and set at 100%.
- The researcher can now calculate which percentage of this 100% is allocated to various brands: the column total is shared by the sum of the column and row total.

---

11   The method that Bronner proposes for correcting the data for the double-jeopardy effect is part of the formula for calculating what is known as the chi quadrate (Swanborn, 1991):

$$\text{chi}^2 = \Sigma \ (f_o - f_e)^2/f_e$$

in which f_o = factual frequency in a cell (o of observed)
in which f_e = expected frequency in a cell (e of expected)

As can be seen from this formula, in order to calculate the chi quadrate, the differences between the expected and real value per cell are summed up and the researcher ultimately arrives at pronouncements on the relationship between two variables: he finds out whether the connection found in the sample is so strong that one can assume with a certain degree of reliability that a connection between the two variables also exists in the population. If that is the case, we speak of a statistically significant connection (for more information on the chi quadrate see Swanborn, 1991; den Boer, Bouwman *et al.*, 1994). When studying brand representation you do not sum up – you look at things cell by cell. Correcting for the double-jeopardy effect is therefore not a statistical test. Only part of the chi quadrate is used.

- Per row (i.e. per trait) we can now calculate the percentage of the allocation each brand has received. In the comfort row, brand A got $50/255 = 19.6\%$ of the allocations. This 19.6% is compared with the column total of brand A (15.7% = the total number of allocations that brand A has received across all brand meanings) by calculating the difference between 19.6% and 15.7% (+3.9). Based on this we can conclude that brand A scores quite high for driving comfort.

In some cases, the ASSPAT method is also suitable to protect research results against the double-jeopardy effect (the method and the way it can correct the results are described in section 20.2, item 33).

The ideal research into brand representation consists of several phases:
(1) Reconnaissance phase (qualitative preliminary research).
(2) Write down the 'spontaneous' reactions to the brand; make a distinction between the associations from the brand and the associations towards the brand.
(3) Standardisation.
(4) Quantitative research.
(5) Analysis of results: try to establish a mutual relationship between variables and between variables and purchasing behaviour, and correct the results for the double-jeopardy effect.

18.3   Forms of interviewing

18.3.1   *Single interviews*

Single interviews are applied to quantitative as well as qualitative research. The big advantage of single interviews is that one can delve deeply into reasonings and motives. The respondent is not influenced by other people and the interviewer can go into detail if necessary. Although in qualitative research nothing can be said in the way of 'most people think that...', we do get insights into the relationships of meanings. On the basis of these relationships a researcher can formulate conclusions with considerable certainty and eventually advise his client on decisions to be taken.

In a single interview the respondents are interviewed one by one. For budgetary reasons, quantitative single interviews are often done by telephone or by mail. A disadvantage of telephone interviews is that the researcher cannot show anything to the respondents and that a lot of resistance is encountered. Furthermore, research has shown that 80% of the approached respondents do not feel like being bothered on the phone and do not want to cooperate. An increasing number of respondents dislike being harassed by telephone with the umpteenth survey. A disadvantage of mail surveys is that the chance of non-response is considerable; a large number of questionnaires are just never sent back by respondents.

The qualitative single interview is carried out on the basis of a checklist that can vary from very structured to quite unstructured. The interview is usually recorded on an audiotape or videotape. A group of people may observe from another room via video camera or a one-way mirror. This group usually consists of the client, an advertising strategist, a researcher and a minutes secretary. To answer a certain question it is usually necessary to do several interviews. The number of interviews held per subject or per problem depends on the goal of the study, the homogeneity of the target group (the more homogeneous the target group, the fewer interviews are needed), the assignment, budget and time. The interviewing method is completely unstructured and the respondent's personal ideas and views can be freely delved into in depth. The disadvantages of this method are that it is expensive, it is always done with a small number of respondents, a cognitive effort is required that would never occur in natural circumstances, and the results are sometimes difficult to categorise under one denominator. Generalisations are not possible. In addition to the single interview described above, there are three other special forms of single interviews in qualitative research (Van Tilburg and Tuitert, 1995).

(1) *Paired interview*

In a paired interview, two respondents are interviewed simultaneously. A researcher chooses to do a paired interview when she is interesting in looking at the interaction between two respondents who are involved in the decision-making process in daily life. For instance, husband and wife decide together on the purchase of a car and a child is screaming in the supermarket because he wants sweets.

(2) *Triangular interviews*

Triangular interviews are those in which three respondents are interviewed simultaneously. Just as with the paired interview, respondents can react to each other. What is special about triangular interviews is that the researcher consciously selects three respondents of different backgrounds (Gordon and Langmaid, 1988). He can choose a loyal user of the researched brand, a loyal user of another brand, and someone who uses the researched brand now and then.

(3)   *Chain conversation*

A chain conversation entails having several consecutive talks. Two variants are possible. In the first variant there is a series of consecutive conversations so the researcher can build up an increasingly better picture of the corresponding subject. The conversations usually take place by telephone, sometimes face-to-face. In each interview the researcher builds on the preceding interviews. The conversations are unstructured due to their reconnaissance nature. In the second variant the researcher shows something to the respondent (e.g. a commercial or a package). This person then has to explain what he has seen to someone else. The researcher now has the opportunity to analyse which information from the commercial is important to the respondent and how information exchange between two persons takes place. Next, the researcher interviews the two persons at the same time in order to find out whether any other aspects have been noticed but not named.

18.3.2   *Group discussions*

Group discussions are always qualitative. They are usually chosen when interaction between respondents is important. Group discussions ensure more spontaneity, creativity and trueness to life in the way consumers speak about a brand, but have the disadvantage that all kinds of undesirable group processes can emerge (such as social influencing). Insight is gained into group effects and the meanings that exist in practice on a specific subject. A group discussion or focus group usually takes place with six to eight respondents and lasts one to two hours. The respondents sit in a circle and the discussion starts with respondents and group leader introducing themselves to each other. Just as with single interviews, the group discussion is recorded on an audiotape or videotape and the client, a researcher and a minutes secretary observe from another room via a closed circuit camera or a one-way mirror. The number of group discussions carried out for one study depends on the question, the homogeneity of the target group, budget and time. In qualitative market research, additional specific types of groups are distinguished from the standard group discussion (Van Tilburg and Tuitert, 1995).

(4)   *Mini-group discussion*

A mini-group discussion takes place between three or four persons. This type of research is used mostly when it is necessary to get insights into individual as well as social processes. Since the group is not too large, subjects can be discussed in depth, while the group process can be kept under control. There is more opportunity for all respondents to talk. Sometimes there are also budgetary reasons for choosing mini-group discussions.

(5)   *Repeated group discussion*

There are two variants of repeated group discussion:

- Several groups are interviewed on the same subject. The most important thing is for the differences between groups as regards norms, values and interests to be shown.
- The same group is asked to come back once or twice to talk about the same subject. Sometimes the respondents are given an assignment to complete in the meantime, or the interruption is to allow the first discussion to sink in or to be reflected on.

(6)   *Extended group discussion*

An extended group discussion takes an extra long time (usually three to four hours). Because of the length of time, various subjects can be discussed more extensively and in depth.

(7)   *Bifocal groups*

Two groups are worked with simultaneously. Each group has six to seven people. A 'normal' group discussion lasting about two hours takes place with one group, while the other group looks on from another room via closed circuit camera. After two hours they exchange groups and the discussion is carried out with the other group while the first group looks on. Afterwards both groups talk further to exchange reactions.

(8)   *Group builds image*

The group of respondents forms pictures, images or ideas of an existing or new product or brand. With a new product the intention is to generate ideas and find out if the respondents have clear needs. With an existing product, a discussion is carried out with the group on ideas in order to eventually adjust the product.

(9)   *Interactive innovation*

In interactive innovation the client (the advertiser) participates in the group discussion. This advertiser plays the role of 'problem owner' and explains a problem to the other participants (for example, 'my sales numbers are dropping'). The other participants are a facilitator, respondents and a writer. The facilitator leads the conversation and the writer is responsible for recording the group memory. He writes down everything that is said and does it in such a way that it is visible to all participants (usually on a flip chart).

(10)   *Synectics*

Synectics is originally the name of an international consultancy agency specialising in innovation and change. The technique of synectics was developed in the 1960s by William Gordon, who wanted to end the rational grounding on which most research was based at that time. The creative thoughts of the respondents are used in a structured fashion to solve a problem with synectics. The technique is used in all areas: in management training, brand development and advertising (Hankinson and Cowking, 1993).

Synectics is only used in group discussions. Six to eight people with very different backgrounds participate in these discussions. An advantage of the heterogeneous composition of this group is that the problem is looked at from different perspectives. A disadvantage is that some participants think that their background is more relevant and important than that of other participants, and want to constantly be speaking. It is the interviewer's task to solve this problem and have the conversation run its course in a structured manner. A sort of manual has been formulated that can help the interviewer accomplish this goal (Hankinson and Cowking, 1993):

- 'Speak for easy listening': use terms and phrases that encourage participants to participate and think.
- 'Associative listening': a remark from one of the participants can provoke a reaction in another participant. This participant will not say anything, will write down what he really wants to say, and will use the remark in a subsequent discussion.
- 'Posit an argument assertion and ask no questions': it is better to have participants react to an argument instead of having them answer a question later. Questions push them in a certain direction and leave little room for creative ideas.
- 'Understanding comes before valuation': participants must first explain clearly what they mean, before interviewers link conclusions to their arguments.
- 'Value someone else's ideas': encourage participants to elaborate on ideas expressed by somebody else.
- 'Use negative reactions as a point of departure for assuming a new direction': do not stay very long with negative reactions or expressions of participants. Use these reactions as an occasion for moving on to a new subject.

- 'Do not make a decision on an idea if it is not really necessary': the interviewer makes a decision on an idea (solution) only when he is certain of it.
- 'Mind your own business': most problems cause other problems. The interviewer should keep asking himself if there is a chain reaction of problems or whether several problems are just part of one single problem. A chain reaction of problems has to be structured and thoughtfully mapped out.
- 'Listen as well as you can': the interviewer should avoid as much as possible misunderstanding the participants.
- 'Speak for yourself': the interviewer shows his own opinion and makes sure others do the same.

The developers of synectics believe they have found a good and creative way of having several people solve a problem together. Work has to be done in a structured way (Hankinson and Cowking, 1993):

- First, the problem is described (e.g. 'I want a new brand name').
- This is followed by a brainstorming session in which participants say what they think and want.
- The interviewer attempts to gain insight into the deeper ideas and intuitive reactions of the participants by using various projective techniques. These techniques are described later in this chapter, in the 'projective techniques toolkit'.
- Select the three or four most common solutions for the problem.
- Evaluate the three or four alternatives. Give advantages and disadvantages for each alternative and expand them with new ideas and insights.
- Next step: move forward to action. Find out if the solution is (legally) possible.

18.4   Aids

18.4.1   *Introduction*

Aids are intended to help respondents arrive at a goal more quickly and easily. Research into brand image has shown these goals to be 'bringing brand responses above water'. Brand responses are usually so abstract or so commonplace that respondents need help to get on the right track or to explain what they mean. In this section we will describe two types of aids: stimulus material and projective techniques.

18.4.2 *Stimulus material*

In quantitative as well as qualitative research, in single interviews and in group discussions, use is made of what is known as stimulus material or cues. A researcher shows stimulus material to the respondents to elicit a reaction or to clearly indicate which brand, product, packaging or advertisement he wants to talk about. Stimulus material exists in all types and sizes. Frequently used types are concept boards (boards on which a product, brand or advertisement idea is pictured), storyboards (boards on which the idea for a commercial is pictured in the form of a comic strip), photos, films (Gordon and Langmaid, 1988), cards with verbal concepts and verbal questions with statements. The use of stimulus material can be very useful, but it is not totally harmless. Respondents are actually influenced by the material and pushed in a certain direction. In research terms, this is known as the suggestive effect of stimulus material. If researchers use it carefully and sensibly, there should not be any problem or danger. When interpreting the results it is very important that the researcher take into account the fact that stimulus material was used.

18.4.3 *Projective techniques*

Projective techniques help respondents to express their thoughts and feelings. An additional advantage is that they make participating in a study more fun and interesting for respondents (Gordon and Langmaid, 1988). Through projective techniques respondents find out things about themselves, they really live it up for an hour, or imagine that they are back in nursery school. Gordon and Langmaid (1998) describe projection as 'the tendency to imbue objects or events with characteristics or meanings which are derived from our subconscious desires, wishes or feelings'.

Most research agencies have plenty of projective techniques. Gordon and Langmaid discovered that these projective techniques can be subdivided into several groups. The classification in Table 18.2 is used as a stepping stone for the projective techniques that have appeared in the literature on research into brands.

ASSOCIATION

(11) *Free association*

Free association is the opposite of aided association. In aided association the respondent has to say something about a brand on the basis of certain stimuli. The stimuli can take different forms: photos, words, films, etc. In free association the respondent can say something about a brand without being directed or held back by stimuli. The researcher gives a brand name and asks

Table 18.2 Projective techniques toolkit.

Association	Completion	Construction (of a fantasy)	Expression
• Free association (or word association) • Secret pooling • Sorting techniques: Photo sort, Relationship sort, Situation sort, Tree sort, Animal sort, Value sort (e.g. personal. drives analysis) • Personification • User typology • Paint box • Planet description	• Sentence completion	• Thematic apperception test • Guided dreams • Projective question • Bubble cartoons/ Ballooning • Scenario technique	• Psychodrawings (e.g. drawing pictures of objects) • Collage • Psychodrama and role playing • Metaphor and analogy

the respondent to say anything that comes to her mind. A disadvantage of free association is that it is difficult for many respondents to express what they want without any help. An advantage is that the chance of blind spots decreases (see footnote, section 26.4). Practice with this technique over time has shown that respondents find it difficult to make associations in one-to-one conversations. In group discussions the associations are generally much 'richer'. Another name for the same technique is 'word association'. The respondent is given one word (the brand name) by the researcher, and is asked to write down everything that comes to her mind.

(12) *Secret pooling*

Secret pooling is a technique used in group discussions. With the help of secret pooling respondents can express feelings they might otherwise not share with group members. Each respondent writes on a note the feelings and thoughts he has on a brand. He folds the note without writing his name on it and throws it in the middle of the table. The notes are read out loud one by one by the researcher and discussed in the group. Secret pooling is used a lot in brainstorming sessions in which respondents are warmed up for the real group discussion. With the help of secret pooling they can structure their thoughts in this phase.

(13)   *Sorting techniques*

The starting point of sorting techniques is the assumption that people find it difficult to indicate what they think of a product or brand, especially if they can only do this with words. Sorting techniques have been developed to give people the opportunity to express their feelings on products and brands without forcing them to have to search for words. Thus important information is expressed that a respondent would not be able to verbalise without the help of sorting techniques. The researcher can get more insights into the intuitive reactions and unconscious associations of respondents. Different sorting techniques have been developed which work more or less similarly. In each sorting technique the respondent is confronted with a number of brands and is given a pile of cards to sort for each brand. The pictures on the cards differ for each technique. The most common variant is the 'photo sort', in which portrait photos of people are pictured in the cards, but many other forms are also possible. Below is a description of the photo sort plus an explanation of the 'animal sort', 'situation sort', 'relationship sort', 'tree sort' and the 'personal drives analysis'. Many variants are possible.

Sorting techniques can be used in group discussions and single interviews, and are usually a supplement to another – more rational – technique. The researcher must validate the pile of cards before the research begins. In practice, this means that he knows exactly what each card represents and what it communicates. The same attributes expressed by the card can be ascribed to the brands. This is called 'projection'.

Examples of sorting techniques

Photo sort
Photo sort makes use of portrait photos of people. Each portrait represents a number of emotions. If we see someone for the first time, we form, albeit unconsciously, a representation of that person. How old is he? Can he be trusted? Photo sort allows people to play the same association game, but with brands instead of persons. For a number of brands, respondents are asked to place the photos they think fit best in any way. The respondents can express themselves through the photos without having to express in words the emotions that the photos stand for. The brands are directly associated with the emotions that the portrait photos invoke. What you need to watch out for as a researcher is respondents regularly using the

Contd

brand as a point of departure and not the people on the photos. Respondents are easily tempted into putting photos together with brands whenever a stereotypical user is pictured in that photo.

Animal sort
Instead of portrait photos, pictures of animals are portrayed. A tiger looks different from a rabbit. It is very important that the pictures are properly validated beforehand: it should be clear to everyone what the pictures express. Paul Heylen (1990) is usually considered as the creator of animal sort. He developed the instrument from his visions on the implicit personality of man and animal.

Tree sort
There are all kinds of variants of this sorting technique. Sometimes the researcher uses pictures of trees. Trees come in all sorts and sizes: there are decorative trees, scary trees, thin and thick trees, and so on. These varieties of trees invoke all sorts of different reactions in people. Some trees make them cheerful, others a little frightened. When it comes to tree sorts, it is also very important that the pictures be properly validated beforehand.

Situation sort
Situation sort is sometimes used to find out what atmosphere is invoked by a brand. Here respondents also have to place cards for a number of brands. These cards picture all kinds of people in various situations. In some cards several people can be seen, while other cards show only one person. People are depicted in a variety of situations: at home, on the beach, in the woods, at the swimming pool. From the validated pictures one can clearly understand whether the people in the picture are having a good time, if they are afraid or if they are partying, etc.

Relationship sort
A lot of attention has been given recently to the relationship between brand and consumer (see Chapter 15). Various types of relationships can be distinguished in daily life. There are relationships between mother and daughter, grandfather and grandchild, boss and employee, boyfriend and girlfriend, man and woman, and so on. The relationships that a consumer has with brands he uses can also differ. He is very brand-loyal within many product categories, and within other product categories he has a brand repertoire from which he makes his choices. It is difficult for consumers to

Contd

describe these relationships. The task becomes easier when, during research, they can distribute some cards among brands that have descriptions of various types of relationships (father–son, husband–wife, bus driver–passenger, etc.).

Value sort

Since the 1960s we have known that values play an important role in the choice process of consumers. In the course of the years various inventories have been made of values that are considered important in people's lives. Several theories have also been developed on the way values influence the choice process. The most prominent value expert is undoubtedly Rokeach. He and many of his followers state that a value can be defined as a 'centrally held, enduring belief which guides actions and judgements across specific situations and beyond immediate goals to more ultimate end-states of existence' (Rokeach, 1973). One can imagine (see also section 10.5.3) that people allow themselves, sometimes unconsciously, to be led by their values when making choices.

To find out whether this also happens with purchasing decisions and which values are the most important with certain products or brands, several research techniques have been developed. The most well known example is the laddering technique, which is described in section 20.2. Sometimes researchers also use a value sort. Various values are described in cards, and respondents have to place these cards with a few selected brands.

'Towards which values do the people who use these brands strive?' A disadvantage of this technique is that respondents consider it rather abstract. It is very difficult to place yourself in someone else's shoes. The fact that the concepts on the cards often have several meanings makes the task even more complicated. It is therefore very important to properly validate the 'value sort' and for the semantics of the terms to be tested. Another disadvantage is that the value inventory of Rokeach is often taken as a point of departure.

Even though Rokeach's research can be called ground breaking, it is also open to a lot of criticism. The assumed universality of these values is questionable. It is quite possible that the values that Rokeach found are only applicable in the middle of the United States in the early 1970s. A more important critical point, the limited empirical foundation, was recognised by Rokeach himself.

There are a lot of problems with the method Rokeach used to arrive at his inventory (Vyncke, 1992). SWOCC constructed a value inventory that is applicable to the Dutch population of 1997 and that also has a proper empirical foundation (Sikkel and Oppenhuisen, 1998) (see page 205).

(14)   *Personification*

The researcher asks the respondent to imagine a brand as if it were a person. If this works, the respondent is invited to associate further: is it a man or a woman? What does he or she look like? What kind of work does the person do? The researcher can gradually start asking about more abstract attributes (e.g. hobbies and ambitions).

(15)   *User typology/stereotyping*

The respondent imagines the average or stereotypical user of a brand and gives a description of the person and his traits (appearance, age, hobbies, occupation). It is different from personification in that personification describes the brand itself, whereas this technique describes the user of a brand.

(16)   *Paint box*

The respondent has to indicate which colours or colour combinations go with a specific brand. The technique is derived from colour psychology. Colour psychologists assume that each colour is associated with certain emotions – for instance, yellow stands for cheerfulness, red for passion and green for calm. By using colours, respondents can express those emotions that they find difficult to verbalise.

(17)   *Planet description*

Planet description is a relatively unknown technique, used mainly in single interviews. The respondent imagines that a brand is a planet and describes what this planet looks like. What do the inhabitants look like? What do they eat? Are there any apartments? What does its flora and fauna look like? Sometimes a respondent is asked to describe space and to see several brands as planets. This way the researcher can get an insight into the whole product category as the respondent experiences it.

COMPLETION

(18)   *Sentence completion technique*

Just like many other projective techniques, this technique comes from clinical psychology and is used mainly during single interviews. The interviewer gives the respondent a vague, unfinished sentence and asks her to complete it. For example: 'I eat corn flakes every day because ...' The interviewer keeps the phrase rather vague on purpose in order to lead the respondent in a certain direction as little as possible.

CONSTRUCTION (OF FANTASY)

(19) *Thematic Apperception Test (TAT)*

The Thematic Apperception Test (TAT) is a projective technique developed in 1953 by the psychologists Morgan and Murray (Engler, 1995). TAT is used in single interviews. The idea is to create a visual environment that fits the brand that will be discussed. Marlboro cigarettes may be linked to horses and empty mountains, and Persil to a cosy home and family life. Respondents have to put themselves in this visual environment and fantasise about what would happen. This fantasy has to be told in the form of a story and there should be a beginning, a middle and an ending. According to the developers of this technique, TAT elicits from respondents the most elementary motives on which their brand choices are based.

(20) *Guided dreams*

A respondent has to imagine that he has had a dream about a certain brand. The researcher asks him to relate this dream. This technique is used in single interviews and resembles Trance research and the Thematic Apperception Test to a certain degree. All these techniques make use of creating and concretising a fantasy.

(21) *Projective questioning*

Projective questioning is used extensively in marketing research. A typical projective question is, 'What do you think most people think of the use of products that have been tested on animals?' Answers to such questions reflect the respondent's own ideas. The respondent feels freer to give a more honest answer to the questions now that it seems as if he is talking about other people.

(22) *Bubble cartoons/ballooning (text clouds in comic strips)*

Respondents are asked to fill in text clouds on a board. Such boards picture several people having a conversation (to be seen in the text clouds). The respondents have to work out what it is they are saying. Figure 18.1 shows an example.

The technique is also useful if the researcher wants to know which interaction takes place between people as a result of a product or a brand. The data can be interpreted qualitatively. It is also possible to elaborate a coding

Figure 18.1 An example of a 'bubble cartoon' (Steel, 1998).

scheme and include in it the various subjects that the respondents throw up. In practice, a combination seems to provide useful information. The qualitative data are supplemented with a coding scheme and an optional statistic board (Gordon and Langmaid, 1988).

(23) *Scenario technique*

With the scenario technique the researcher tries to find out which behavioural scenarios respondents use in various situations. These are often situations in which a brand choice is made and the researcher gets more insight into behaviour during consumer decisions. Before the research starts, the researcher maps out different scenarios. A scenario could go something like this:

> Martin is on his way to the station. He realises that he has forgotten his wallet, but luckily he still has five guilders in change in his pocket. He wants something to eat on the train, and goes to the kiosk. He sees sandwiches, chewing gum and various chocolate bars. 'It's going to be a chocolate bar,' he thinks. But which?

The respondent is presented with several scenarios and indicates how he would react in such situations and why. The scenario technique is generally used in single interviews and less often in group discussions. A disadvantage of this technique is that the respondents are very limited in their freedom of expression. There is no possibility of adjusting a scenario or coming up with one's own version of it (Van Tilburg and Tuitert, 1995).

EXPRESSION

(24) *Psychodrawings*

A psychodrawing is a representation of the associations that a respondent has with a brand or a product. It is important that the respondent be encouraged to explain what she has drawn and why. It is better to use this technique in a group discussion so that the drawings can be discussed with the whole group. The idea behind it is that the use of colour and form can help the respondents express their ideas and feelings. A disadvantage is that the technique is time-consuming and expensive. Another disadvantage is that many people think they cannot draw very well and are terrified of showing their 'mess' to other group members or to the researcher. It is usually necessary to supplement psychodrawings with another technique. An advantage is that, while drawing, associations that respondents cannot or do not want to mention come up.

An alternative is the technique of *drawing pictures of objects*. Respondents have to make drawings of objects or articles that are related to the brand – albeit indirectly. A researcher can say to a respondent, 'Imagine you are stepping into your dream car ... What does it look like? Try drawing it'.

(25) *Collage*

The collage technique is regularly used in group discussions. Respondents are assigned to make a selection from a pile of magazine pictures they consider are related to a brand. After cutting out the pictures they make a collage of them. In some cases every respondent makes a collage, and at other times there is group work. In yet other cases the whole group makes one single collage. The larger the groups, the greater the spontaneity, creativity and trueness-to-life in the way respondents talk about the brand. When the collages are ready, the researcher asks whether the respondents have found certain pictures that would fit the brand. This technique only works if the respondents are given the chance to explain what they have done and why.

(26) *Role playing and psychodrama*

Role playing and psychodrama can only be used in group discussions. Two variants are possible. In the first variant the interviewer explains that the respondents have to act in a theatre play or a role play and gives each respondent a role. The play is of course related to a situation in which a brand or product is evaluated by a number of people. Since the respondents can hide behind their roles, it is easier for them to say or do certain things. In some cases the interviewer participates actively in the role playing, at other times he only observes. There is an important difference between role playing and psychodrama. In psychodrama the respondent does not have to empathise with someone else, but plays himself (in relation to a brand); the respondent has to imagine, for example, that various brands are playing a poker game. He has to describe how the various brands behave. The difference from the first variant is that the respondents do not have to play roles; they are just themselves and describe the brands (Van Tilburg and Tuitert, 1995).

(27)   *Metaphor and analogy*

This technique is used in single interviews and in group discussions. The respondent is asked something like, 'Imagine that a BMW is an animal – what animal would it be?'. The explanation of the respondent is at least as important as the metaphor itself.

18.5   Conclusion

In colloquial language as well as in scientific literature, the term research is used for any well intentioned attempt to study a problem systematically and, perhaps, produce a solution. A problem is central in every study. That sounds like an open door, but in practice it seems that the research instrument often controls the method: the problem is distorted and adjusted in such a way that it can be easily studied or it enables the research agency to use its own standard instrument. Respondents sometimes find it difficult to explain to a researcher exactly what they mean and sometimes do not completely understand what a researcher means (or which brand or commercial he is talking about). In the first case a researcher can make use of projective techniques, and in the second case he can use stimulus material. What is important is that, while interpreting the results, the researchers are aware of the fact that such aids have been used.

Some researchers consider brand representation to be a sum of all elements that are stored in memory about a brand. Various scientists, researchers and marketers have published work on 'the brand as an associative network'. They implicitly posit that the brand representation is equivalent to this associative network, or claim that, at any rate, it is strongly derived from it. In Part Two of this book we tried to organise into separate components all the information stored in our memory with relation to a brand. The seven components that are distinguished are used in the following chapters as a hook on which to hang, as it were, the various research techniques.

Chapter 19

Research into Brand Awareness

19.1   Introduction

In Part Two of this book brand awareness was defined as: 'the presence of a brand name and the other related identification marks in long-term memory and the ability to retrieve this information into the working memory'.

The strength of a brand is partially evaluated on the basis of its awareness: 'How many people know the brand in the world, even if just by name?' According to Kapferer (1997), this is an obvious standard. The brand is a symbol and says something about the number of people that recognise the meaning of a brand and are aware of the promise that this symbol wants to express. Furthermore, research has shown that there is a strong correlation between buying and using brands, and the relative spontaneous awareness of these brands (see e.g. Ehrenberg, 1974, Schuring, 1995, and Part Two of this book). People activate more quickly the names of brands they themselves use or have used in the recent past. They usually name first the brand they consider as 'their' brand.

By using the brand, perceiving it and being confronted with it through advertising, consumers learn about its meanings. As was described earlier, all this information is connected associatively to the brand name. The richer this associative network is, and the stronger the associations, the greater chances are of consumers thinking of 'Dulux' when they want paint and 'Andrex' when they need toilet paper.

A lot of information stored in memory with which nothing has happened in a long time gets 'buried'. Forgetting does not necessarily mean that certain information has disappeared from memory, only that people are unable to access it. In other words, the presence of a brand name in memory is not enough: people should be able to retrieve the name. This description corresponds with the way brand awareness is measured nowadays.

Three levels of brand awareness are usually distinguished:

(1) Spontaneous brand awareness
(2) Aided brand awareness (or brand recognition)
(3) 'Top of mind' awareness.

In the next section we will discuss how these forms of brand awareness can be researched.

19.2 Techniques to measure brand awareness

(28) *Measuring spontaneous brand awareness*

We should mention here that spontaneous brand awareness does not really exist. The respondent is always aided, since the interviewer asks for brands she knows within a certain field (e.g. a certain product category). Indicating a field can be seen as a stimulus or cue. Spontaneous recall is measured by asking the respondent about the brands she knows in a certain product category. 'Which brands do you know in product category X, even if just by name?'

(29) *Measuring aided brand awareness*

The brand recall (brand awareness) is measured in a low consciousness level. On the basis of stimulus material, the consumer has to indicate whether he has seen the brand previously (for instance in an advertisement). In practice, measuring aided brand awareness is done in many ways. The researcher can show a package or mention a brand name and ask the respondent whether he recognises this packaging or name (in the latter case we speak of measuring brand recognition).

(30) *Measuring TOMA (top of mind awareness)*

Measuring brand awareness is only useful for relatively new brands. With large established brands, the awareness is already nearly at its maximum and the brand saliency is measured. Brand saliency can be measured with TOMA: the brand named *first* when being asked 'Which brands do you know from product category X, even if just by name?'

(31) *Tachitoscopic research*

The tachitoscope is a device with which a brand name, a logo, the packaging or an advertisement can be shown to the respondent during a short period (from 0.001–2 seconds). The respondent sees the brand name, logo, package or advertisement during a variable number of (thousandths of) seconds and is interviewed after each exposure. This interview serves to find out to what degree identification of and communication with the brand have taken place (Aans, 1996).

Chapter 20

Research into Brand Meanings

20.1 Introduction

In this book brand meanings are described as 'the mental links of a brand name to cognitions in long-term memory'. Brand meanings are the perceived traits of a brand that the consumer uses as an evaluative criterion. Sometimes a brand meaning flows directly from the function of the product and other times an abstract or symbolic meaning is linked to a brand with the help of communication. In spite of the fact that this depends upon perceptions of individuals, brand meanings are relatively constant and objective, even though every individual links his own evaluative opinion to them. A person who likes design consciously chooses an Italian car. Someone else might also perceive that the car comes from Italy, but finds it unattractive precisely for that reason. This also applies to symbolic attributes: objectively speaking, a certain user type 'belongs' with a certain brand (we recognise a 'real' BMW 500 driver and a 'real' Cosmopolitan reader). The evaluation of these perceived user types varies from individual to individual. At the beginning of Chapter 10, brand meanings were separated into groups (see box 'Categories of brand meanings'). In section 20.2 we will discuss techniques for researching the meanings.

20.2 Techniques to measure brand meanings

(32) *Repertory grid*

The repertory grid is used to discover the different dimensions that people use when they interpret and evaluate brands. The researcher keeps putting out sets of three cards from a stack in front of a respondent or a group of respondents. These cards have names, logos or pictures of brands on them. The respondent is required to indicate which two brands have something in common, what that common thing is, and why the third brand does not have it. The researcher keeps giving the respondents different trios of stimuli until she cannot make trios any more. The techniques can be used during single interviews and group discussions.

The repertory grid has come out of Kelly's 'construct theory'. According to Kelly, people form an image of the world around them. This image arises on the basis of a construct – a way in which two or more issues are the same and thus different from a third issue. Constructs are always bipolar (e.g. good–bad, beautiful–ugly). People give meaning to the world by simultaneously noticing differences and similarities. A chair is a chair because it looks like something you previously called a chair. On the basis of these constructs, people develop hypotheses and expectations which they constantly test and adjust (Van Tilburg and Tuitert, 1995).

(33)   *ASSPAT*

ASSPAT stands for 'association pattern method'. The method is used only during single interviews. The respondent is presented with a 'compartmentalised pattern'. A few years ago the brands were mentioned in the rows and their possible attributes were mentioned in the columns. The respondent was asked to put a cross for each brand that he considered possessed the relevant attributes. In more recent years, practical considerations have 'capsised' the pattern so that the columns have the brands and the rows contain their attributes (see Table 20.1). The result is a pattern in which crosses indicate which brands are associated with which attributes. A big advantage of this is that brands are constantly being evaluated in relation to one another. A disadvantage is that the evaluation per brand is not very differentiated. Correspondence analysis is generally used to analyse the data further (Van Tilburg and Tuitert, 1995; Research International, 1997b).

If the expected results are calculated per cell and these values are compared with the actual cell values, it is possible to protect the results against the double-jeopardy effect (see section 18.2).

Table 20.1   An example of ASSPAT

	Brand 1	Brand 2	Brand 3	Brand 4	Brand 5	None of these
Healthy						
Good price/quality ratio						
Has a fresh taste						
Natural ingredients						
Nice advertisements						

An example of cognitive response analysis

When you mention the name Cadbury, what do you think of? You may say anything that enters your mind: thoughts, ideas, feelings, packaging, taste, advertising. These can be positive, negative or neutral thoughts:

	Positive	Neutral	Negative
1.	☐	☐	☐
2.	☐	☐	☐
3.	☐	☐	☐
4.	☐	☐	☐
5.	☐	☐	☐

(34) *Cognitive response analysis*

Several market research agencies use the technique of cognitive response analysis (CRA) to generate the reactions that a stimulus (a brand) invokes in respondents. The point of departure of the technique (as used by, for example, Research International) is the hypothesis that a stimulus (advertising, packaging, brand name, logo) that leads to an active mental process will have more of an effect than advertising in which that is not the case. The second hypothesis is that a stimulus that leads to a response that is found relevant by the consumer will be more convincing (Research International, 1997a).

In CRA the respondent names all the reactions that a presented stimulus (the brand) invokes in him during a period determined beforehand (e.g. three minutes). The respondent is then asked to name a feeling (either positive, negative or neutral) associated with each reaction. An example is shown above.

When interpreting results, some market research agencies impute significance to the number of reactions that the respondent has given in connection with the speed with which these are given. For example, the marketing research agency Signicom (1994) makes a distinction between direct, spontaneous reactions and reactions that are given after some time, or secondary reactions. In this research, spontaneous associations are part of those reactions that the brand invokes within thirty seconds.

(35) *Goose board method*

The goose board method is used in single interviews. The respondent gets a stack of cards (a multiple of four) on which attributes of brands are pictured. It is necessary for the analysis that the number of cards be divisible by four.

The respondent keeps getting a new set of four cards and has to order them. This ordering can be done in different ways. For instance, the respondent can indicate their order of importance, or which of the four attributes fits best with a certain picture. The respondent has to explain clearly why he is using a certain order. These reactions are written down. By using the goose board method, the researcher gains an insight into the image that the respondent has of a brand. On the basis of this order she can determine which attributes of the brand the respondent finds most important (Van Tilburg and Tuitert, 1995).

Consumers find it difficult to indicate which attributes they actually use when choosing a brand. In reality, this choice is often unconscious and, consequently, so is an ordering of attributes. By continuously considering foursomes of attributes, the task of the respondent becomes more orderly. A disadvantage of this technique is that the respondent constantly has to make a forced choice between the attributes. It remains to be seen how realistic this is. And who knows, at the point of purchase a consumer may choose a brand based on several attributes.

(36) *The Brand Personality Scale (BPS)*

Several decades ago, academics and practising professionals discovered that brands are not bought exclusively for functional reasons. It is particularly *after* the purchase of a brand article that the values that are added to a brand become important to a consumer. Franzen and Hoogerbrugge (1996) speak of the 'symbolic function of a brand'. Consumers evaluate the meaning of different brands in order to find out whether they say the right things about them. They look at what the brands symbolise, and on that basis decide whether or not to use a certain brand.

To get an insight into the how and why of this symbolic function, researchers and practising professionals have focused on the interactions between the personality of a consumer on the one hand and the brand on the other (Aaker, 1996); for example whether an extraverted person chooses different brands from those selected by an introvert.

Jennifer Aaker (1996), a researcher at the University of California in Los Angeles, is startled by the fact that hardly any efforts have been made to develop a conceptual structure that gives insight into the personality of brands. Aaker understands brand personality to be the human attributes that are associated with a brand. This brand personality is not product related but has a symbolic function. She carried out a study based on the 'Big Five' personality traits, a well known list from personality studies (see also section 10.6.2). These Big Five are openness, conscientiousness, extraversion, agreeability and neuroticism (a mnemonic device: the first letters of the Big Five form the word 'ocean') (Engler, 1995). The purpose of this study was to develop an instrument to map out the brand personality. Aaker compared the lists that are

The Brand Personality Scale (Aaker, 1997)

- **Sincerity**

Down-to-earth:	family-oriented, small-town, conventional, blue-collar, all-American
Honest:	sincere, real, ethical, thoughtful, caring
Wholesome:	original, ageless, classic, old-fashioned
Cheerful:	sentimental, friendly, warm, happy

  Examples of brands are: Kodak, Campbell's and Douwe Egberts

- **Excitement**

Daring:	trendy, exciting, off-beat, flashy, provocative
Spirited:	cool, young, lively, outgoing, adventurous
Imaginative:	unique, humorous, surprising, artistic, fun
Up-to-date:	independent, contemporary, innovative, aggressive

  Examples of brands are: Porsche, Benetton and Absolut

- **Competence**

Reliable:	hardworking, secure, efficient, trustworthy, careful
Intelligent:	technical, corporate, serious
Successful:	leader, confident, influential

  Examples of brands are: IBM, American Express and ABN/AMRO

- **Sophistication**

Upper class:	glamorous, good-looking, pretentious, sophisticated
Charming:	feminine, smooth, sexy, gentle

  Examples of brands are: Mercedes, Revlon and Lexus

- **Ruggedness**

Outdoorsy:	masculine, Western, active, athletic
Tough:	rugged, strong, no-nonsense

  Examples of brands are: Levi's, Marlboro and Nike

used in psychology and in market research, and which are based on the Big Five, with each other and arrived at a list of 133 personality traits. To check that these traits are adequate for research into brand personality, she asked a small number of respondents (sixteen) to make a free association. These respondents had to think of a number of brands selected by Aaker and write down the personality traits that came to their minds. This test produced as many as 295 personality traits and brought the total to 209 traits. To reduce the number, Aaker asked twenty-five respondents to evaluate, with the help of a scale technique, how relevant they thought the traits were. A total of 114 traits remained, which Aaker used for a large quantitative analysis in which 600 respondents were asked to score several brands on the 114 remaining traits. A factor analysis of the results produced the Brand Personality Scale (see box on previous page).

The basis of the instrument is formed by Aaker's findings that a brand personality consists of five dimensions: honesty, excitement, competence, distinction (sophistication) and ruggedness. Each dimension is in turn made up of a number of factors (a total of fifteen), and in order to map out these factors Aaker developed statements (linked to the fifteen factors). Respondents can indicate on scales to what degree they agree with a certain statement. By looking at the scores of different respondents for one specific brand, the researcher gets a picture of the dimension(s) that are particularly applicable to that brand (Aaker, 1996).

(37)   *Laddering*

The technique of laddering is a method whereby questions are continually asked until a terminal value is achieved, and is used regularly in market research to discover the underlying motivations for purchasing products. Laddering is a qualitative technique that produces the best results during single interviews. A card with meaning structures is made for each respondent. The card is in the form of a ladder and consists of the following elements:

- Products or product types
- Attributes (the attributes of products)
- Functional implications (the consequences of the attributes for the usage of the product)
- Psychological implications (how does the respondent experience the attributes of the product?)
- Instrumental values
- Terminal values.

The card indicates which attributes a product or brand must have, according to the respondent. The technique can produce quantitative information if the elements that appear in qualitative ladders are structured and are then presented to the respondents in a closed questionnaire (Sikkel, 1994).

Laddering – an example

When a researcher asks a respondent: 'Why do you always use products from The Body Shop?', it seems that this question can be answered in different ways. A possible answer is:

'Products of The Body Shop are not tested on animals.'

The researcher can go on asking: 'Why do you think it is important that products not be tested on animals?' A possible answer is:

'The use of these products does not cause any damage to nature and the world.'

The researcher can now ask: 'Why do you not want to cause any damage to nature and the world'? An answer might be:

'I want my children to grow up in a world full of beauty and love.'

This last answer appears in Rokeach's values inventory and is a terminal value. There is no point in continuing to ask questions after this answer.

Chapter 21

Research into Brand Emotions

21.1 Introduction

Brand emotions are the mental links of a brand name to emotions that can be distinguished on the basis of their nature and intensity. In Part Two it became clear that, when defining and studying brand emotions, all kinds of things can go wrong, and often do. A distinction between emotions and feelings is seldom made. A lot of use is made of lists with basic emotions. This can be very handy and speedy, but there is great scientific discord on whether basic emotions exist and which these might be. Furthermore, there is rarely any research into the *intensity* of an emotion, only its nature. In this part we explain that two types of 'emotional' brand responses are possible.

First, the confrontation with the brand can invoke an affective response. Affective responses are not the same as emotions, and they are not specific either. At best, people experience brands as pleasurable versus non-pleasurable. There is also the question of whether the affective reaction that dominates everything is not a feeling of confidence. Many people experience confidence as something positive. They buy Persil because of this confidence and not because of warmth or togetherness. The affective reactions to brands are usually too weak to register with standard instruments for measuring emotions; FACS, for instance, will produce nothing (see section 11.2.5). In quantitative research they can be measured with semantic differentials.

Secondly, the emotion can be used as a 'benefit'. Emotions are strategically linked to the brand name. Consumers recognise that a certain emotion belongs with a brand, but do not experience the emotion. Linking a brand name to an emotion ensures that the brand distinguishes itself from the competition and thus becomes more relevant for consumers. Sutherland writes in his book *Advertising and the Mind of the Consumer* that just as certain *information* can be associated with a brand (e.g. safety and Volvo), so an *emotion* can also be associated with a brand: if we consider safety important, Volvo is the symbol, and if we think that driving pleasure is important, a BMW fits better.

Several research techniques have been borrowed from psychology. After some adjusting they appear to have become suitable for brand and advertisement research. These techniques tend to be quite expensive because they require the use of very advanced equipment. At present, the techniques described in the following section are not used widely in marketing and advertising research; when they are used, it is mainly to measure advertising responses rather than mental brand responses. For the sake of completeness, though, we have included them in the overview.

21.2 Techniques for measuring brand emotions

(38) *Psychophysiological research*

In psychophysiological research, a connection – usually quantitative – is sought between the values of a physical variable (e.g. body temperature, amount of sweat, heartbeat) and the mental perceptions that go together with it. The following examples of physiological research (borrowed from Aans, 1996) are seldom or never used for market research. They are very expensive and it is extremely difficult to find respondents who want to collaborate in such research. The research results that are known in the field of brands and advertising come largely from psychologists who have used an advertisement as a stimulus when developing a technique.

- *Research into brain waves and hemispheric asymmetry*
  Brain waves can be measured by means of electrodes attached to the head. With a PET scan, researchers can also see which brain areas are activated when the respondent is confronted with a stimulus. Krugman (1971) and Cacioppo and Petty (1983) used this method to do research into the physiological effect of an advertisement. It is also possible to find out which reactions a brand name invokes in the brain of a respondent.

- *Voice analysis*
  The frequencies and intensity of the voice are measured by voice analysis. The idea behind this is that perception of an intense stimulus changes the brain system. This change manifests itself in the voice of the respondent, which may become louder, higher and faster, or languid and slow.

- *Heartbeat research*
  The electrical manifestations that take place with every heartbeat are measured with an electrocardiogram (ECG). Research has shown that the heart beats faster when processing emotional advertisements and slower when processing statements of a more cognitive nature (Thorson, 1991). It is easy to imagine that a brand that distinguishes itself from its competitors

by using more emotionally loaded advertisements (for instance John Smith, which distinguishes itself with humour) makes the hearts of respondents beat more quickly.

- *Research into natural observable bodily responses*
The facial expressions and head movements of respondents on seeing a brand name (or logo or packaging) can be registered and studied with a videotape. The method works better when respondents do not know beforehand that they are being observed. After all, bodily reactions can be kept very much under control (Aans, 1996).

- *Eye movement technique*
This technique is regularly used experimentally to measure reactions to advertisements. The respondent sees the advertisement through binoculars. An infrared ray is reflected into the eye, registering which points in the advertisement have been looked at, the direction of the gaze and the duration of the fixation. This way the elements that attract attention become clear. After registration a qualitative interview is carried out with the respondent to measure why certain elements of the advertisement received more attention than others. In fact, attention can have a positive as well as a negative effect (Aans, 1996). In the autumn of 1997, a new method of automatically measuring eye movements was introduced in the Netherlands. This method is called Verify and, in addition to the eye movement registration research, offers its clients a databank that is updated daily and provides information on the attention consumers pay to newspapers and commercials (Parker Brady, 1997).

   Instead of advertisements, it is possible to ask the respondent to look at a brand name, logo or packaging. Other qualitative and quantitative research has shown that almost nobody knows what logo is depicted on a bottle of Guinness. By using eye movement registration, researchers can find out what consumers *do* look at when they see a bottle of Guinness.

- *Galvanic skin reaction (GSR)*
Galvanic skin reaction is a measure of the electrical response of the skin, measured with a galvanometer. Put simply, GSR measures the amount of sweat and/or goosebumps that a respondent produces when perceiving a stimulus. Two techniques are usually applied in psychology: the Féré method, which measures changes in the skin condition with the passage of electrical current, or the Tarnachov measurement, which measures currents produced by the body itself (Reber, 1997). The mother of a 15-year-old boy will be able to produce sweat when seeing the brand name 'Nike'. She thinks this brand of shoes is too expensive, but her son is threatening not to go to school any more if she does not buy them for him.

(39) *Verbal research*

Verbal research measures the verbal reactions to a brand name (or the logo or packaging) with pre-coded answer possibilities or with spontaneous reactions that are coded afterwards. Respondents are often asked to indicate on a scale to what degree a brand invokes a certain emotion (see Figure 21.1). The researcher can also use semantic differentials (see item 55 in section 23.2).

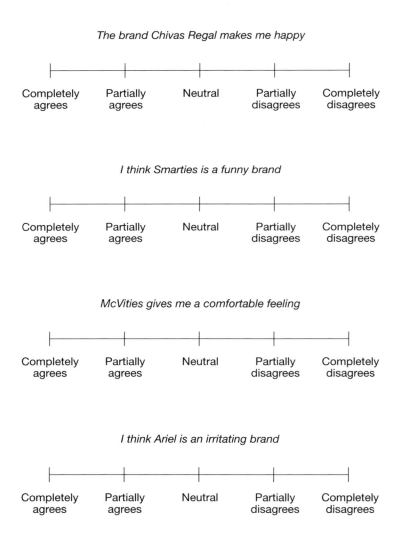

The brand Chivas Regal makes me happy

| Completely
agrees | Partially
agrees | Neutral | Partially
disagrees | Completely
disagrees |

I think Smarties is a funny brand

| Completely
agrees | Partially
agrees | Neutral | Partially
disagrees | Completely
disagrees |

McVities gives me a comfortable feeling

| Completely
agrees | Partially
agrees | Neutral | Partially
disagrees | Completely
disagrees |

I think Ariel is an irritating brand

| Completely
agrees | Partially
agrees | Neutral | Partially
disagrees | Completely
disagrees |

Figure 21.1 Verbal reactions to a brand name.

(40)   *Self Assessment Manikin (SAM)*

SAM is based on the Pleasure Arousal Dominance model (PAD) of Mehrabian and Russell. Research done by these two psychologists in 1977 showed that emotions consist of three independent and bipolar dimensions:

(1) Pleasure versus dissatisfaction
(2) Degree of arousal (high versus low)
(3) Dominance versus submission.

These dimensions can take place independently of one another and are graphically depicted in SAM in Figure 21.2.

The series of graphic depictions for dimension 1 begins with a happy, laughing doll and ends with an unhappy frowning doll. The degree of arousal is indicated with a series of five dolls who have at the extremes a sleepy doll with closed eyes and an excited doll with open eyes (and a kind of explosion in its belly). The third dimension is indicated with a series of dolls that become increasingly larger: a submissive doll is small and a dominant doll hardly fits within the frameworks of this picture (Morris, 1995). Respondents can indicate their emotional state by pressing a button under the picture that best fits that emotional state. There are several methods of evaluating SAM. First, pleasure, arousal and dominance scores can be given to every advertisement. This is how we can see if the goal of the advertiser has been achieved. Secondly, every brand can be placed in a 'pleasure–arousal' matrix. Brands that fall into the same quadrant can be compared with each other (Aans, 1996).

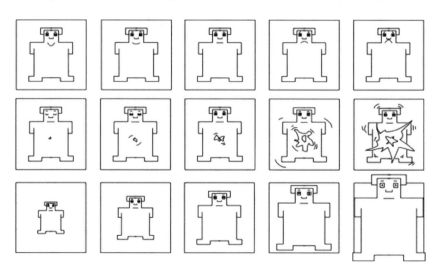

Figure 21.2   Graphic depiction of SAM (Morris, 1995). Reprinted from the *Journal of Advertising Research* © 1995, the Advertising Research Foundation.

Chapter 22

Research into Brand Positioning

22.1　Introduction

Brand positioning is defined as 'the classification of a brand into a group or subgroup of other brands on the basis of the most characteristic common traits and the distinction of a brand from other brands within that group or subgroup on the basis of its most characteristic differences'. This component of the mental brand response is very difficult to distinguish from the other components in research. Consumers are faced daily with a large number of brands within one and the same product category and must make a choice. Researchers, advertisers and publicists are therefore not only interested in how consumers evaluate a certain brand, but even more in the degree to which and the way in which other brands are involved in the choice process. To what degree and with regard to which attributes is a brand unique compared to the competition? To get answers to such questions, several brands are almost always involved in image research. For that reason, practically every technique for measuring brand representation is in fact a positioning technique.

As became clear in section 12.2, consumers place brands with common traits into groups in their memories. Different researchers have different views on the categories that people make in their brain. Some claim that all brands belonging to the same product category are in one group, and others say that consumers categorise all the brands that fit into their value system (for more information, see also section 12.3). This difference has important implications for research: for instance, can researchers use standard measuring instruments to research different product categories? In other words: does it make sense to pose the same questions when it comes to toilet paper and cars? Most research agencies do not think so. They make up a new questionnaire for each product category (or change part of it). The advertising agency Y&R thinks it is possible and uses the 'brandscape' of Biel (see section 12.3) as a basis for its brand research, having respondents evaluate brands from all product categories on the same 'statements'.

The techniques used to get an insight into brand positioning can be roughly divided into two groups:

- Respondents are asked to divide various brands into groups
- Respondents evaluate brands on a number of attributes or traits, after which they are classified into groups on the basis of their profiles.

This splitting is central to the classification of techniques in the following section.

22.2   Techniques for measuring brand positioning

GROUPING

(41)   *Natural grouping*

In natural grouping the respondent is asked to split a collection of brands (usually depicted in photographs) into two groups. In turn, each subgroup has to be split in two. In every splitting, the respondent is asked to indicate the reasons for the splitting and to describe the groups that emerged. The actions are repeated until the respondent cannot think of another reason to make a new group. The researcher gains an insight into the brands that resemble each other, according to the respondent, and the reasons why.

(42)   *Market Structure Audit (MSA)*

The Market Structure Audit was developed by BBDO and is fully derived from natural grouping. With MSA, BBDO analyses the competition ratios between brands, and the main market segments are determined from the consumer's point of view. Respondents are asked to divide brands into groups. The brands that resemble each other in any way at all fall into one group. The respondents have to keep explaining why they put certain brands in a group. By using cluster analysis the research results are processed and analysed. The distance between the clusters indicates how strongly certain brands differ from each other. In many cases it seems that consumers find it difficult to indicate why some brands resemble another and others do not. The photo sort (see projective techniques toolkit) can be used as an aid (BBDO, 1990).

ALLOCATING ATTRIBUTES/TRAITS TO DIFFERENT BRANDS

(43)   *Delta diagnosis*

Delta diagnosis is used when it is important to obtain broad insights into the position of various brands with regard to one another. How large are the differences that are perceived by the consumer? Delta diagnosis evaluates strengths and weaknesses of brands at instrumental as well as expressive levels, and takes into account the decision-making process of the consumer. The delta is the fictional space in which various evaluation aspects of three brands are evaluated with regard to one another by the consumer. A respondent places cards with a product trait in such a way in the delta that it is closest to the brand it fits best. The cards can contain words and concepts as well as photographs from the photo sort. There is also a card that represents the respondent's own brand preference (the 'me' card). With this card the respondents make the mental trade-off, just as they do when they choose between brands. The results allow a direct reading of the attractiveness of the position of a brand, while an insight also arises into the 'closeness' of competing brands.

(44)   *TOMI (top of mind image)*

An important difference between TOMI and other positioning techniques is that in TOMI the following question is asked first: 'If you were to buy product X tomorrow, which brands would you consider?' In this way a filter can be built in, and the researcher believes he is getting a more realistic view of the brands that the consumer experiences as the competition. The respondent then has to score the brands she answered with in the previous question on several attributes. She does this by indicating with a grade to what degree a trait fits with a brand. The researcher keeps using two attributes as coordinates in a coordinate system in which she indicates the place of various brands (ISEO, 1996).

(45)   *Locator*

The Locator technique was developed by Research International. The technique measures the mutual relationship between brands and is therefore a positioning technique. The image each respondent allocates to a brand is observed and this is related to that person's preference structure. In fact, two things are measured: how the respondent sees the brand and how he evaluates the brand with regard to the competition.

   To measure the brand image, respondents have to evaluate three to eight brands on a number of attributes. These attributes are selected beforehand by the researcher. The dimensions that determine the image are identified with the help of factor analysis.

To measure brand preference, CSP (constant sum preference) is used. Respondents have to distribute a number of points (usually eleven) over two brands. An example:

'Distribute eleven points over brand A and brand B to indicate your preference.'

A respondent gives, say, seven points to A and four to B (Research International, 1995). The results of CPS are combined later with those of image measurement. This can be done in two ways:

- *Ideal point modelling.* In bipolar evaluation it is possible to determine an 'ideal point'. This is the point at which the distance of each of the products is inversely proportional to the preference.
- *Vector modelling.* This model is suitable for data that are collected with unipolar scales. A smallest quadrant regression method is used to establish a line that is most fitting for the data.

By using Locator, the researcher looks at which attributes can make an important contribution to the image and the preference. Brand A may be very beautiful, while brand B may be very durable (image). Consumers choose brand A because of the price (preference for A). The researchers can also carry out simulations using Locator. During the study the researcher changes the image of a brand a few times (by using other attributes in the description of a brand) and looks at how this affects the preference (Research International, 1995).

(46) *Quality planning (QP)*

Consumers are confronted daily with an enormous amount of information. The number of advertisements that a consumer is faced with every day has also increased. Calculations in the United States indicate that the number of advertisements and commercials printed and broadcast increased by 103% between 1967 and 1982. This number is expected to have doubled between 1983 and 1998 (Franzen, 1992). At the same time, society has become strongly individualised in recent years. The media have taken advantage of this individualisation by strongly segmenting. This can be seen in the fact that consumers can now choose from hundreds of magazine titles and television stations: there is something for everyone. With this growth in and segmentation of the media supply, a new problem has emerged for the advertiser: it is becoming increasingly difficult to determine which media and which media titles she should select in order to place her advertisements. This problem could probably be solved by using the technique of Quality Planning (QP).

The developers of QP, the Dutch market research agency MarketResponse and the publishing company VNU, assume that the most effective communication takes place when a brand and a periodical represent corresponding values. Correspondence between the brand and the environment in which the information on this brand is given allegedly stimulates the clarity of the positioning and the effectiveness of the message. The theoretical foundation of this hypothesis is in fact quite vague and there is no empirical proof as yet. It is plausible, however, that harmony between brand and medium works better than contrast between them, but this hypothesis still has to be researched further (Lamme and Gameren, 1993).

In QP, periodicals and brands are placed in a cube, a three-dimensional space in which the following coordinates can be distinguished:

- Coordinate with psychological orientation (extrovert versus introvert)
- Coordinate with sociological orientation (ego-oriented versus group-oriented)
- Coordinate with behavioural orientation (conforming to the norms versus individualistic behaviour).

Placing brands and periodicals is done by interviewing readers of the publications. These people have to indicate, from a collection of 'basic concepts', to what degree these fit a certain article or brand. The collection of basic concepts consists of occupations, hobbies and character traits of people. The correlation between a title and a brand is apparent from the distance between them in the cube. The results are processed and analysed with special software (Lamer and Gameren, 1993).

(47) *IMPMAP*

Implicit Personality Mapping (IMPMAP) was developed by the British marketing agency Infratest Burke. Sampson (1993), one of the developers of IMPMAP, claims that consumers choose brands on the basis of the personality of these brands. The brand personality, together with the brand identity, form the image of a brand. According to Sampson, the identity of a brand emanates from the explicit, rational attributes of a brand: ice-cream of the brand Häagen Dazs is natural, exuberant, delicious and refreshing. The personality of a brand is formulated on the basis of reactions of consumers to the implicit traits: Häagen Dazs is hip, cool and exciting. Sampson believes that most research techniques only measure the explicit attributes of a brand and he says this is only half of the story: we have to measure the implicit as well as the explicit attributes of brands. This would be possible by using IMPMAP.

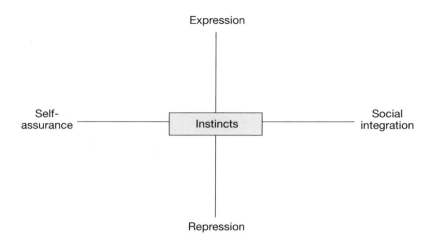

Figure 22.1 The expression and repression of instincts (Heylen *et al.*, 1995).

The basis of IMPMAP is formed by the theory of Paul Heylen (1990; Heylen *et al.*, 1995). Following on Freud, Heylen claims that people use two dimensions to give meaning to the world around them. On the one hand, the behaviour of people is determined by innate instincts. On the other hand, people learn at a young age that they have to adapt themselves to the norms and values of society. There is a constant tension between these instincts and the demands of a culture and a society. People are constantly confronted with the choice of expressing or repressing their instincts and how to do this: in an active, masculine, self-assured manner, or in a passive, sensitive, feminine manner, with social integration and harmony as the ultimate goal (Figure 22.1).

Sampson believes that this space can be filled further. He has indicated a number of possible behaviours in the two-dimensional space (Figure 22.2).

From Figure 22.2 it is a small step to the final IMPMAP model (Figure 22.3).

The eight 'pieces of cake' represent eight personality traits: extrovert, introvert, warm, cold, affiliating, assertive, subdued and energetic.

The researcher selects beforehand several explicit attributes and several brands. The respondent has to allocate these attributes to the selected brands. The respondent is then given three stacks of cards which he has to distribute over the brands.

One of the stacks consists of six close-up photographs depicting men and women. There is a picture of a stereotypical man, a feminine man, a masculine man, a stereotypical woman, a masculine woman and a feminine woman.

The second stack helps provide insight into the various 'gratifications' that the brands can fulfil. This stack of cards is also called the 'morphology set'. The respondent is given eight pictures depicting bodily postures. There is a picture of an active posture, a passive posture, and a feminine and a masculine

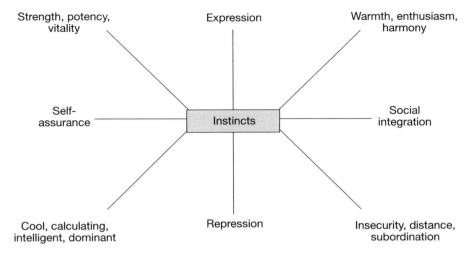

Figure 22.2 Human behaviour according to Heylen *et al.* (1995).

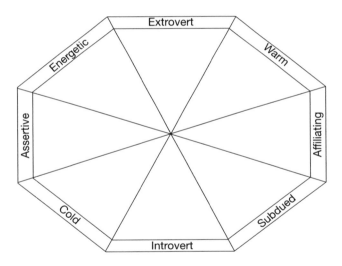

Figure 22.3 IMPMAP (Sampson, 1993).

posture and two pictures of people who are self-absorbed (in an active manner, e.g. 'reading', and in a passive manner, e.g. 'staring'). Finally, there is a picture of someone in a posture that is in harmony with the surroundings and a picture of someone committing a misdemeanour.

A third stack has to bring out the deeper meaning of brands for the respondent. The cards (a total of eight) depict pictures of animals. These animals represent successively life, potency, assertiveness, vulnerability, death, impotence, submission and fertility.

Based on the results of the above-mentioned sorting techniques, the brands (with their corresponding attributes) can be placed in the IMPMAP space (Sampson, 1993; Heylen *et al.*, 1995).

(48) *Marketing analysis according to the psychodynamic approach*

All the research carried out by the Benelux market research agency Censydiam and all the research techniques developed by the agency are oriented towards the psychodynamic approach. The consumer is approached more from the inside out, and researchers attempt to penetrate into the 'deeper self'. Several theories of Dichter, Freud, Jung and especially Adler are used as a basis for this psychodynamic thinking. In 1994 four researchers at Censydiam – Callebout, Janssens, Lorré and Hendrickx – published a book in which they discuss the working method of Censydiam and the importance of in-depth psychological market research. It is interesting to start by describing the train of thought of Adler (on which Censydiam bases itself) and to explain the way Censydiam translates Adler's theory into research. For a more detailed description, see Callebout *et al.* (1994).

According to Adler, all people have a 'community spirit' in themselves, a natural urge to connect to others. He calls this urge 'belonging'. At the same time, all people strive towards superiority: they want to be the best. One striving is almost always in conflict with the other. The basis of Adler's theory is people's feeling of inferiority. He calls this 'organ inferiority' because the feeling comes from the thoughts people have that their organs do not work any more.

Every child is confronted early in life with the fact that adults are stronger. We carry this feeling the rest of our lives. We become angry at the feeling and strive towards superiority. There are two ways in which we can deal with our inferiority organ (Callebout *et al.*, 1994):

- The masculine method: being good at something else (compensating)
- The feminine method: passiveness and despondence, manifesting itself in a large inferiority complex: 'some brands are too good for me'.

To explain how this train of thought is translated into research, we will use a study into the automobile market carried out by Censydiam which has been regularly published in specialised journals in recent years.

The dimension derived from the theory of Adler is shown on the horizontal coordinate of Figure 22.4. The vertical coordinate gives a distinction between brands that are bought primarily for functional reasons and brands that are chosen for their emotional or symbolic value. Using, for example, 'animal sort' and 'occupational sort', respondents allocate the brands to the various quadrants in the coordinate system.

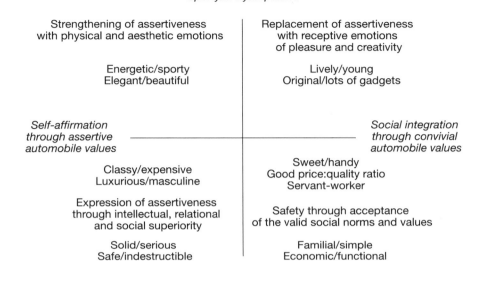

Emotional relationship
Sporty/lively/impulsive

Strengthening of assertiveness
with physical and aesthetic emotions

Replacement of assertiveness
with receptive emotions
of pleasure and creativity

Energetic/sporty
Elegant/beautiful

Lively/young
Original/lots of gadgets

Self-affirmation
through assertive
automobile values

Social integration
through convivial
automobile values

Classy/expensive
Luxurious/masculine

Sweet/handy
Good price:quality ratio
Servant-worker

Expression of assertiveness
through intellectual, relational
and social superiority

Safety through acceptance
of the valid social norms and values

Solid/serious
Safe/indestructible

Familial/simple
Economic/functional

Indestructible car/familial car
Calm/less harmful/reliable car
Functional relationship

Figure 22.4 The technique applied to the Belgian automobile market (Callebout *et al.*, 1994).

(49)   *The BrandAsset Valuator*

The BrandAsset Valuator was developed for and by the Young and Rubicam (Y&R) group, an international advertising agency with branches in almost every country in the world; as well as in the Netherlands, fieldwork is being done in twenty-three countries all over the world. This has produced an enormous databank with facts and figures on more than 7000 brands in all kinds of product categories. Because the measurements are done once every several years (studies were done in 1993 and 1997), it is possible to evaluate whether and how various brands have developed. The following description of the BrandAsset Valuator is based on an article by and a conversation with Jos Ahlers from Y&R-Netherlands (Ahlers, 1997a,b).

Although the BrandAsset Valuator is not based on an extended theoretical framework (Ahlers, 1997a), we are still able to clearly trace back the ideas of people such as Aaker, Biel and Kapferer. The basic idea of the BrandAsset Valuator is that it is the consumer and not the producer who determines the value of a brand. Only when a marketing strategist knows what the strength of his brand is in the eyes of the consumer can he develop an effective marketing strategy; the fact that respondents have to evaluate brands outside the context of product categories is clearly derived from the 'brandscape' invented by Biel (see section 12.3).

The idea that a brand undergoes a life cycle that irrevocably ends in death is rejected by Y&R. Brands can be 'managed' in such a way that they stay young and healthy. The basic idea behind this is formed by the four pillars of brand strength, distinguished by Y&R, which together determine what position the brand takes in the world of the consumer and are defined as follows (Ahlers, 1997a):

- *Differentiation:* How unique is a brand?
- *Relevance:* To what degree does the brand (and the way it differentiates itself) answer to personal needs?
- *Valuing:* How much esteem do consumers have for the brand?
- *Familiarity:* To what extent is the brand part of the consumer's daily life?

The four pillars determine the current strength and the future potential of a brand. In Figure 22.5 we can see how the brand value comprises several constructs.

Scores on the factors of differentiation and relevance are combined into a dimension of brand strength (vitality), and this combination provides an insight into the future potential of the brand. When a brand has a differentiated potential and seems to be relevant for large groups of consumers, then it clearly still has growth possibilities after all. Authority of a brand, a representation of the current strength, is determined by combining scores on 'valuing' and 'reliability'. These pillars indicate what a brand has achieved up to now. If a brand is highly valued and at the same time many consumers are very familiar with the brand, that says something about how strongly a brand is rooted in society (Ahlers, 1997a).

The BrandAsset Valuator is a quantitative study using a representative sample of consumers. The list of brands that are included in the research

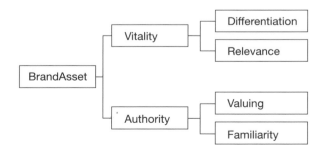

Figure 22.5 Brand value (BrandAsset) and the underlying constructs (Ahlers, 1997a).

consists of global and local brands. Global brands are those that have had exposure in all countries. In addition, local Y&R branches can also add relevant brands to the study. This has produced a total list of more than 7000 brands in 113 product categories. The evaluation of the brands takes place outside the context of product categories. The goal is to have the respondents evaluate the brands in relation to all the brands they know and not only in relation to a previously determined 'competitive set', which is more common in traditional market research. In fact, the questionnaire consists of three parts:

- Respondents evaluate how the various brands score on the four pillars. In some pillars they can indicate this by using a 7-point scale, and in others by using yes/no answers.
- Respondents can indicate with yes/no answers how various brands score on a large number of 'general' attributes. Examples of such attributes are 'fun', 'luxurious', 'cheap', etc.
- Here the spontaneous and aided brand awareness is measured, as well as category use (do you drive? do you smoke?), current usage (do you ever buy Guinness? did you buy Guinness this week?), media consumption, and a scale that makes psychosocial segmentation possible (Young and Rubicam's Cross-Cultural Consumer Characterisations).

(50)   *Cube thought model*

'A map comes about on the basis of measurements of distances that are indicated on a scale. The topography of a market is more difficult to map out, because the markets are constantly in motion due to the influence of all kinds of factors' (ISEO, 1996). Another difficulty is that every consumer has a different image of the market and this image is stored in memory. The only way of getting access to this image is by using properly structured psychological theories. The consumer seems always to use three dimensions in his attitude to the market: an evaluation dimension, a potency dimension and an action dimension. Sometimes these dimensions are also translated into emotion, cognition and conation (behaviour) by the Dutch market research agency ISEO. Dimensions that are important in a given situation are determined market by market or for each market segment with the help of preliminary research. These 'specific' dimensions form the structure of a cube. Respondents indicate which place a brand takes on each of the dimensions. Using this information the researcher can give each brand a place in the cube (ISEO, 1996).

Chapter 23
Research into Brand Attitude

23.1 Introduction

In this book, brand attitude is described as 'the durable evaluation with regard to a brand that is based on the consideration of positive and negative traits of the brand and that has implications for behaviour with regard to the brand'. Since the 1950s a lot of attention has been paid to measuring attitudes. This has resulted in an innumerable amount of models and methods that can provide insights into the attitudes of people. This stems largely from the interest many researchers have in being able to make predictions about people's behaviour on the basis of insights into their attitudes. The fact that many researchers do not succeed in showing the relationship between attitude and behaviour can be ascribed to a methodological fault that they make. According to Fishbein and Ajzen (1975), every behaviour consists of the components of action (what the person does), goal (of the action), context (in which the action takes place) and time (during which the action takes place). Only when the attitude and the behaviour have been specifically defined on the basis of these components is it possible to establish a relationship. Most attitude measurements are oriented exclusively towards the goal of behaviour. The brand attitude is usually measured with scale techniques. These scales are discussed in section 23.2. The scales can also be used to measure other concepts such as the brand behavioural tendency. Since they are known mostly as methods for measuring attitude, they are discussed in this chapter.

23.1.1 *Brand attitude and brand preference*

In many books and articles on brands and advertising, brand preference is used as a synonym for brand attitude. This is not entirely accurate. Franzen (1998) describes brand preference as 'the situation in which a consumer gives relative preference to a specific brand over other brands in the consideration set'. It is a misconception to think that this consideration set includes all the brands towards which consumers have a positive attitude. People buy products without thinking much about it on a daily basis: this is a low involvement situation. The attitudes towards brands in such product categories can be called more neutral than positive. Still, consumers develop a preference for a number of brands. This phenomenon could be explained by the fact that certain brands are larger than others and therefore more prominently present in the surroundings of a consumer. The brand she develops a preference for is just the first brand that comes to her mind. More research would be necessary in order to make well founded pronouncements on why people develop preferences. Not all brands have an equal preference position within a consideration set. It is relevant to measure these differences in preference because there could be a positive relationship with the scope and stability of the market share. This means that, on the basis of insights into the brand preferences of a representative consumer sample, we can make predictions on the market share of this brand. Several methods have been developed to research brand preference. Sometimes a simple question such as: 'Next time you buy product X, which brands will you consider?' is used. Other methods are the constant sum method, brand ranking and the price trade-off method. These methods will be discussed extensively in the following section.

23.2 Techniques for measuring brand attitude

(51) *Likert scale*

The Likert scale was developed by R. Likert and, together with the Guttman scale, it has become one of the most popular methods for measuring attitudes (Van der Pligt and De Vries, 1991). Likert asked respondents to indicate to what degree they agreed with pronouncements that expressed either a positive or a negative attitude towards the object. Five-point scales are generally used for this (see Figure 23.1).

The evaluation of respondents is given a number between 1 and 5. The example in Figure 23.1 shows that a respondent who thinks very positively about the brand Douwe Egberts will answer '5' for every statement. This respondent will get a total score of 15.

Once all respondents have given their reactions to the statements, they are subdivided into groups: 25% of the sample that reacted most favourably to the attitude object, 25% of the sample that reacted most unfavourably to the attitude object, and the remaining less pronounced 50%. Afterwards a selection of statements is made: statements in which the supporters usually agree and opponents do not (and vice-versa) apparently discriminate well between two groups and are included in the attitude measuring instrument (Van der Pligt and De Vries, 1991).

1   If a shop does not sell Douwe Egberts coffee, I go to another shop

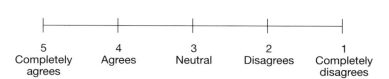

5	4	3	2	1
Completely	Agrees	Neutral	Disagrees	Completely
agrees				disagrees

2   I always have Douwe Egberts coffee at home

5	4	3	2	1
Completely	Agrees	Neutral	Disagrees	Completely
agrees				disagrees

3   I only drink Douwe Egberts brand coffee

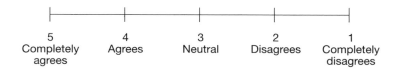

5	4	3	2	1
Completely	Agrees	Neutral	Disagrees	Completely
agrees				disagrees

Figure 23.1   The Likert scale.

(52)   *Guttman scale*

Guttman constructed his attitude scale in 1944. He formulated a series of statements 'with increasing favourableness' with regard to an object (Van der Pligt and De Vries, 1991). A turning point can be determined for each respondent where the person no longer agrees with statements beyond this point. The attitude of the respondent can be encapsulated in one figure with a perfect Guttman scale. This figure also indicates which statement a respondent has or has not agreed with.

(53)   *Thurstone scale*

All the scales used in the social sciences are derived from the work of the psychometrist L.L. Thurstone and based on the general psychophysiological technique known as the 'method of similar intervals'. The general procedure for constructing such scales is as follows: the researcher presents several statements on a certain issue (e.g. the Church, the death penalty, buying shampoo at the Body Shop) on cards and asks a large number of evaluators to sort them into various stacks (e.g. eleven), varying from 'strongly disagree' to 'strongly agree'. For each statement the percentage of evaluators that puts the statements on a certain stack is calculated, and this percentage constitutes the basis for the calculation of a scale value (e.g. the median) that indicates where the statements belong in an underlying scale. Once the statements have been ordered on a scale, they can be presented to respondents, who at that point can only answer 'agree' or 'disagree'. Their score consists of the average or median of the scale values of the statements they agreed with. In fact, this scaling technique departs from the idea that the scale value of a stimulus or statement is probabilistic, just as the position of the respondents is (Reber, 1997).

(54)   *The attitude scale of Achenbaum*

Achenbaum developed an attitude scale on which three levels are indicated: acceptance, unfamiliarity/indifference, and rejection. The area of acceptance points towards the brands that are included in the consideration set. The area of rejection contains the brands that are not seen as acceptable or are clearly rejected. Between these two areas a group of brands can be found about which the consumer feels insecure or indifferent (Franzen, 1998).

Area of acceptance
- Unique: This is my favourite brand. If it isn't there, I go to another store.
- Preference: This is a good brand, which I buy regularly.
- Acceptance: This is a regular brand, but I am only buying it because no better brands are available.

Area of unfamiliarity/indifference
- Indifference: This brand doesn't mean a lot to me. I don't know if it is good or not. I don't know if I would buy it.
- Unfamiliarity: I have never heard of this brand.

Area of rejection
- Rejection: This is a brand I don't like. I would not buy it, but there are worse.
- Disapproval: This is one of the worst brands. I would never buy it.

(55)   *Semantic differentiation scales*

The semantic differential was developed by Osgood *et al.* (1957) and is one of the most popular methods for mapping out evaluations of objects (and thus attitudes). In most scale techniques respondents are asked to indicate to what extent they agree with certain statements. In the semantic differential, respondents are asked to evaluate a specific object on a set of semantic scales.

These scales are defined by daily verbal contradictions with a neutral middle. They usually consist of seven differentiated steps. An example of a semantic differential is given in section 11.3.1. Care is recommended when selecting pairs of words. It is actually very possible for the attitude of the researcher to lead to a biased selection that puts a certain attitude in a more favourable light.

After an enormous amount of research, Osgood *et al.* (1957) arrived at the conclusion that there are three dominant, independent dimensions that people use to evaluate objects:

(1) Evaluation (good versus bad)
(2) Potency (strong versus weak)
(3) Activity (active versus passive).

(56) *Projective differentiation scales*

The projective differentiation scale is an extension of the semantic differentiation scale. The opposed word pairs are replaced by pictures that express an opposite emotion. The pictures can be ink spots, pictures of people or animals, etc. Respondents have to indicate where a brand is on a scale whose extremes are opposite pairs of emotions (Vaughn, 1989). An example is shown in Figure 23.2.

(57) *Indirect measurements*

Under some circumstances, the brand attitude is assessed with a special method. In this method the researcher tries to eliminate the use of language as much as possible. An example of what is known as 'indirect measurements' is the use of psychophysiological dimensions. Muscular movements around the mouth give an indication of cognitive activity and the pupil size indicates the scope of the attention with which a respondent processes a certain message (Van der Pligt and De Vries, 1991).

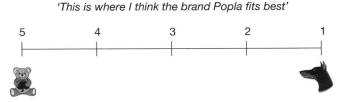

'This is where I think the brand Popla fits best'

Figure 23.2 Projective differentiation scale.

(58) *'Unobtrusive' measurements*

Measurements may be described as unobtrusive when a respondent does not realise that he is being observed or what the purpose of a study is. Unobtrusive measurements are used to solve a number of frequent problems. Problems can arise when recruiting respondents and when the reactions of respondents depend on the effects of social desirability. Examples of unobtrusive measurements are walking around in the supermarket to see which products and brands people buy and taking a look into people's homes to see which brands they use (Van der Pligt and De Vries, 1991).

23.3 Techniques for measuring brand preference

(59) *Constant sum method*

With this method respondents can express their relative brand preference by distributing several points (the constant sum) over the brands that they are considering. There are various ways of applying this method. Respondents are generally asked to distribute eleven points over the same two bands (Franzen, 1998).

Several variants on the constant sum method have now been developed. Sometimes a respondent has to distribute points over a larger number of brands, or over all brands within a product category. In his book *The Laws of Choice*, Marder (1997) describes a version of the constant sum method that resembles very much the way in which consumers choose between brands in daily life. According to Marder, the constant sum method is unique with regard to other research techniques because, when evaluating a brand, consumers are forced to involve evaluations of other competing brands. He claims that this approaches the situation in which consumers choose between brands in daily life: they stand in front of a shelf and compare different brands. Marder gives respondents a book in which each page is devoted to describing the packaging of a brand, with a short description of the added value of each brand (for instance, Ariel washes thoroughly clean, Persil is the brand to use if the wash has to be really white, Bold is a 2-in-1 laundry detergent with fabric softener, and so on). Respondents have to distribute several points over the brands in the book (Marder, 1997).

(60) *Brand ranking*

With brand ranking, as the name implies, the respondent is asked to order a number of brands. The brand that gets most of the preferences gets a high score or reaches the top of the list. Over the years advanced ways have been

Table 23.1 An example of brand ranking.

	Taste	Preparation time	Nutritious	Healthy
How do you evaluate brands that you know on the basis of the mentioned attributes/traits? You can indicate your evaluation with the help of a grade report. Number 1 means 'very bad' and number 10 means 'very good'.				
Brand A	...	...	...	...
Brand B	...	...	...	...
Brand C	...	...	...	...
Brand D	...	...	...	...

devised to do such research. An example is shown in Table 23.1 (Hoogerbrugge, 1996).

(61) *Price trade-off method*

This method calculates the percentage of buyers for a number of brands in contrasting scenarios. On the basis of the results, good predictions can be made on the price elasticity and the related market shares of these brands. It also gives an indication of how far brands can afford a higher price level than that of the competitors (Research International, 1997a). The method works as follows: a respondent is shown a number of brands (e.g. roll-your-own tobacco). The researcher keeps sketching a situation in which there is a price increase and the respondent has to choose which brand he would buy in this situation.

A fictional example: let's say that your point of departure is the situation as it is in real life, i.e. with the actual prices that are charged in the store. In this situation, respondent A has a clear preference for Drum. The researcher asks what the respondent would do if Drum increased its price by twenty-five cents. The respondent answers that he would still choose Drum. If Drum became another fifty cents more expensive, he would switch to Van Nelle. If Van Nelle then became 25 cents more expensive, he would go back to Drum. If Drum became even more expensive, he would then decide it was not worth it and would switch to Brandaris (Table 23.2).

Table 23.2 An example of the price trade-off method.

Brand and store price	Drum (¢ 5.00)	Van Nelle (¢ 4.75)	Samsom (¢ 4.75)	Brandaris (¢ 4.70)	Jacob's (¢ 4.55)
+ ¢ 0.25					
+ ¢ 0.25	x				
+ ¢ 0.25	x				
+ ¢ 0.25	x				
+ ¢ 0.25	x	x		x	

The market research agency Research International has developed a special version of the price trade-off method called BrandYard[12] for the advertising agency Ogilvy and Mather. BrandYard is a technique to measure the strength of a connection that exists between an individual consumer and a brand. Just as in the price trade-off method, the consumer is shown several brands and the researcher keeps sketching a situation in which a change takes place. The consumer has to choose which brand he would buy after this change. Unlike the price trade-off method, there is not always a price change: what is looked at is the number of steps a consumer takes staying with his brand if the brand proposition is made less attractive (Ogilvy and Mather, 1997). Here is an example of a brand proposition that is decreasingly attractive:

(1) Ariel washes thoroughly clean.
(2) Ariel washes very clean.
(3) Ariel washes out most stains.
(4) Ariel cannot fight the really stubborn stains.
(5) Ariel does not wash very clean.

The researcher observes at which proposition the respondent tends to switch to the competition.

---

12 Together with the BrandGrid, BrandYard forms the Customer Ownership, the term used at Ogilvy and Mather to indicate:

- Which *value* an individual consumer will have for the brand in the future
- To what degree the brand in question satisfies the needs of the consumer
- How strong the connection is between an individual consumer and the brand, and which values constitute the basis for this connection.

The way BrandYard works has already been described. In the BrandGrid, statements on a brand and its main competitors are used to obtain quantified insight into the emotional and rational associations that are made with a brand.

Chapter 24

Research into Brand Behavioural Tendencies

24.1   Introduction

Brand behavioural tendency is the tendency anchored in memory to keep buying a brand (the acquired purchasing habit). After all, every advertiser is interested in getting a sale: the beautiful stories about the brand image and the attitude with regard to the brand have to be translated into hard sales figures. Predicting behaviour on the basis of insight into the components of the brand representation is difficult, maybe even impossible. Behaviour is actually determined by psychological as well as environmental factors, and a lot of purchasing behaviour, especially for products with low involvement, is habitual. Without being aware of it, people pick the same products and brands from the shelves again and again. These are usually products and brands they have been using for a long time (Franzen, 1998). The brand purchasing tendency points not only to the actual purchasing, but also to a concrete plan or intention to show certain behaviour in the near future. In durable goods, such as cars and washing machines, Van Westendorp (1996) recommends establishing the information intention instead of the purchasing intention (i.e. by counting the incoming reactions on a customer service number).

   If you want to study or predict whether respondents are planning to buy a certain brand, it is better if you ask directly. This usually takes place with the help of scale techniques. A great disadvantage of such scale techniques is that respondents can only give a reaction to propositions that have been made up beforehand by the researcher. Another disadvantage is that questions on intended purchasing behaviour are, in fact, more attitude measurements than actual behavioural tendencies. Yet another disadvantage is that questions on behaviour are not that reliable. Respondents may think that they buy Knorr soup, but what their kitchen cabinets really contain are packages of Heinz. An elegant, and expensive, alternative to the use of scale techniques is mapping out as many behavioural determinants as possible. In marketing terms this is also called brand monitoring (for more information, see Franzen, 1998).

24.2 Techniques for measuring brand behavioural tendencies

(62) *Brand monitoring*

According to many researchers, it is impossible to make predictions on purchasing behaviour based on insights into the image of a brand. They claim that, in order to say anything meaningful about this purchasing behaviour, we have to keep constantly registering as many behavioural determinants as possible (nature of the market, competition, social development, seasonal influences, distribution channels, price changes, etc.). Studying behavioural determinants usually takes place quantitatively. Market research agencies such as AC Nielsen and GfK produce figures related to the distribution degree and the market share, and the advertising agency in question has an insight into advertising expenditure. In addition, a representative sample of respondents are regularly asked to fill in long questionnaires. A disadvantage is that this is how researchers get a large amount of information to choose from and that all this information has to be interpreted. To take care of this problem, theories and corresponding models have been developed. With these techniques and models, the quantitative data can be placed in spreadsheets to allow multivariate analysis and other statistical calculations (Schuring and Vogel, 1998).

The term brand monitoring is sometimes confused with advertising tracking. The difference between these two techniques is not clear to everyone and both tracking variants are not mutually exclusive. The difference is based on where the point of gravity of the measurements lies: in the effectiveness of advertising (advertising tracking) or in the position of the brand in the market (brand monitoring) (Hoogerbrugge, 1996).

(63) *Scale techniques*

The following are some examples for measuring the purchasing intention with propositions and scales (Hoogerbrugge, 1996):

'Next time you need product X, will you tend to buy brand Y?'

☐ 5 definitely

☐ 4 probably

☐ 3 maybe

☐ 2 probably not

☐ 1 definitely not

'Do you intend to buy this brand/product in the next 3 (7, 10, 12, 30) (days/weeks/months/years)?' (indicated term depends on the type of product)

☐ yes

☐ no

☐ don't know/no opinion

'Which answer would you choose to show the likelihood of you or another family member buying brand X in the next X weeks?'

Scale	Purchasing likelihood
☐ 100 completely sure	(100 in 100)
☐ 90	(90 in 100)
☐ 80	(80 in 100)
☐ 70	(70 in 100)
☐ 60	(60 in 100)
☐ 50	(50 in 100)
☐ 40	(40 in 100)
☐ 30	(30 in 100)
☐ 20	(20 in 100)
☐ 10	(10 in 100)
☐ 0 absolutely no chance	(0 in 100)

Similar questions can also be posed on the likelihood of people asking for information. In some advertisements there is a customer service number that consumers can call to request information. In an interview, respondents can be asked the degree to which they are willing to call such a number.

'Let's say you see this advertisement in a magazine. There is a customer service number where you can request additional information. Are you willing to call this number?'

☐ 5 definitely

☐ 4 probably

☐ 3 maybe

☐ 2 probably not

☐ 1 definitely not

(64) *BrandWatcher*

There is a research centre associated with Erasmus University in Rotterdam, called CMM (Centre for Research into Brands and Brand Policy). Researchers at this centre have developed the BrandWatcher questionnaire,[13] based on literature research, case studies of six brand article makers, in-depth interviews with 72 consumers and three group discussions. This questionnaire consists of five blocks of questions (see box overleaf).

The developers of the BrandWatcher claim that a relationship can be established between the brand positioning on the one hand and brand choice and brand loyalty on the other by using the answers given on the questions from the five blocks, and that on the basis of their analysis they can predict which functional and symbolic association will play a decisive role in the final purchasing decisions (Sloot and Bunt, 1996).

---

13 One of the main results of the qualitative preliminary research is that consumers do not form a homogeneous mass, but are instead very pluriform as far as their behaviour and attitude are concerned. A cluster analysis based on the behavioural and attitude questions has been made using the WARD cluster method, in order to segment the market. The following brand loyalty typologies were found (Sloot and Bunt, 1996): ambassadors, loyalists, variety seekers, habit purchasers and switchers.

(1) **Behavioural questions**
A determination is made of which brands within a certain product category respondents have at home, the frequency of use of those brands, and the distribution channels used.

(2) **Cognitive questions**
Here the spontaneous and aided awareness of the researched brands is asked about. A question is also included on the brands people consider taking home occasionally.

- Which brands do you know, even if just by name?
  (determining spontaneous name awareness)

- Do you know the following brands?
  (determining assisted name awareness)

- Which brands do you consider taking home occasionally?
  (determining the consideration set)

(3) **Attitude questions**
Based on other research by Sloot and Bunt (1996) and the Marketing Scales Handbook (Bruner and Hensel, 1992; 1996), it has been established that a number of aspects can provide an insight into the product and brand bonding of consumers. Each aspect is measured with two propositions on a 5-point scale (1 = completely agrees, 5 = completely disagrees). The aspects with their corresponding propositions are indicated below:

- Product involvement
  Compared with others, I am very interested in brand X.
  I know a lot about brand X.

- Recommendation
  I like to talk with others about my favourite brand.
  I like to recommend my favourite brand to others.

- Complaints
  If the store where I usually buy product X stopped carrying my usual brand, would I say something about it?
  If the store where I usually buy product X stopped carrying my usual brand, would I tell others if they bought the same product X in the same shop?

Contd

- Variety seeking
  Even though I am satisfied with product X, I still alternate between brands regularly.
  I alternate between brands regularly to try new things.

- Perception of equality (indicates the degree to which consumers see functional and emotional differences between various brands)
  Most brands within product category X taste (smell, feel, etc.) the same.
  Most brands radiate the same mood.

- Price awareness
  With product category X I always watch the price.
  With product category X I always watch for price offers.

- Switch sensitivity (switching or not switching in an out-of-stock situation, a situation seen in the literature as the hardest measurement of brand loyalty)
  If my steady brand X is not available in a certain store, I buy it somewhere else.
  If my steady brand X is not available in a certain store, I buy another brand.

- Brand involvement
  Within product category X, I don't care which brand I buy.
  I have a strong preference for one specific brand within product category X.

(4) **Brand association questions**
In this block two competing brands are evaluated on a number of relevant functional and a number of symbolic positioning elements. The relevant positioning elements emerge on the basis of in-depth interviews with experts. The functional positioning elements are related to instrumental brand attributes, the symbolic positioning elements are related to the radiation of a brand.

(5) **Background questions**
As a check on the survey's representativeness and the ability to describe various segments and target groups, the following backgrounds are included in the BrandWatcher list: gender, age, household, civil status, professional situation, level of education, income and province.

Chapter 25

Research into Brand Relationships

25.1 Introduction

In Part Two of this book brand relationships are defined as the two-sided involvement between a consumer and a brand, consisting of the components of interaction, communication, reciprocity and continuity:

(1) *Interaction:* a relationship has to do with a series of interactions between a consumer and a brand that know each other and in which each interaction in the series can be influenced by previous interactions between participants and by expectations over future interactions.

(2) *Communication:* relationships cannot exist without communication. The effect of a communicative message is that someone else is influenced or could be influenced by it. It is irrelevant whether this message is sent intentionally or not. In communication between relationship partners we also speak of relationship proposals (Drost, 1996). Two types of relationship proposals can be distinguished on a general level: proposals over the balance of power (is a brand an expert in a certain area?) and proposals related to affinity (are brand and consumer friends for life?). The communication between consumer and brand is expressed in advertising and in reactions of consumers to messages of the brand (special customer service numbers).

(3) *Reciprocity:* an important characteristic of every relationship is that the partners influence each other reciprocally. The partners form an image of each other based on previous interactions and communication. This image goes together with feelings and cognitions and ensures the emergence of expectations about future interactions. The reciprocity manifests itself very clearly in close relationships.

(4) *Continuity:* continuity means that a relationship reaches further than one isolated meeting or interaction. There is a concatenation of interactions over a longer period of time. Previous interactions influence future interactions and thus the nature and intensity of the relationship.

Lately, a distinction is being increasingly made between relationships that consumers enter into with brands and the relationships that arise between consumers via a brand (see Geursen, 1994, 1998; Langer, 1997). Here a brand becomes a network of and for consumers who share a certain interest, a problem, a challenge, an image or a dream. The brand is a creator of conditions: it creates possibilities for contact.

A great deal of research into brands still has to be carried out. Many questions remain unanswered, such as the way a relationship can be delimited. Essential research into the relationship between brands and consumers has been carried out by Langer (1996) and Fournier (1994). In the extension of her projects on the relationships between brand and consumer, Fournier developed a research instrument to map out this relationship. This technique, Brand Relationship Quality, will be discussed extensively in the following section. Two other methods for measuring brand relationships were developed by The Research Business, a renowned market research agency in Great Britain. The Research Business developed a large number of propositions that respondents are asked to evaluate on 7-point scales, and an instrument known as the 'me map'. These methods will also be described later in this chapter.

25.2 Techniques for measuring brand relationships

(65) *Brand Relationship Quality (BRQ)*

Susan Fournier carried out extensive research into brand relationships. In addition to new insights into the phenomenon of brand relationships, this produced a research instrument, the Brand Relationship Quality (Fournier, 1994). Fournier claims that all strong relationships originate in an instrumental product performance. This could be the result of the fact that Fournier has carried out research mainly into fast moving consumer goods. Fournier says that the BRQ standard is designed primarily for packaged consumer goods.

Based on three in-depth interviews with female respondents, Fournier arrived at the conclusion that a relationship consists of several facets. A large-scale quantitative study has led to an insight into the nature of these facets:

(1) Quality of the partner
(2) Love

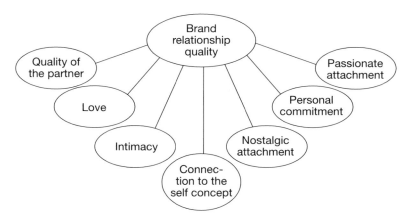

Figure 25.1 The Brand Relationship Quality (Fournier, 1994).

(3) Intimacy
(4) Connection to the self concept
(5) Nostalgic attachment
(6) Personal commitment
(7) Passionate attachment.

These facets constitute the basis of the Brand Relationship Quality, an instrument to research the relationship between consumer and brand.

The seven facets are additive: if a certain facet is missing in a person/brand relationship, the general quality of the relationship is lower than in a relationship in which all facets score high (Figure 25.1).

Fournier operationalised the facets and put them into statements. Respondents can indicate on scales how far they agree or disagree with these statements. Examples of statements for the various facets are:

(1) Quality of the partner
    'This brand takes good care of its clients.'
    'This brand has always been good to me.'
    'This brand always interests me.'
(2) Love
    'I really like this brand.'
    'I really love this brand.'
(3) Intimacy
    'I know a lot about this brand.'
    'I feel close to this brand.'
    'I feel at home with this brand.'

(4) Connection to the self concept
'This brand says a lot about the type of person I want to be.'
'This brand says something about what I consider important in life.'
'This brand and I are similar.'

(5) Nostalgic attachment
'This brand reminds me of things past.'
'This brand makes me think of people who are important to me.'

(6) Passionate commitment
'I will always be there for this brand.'
'I will remain with this brand through good and bad times.'

(7) Passionate attachment
'I feel very attracted to this brand.'
'In some ways I am addicted to this brand.'

The score on the statements provides an insight into the way consumers view a brand and into which reasons are important for entering a long-term relationship.

(66)   *Statements and scales*

Swan (1995), a researcher at the market research agency The Research Business in Great Britain, indicates that brand experience is strongly determined by the relationship a consumer has with the brand. Questions such as 'How does the brand fit my needs?' and 'What do my friends think about the brand?' play an important role. Consumers are increasingly dealing with the question, 'What does the brand think about me?' (does the brand understand what I need, does it understand something about my views on life, does it appreciate my loyalty), 'Does the brand respect me?'

As an instrument, Swan uses a number of propositions that have to be evaluated on scales. As an example, he gives the following propositions:

- Brand X is really a brand for me.
- Brand X is my type of brand.
- I like brand X.
- I am interested in brand X.
- Brand X means a lot to me.
- I feel attracted to brand X.
- Brand X has a dominant presence.
- Brand X is an interesting brand.
- I have the idea that I know a lot about brand X.
- Brand X is important to me.

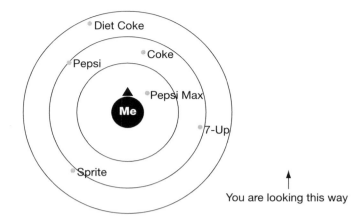

Figure 25.2   The 'me map' created by The Research Business (Swan, 1995).

(67)   *Me map*

A researcher can find out what relationship a respondent has with the brand in her surroundings by using all kinds of projective techniques (especially the 'relationship sort'; see the projective techniques toolkit in section 18.4.3). He can also show the strength of the relationships (for instance, the husband/wife relationship is stronger than the bus driver/passenger relationship). A 'me map' can show the distance that a respondent experiences between herself and various brands (see Figure 25.2).

(68)   *The conversion model*

The conversion model was developed in the late 1980s in South Africa by Hofmeyr and Rice of the Research Surveys agency. The model consists of a combination of questions that can be used to measure the degree of commitment of consumers to a brand in relation to alternative brands. This commitment consists of four dimensions and is measured per dimension (Brinkman, 1998; Franzen, 1998) (see Table 25.1).

The scores on the four dimensions are used to classify users and non-users of a brand into segments. The conversion model distinguishes eight segments: the first four for users and the last four for non-users of the researched brand (Franzen, 1998):

- *Committed:* users who are not likely to change in the near future. They remain loyal to the brand through thick and thin.

Table 25.1 The conversion model: dimensions, descriptions and questions.

Dimension	Description	Question
Need satisfaction	The degree to which a brand satisfies needs and expectations	The satisfaction with the brand is measured on a 10-point scale
Evaluation of alternatives	Attractiveness of alternatives	Respondents give (on a 7-point scale) their overall evaluation for each brand they know within the product category
Interest	Degree of involvement in the brand choice	Interest is measured with two questions: 1) respondents indicate on a 5-point scale how important they find the choice for a certain brand 2) respondents are asked how often they have bought the brand in the past twelve months
Movement	Tendency to change	Respondents are asked which of the next three claims applies best to the brand used in the last twelve months: 1) there are many good reasons to keep using the brand and few reasons to change brands 2) there are many good reasons to keep using the brand but there are also good reasons to change brands 3) there are few reasons to keep using the brand and many to change brands.

- *Loyals:* users who are not likely to change in the short term; their bonding is so strong that they will not desert that easily.
- *Hesitants:* users in whom the first hesitations can be detected. Their loyalty is below average and they are starting to focus on other brands/organisations.
- *Near deserters:* users who are at the crossroads, just about to change.
- *Available:* non-users who have a warmer feeling towards the brand than towards their current brand(s).
- *Doubters:* non-users who are wavering between their current brand and the brand that is the subject of research.
- *Latent:* non-users who probably remain loyal to their current brand(s).
- *Unapproachable:* non-users with a strong preference for their current brand(s).

Table 25.2 shows how Heath (1997) placed the segments.

Table 25.2   Segments in the conversion model.

Reliable users		Vulnerable users			
Committed	Loyal	Hesitant	Near deserters		
		Approachable non-users		Unapproachable non-users	
		Available	Doubters	Latent	Unapproachable

Source: Heath, 1997.

The extent of the eight bonding segments is measured per brand. By distributing the various brands from the same product category, which brands are vulnerable and which brands have little to fear becomes visible. An important analysis point of entry is to pick up the hesitants and the near deserters of the brand and to see if these people can be included among the available ones or doubters in other brands. The back and forth movement between near deserters and the available category is especially important (Franzen, 1998). They are responsible for the penetration development, and this development is the most important variable for explaining the market share. The disadvantage of the classification of consumers according to the conversion model is that some groups of consumers cannot be classified separately into one of the segments. Non-product users, ex-product users and convinced non-users are classified in the last segment, but differ in their advertising and promotion needs. New product users and brand switchers are classified mainly in the segment of near deserters, but also need a separate communication strategy (Brinkman, 1998).

Chapter 26

Holistic Brand Research

26.1 Introduction

'Movement, alternation and speed are integrated into our perception and planning by recognising patterns in space and time. Our grip is not based anymore on static images or structure (for instance, in most cases, an organisational scheme does not say anything anymore about how an organisation works). In fact, what we followed in the business world was only loose facts in time, and not wholes. After all, we are still doing biannual research into all sorts of loose elements, such as the familiarity of a name. Even the Gestalt of an image is unravelled in loose values, all of which get a score. You can listen analytically to music and recognise loose notes, themes or even patterns. If you really want to go into the deeper meaning of the piece, you have to turn off your analytical spirit and enjoy the consonance as a whole.' (Geursen, 1994)

Gestalt is a German word that means roughly 'shape' or 'form'. The most essential feature of the term is that it indicates connected wholes, complete structures or 'totals' whose nature cannot be discovered through a simple analysis of the components. This is summed up in the well known aphorism: 'The total (i.e. the Gestalt) is more than the sum of the parts'. This principle constitutes the core of the Gestalt psychology movement (Reber, 1997).

Many researchers and even more practising professionals see a brand image as a Gestalt, a holistic whole that cannot be unravelled into loose elements. In the following section we will give an overview of research techniques that are currently used to map out the holistic image.

In this overview a distinction is made between the various techniques by asking the question: 'Who brings out the attributes, the respondent or the researcher?' If the respondent brings out the attributes, we speak of an explicit method, and if the researcher comes up with them beforehand, it is an implicit method (Van Herk *et al.*, 1995). In addition to these explicit and implicit methods, there are also techniques that use a 'free method' and techniques that follow a clear structure. We speak of a 'free method' if open questions are asked about a brand and a product, after which freely expressed information and evaluations about the brand come forward. A structure method is a method in which a respondent is interviewed following a specific structure.

Gestalt psychology

Gestalt psychology is a school of psychology founded in Germany around 1910. Originally, Gestalt psychology was the counterbalance of structuralism and posited that psychological phenomena could only be understood if seen as ordered, structured wholes (or Gestalts). It directly attacked the structuralistic standpoint that maintained that phenomena could be introspectively analysed into primitive perceptual elements (such as the seven components of the mental brand response [see section 8.3.1]). According to the Gestalt point of view, such an approach ignored the notion of the whole, the 'being' of a phenomenon that forms a unit (Reber, 1997).

'Gestalt psychologists focus on people's experience of dynamic wholes, and elementalists focus on the expert's ability to break the whole into pieces. As an illustration of the difference between Gestalt and elemental approaches, think of a song in your mind. A song can be perceived as a series of individual notes (elemental) or as a melody that emerges from the relationships among the notes (Gestalt). The emergent structure is lost by analysing it into its sensory elements, in the Gestalt view. Gestalt psychologists saw the mental chemistry metaphor of the elementalists as misguided because a chemical compound has properties not predictable from its isolated elements. Similarly, the perceptual whole has properties not discernible from the isolated parts. For example, the note middle C can seem high in the context of many lower notes or low in the context of many higher notes, but it would not stand out at all in the context of other notes close to it. Psychological meaning goes beyond raw sensory parts to include the organisational structure people impose on the whole' (Fiske and Taylor, 1991).

26.2 The free format method

(69) *Trance research*

Trance research has been increasingly used in recent years to obtain insights into meanings that people allocate to brands. Developers of trance research describe trance as a very light form of hypnosis that has nothing to do with loss of control of the respondent. By putting the respondents into trance, many barriers come down and they can talk freely and openly about all kinds of subjects. The most important requirements for the success of trance research are giving a proper explanation to the respondent and the respondent trusting the researcher. In addition, the 'depth' of the trance is very important. A respondent is usually brought under hypnosis by means of a language method; the interviewer begins to talk more slowly (Van Tilburg and Tuitert, 1995), he agrees with the respondent that a certain number stands for the depth of the trance level and the respondent can indicate with a finger movement whether this level has been reached (Polter and Van Fessen, 1991). Of course, not every researcher is capable of applying such a technique and it may be necessary to hire a trained interviewer. This can increase the costs of the research considerably. Another disadvantage is that many people wonder how ethical such research is.

The technique is very useful if a researcher wants to know more about emotions that play a role in brand experience. According to Polter, a pioneer of trance research, the technique can be used to help creative researchers in their work. Trance research is also a technique that fits well with the spirit of the times. Nowadays people are trying to find answers 'inside themselves' to different questions. They join New Age movements and take yoga classes. Trance is a means *par excellence* to search deep in a respondent's head for answers. A great disadvantage is that it is not yet quite clear whether the answers from people's unconscious have anything to do with future purchasing behaviour. Some researchers have also been disappointed with the amount and quality of information that emerges with this technique (sometimes the respondents only mumble something or other).

26.3   The implicit method

(70)   *Brand fitness*

Brand fitness is a technique that was developed by BBDO; consumers select a certain brand on the basis of several dimensions. For instance, a brand should possess certain functional attributes, but it should also invoke a certain feeling in people. Furthermore, consumers involve in their decision the values that a brand represents. A research technique has been developed in the past for each of these dimensions (attributes, feelings, values). To measure which attributes a brand possesses and which feelings it invokes, attribute sort and photo sort have been developed. Insight into the values can then be gained using, for example, the personal drive analysis. All these techniques have already been described extensively.

Brand fitness operates as follows: the names of several competing brands are depicted on plates. These plates are placed on the table, facing the respondent. The respondent then gets three stacks of cards (attribute sort, photo sort and PDA) and has to allocate these stacks one by one and card by card to the brands. He does not have to explain why he makes a certain choice. The research data are depicted graphically using correspondence analysis. An image of the market emerges, with each brand surrounded by a cluster of attributes, photos and values.

An advantage of the technique is that it shows at a glance how consumers perceive the market but the technique has some disadvantages as well. Brand fitness is actually a combination of three qualitative techniques that are being analysed quantitatively. This does not necessarily have to be a problem if the researcher takes certain factors into account. First, he has to make sure the sample is large enough. Secondly, he should be careful when drawing conclusions; the graphic map appears to show a clear and detailed picture of the market, while in fact it is only the subtleties which can be read. Finally he needs to be aware that all the shortcomings of attribute sort, photo sort and PDA are incorporated in brand fitness.

(71) *Transactional analysis*

Transactional analysis was developed by Dr Eric Berne in 1957. The technique comes from psychotherapy and attempts to provide an insight into the way the brain functions and why people behave the way they do. The vocabulary that researchers use is carefully chosen and extensively researched. Berne is of the opinion that there should not be a difference between the use of language in daily life and in research practice. He believes transactional analysis is so essential that it should be accessible to and comprehensible by everyone. The technique seems to be mainly suitable for people who are not afraid to change.

Since its development, transactional analysis has frequently been used in hospitals, prisons and juvenile centres, and later on it became popular for management training. At present, attempts are being made to apply the technique to brands (Blackston and Holmes, 1983; Verlinden, 1994). We will now give a short description of the technique as described by Berne and as it is used in psychotherapy (Harris, 1992).

Transactional analysis in general

Penfield, a neurosurgeon from Montreal, claims that as early as birth (or even before) we start registering all the data that have entered our consciousness. The registrations are not only events from the past, but also the feelings that are connected to those events. The event and the feeling that is invoked by it, are unbreakably linked in the brain; one cannot be invoked without the other. If there is cause for it, the registrations take place in the present. This 'taking place in the present' is called a recollection. In other words, a recollection is the reproduction of that which a person has seen and heard, felt and understood (Harris, 1992).

After years of research, the psychologist Berne arrived at the conclusion that people have many sides to their character. This multifaceted character is also called a dualistic nature and was described earlier by Plato and Freud. Proof can be found in daily life for the multifaceted character of people: the people that surround us constantly undergo changes. Many people are completely 'different' at work, at the sports club and at home. The changes in character manifest themselves in attitude, appearance, word and gesture. Berne claims that the changes emanate from the three 'ways of being' (or phenomenological representations) that are present in all people (Clarkson, 1992; Harris, 1992):

- The Parent
- The Child
- The Adult.

The Parent: In the Parent, all the admonitions, rules and laws are stored that the child hears from her parents (biological or not) or observes in the first years of life. Young children trust their parents blindly and see no reason at all to control their statements. They accept them without thinking and store them in their memory. These registrations in memory cannot be removed: they stay with the person throughout her life. The internal Parent acts as a protector because, with the help of her Parent, the person knows how to act in every difficult situation. The experiences with older close relatives or other authority figures are also registered in the Parent. Additionally, television has also become an important provider of information in the Parent.

The Child: In the Child all internal events are registered: the reactions of the small person to what he hears and sees, what he feels and, later, what he understands. Small children are not yet able to understand where their parents' angry look comes from. They do not understand that it comes from breaking an expensive vase or smearing food on the curtains. They only see an angry look and that look brings about feelings they do not like. On the basis of these negative feelings, the small person quickly arrives at the conclusion 'I am not OK'. This conclusion is fixed permanently in memory and stays there even after the child grows up. Of course, children are also confronted with positive feelings. Parents react happily the first time their baby laughs, the first time it utters 'ma', etc. The negative feelings will always dominate in the Child. The child also stores in it the natural urge young people have to examine and touch everything. On the one hand, this urge brings about the expected angry looks; on the other hand, it stimulates each person's curiosity and creativity.

The Adult: After about ten months, the child is capable of influencing her surroundings. She starts understanding something about how causality works: if I do this, my parents will respond like that. With this concept the third 'way of being' is developed: the Adult. The Adult collects data from the world around her and develops a thought-out, rational view of life. Two important tasks of the Adult are testing the information in the Parent (is what my parents say and do right?), and testing the expressions of feeling in the Child (is it proper to react very angrily and start throwing books around?).

The main conclusion from the preceding is the fact that every person carries with them a feeling that they are not 'OK'. Even when still very young, children get the idea that everyone knows and can do everything better than themselves, and they develop the feeling of 'I am not OK – you are OK'. In some people the feeling has such an influence that they have trouble functioning in society. Transactional analysis concentrates not so much on describing an individual, but on how several people act and interact in a given situation. Within this context, Berne uses the term 'transaction', meaning that a transaction consists of a stimulus from one person and a reaction from another person. In turn, this reaction becomes a stimulus for the first person, who reacts to it. Who is speaking: the insecure or creative Child, or the 'all-knowing' Parent (Clarkson, 1992; Harris, 1992)? By using transactional analysis, people can learn that they *are* OK. They have to become aware of the fact that they are responsible for what happens in the future. They have to change, develop self-control and realise that they are completely free in the choices they make (Clarkson, 1992; Harris, 1992).

Transactional analysis applied to brands

Blackston and Holmes (1983) believe that all marketing and advertising efforts have as their goal the creation of a Gestalt of a brand. This Gestalt gives consumers, in addition to the basic requirements for quality, a reason or motivation to decide to make a purchase and a motivation to enter a long-term relationship with the brand.

The first step necessary in order to apply transactional analysis to brands is to ensure that respondents see the brand as a person. The respondent has to 'convert' the brand into a person in his memory and think about which personal traits it possesses. The basis of every brand is the functional product (Pepsi is a soft drink in the first place). The functional product fulfils in a completely rational way the basic needs of the consumer. Consumers do not choose a brand merely because of these functional attributes. They are more attracted to some brands than to others. The power of attraction emanates from the 'added attributes' of the brand (such as the symbolic and emotional value). Based on knowledge from transactional analysis, the rational functional product is called the rational Adult (Verlinden, 1994).

Transactional analysis uses an open-ended questionnaire; in some questions, respondents indicate with projective techniques what they think of a subject

(Blackston and Holmes, 1983). This ensures that respondents are free to make associations. The results of the research are analysed according to the principles of transactional analysis. Here use is made of a 'code' developed by Eric Berne.

The relationship a consumer has with a brand can be analysed in terms of the 'Ego state' of the consumer (Adult, Parent, or Child) and the 'Ego state' that is projected by the consumer onto the brand. Blackston and Holmes (1983) posit that classification of transactions between consumers and brands on the basis of their Ego state makes it possible to recognise the mutual influences in the relationships between consumers and brands that lead to their positive and negative exposure to these brands. The reactions of respondents can be linked to functional and emotional needs and conditions. In Berne's terminology, 'Parent' stands for authority. When there is a positive relationship, this means reassurance and protection. In a negative relationship it means disapproval, criticism, authoritative practices. 'Adult' means objectivity. In a positive relationship this means functional values, and in a negative relationship it means low involvement. 'Child' means instinct/emotion. In a positive relationship this is expressed as warmth, pleasure and sensuality, and in a negative relationship it expresses itself in hostility, fear, vengefulness (Blackston and Holmes, 1983).

The way in which the Ego states of consumer and brand are combined determines the results of the transaction. Berne places all possible transactions into successful (complementary) and unsuccessful (crossed) categories. Figure 26.1 gives a few examples.

The Dutch researcher Verlinden (1994) claims that we can distinguish four types of dimensions that describe the relationship between consumer and brand:

- The first dimension is based on the demanding nature of people and their rational expertise.
- The second dimension is based on emotions: the need for comfort, care and gentleness.
- The third dimension stands for originality, non-conformism, 'having fun in life'.
- The fourth dimension stands for class, show, eye-catching image and lifestyle.
- Consumers identify brands as successful if they have at least three of these dimensions (Verlinden, 1994). A graphic depiction is given in Figure 26.2.

According to Verlinden, researchers use photo sort and the collage technique to find out which dimensions respondents allocate to a brand (Verlinden, 1994).

Consumer   **Brand**

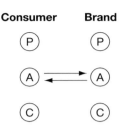

The brand is recognised as delivering functional values: performance, efficiency. If there are no other sorts of transaction, then the relationship is devoid of any emotive values.

Consumer   **Brand**

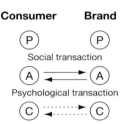

There is a complete complementarity at both levels of the relationship. In addition to satisfying functional needs, the consumer's relationship with the brand is rich in emotive content.

Consumer   **Brand**

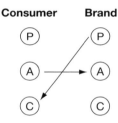

While recognising the functional values of the brand, the consumer perceives it as exacting too great a price for using it. The brand may be seen as 'too good' and often too expensive (too high a price in real terms as well as in psychological terms) hence giving rise to feelings of inadequacy or guilt in relation to using the brand.

P = Parent
A = Adult
C = Child

Figure 26.1   Examples of successful and unsuccessful relationships between consumer and brand (Blackston and Holmes, 1983).

(72) *BrandWorks*

Two British researchers, Gordon and Restall (1992), claim that people choose brands not only on the basis of functional attributes, but also on feelings and associations that the brands awaken in them. Gordon and Restall call these feelings 'tonal qualifiers' (how do people feel with regard to a brand?). All other information is stored in memory in a way the two researchers call the 'brand fingerprint'. In this fingerprint a distinction is made between feelings, smell, hearing and visual information (see Figure 26.3). Based on all this

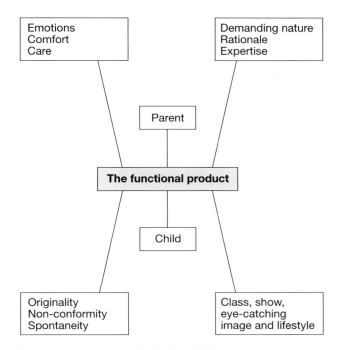

Figure 26.2 Four brand dimensions (Verlinden, 1994).

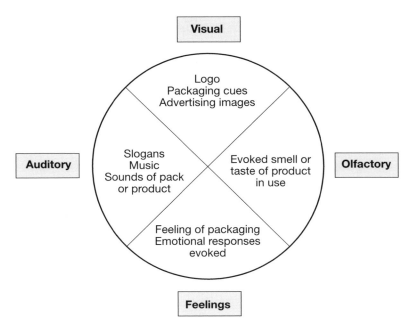

Figure 26.3 The brand fingerprint (Swan, 1995).

sensory information, people form an image of a brand, or a brand image. Gordon and Restall developed together with BrandWorks a technique to map out this brand image. The technique assumes that a brand, just like a diamond, consists of a number of facets: *brand saliency* (the relevance of the brand for different groups of people); *user imagery* (the users of the brand); *occasion imagery* (the context in which the brand can best be used); *service imagery* (especially important for travel, retail and financial brands: how helpful is a bank in its service?); *product/functional imagery* (how respondents think the product works); *brand personality* (the kind of person the brand would be). These facets determine, just as in a diamond, the beauty and value of a brand. The facets are measured with questionnaires developed by Gordon and Restall (1992).

26.4 The explicit method

(73) *ZMET: The Zaltman Metaphor Elicitation Technique*

With the Zaltman Metaphor Elicitation Technique researchers attempt to find out how people 'experience' products and brands. They do this by looking for the 'deeper meanings' that a consumer allocates to a brand and the abstract thoughts that the consumer has on the brand. During this search, metaphors and visual stimuli are used. A metaphor is generally described as a style figure in which a word is replaced by another word. Metaphors can help clarify additionally or explain more powerfully what is meant. The basis of a metaphor is the knowledge that there is a certain degree of correspondence between the words that replace each other. Some psychologists claim people constantly use metaphors to give meaning to the world around them. They compare new information with information that is already stored in memory. The old information becomes, as it were, a metaphor for the new information. Zaltman uses this phenomenon in his research technique. He lets respondents talk about brands and encourages them to express their thoughts on these brands by using pictures and photos (Zaltman and Higie, 1993, 1995).

In addition to metaphors, Zaltman uses visual stimuli in his research. There is a lot of disagreement on whether information is stored in memory in the form of words (verbally) or images (visually). Respondents used always to have to explain in words during interviews and group discussions what they thought of something; this proved very difficult, especially when abstract concepts such as 'satisfaction' had to be expressed. A researcher can solve this problem by using visual stimuli (such as films, photos and pictures). Respondents no longer need to explain in words how satisfied they are with a brand, but can point to a picture of a satisfied-looking man.

The use of visual stimuli during research is in keeping with the fact that so much communication is currently visual or non-verbal. Children become accustomed to seeing an enormous number of images and pictures. Zaltman believes that the use of metaphors and visual stimuli is necessary for carrying out proper research. With these two aids an atmosphere is created that helps respondents evoke the image they have of a brand (Zaltman and Higie, 1995).

Actually, ZMET is not a new technique, but a research approach in which various techniques (laddering, repertory grid, photo sort and collage) are combined. Around twenty consumers are selected to participate in the study, and they are given information on the research topic (for instance, they hear that the study is about 'coffee'). They are given a disposable camera and assigned to take pictures; they also collect images from periodicals, books, newspapers and other sources to show what the topic means to them. Seven to ten days later, a single interview takes place in the form of a guided conversation, consisting of ten steps (Zaltman and Higie, 1993):

(1) Description of the images: the respondent describes the pictures and photographs she has collected and explains why she has chosen these in particular.

(2) Missed pictures: the interviewer asks if the respondent has been unable to find or take certain pictures that fit the topic. She has to indicate what these pictures would look like.

(3) Distributing and naming groups: respondents are asked to allocate the pictures to groups and name them. If the research topic is 'coffee', the following groups could be made: healthy, luxurious and cheap. The respondent can make as many groups as she feels necessary. This way it becomes clear which traits and attributes of a brand are important according to the respondent.

(4) Filtering constructs: the researcher tries to find out why the respondents have grouped the pictures in a certain way. To this end, he uses the 'construct theory' of Kelly, which is also applied in the repertory grid (described in section 20.2). The researcher keeps selecting three pictures (from the respondent's stack) and the respondent has to indicate which two pictures resemble one another and thus differ from the third. She also has to indicate why the two pictures are similar. This way the reasons for the grouping of the pictures are brought out.

(5) The most representative image: the respondent has to indicate which picture is the most representative for the image she has of the brand.

(6) Contrasting pictures: the respondent has to describe or point to a picture that contrasts with the image she has of a brand.

(7) Sensory information: the respondent describes the subject with all her senses: which smell, colour, taste and sound fit best with the subject?

(8) The mental map: the interviewer names all the arguments and aspects that the respondent has brought forward and checks if this list is complete. The respondent can still indicate whether she thinks something is missing. The

respondent then makes a list of all the aspects and describes the relationships between them. It does not matter if no relationship can be described between issues: what is important is the main relationships.

(9) The summarising image: from the pictures the respondent has brought with her, a collage is made that portrays the 'most representative image'.

(10) Data analysis: putting together a consensus map in which the data of all the interviews are integrated. The researcher tries to make a map in which he includes all the rationales mentioned in the interviews.

The ZMET ensures that researchers gain an insight into the image that respondents have of a brand or product. The deeper motives and emotions and the intuitive reactions of respondents can be brought to the surface. The technique claims to make it possible to communicate better with respondents who are visually oriented (as we all are to some extent), or about brands and products with an important visual element. Respondents are repeatedly asked to explain in words why they chose a certain image. An important advantage is that the respondent is put in a position where she herself can bring up the stimuli used during research. The respondent is not limited in her answers and the chance of 'blind spots'[14] decreases. However, this advantage can also be a disadvantage; the researcher has to prevent respondents from being too free to become 'creative' without a connection to the research subject. Another disadvantage is that the data analysis in step ten is done by one single researcher. He sees the results from the interviews 'through his own spectacles' and can shift the consensus map in a direction that best fits his own frame of reference. Another disadvantage is the fact that Zaltman takes only verbal and visual information into account, although this in itself is already a big improvement compared with other research; but psychologists now agree that, in addition to verbal and visual information, sounds and smells are also stored in memory.

This long list of disadvantages does not mean that the Zaltman Metaphor Elicitation Technique is no good. The technique is still in its development phase, and further research (including research into the validity and reliability of the instrument) has to show whether ZMET can be deployed as a valuable research instrument.

---

14 There is a 'blind spot' when a researcher does not bring certain information to the surface during his study, even though this information is present. If the researcher himself selects stimuli or cues beforehand, there is a chance he may have forgotten something and did not include some stimuli in his research. The respondent answers on the basis of the stimuli, but does not get the chance to say something about a subject that was forgotten by the researcher.

(74) *Multi Dimensional Scaling*

In Multi Dimensional Scaling (MDS) respondents have to give preferences or similarity evaluations on pairs of brands. These similarity scores can be derived by the researcher himself from previously obtained information on the brands. Respondents are usually asked directly to give their similarity evaluation by indicating the similarity between two brands on a 7-point scale. The brands can then be put on a coordinate system, and the distances between the brands would indicate the degree of similarity (Van Herk *et al.*, 1995).

Chapter 27

New Forms of Research

Research agencies and the research departments of advertising agencies seem to have (re)discovered three 'new' forms of research lately. This has emerged particularly during the expert interviews. For reasons of confidentiality, in this chapter we will not mention names of companies or persons who are working with a certain technique or are developing an instrument.

Three research methods will be discussed: 'narrative', 'observation' and 'panel research'. These research methods are certainly not new. Telling stories as a research engine has existed since the psychologist Adler emphasised its importance in the 1930s, and observation may be even older. Still, these methods seem to be getting more attention lately. Panel research is a logical result of the technological developments and the 'trendwatch' movement.

27.1 Narrative

McAdams (1994) explains that people are storytellers by nature. In each of our cultures we encounter variants of stories such as folklore, legends, myths, chronicles, pantomimes, movement and dance, and even the news. The story forms a natural means of organising various forms of information. Telling stories is a fundamental way of expressing ourselves and conveying our experiences to others.

Geursen (1994) writes: '"A man comes to his house, inserts the key in the keyhole, hesitates, and comes in. He picks up the mail and ..." I stop here, because with these few words I have already put you in the mood of the story, inside the power of the story. [...] We are going to tell even more stories. That is a trend, even in the business world. This way we look for the essence of why we are together on this Earth – for something more than just giving each other tables with the latest electoral gain or sales figures. Telling stories and listening to them is a gift of mother nature. Stories have a certain grip on the imagination. Stories are also exceptionally suited for social negotiation, because they help you learn to distinguish the dancer from the dance, so to speak. A story is, after all, *someone's* story. Stories can give a person and a brand a profile. They are about personal meanings. [...] An interesting characteristic of a story is that it doesn't matter if it is made up or based on real facts. One doesn't ask that, because either way the strength of the story does not get lost. What's more, objectivity does not exist, because everyone interprets the world that surrounds them in their own way. The world is not etched in our memory the way a film is projected on the movie screen. We look with our brain and our feelings, not just with our eyes. No single story can describe all the aspects of an event, there is always a vision, a standpoint. We are in the habit of becoming the stories we tell. This way, stories become reality and vice-versa. You cannot separate the two.'

An increasing number of books and articles on advertising and communication are discussing the importance of stories. These books and articles are often written by the same people who publish regularly on post-modern times and the chaos theory. In scientific literature the importance and relevance of telling stories is also emphasised regularly. Jerome Bruner, a recognised psychologist, in his best-seller *Acts of Meaning* (1990), claims that the function of a story is to have members of a culture develop an expectation about who they are or to help them understand themselves and the world around them. Bruner illustrated this on the basis of a study in which he asked people to tell their life stories. This was not so much about what had really happened in their lives, but about what the person thought he had done, why he thought he had done that, in what situation he thought he was, and so on. According to Bruner, the form of the story often says more than the contents. From within this form, the meanings emerge that people allocate to the events in their lives and therefore to themselves (Drenth, 1996).

In several projective techniques, discussed in section 18.4.3, telling stories plays an important role. In the Thematic Apperception Test, respondents are asked to imagine a certain situation and tell a story from this situation. The difference with telling stories is that this last method is less structured: respondents have to be able to tell their stories without any inhibitions or limitations.

A step further: 'the brand as a story' (Verheul, 1997)

Some brands tell (e.g. in advertisements) something about the organisation behind the brand (makers), about the users or the brand development, or about the country of origin (where does the brand come from?). This makes possible the creation of a form of cooperation between the brand and the consumer. There is an interaction and the consumer is, as it were, part of the brand. The consumer can create his own reality with the information that is offered to him.

A disadvantage of telling stories is that it is a very linguistic method. The psychologist Adler was the first to give a theoretical basis to the importance of telling stories, establishing quite early on that people need projective aids to give verbal expression to their thoughts and feelings.

27.2   Observation

'In a research room, people claim other things than those they do in reality. For instance, they say flatly that they always buy packets of Knorr, and they describe in detail the colours and forms of the Knorr packets. When the researcher looks in their kitchen cabinets, what he finds are packages of Maggi. And then the respondent says: "Oh, did I say I used Knorr? I meant Maggi, of course."' (Asselbergs, 1997)

Collecting information on the way people deal with brands can be done essentially in two ways: through observation and through interviewing (by telephone, in writing or face-to-face). Interviewing has been extensively described in previous chapters. This section focuses on observation as a research instrument. In psychology, an observational research instrument is described as 'every procedure or technique for the accurate observation in non-experimental research'. The means used include audio and video equipment, chronometers, lists with behaviours that have to be noticed (Reber, 1997) and scanning equipment (when buying in supermarkets).

The major advantage of observation is that there is little chance of distortion due to consumers giving socially desirable answers or saying things that the researcher wants to hear. It enables the researcher to collect 'original' data that are not distorted by the consumer's unwillingness or lack of expertise to report on his purchasing behaviour. For this reason, the observation method is also suited to collecting 'difficult' information, such as unconscious behaviour, behaviour that cannot be remembered, or behaviour about which people would rather not speak or even lie. Through observation the researcher is capable of overseeing the entire event, something that is more difficult through interviewing. For example a project is being carried out in which researchers observe people in supermarkets, writing down their behaviour: at which shelves they stop; which products they take; which messages they look at; whether they also look at products situated above eye-level; how many different products within a certain product category they take before making a choice, etc. It is clear that it would be hard to make an interviewing method produce the same complete and reliable information as a properly set up observation project. Observation of phenomena in which the cooperation of the research subject is required enables the researcher to establish phenomena and reactions that he could never establish any other way (De Pelsmacker and Van Kenhove, 1994). Observation also has disadvantages, of course. Sometimes people act differently if they notice that someone is watching them.

Besides, observation is very expensive and time-consuming, and its interpretation is very difficult (ultimately, researchers want to know *why* someone behaves the way they do).

Observation is widely used to map out target groups; using a segmentation technique such a VALS, or the 4 Cs (Cross-Cultural Consumer Characteristics) of Y&R, or Socioconsult of the Dutch research agency Motivaction, a framework can be created. With these techniques a researcher can determine the sociodemographic traits of a group, the values of the members of that group, and the periodicals they subscribe to. By using observation, the framework is given some shape: the people that are part of a segment 'come to life'. What do they look like? What kinds of clothes do they wear? How do they talk and what do they talk about? Where do they go on holiday and what do they do there? What does their living room look like?

Many research and advertising agencies employ people who film in the street, in cafes, in school playgrounds, in kitchens, etc. what different people do and which brands they use, whether they use a certain brand alone and in private, or whether they use it with a large group of people around them? Do different people use a certain brand at the same time? What do people who use a certain brand look like (what clothes do they wear, what does their hair look like)?

It is not always necessary for a researcher to go out with a video camera or a memo pad. In some research agencies, respondents can borrow a video or photo camera for a specific period of time in order to record as many moments as they can of their daily life. It goes without saying that the brands they use will become obvious.

27.3   Panel research

A panel is a group or sample whose members have been chosen from within the population according to certain criteria. This group or sample is generally subject to occasional research during a prolonged period of time. A panel can be chosen in such a way that (a) the selected group is clearly non-representative of the population, or (b) the group is more representative than would be expected of a randomly composed group of the same size. To effect such a selection, use is made of stratified sampling (Reber, 1997).

Technological developments have made it possible to follow a group of people (with their approval) and register all kinds of information about them. A researcher tries to keep close track of how old these people are, how many children they have, which television programmes they watch, which products they buy, how often and to which countries they go on holiday, etc. This way an enormous data file with detailed information on a selected group of people is produced.

Single source research (Franzen, 1998)

Sales figures are made up of two variables: the number of users of the brand (the 'penetration') and the average purchasing frequency of these users (and, of course, the average amount purchased). A group of people are given a scanner for a certain period of time to register all their purchases. In this way the development of the penetration and of the purchasing frequency of the various brands within a product category can be established. By also registering the TV viewing behaviour in the same households (the single source principle), it has become possible to establish direct connections between advertising exposures and purchasing behaviour at a household level. The number of 'opportunities to see' per household are calculated from the viewer behaviour data. The purchases per household are then related to the number of received 'opportunities to see' in the same household. In particular, the purchasing behaviour of the households that received one or more 'opportunities to see' is compared with that of households without advertising exposures.

One of the advantages of this type of research is that the members of the household panel are exposed to the same market influences. Only the advertising input or the advertising consumption varies. The differences in effectiveness that are established in various commercials or advertisements can thus be directly ascribed to the advertisement. We have to deal less with the problem of isolating the advertising effects from those of other marketing mix variables, as is the case with modelling. A second advantage is that the effectiveness of the advertisements is not measured in isolation, but under normal conditions. Especially when it comes to the activities of competing brands, 'negative' effectiveness of campaigns is often observed. This could be the result of a difference in advertising pressure between the research brand and its competitors. A 'disadvantage' of the single source method is that we obtain little information on the causes due to which a campaign does or does not sort effects, which makes adjustments difficult. For instance, we were able to observe that a campaign does not work, or works sub-optimally, but were not able to trace this back to the strategy of the message or creation.

There is a special form of panel research that is known as 'single source research'. In single source, a researcher may register which advertisements a certain group of people are confronted with, and which brands and products those people buy.

Chapter 28

Final Reflections

The likelihood is that Part Three of this book will leave readers with a strange aftertaste: such a colourful collection of research techniques – what is the point of it? A researcher may have hoped to get an answer to questions such as 'Which technique should I choose in situation X?' and 'How is brand representation connected with the market share?'. It has proven impossible to give unambiguous answers to such questions. There are many 'brand gurus' and each guru has his own vision. Different research techniques emanate from these visions. Each guru is right, every vision is correct and, consequently, every technique is useful! Comparing techniques without looking at the visions behind them is the same as comparing apples with oranges. The ideal method does not exist and, within one vision, many roads lead to Rome.

An important question that could be asked when researching brand representation is whether use can be made of a qualitative or a quantitative method. It is often easier for an advertiser to base decisions on a quantitative study, measuring quantitatively the results of an earlier qualitative study. Regarding the question of whether this is always necessary or even possible, opinions are split. Is it possible, for example, to measure quantitatively the relationship a consumer has with a brand? Can you expect a respondent to indicate on a scale of 1 to 7 how much he loves Vaseline? The concept of brand relationships has stemmed largely from the idea that the relationships people have with others can be compared to the relationships they enter into with brands. Can you expect people to indicate on a scale how much they love their parents and their spouse? And can you then compare those numbers? The doubts that the authors themselves have on the subject is expressed in a poem by Jules Deelder (1994) (overleaf).

It should be remembered that, when researching brands, it is extremely important to make a distinction between the users and the non-users of a brand. People have to make so many choices in their lives, and research has shown that the choices of everyday things (such as a tube of toothpaste) in particular are based on wafer-thin decision-making processes: they just get it over with, often having all sorts of mixed reasons for their choice. Various psychological studies and theories have taught us that people do not like being confronted after the fact with the question of whether they made a good

What do all those formulas and figures from research actually mean?

Some believe
that
the bliss
can be reached
along many roads
and they
like to use
the saying

'CaS plus $2O_2$
gives
$CaSO_4$'

This is
in no way
the case, though,

Rather the contrary
takes place!

Thus people
continue on their way,
warned.

Jules Deelder, 1994

choice, and that they tend to justify their choices afterwards with a lot of bravado. In research into the image of a brand, respondents who use the brand in question are positive about this brand on all fronts: the advertisement is nice (at any rate, better than that of its competitors), the maker is probably environmentally conscious, there is a good price : quality ratio, and so on. Within this context, it is important to refer to the double-jeopardy effect in research. In section 18.2 we explained that, as a result of this effect, respondents allocate most associations to major brands (the market leaders). When this group includes fans of a major brand (frequent users), this effect is even more enhanced. In this final part of the book we have offered several suggestions to correct the research results in order to overcome the double-jeopardy effect.

Appendix

The interviewed experts:

Pim Asselbergs	IPM
Jos Ahlers	Consult (part of the Y & R group)
Willem Brethouwer	MarketResponse
Fred Bronner	Veldkamp/Marktonderzoek
René Brounts	Ogilvy & Mather
Goos Geursen	FHV/BBDO
Terry Häcker	Research International
Adriaan Lamme	MarketResponse
Hans Ophof	FHV/BBDO
Anjo Schreuder	Schreuder, Petrescu en Vunderink
Frits Spangenberg	Motivaction
Bert de Vries	ISK
Ron Walvisch	Saatchi & Saatchi
Richard Wolking	Wolking Research Strategy BV
Erik Wünsch	Schaeffer Wünsch Has

Bibliography

Aaker, D.A. (1991) *Managing Brand Equity: Capitalizing on the Value of a Brand Name*. The Free Press, New York.

Aaker, D.A. (1996) *Building Strong Brands*. The Free Press, New York.

Aaker, J.L. (1996) *Conceptualizing and Measuring Brand Personality, UCLA Working Paper No. 262*. The John E. Anderson Graduate School of Management, UCLA, Los Angeles.

Aaker, J.L. (1997) Dimensions of measuring brand personality. *Journal of Marketing Research* **34**, 347–456.

Aans, N. (1996) *Emoties en Reclame: Associatievorming tussen Merk en Emotie*. Masters thesis, University of Amsterdam.

AC Nielsen (1999) *SMA-Merk en Consument*. AC Nielsen internal document, Diemen.

Acuff, D.S. (1997) *What Kids Buy and Why*. The Free Press, New York.

Adformatie (1996) Merkplacebo's. *Adformatie*, 3/10/1996.

Agres, S.J. & Dubitsky, T.M. (1996) Changing needs for brands. *Journal of Advertising Research* **36**, January/February, 21–30.

Ahlers, J.B.A. (1997a) *De BrandAsset Valuator als Ondersteuning bij het Ontwikkelen van Strategie*. Y&R internal document, Amsterdam.

Ahlers, J.B.A. (1997b) Personal communication with Consult/Y&R, Amsterdam.

Ajzen, I. (1988) *Attitudes, Personality, and Behavior*. Open University, Milton Keynes.

Ajzen, I. & Fishbein, M. (1977) Attitude–behavior relationships: a theoretical analysis and review of empirical research. *Psychological Bulletin* **84**, 888–918.

Alba, J.W. & Hasher, L. (1983) Is memory schematic? *Psychological Bulletin* **93**, 203–231.

Alba, J.W. & Hutchinson, J.W. (1987) Dimensions of consumer expertise. *Journal of Consumer Research* **13**, March, 411–454.

Alba, J.W., Hutchinson, J.W. & Lynch, J.G. (1991) Memory and decision making. In *Handbook of Consumer Behavior*. (T.R. Robertson & H.H. Kassarjian, eds.). Prentice-Hall, Englewood Cliffs, New Jersey.

Aleksander, I. & Morton, H. (1993) *Neurons and Symbols: the Stuff that Mind is Made of*. Chapman & Hall, London.

Alleborn, J.P. (1994) The relationship of a brand's quality (value) to a brand's sales, profitability, and stock market performance. *ARF February 14–15, Brand Equity Workshop (Building Brand Equity: The Lead Role of Research in Managing the Power of Brands)*, 95–108.

Alpert, M. (1971) Identification of determinant attributes: a comparison of methods. *Journal of Marketing Research* **8**(2), 184–191.

Anderson, J.R. (1976) *Language. Memory and Thought*. Lawrence Erlbaum Associates, Hillsdale, New Jersey.

Anderson, J.R. (1983) A spreading activation theory of memory. *Journal of Verbal Learning and Verbal Behavior* **22**, 261–295.

Anderson, J.R. (1984) Spreading activation. In *Essays in Learning and Memory*. (J.R. Anderson & S.M. Kosslyn, eds). W.H. Freeman, New York.

Anderson, J.R. (1995) *Learning and Memory: an Integrated Approach*. John Wiley & Sons, New York.

Anholt, S. (1998) Nation-brands of the twenty-first century. *Journal of Brand Management* **5**(6), 395–406.

Arnold, M.B. (1960) *Emotion and Personality*. Columbia University Press, New York.

Asselbergs, P. (1987) *Image in Historisch Perspectief*. IPM internal document, Rotterdam.

Asselbergs, P. (1997) Personal communication with IPM, Rotterdam.

Atkinson, R.C. & Shiffrin, R.M. (1968) Human memory: a proposed system and its control processes. In Spence, K.W. (ed.). *The Psychology of Learning and Motivation: Advances in Research and Theory, vol. 2.* (K.W. Spence, ed.) Academic Press, New York.

Atkinson, R.C. & Shiffrin, R.M. (1971) The control of short-term memory. *Scientific American* **225**, 82–90.

Averill, J.R. (1982) *Anger and Aggression: an Essay on Emotion*. Springer Verlag, New York.

Baars, B. (1988) *A Cognitive Theory of Consciousness*. Cambridge University Press, Cambridge.

Bacon, L.D. (1994) *Linking attitudes and behavior*. American Marketing Association, San Francisco.

Baddeley, A. (1990) *Human Memory: Theory and Practice*. Lawrence Erlbaum Associates, Hove/London.

Baddeley, A.D. & Hitch, G. (1974) Working memory. In *The Psychology of Learning and Motivation, vol. 8* (Bower, G.H., ed.). Academic Press, New York.

Bahrick, H.P. & Hall, L.K. (1991) Lifetime maintenance of high school mathematics content. *Journal of Experimental Psychology: General* **120**, 20–33.

Baldinger, A.L. & Rubinson, J. (1996) Brand loyalty: the link between attitude and behavior. *Journal of Advertising Research* **36**(6), 22–34.

Bandura, A. (1986) *Social Foundations of Thought and Action: a Social Cognitive Theory*. Prentice-Hall, Englewood Cliffs, New Jersey.

Bargh, J.A. (1997) The automaticity of everyday life. In *The Automaticity of Everyday Life: Advances in Social Cognition, vol. 10* (R.S. Wyer, ed.). Lawrence Erlbaum Associates, Hillsdale, New Jersey.

Barsalou, L.W. (1993) Flexibility, structure and linguistic vagary in concepts: manifestations of a compositional system of perceptual symbols. In *Theories of Memory*. (A.F. Collins, S.E. Gathercole, M.A. Conway, & P.E. Morris, eds). Lawrence Erlbaum Associates, Hillsdale, New Jersey.

Bartlett, F.C. (1932) *Remembering: A Study in Experimental and Social Psychology*. Cambridge University Press, Cambridge.

BBDO (1990) *Reclamestrategieontwikkeling en Onderzoek bij FHV/BBDO*. FHV/BBDO internal document, Amstelveen.

BBDO Worldwide (unpublished). *BBDO's Emotional Measurement System*. BBDO internal document, New York.

Beach, L.R. (1993) Image theory: an alternative to normative decision theory. *Advances in Consumer Research,* **20**, 235–238.

Bear, M.F., Connors B.W. & Paradiso M.A. (1996) *Neuroscience: Exploring the Brain*. Williams & Wilkins, Baltimore, Maryland.

Beekman, Y. (1995) *Het Imago van Automerken*. Masters thesis, University of Amsterdam.

Beijk, J. & van Raaij, F.W. (1989) *Schemata, Informatieverwerking, Beïnvloedingsprocessen en Reclame: Pre-Advies aan de VEA*. VEA, Amsterdam.

Bergsma, A. (1995) *Emoties en Kwaliteit van Bestaan*. Het spectrum, Utrecht.

Bergsma, A. (1996) *Het Brein ons Innerlijk Universum*. Stichting Educatieve Omroep Teleac, Utrecht.

Biel, A. (1991) The brandscape: converting brand image into equity. *Admap,* October.

Biel, A.L. & Bridgewater, C.A. (1990) Attributes of likeable television commercials. *Journal of Advertising Research* **30**(3), 38–44.

Bjork, R.A. & Bjork, E.L. (1992) A new theory of disuse and an old theory of stimulus fluctuation. In *From Learning Processes to Cognitive Processes: Essays in Honor of William K. Estes, vol 2* (A.F. Healy, S.M. Kosslyn & R.M. Shiffrin, eds). Lawrence Erlbaum Associates, Hillsdale, New Jersey.

Blackston, M. (1993) Beyond brand personality: building brand relationships. In *Brand Equity and Advertising: Advertising's Role in Building Strong Brands* (D.A. Aaker, & A.L. Biel, eds). Lawrence Erlbaum Associates, Hillsdale, New Jersey.

Blackston, M. & Holmes, M. (1983) The use of transactional analysis in the development of a new brand's personality. *ESOMAR Seminar on New Product Development*. ESOMAR, Athens, pp. 105–128.

Boom, E.J. & Weber, A.A. (1994) *Consumentengedrag: Aanknopingspunten voor Marketingstrategie*. Wolters-Noordhoff, Groningen.

Bor, J., Petersma, E. & Kingma, J. eds (1995) *De Verbeelding van het Denken: Geïllustreerde Geschiedenis van de Westerse en Oosterse Filosofie*. Uitgeverij Contact, Amsterdam/Antwerp.

Bouman, H. (1998) Topmanagement krijgt eindelijk oog voor het bedrijfslogo. *Management Team* 11/9/1998.

Boush, D.M. (1993) Brands as categories. In *Brand Equity and Advertising: Advertising's Role in Building Strong Brands* (D.A. Aaker, & A.L. Biel, eds). Lawrence Erlbaum Associates, Hillsdale, New Jersey.

Bouts, J.M. & Mackor E.O. (1991) Merkassociaties bij banken. *Tijdschrift voor Marketing,* March, 52–57.

Bower, G.H. (1992) How might emotions affect learning? In *The Handbook of Emotion and Memory: Research and Theory* (S.-Å. Christianson, ed.). Lawrence Erlbaum Associates, Hillsdale, New Jersey.

Bremer, D. (1996) *Merkrelaties*. Masters thesis, University of Amsterdam.

Brinkman, W. (1998) *Het Conversie Model en Tijdschriften: een nieuwe onderzoeksmethode voor VNU Tijdschriften*. Masters thesis, University of Amsterdam.

Bronner, A.E. (1981) Ontwikkelingen in image-onderzoek. *Jaarboek van de Nederlandse Vereniging van Marktonderzoekers*. Dutch Association of Market Researchers, Amsterdam.

Bronner, A.E. (1993) Het double-jeopardy-effect en de Merkenmonitor. *Onderzoek,* April.

Bronner, A.E. (1997) Personal communication with Bureau Veldkamp/Marktonderzoek, Amsterdam.

Brouwer, J.D. & Weijde, J., van der (1998) *De Winkelende Consument: Beslissinggedrag In De Supermarkt Nader Bekeken.* Masters thesis, Erasmus University Rotterdam.

Brown, S. (1995) Postmodern marketing research: no representation without taxation. *Journal of the Market Research Society,* **37**(3), 287–310.

Brown, T. (1998) Het imago in de marketing. Corporate associaties in de marketing: antecedenten en consequenties. *Tijdschrift voor Strategische Bedrijfscommunicatie,* **4**(3).

Brown, T.J. & Dacin, P.A. (1997) The company and the product: corporate associations and consumer product responses. *Journal of Marketing* **61** (January), 68–84.

Bruner, J.S. (1990) *Acts of Meaning: the Jerusalem – Harvard Lectures.* Harvard University Press, Cambridge, Mass.

Bruner, G. & Hensel, P. (1992) *Marketing Scales Handbook: a Compilation of Multi-Item Measures, vol. 1.* American Marketing Association, Chicago.

Bruner, G. & Hensel, P. (1996) *Marketing Scales Handbook: a Compilation of Multi-Item Measures, vol. 2.* American Marketing Association, Chicago.

Buzzel, R.D. & Gale, B.T. (1987) *The PIMS-Principles: Linking Strategy to Performance.* The Free Press, New York.

Cacioppo, J.T. & Petty, R.E. (1983) *Social Psychophysiology.* The Guilford Press, New York.

Callebout, J., Janssens, M., Lorré, D. & Hendrickx, H. (1994) *The Naked Consumer: the Secret Motivational Research in Global Marketing.* Antwerpen: Censydiam Institute, Antwerp.

Calvin, W.H. (1996) *The Cerebral Code.* MIT Press, Cambridge, Mass.

Cantor, N. & Kihlstrom, J.F. (1989) Social intelligence and cognitive assessments of personality. In *Advances in Social Cognition, vol 2* (R.S. Wyer, & T.K. Srull, eds). Lawrence Erlbaum Associates, Hillsdale, New Jersey.

Carlston, D.E. (1992) Impression formation and the modular mind: the associated systems theory. In *The Construction of Social Judgements* (L.L. Martin & A. Tesser, eds). Lawrence Erlbaum Associates, Hillsdale, New Jersey.

Carter, R. (1998) *Mapping the Mind.* Weidenfeld & Nicolson, London.

Case, R. (1984) The process of transition: a neo-Piagetian view. In *Mechanisms of Cognitive Development* (R. Sternberg, ed.). Freeman, New York.

Case, R. (1985) *Intellectual Development: Birth to Adulthood.* The Academic Press, New York.

Castleberry, B.S. & Ehrenberg, A.S.C. (1990) Brand usage: a factor in consumer beliefs. *Marketing Research,* June.

Censydiam (1998) *Studie Naar het Imago van 30 Automerken en 85 Modellen: Vierde Meting.* Censydiam internal document, Almere.

Centerdata (1999) *Analyse van de Percepties van Nederlandse Biermerken.* Unpublished.

Chaiken, S., Liberman, A. & Eagly, A.H. (1989) Heuristic and systematic processing within and beyond the persuasion context. In *United Thought* (J.S. Uleman & J.A. Bargh, eds). Guilford Press, New York.

Churchland, P.M. (1994) *The Engine of Reason, the Seat of the Soul: a Philosophical Journey into the Brain*. MIT Press, Cambridge, Mass.

Clarkson, P. (1992) *Transactional Analysis Psychotherapy: an Integrated Approach*. Routledge, London.

Cohen, G., Kiss, G. & Le Voi, M. (1993) *Memory: Current Issues*, 2nd edn. Open University Press, Buckingham.

Cohen, N.J. & Squire, L.R. (1980) Preserved learning and retention of pattern analysing skill in amnesia: dissociation of 'knowing how' and 'knowing that'. *Science* **210**, 207–209.

Collins, A.M. & Loftus, E.F. (1975) A spreading activation theory of semantic memory. *Psychological Review* **82**, 407–428.

Collins, A.M. & Quillian, M.R. (1972) Experiments on semantic memory and language comprehension. In *Cognition and Learning* (L.W. Gregg, ed.). John Wiley & Sons, New York.

Coltheart, M. (1978) Lexical access in simple reading tasks. In *Strategies of Information Processing* (G. Underwood, ed.). Academic Press, London.

Crick, F. (1994) *The Astonishing Hypothesis: the Scientific Search for the Soul*. Touchstone Books (Simon & Schuster), London.

Damasio, A.R. (1994) *Descartes' Error: Emotion, Reason, and the Human Brain*. Avon Books, New York.

Dammler, A. (1998) Marken für kids. *Werben & Verkaufen*, 11/98, 24.

De Chernatony, L. (1993) Categorizing brands: evolutionary processes underpinned by two key dimensions. *Journal of Marketing* **9**, 173–188.

De Chernatony, L. & McDonald, M.H.B. (1992) *Creating Powerful Brands: The Strategic Route to Success in Consumer, Industrial and Service Markets*. Butterworth-Heinemann Ltd, Oxford.

De Chernatony, L. & McWilliam, G. (1990) Appreciating brands as assets through using a two dimensional model. *International Journal of Advertising* **9**(2), 111–119.

Deelder, J. (1994) *Renaissance: Gedichten '44–'94*. Uitgeverij de Bezige Bij, Amsterdam.

Defoe, D. (1908) *The Life and Strange Surprising Adventures of Robinson Crusoe, of York, Mariner, as Related by Himself*. Altemus, Philadelphia.

De Groot, A.D. (1997) Intuïtie is onmisbaar voor schakers. *NRC Handelsblad*, 27/5/1997.

DeKimpe, M. & Hanssens, D. (1995) Empirical generalizations about market evolution and stationarity. *Marketing Science* **14**(3), part 2.

De Man, J. (1995) De mens als machine. *HP de Tijd,* December.

Den Boer, D.J., Bouwman, H., Frissen, V. & Houben, M. (1994) *Methodologie en Statistiek voor Communicatie-ondezoek*. Bohn Stafler Van Loghum, Houten/Zaventem.

Dennett, D.C. (1991) *Consciousness Explained*. Penguin Books, London.

Dennett, D.C. (1996) *Kinds of Minds: Toward an Understanding of Consciousness*. HarperCollins, New York.

De Pelsmacker, P. & van Kenhove, P. (1994) *Marktonderzoek: Methoden en Toepassingen*. Garant, Leuven/Apeldoorn.

Descartes, R. (1985) The passions of the soul. In *The Philosophical Writings of Descartes, vol. 1* (J. Cottingham, R. Stoothoff, & D. Murdoch, eds). Cambridge University Press, Cambridge.

De Vries, H. (1997) *Het Draait om de Kern: een Onderzoek naar Kernassociaties die Consumenten hebben met Merken*. Masters thesis, University of Amsterdam.

Dickson, P.R. & Sawyer, A.G. (1986) Point-of-purchase behavior and price perceptions of supermarket shoppers. *Marketing Science Institute, Working Paper No. 86–102*. MSI, Cambridge, Mass.

DMB&B (1994) *A New Strategy for Leadership*. DMB&B internal document, London.

Donius, J.F. (1994) Brand equity: a holistic perspective. *ARF Brand Equity Workshop*, New York, February 15–16.

Doob, L.W. (1947) The behavior of attitudes. *Psychological Review* **54**, 135–156.

Dowling, G.R. & Uncles, M. (1997) Do customer loyalty programs really work? *Sloan Management Review*, Summer.

Doyle, P. (1989) Building succesful brands: the strategic options. *Journal of Marketing Management* **1**, 77–95.

Drenth, T. (1996) *Het merk als Symbool*. Masters thesis, University of Amsterdam.

Drost, D.M. (1996) *Mensen Onder Elkaar: Psychologie van Sociale Interacties*. De Tijdstroom, Utrecht.

Dru, J.M. (1996) *Disruption: Overturning Conventions and Shaking up the Marketplace*. John Wiley & Sons, New York.

Dyson, P., Farr, A. & Hollis, N. (1996) Understanding, measuring, and using brand equity. *Journal of Advertising Research*, **36**(6), 9–21.

Eagly, A.H. & Chaiken, S. (1993) *The Psychology of Attitudes*. Harcourt Brace Jovanovich, Orlando, Florida.

Ebbinghaus, H. (1885) *Memory: A Contribution to Experimental Psychology*. Dover, New York.

Edelman, G.M. (1993) *Klare Lucht, Louter Vuur*. Bert Bakker, Amsterdam.

Ehrenberg, A.S.C. (1969) Towards an integrated theory of consumer behaviour. *Journal of the Market Research Society* **11**(4).

Ehrenberg, A.S.C. (1974) Repetitive advertising and the consumer. *Journal of Advertising Research* **14**(2).

Ehrenberg, A.S.C. (1997) B.E. or not B.E. *Advertising Research Foundation 43rd Annual Conference*. ARF, New York.

Ehrenberg, A.S.C. & Uncles, M.D. (1995) *Dirichlet-Type Markets: a Review, Part 1: Patterns and Theory*. South Bank University, London.

Ehrenberg, A.S.C. & Uncles, M.D. (1999) *Understanding Dirichlet-Type Markets, Research Report 1 (revised version)*. South Bank University, London.

Ehrenberg, A.S.C., Barnard, N. & Scriven, J. (1997) Differentiation or Salience. JOAB Report 5. *Journal of Advertising Research* **37**(6), 7–14.

Ekman, P. (1989) The argument and evidence about universals in facial expressions of emotions. In *Handbook of Social Psychophysiology* (H. Wagner & A. Manstead, eds), pp. 143–164. Wiley, Chichester.

Ekman, P. (1992) An argument for basic emotions. *Cognition and Emotion* **6**(3/4), 169–187.

Ekman. P. & Friesen, W.V. (1976) Measuring facial movement. *Environmental Psychology and Nonverbal Behavior* **1**(1), 56–75.

Ekman, P. & Friesen, W.V. (1978) *Investigator's Guide to the Facial Action Coding System, Part II*. Consulting Psychologists Press, Palo Alto, California.

Ekman, P., Friesen, W.V. & Ancoli, S. (1980) Facial signs of emotional experience. *Journal of Personality and Social Psychology* **39**, 1125–1134.

Ekman, P., Friesen, W.V. & Ellsworth, P. (1982) What emotion categories or dimensions can observers judge from facial behavior? In *Emotion in the Human Face* (P. Ekman, ed.). Cambridge University Press, New York.

Engel, J.F., Blackwell, R.D. & Miniard, P.W. (1990) *Consumer Behavior*, 6th edn. The Dryden Press, Chicago.

Engler, B. (1995) *Personality Theories: an Introduction,* 4th edn. Houghton Mifflin Company, Boston.

Eysenck, M.W. & Keane, M.T. (1995) *Cognitive Psychology: a Student's Handbook,* 3rd edn. Lawrence Erlbaum Associates, Hillsdale, New Jersey.

Fajer, M.T. & Schouten, J.W. (1995) Breakdown and dissolution of person–brand relationships. *Advances in Consumer Research* **22**, 663–667.

Farr, A. (1998) Brand values: is size all that matters? *Admap,* May.

Farr, A. (1999) Does your brand have the energy to compete? *Admap,* April.

Farr, A. & Hollis, N. (1997) What do you want your brand to be when it grows up: big and strong? *Journal of Advertising Research* **37**(6).

Fazio, R.H. (1989) On the power and functionality of attitudes: the role of attitude accessibility. In *Attitude Structure and Function* (A.R. Pratkanis, S.J. Breckler, & A.G. Greenwald, eds). Lawrence Erlbaum Associates, Hillsdale, New Jersey.

Ferguson, M. (1989) *The Aquarian Conspiracy*. Paladin, London.

Festinger, L. (1957) *A Theory of Cognitive Dissonance*. Stanford University Press, Stanford.

Festinger, L. & Carlsmith, J.M. (1959) Cognitive consequences of forced compliance. *Journal of Abnormal and Social Psychology* **58**, 203–210.

Fischer, A.H. (1991) Sociale cognitie en emoties. In *Cognitieve Sociale Psychologie* (N.K. de Vries & J. van Pligt, eds). Boom, Meppel.

Fishbein, M. (1967) *Readings in Attitude Theory and Measurement*. John Wiley & Sons, New York.

Fishbein, M. & Ajzen, I. (1975) *Beliefs, Attitude, Intention and Behavior: An Introduction to Theory and Research*. Addison-Wesley, Reading, Mass.

Fiske, S.T. & Taylor, S.E. (1991) *Social Cognition*, 2nd edn. McGraw-Hill, New York.

Fodor, G. (1983) *The Modularity of Mind*. MIT Press, Cambridge, Mass.

Fornell, C., Johnson, M.D., Anderson, E.W., Cha, J. & Everitt Bryant, B. (1996) The American Satisfaction Index: nature, purpose and findings. *Journal of Marketing* **60**, October.

Forsyth, D.R. (1990) *Group Dynamics,* 2nd edn. Brooks/Cole, Monterey, California.

Fournier, S.M. (1994) *A Consumer–Brand Relationship Framework for Strategic Brand Management*. Doctoral dissertation, University of Florida.

Franzen, G. (1992) *Hoe Reclame Echt Werkt: Bevindingen uit Empirisch Onderzoek*. Kluwer Bedrijfswetenschappen, Deventer.

Franzen, G. (1998) *Merken en Reclame: hoe Reclame-Effectiviteit Brand-Equity Beïnvloedt*. Kluwer Bedrijfsinformatie, Deventer.

Franzen, G. & Holzhauer, F. (1987) *Het Merk: Serie uit Acht Delen (ter gelegenheid van het 25-jarig bestaan van FHV/BBDO)* Kluwer Bedrijfsinformatie, Deventer.

Franzen, M.P. & Hoogerbrugge, M.C. (1996) *Het Merk op Weg naar de 21ste Eeuw*. SWOCC (University of Amsterdam), Amsterdam.

Franzen, M.P., Schuring, R.J. & Sikkel, D. (1998) *Brand-equity bier- en margarinemerken*. Unpublished.

Frege, G. (1952) On sense and reference. In *Translations from the Philosophical Writings of Gottlob Frege* (P. Geach, & M. Black, eds). Basil Blackwell, Oxford.

Fridlund, A.J. (1991) The sociality of solitary smiling: potentiation by an implicit audience. *Journal of Personality and Social Psychology* 60, 229–240.

Frijda, N. (1986) *The Emotions*. Cambridge University Press, Cambridge.

Frijda, N. (1991) *Emotion*. Unpublished, University of Amsterdam.

Frijda, N. (1993) *De Psychologie Heeft Zin*. Prometheus, Amsterdam.

Gazzaniga, M.S. (1998) The split brain revisited. *Scientific American*, July, 33–39.

Geursen, G. (1994) *Virtuele Tomaten en Conceptuele Pindakaas: hoe Interactiviteit, Zelforganisatie en Bewustzijnsverruiming de Marketing op zijn Kop Zetten*. Kluwer Bedrijfswetenschappen, Deventer.

Geursen, G. (1996) De waarden ontwaard. *Adformatie*, 16/6/1996.

Geursen, G. (1998) De opkomst van het netmerk. *Source* 3.

Gilmore, F., ed. (1997) *Brand Warriors: Corporate Leaders Share Their Winning Strategies*. HarperCollins Business, London.

Glass, A.L. & Holyoak, K.J. (1986) *Cognition*, 2nd edn. McGraw-Hill, London.

Glassman, W.E. & Geluk, H. (1998) *Stromingen in de Psychologie*. Uitgeverij Intro, Baarn.

Gleitman, H. (1991) *Psychology*, 3rd edn. W.W. Norton & Company, New York.

Goessens, C. (1995) *GVR Monografie 3: Likability en Reclame-effect*. Genootschap voor Reclame, Amsterdam.

Goleman, D. (1995) *Emotional Intelligence: Why it Can Matter More than IQ*. Bloomsbury Publishing, London.

Gordon, W. & Langmaid, R. (1988) *Qualitative Market Research: a Practitioner's and Buyer's Guide*. Gower Publishing Company, Aldershot.

Gordon, W. & Restall, C. (1992) Brands – the missing link: Understanding the emotional relationship. *ESOMAR Seminar: The Challenge of Branding Today and in the Future*. ESOMAR seminar, Brussels.

Gorsuch, R.L. (1970) Rokeach's approach to value systems and social comparisons. *Review of Religious Research* 11, 139–143.

Gould, J.L. & Gould, C.G. (1998) Reasoning in animals. *Scientific American Presents* 9(4), 52–59.

Graf, R. & Schacter, D.L. (1985) Implicit and explicit memory for new associations in normal subjects and amnesic patients. *Journal of Experimental Psychology: Learning, Memory, and Cognition* 11, 501–518.

Gray, J.A. (1982) *The Neuropsychology of Anxiety*. Oxford University Press, Oxford.

Greenfield, S.A. (1995) *Journey to the Centers of the Mind: Toward a Science of Consciousness*. W.H. Freeman and Company, New York.

Greenspan, S.I. (1997) *The Growth of the Mind and the Endangered Origins of Intelligence*. Addison-Wesley, Reading, Mass.

Grunert, K.G. (1988) *A Method to Estimate Cognitive Structure from Qualitative Data in Market Research: Working Paper no. 12*. Denmark: Aarhus School of Business Administration & Economics, Denmark.

Grunert, K.G. (1996) Automatic and strategic processes in advertising effects. *Journal of Marketing* 60, October, 88–101.

Häberle, E. (1989) Die Marke Macht's. *Werben und Verkaufen*, 09/04/1998, no. 4, 8–9.

Häcker, T. (1993) ASSPAT: 'handige truc' voor image-onderzoek. *Onderzoek*, May.

Hallberg, G. (1995) *All Consumers Are NOT Created Equal: the Differential Marketing Strategy for Brand Loyalty and Profits*. John Wiley & Sons, New York.

Han, M.C. (1989) Country image: halo or summary construct? *Journal of Marketing Research* **26**, May.

Hankinson, G. & Cowking, P. (1993) *Branding in Action: Cases and Strategies for Profitable Brand Management*. McGraw-Hill, London.

Hansen, F. (1998) From life style to value systems to simplicity. *Advances in Consumer Research* **25**.

Harris, P.L. (1989) *Children and Emotions: the Development of Psychological Understanding*. Blackwell, Oxford.

Harris, T.A. (1992) *Ik ben o.k.; Jij bent o.k.: Hoe Kunnen wij Leven en Laten Leven*. Uitgeverij Ambo, Baarn.

Hastie, R. & Park, B. (1986) The relationship between memory and judgment depends on whether the judgment task is memory-based or on-line. *Psychological Review* **93**(3), 258–268.

Hätty, H. (1989) *Der Markentransfer*. Physica, Heidelberg.

Heath, R. (1997) *Brand Commitment as the Predictor of Advertising Effect*. Taylor Nelson AGB, London.

Heath, R.L. & Fogel, D.S. (1978) Terminal and instrumental? An inquiry into Rokeach's value survey. *Psychological Reports* **42**, 1155–1158.

Hebb, D. (1949) *Organization of Behavior*. John Wiley & Sons, New York.

Heylen, J.P. (1990) De impliciete persoonlijkheid. *Onderzoek*, 27/11/1990.

Heylen, J.P., Dawson, B. & Sampson, P. (1995) An implicit model of consumer behaviour. *Journal of the Market Research Society* **37**(1).

Higgins, E.T. (1987) Self-discrepancy: a theory relating self and affect. *Psychological Review* **94**, 319–340.

Hinde, R.A. (1997) *Relationships: A Dialectic Perspective*. Psychology Press, Hove, East Sussex.

Hinton, G.E. (1989) Connections learning procedures. *Artificial Intelligence* **40**, 185–234.

Hirschman, E.C. (1980) Attributes of attributes and layers of meaning. In *Advances in Consumer Research, vol. 8* (J. Olson, ed.). Association for Consumer Research, Provo, Utah.

Hirschman, E.C. (1998) Afterwords: some reflections on the mind's eye. In *Representing Consumers: Voices, Views and Visions* (B.B. Stern, ed.). Routledge, London.

Hite, C. & Hite, R.E. (1995) Reliance on brand by young children. *Journal of the Market Research Society* **37**(2), 185–193.

Holden, S.J.S. (1993) Understanding brand awareness: let me give you a c(l)ue. *Advances in Consumer Research* **20**, 383–388.

Holden, S.J.S. & Lutz, R.J. (1992) Ask not what the brand can evoke; ask what can evoke the brand? *Advances in Consumer Research* **19**, 101–107.

Holler, J. (1993) *Het Nieuwe Brein een Ontdekkingsreis door de Fascinerende Wereld van het Hersenonderzoek* [translation of *Das Neue Gehirn*]. Panta Rhei, Katwijk aan Zee.

Hoogerbrugge, M.C. (1996) *Tracking*. SWOCC, Amsterdam.

Hovland, C.I., Janis, I.L. & Kelley, H.H. (1953) *Communication and Persuasion: Psychological Studies of Opinion Change*. Yale University Press, New Haven.

Howard, J.A. (1977) *Product Hierarchy: Consumer Behavior in Marketing Strategy*. Prentice-Hall, New Jersey.

Howard, J.A. & Sheth, J. (1969) *The Theory of Buyer Behavior*. John Wiley & Sons, New York.

Howes, M.B. (1990) *The Psychology of Human Cognition: Mainstream and Genevan Traditions*. Pergamon Press, New York.

Hoyer, W.D. (1984) An examination of consumer decision making for a common repeat purchase product. *Journal of Consumer Research* **11**, 822–829.

Isen, A.M. (1993) Positive effect and decision making. In *Handbook of Emotions* (M. Lewis & J.M. Haviland, eds). The Guilford Press, New York/London.

ISEO (1996) *Beschrijving van Onderzoekstechnieken*. ISEO internal document, Leiden.

Izard, C.E. (1971) *The Face of Emotion*. Appleton-Century-Crofts, New York.

Jackendoff, R. (1994) *Patterns in the Mind – Language and Human Nature*. Basic Books, New York.

James, W. (1884) What is an emotion? *Mind* **9**, 188–205.

Jansen, K. (1999) Haitinks jaren. *NRC Handelsblad*, 1/3/1999.

John, D.R. & Sujan, M. (1990) Age differences in product categorization. *Journal of Consumer Research* **16**, 452–460.

Johnson, W., Emde, R.N., Pannabecker, B., Sternberg, C. & Davis, M. (1982) Maternal perception of infant emotion from birth through 18 months. *Infant Behavior and Development* **5**, 313–322.

Johnson-Laird, P.N. (1988) *The Computer and the Mind: an Introduction to Cognitive Science*. Harvard University Press, Cambridge, Mass.

Jones, J.P. (1995) *How Advertising Works: the Role of Research*. Sage Publications, Thousand Oaks, California.

Kalat, J.A. (1995) *Biological Psychology*, 5th edn. Brooks/Cole Publishing Company, Belmont.

Kandel, E.R., Schwarz, J.H. & Jessell, T.M., eds. (1991) *Principles of Neural Science*. Elsevier, New York.

Kapferer, J.N. (1997) *Strategic Brand Management*, 2nd edn. Kogan Page, London.

Kapferer, J.N. (1998) Why are we seduced by luxury brands? *Journal of Brand Management* **6**(1), 44–49.

Keller, K.L. (1993) Conceptualizing, measuring, and managing customer-based brand equity. *Journal of Marketing*, January.

Keller, K.L. (1998) *Strategic Brand Management: Building, Measuring, and Managing Brand Equity*. Prentice-Hall, New Jersey.

Kihlstrom, J.F. (1987) The cognitive unconscious. *Science* **237**.

Kihlstrom, J.F. & Klein, S.B. (1994) The self as a knowledge structure. In *Handbook of Social Cognition, vol. 1; Basic Processes*, 2nd edn (R.S. Wyer & T.K. Srull, eds). Uitgever, Plaats.

Kranenberg, A. (1998) Vroeg oude meisjes. *Volkskrant*, 7/3/1998.

Krishnan, H.S. (1996) Characteristics of memory associations: a consumer-based brand equity perspective. *International Journal of Research in Marketing* **13**, 389–405.

Krugman, H.E. (1971) Brain wave measure of media involvement. *Journal of Advertising Research* **11**, 3–9.

Lai, A.W. (1995) Consumer values, product benefits and customer value: a consumption behavior approach. *Advances in Consumer Research* **22**.

Lamme, A. & Gameren, M. (1993) Quality planning: een model en methode voor kwalitatieve mediaplanning. *Blad/Dossier* **6**, June.

Langer, J. (1997) What consumers wish brand managers knew. *Journal of Advertising Research*, **37**.

Laroche, M., Rosenblatt, J.A. & Brisoux, J.E. (1986) Consumer brand categorisation: basic frameworks and managerial implications. *Marketing Intelligence and Planning*, **4**(4).

Larsen, R.J. & Diener, E. (1992) Promises and problems with the circumplex model of emotion. In *Review of Personality and Social Psychology, vol. 14: Emotional and Social Behavior* (M.S. Clark, ed.). Sage, Newbury Park, California.

Lashley, K.S (1950) In search of the engram. *Symposia of the Society for Experimental Biology* **4**, 454–482.

Lawson, R. (1998) Customer knowledge structures: networks and frames. *Advances in Consumer Research* **25**.

Lazarus, R.S. (1991) *Emotion and Adaptation*. Oxford University Press, New York.

LeDoux, J.E. (1993) Emotional networks in the brain. In *Handbook of Emotions* (M. Lewis, & J.M. Haviland, eds). Guilford Press, New York.

LeDoux, J.E. (1996) *The Emotional Brain the Mysterious Underpinnings of Emotional Life*. Touchstone, New York.

Leyens, J.P. & Dardenne, B. (1996) Basic concepts and approaches in social cognition. In *Introduction to Social Psychology: a European Perspective* (M. Hewstone, W. Stroebe, & G.M. Stephenson, eds), 2nd edn. Blackwell, Oxford.

Locke, J. (1924) *An Essay Concerning Human Understanding (vols. 1 & 2)*, A.C. Fraser, ed. Dover Publications, New York.

Lockhart, S.R. (1989) The role of theory in understanding implicit memory. In *Implicit Memory: Theoretical Issues* (S. Lewandowsky, J.C. Dunn & K. Kirsner, eds). Hillsdale, New Jersey: Lawrence Erlbaum Associates.

Loftus, E.F. & Loftus, G.R. (1980) On the permanence of stored information in the human brain. *American Psychologist* **35**, 409–420.

Maathuis, O.J.H. (1999) *Corporate Brands: the Value of the Corporate Brand to Customers and Managers*. Thesis, Erasmus University, Rotterdam.

McClelland, J.K. & Rumelhart, D.E. (1986) Amnesia and distributed memory. In *Parallel Distributed Processing: Explorations in the Microstructure of Cognition, vol. 2: Psychological and Biological Models* (D.E. Rumelhart, J.K. McClelland & The PDP Research Group, eds). Bradford, Cambridge, Mass.

McEwen, B.S. & Schmeck, H.M. (1994) *The Hostage Brain*. The Rockefeller University Press, New York.

McDougall, W. (1926) *An Introduction to Social Psychology*. Luce, Boston.

MacLean, P.D. (1954) Studies on limbic system ('visceral brain') and their bearing on psychosomatic problems. In *Recent Developments in Psychosomatic Medicine* (E.D. Wittkower & R.A. Cleghorn, eds). Lippincott, Philadelphia.

MacLean, P.D. (1973) A triune concept of the brain and behavior. In *Hincks Memorial Lectures* (T.J. Boag, & C. Campbell, eds). University of Toronto Press, Toronto.

Mandler, G. (1980) Recognizing: the judgment of previous occurence. *Psychological Review* **87**(3), 252–271.

Mandler J.M. (1984) *Stories, Scripts and Scenes: Aspects of Schema Theory*. Lawrence Erlbaum Associates, Hillsdale, New Jersey.

Marder, E. (1997) *The Laws of Choice*. Simon & Schuster, London.

Medin, D.L. & Schaffer, M.M. (1978) A context theory of classification learning. *Psychological Review* **85**, 207–238.

Mehrabian, A. & Russel, J. (1977) Evidence for a three-factor theory of emotions. *Journal of Research in Personality* **11**, 273–294.

Menon, G. & Wänke, M. (1998) Accessibility revisited: when and how it is diagnostic for consumer judgments. *Advances in Consumer Research* **25**.

Mervis, C.B. & Rosch, E. (1981) Categorization of natural objects. *Annual Review of Psychology* **32**, 89–115.

Miller, G.A. (1981) Trends and debates in cognitive psychology. *Cognition* **10**, 215–226.

Mishkin, M. & Appenzeller, T. (1987) The anatomy of memory. *Scientific American*, **256**, 80–89.

Mishkin, M., Malamut, B. & Bachevaller, J. (1984) Memories and habits: two neural systems. In *Neurobiology of Learning and Memory* (G. Lynch, J.L. McGaugh, & N.M. Weinberger, eds), pp. 65–77. Guilford Press, New York.

Moens, J.P.G. (1999) *Merkimago en behoeftenbevrediging: een psychodynamische benadering van merken*. Presentation to the Stichting Wetenschappelijk Onderzoek Commerciële Communicatie, Amsterdam.

Morris, J.D. (1995) Observations: SAM: the Self-Assessment Manikin – an efficient cross–cultural measurement of emotional responses. *Journal of Advertising Research* **35**(6), 63–38.

Moscovici, S. (1981) *L'Age des Foules*. Fayard, Paris.

Mosmans, A.P. & van der Vorst, R., eds (1997) *MarketingWijzer: Merkenbeleid*. Kluwer Bedrijfsinformatie, Deventer.

Mosmans, A. & van der Vorst, R. (1998) Brand based strategic management. *Journal of Brand Management* **6**(2), 99–110.

Mowrer, O.H. (1960) *Learning Theory and Behavior*. John Wiley & Sons, New York.

Murre, J.M.J. (1997) Implicit and explicit memory in amnesia: some explanations and predictions by the TraceLink model. *Memory* **5**(1/2), 213–232.

Murre, J.M.J. (1999) *Briefwisseling met de auteurs over deel I van dit boek*. University of Amsterdam, Amsterdam.

Murre, J.M.J. & Sturdy, D.P.F. (1995) The connectivity of the braIn multi-level quantitative analysis. *Biological Cybernetics* **73**, 529–545.

Nash, J.M. (1997) Fertile minds. *Time*, 10/2/1997.

Nawas, M.M. (1986) *Inleiding tot de Persoonlijkheidsleer*. Dekker & Van de Vegt, Nijmegen.

Nedungadi, P. (1990) Recall and consumer consideration sets: influencing choice without altering brand evaluations. *Journal of Consumer Research* **17**, December.

Oatley, K. & Johnson-Laird, P.N. (1987) Towards a cognitive theory of emotions. *Cognition and Emotion* **1**, 29–50.

Ogilvy & Mather (1997) *Customer Ownership: BrandYard & BrandGrid*. Confidential document, Amsterdam.

Ortony, A. & Turner, T.J. (1990) What's basic about basic emotions? *Psychological Review* **97**, 313–331.

Osgood, C.E., Suci, G.J. & Tannenbaum, P.H. (1957) *The Measurement of Meaning.* University of Illinois Press, Urbana.

Özsomer, A. & Cavusgil, S.T. (1991) *Country-of-origin effects on product evaluations: a sequel to bilkey and nes review.* American Marketing Association, San Francisco.

Palmer, S.E. (1975) Visual perception and world knowledge: notes on a model of sensory-cognitive interaction. In *Explorations in Cognition* (D.A. Norman, D.E. Rumelhart, & the LNR Research Group). Freeman, San Francisco.

Panksepp, J. (1982) Toward a general psychobiological theory of emotions. *Behavioral and Brain Sciences* **5**, 407–467.

Parker Brady, R. (1997) De registratie van het onbewust kijken. *Nieuwstribune,* 16/10/1997.

Parsons, A.J. (1996) Nestlé: the visions of local managers – an interview with Peter Brabeck-Letmathe, CEO elect, Nestlé. *The McKinsey Quarterly,* **2**.

Pavio, A. (1986) *Mental Representations: a Dual Coding Approach.* Oxford University Press, New York.

Pearce. J.C. (1992) *Evolution's End.* Harper, San Francisco.

Perfect, T.J. & Askew, C. (1994) Print adverts: not remembered but memorable. *Applied Cognitive Psychology* **8**, 693–703.

Perfect, T.J. & Heatherley, S. (1996) Implicit memory in print ads. *Admap,* January, 41–42.

Peter, J.P. & Olson, J.C. (1993) *Consumer Behavior and Marketing Strategy.* Irwin, Homewood, Illinois.

Petty, R.E. & Cacioppo, J.T. (1986) *Communication and Persuasion: Central and Peripheral Routes to Attitude Change.* Springer-Verlag, New York.

Piaget, J. & Inhelder, B. (1973) *Memory and Intelligence* Routledge and Kegan Paul, London.

Pieters, R.G.M. (1989) Laddering: en nieuwe ontwikkeling in segmentatie. *Tijdschrift voor Marketing,* October, 30–41.

Pieters, R.G.M. & van Raaij, W.F. (1992) *Reclamewerking.* Stenfert Kroese Uitgevers, Leiden.

Pinker, S. (1994) *The Language Instinct: the New Science of Language and Mind.* Penguin, London.

Pinker, S. (1997) *How the Mind Works.* Penguin, London.

Plutchik, R. (1962) *The Emotions: Facts, Theories, and a New Model.* Random House, New York.

Plutchik, R. (1980) A general psychoevolutionary theory of emotion. In *Emotions: Theory, Research, and Experience: vol. 1. Theories of Emotion* (R. Plutchik & H. Kellerman, eds). New York: Academic Press.

Poiesz, Th.B.C. (1989) Image concept: its place in consumer psychology. *Journal of Economic Psychology,* **10**, 457–472.

Polter, J. & van Fessen, A. (1991) Psycholoog Polter laat bij ISK mensen ècht de geest krijgen. *Adformatie* 12/5/1995.

Quillian, M.R. (1968) Semantic memory. In *Semantic Information Processing* (M. Minsky, ed.). MIT Press, Cambridge, Mass.

Raaijmakers, J.G.W. (1996) Personal communication. Amsterdam.

Raaijmakers, J.G.W. & Shiffrin R.M. (1981) Search of associative memory. *Psychological Review* **88**(2).

Reber A.S. (1997) *Woordenboek van de Psychologie*. Bert Bakker, Amsterdam.

Reder, L.M. & Ross, B.H. (1983) Integrated knowledge in different tasks: positive and negative fan effects. *Journal of Experimental Psychology: Human Learning and Memory* 8, 55–72.

Research International (1995) *The Research International Approach to Brand Image Analyses*. Research International internal document, Rotterdam.

Research International (1997a) *Solutions...: een Compendium van Research Technieken*. Research International internal document, Rotterdam.

Research International (1997b) *Image Onderzoek d.m.v. ASSPAT*. Research International internal document, Rotterdam.

Richardson, J.T.E. (1984) Developing the theory of working memory. *Memory and Cognition* 12, 71–83.

Ries, A. & Ries, L. (1998) *The 22 Immutable Laws of Branding: How to Build a Product or Service into a World-Class Brand*. HarperCollins, New York.

Ries, A. & Trout, J. (1972) Positioning. *Advertising Age*, May.

Rijkenberg, J. (1998) *Concepting: het Managen van Concept-merken in het Communicatiegeoriënteerde Tijdperk*. BZZTôH, The Hague.

Rinnooy Kan, E. (1996) *De Stad als Merk*. www.design-inst.nl/activities/2d/tl/legible_city/lc8_speaker.

Roediger, H.L. (1990) Implicit memory: retention without remembering. *American Psychologist* **45**, 1043–1056.

Rokeach, M. (1973) *The Nature of Human Values*. The Free Press, New York.

Rook, D. (1985) The ritual dimension of consumer behavior. *Journal of Consumer Research,* 12/12/1985, 251–264.

Rosch, E. & Lloyds, B.B., eds (1978) *Cognition and Categorization*. Lawrence Erlbaum Associates, Hillsdale, New Jersey.

Rosch, E. & Mervis, C.B. (1975) Family resemblances: studies in the internal structure of categories. *Cognitive Psychology* 7, 573–605.

Rose, S. (1993) *The Making of Memory: from Molecules to Mind*. Bantam, London.

Roth, M.S. & Romeo, J.B. (1992) Matching product category and country image perceptions: a framework for managing country-of-origin effects. *Journal of International Business Studies* **23**(3), 477–497.

Rumelhart, D.E. & Norman, D.A. (1983) Representation in memory. In *Handbook of Experimental Psychology* (R.C. Atkinson, R.J. Herrnstein, G. Lindzey, & R.D. Luce, eds). John Wiley & Sons, New York.

Rumelhart, D.E. & Norman, D.A. (1985) Representation of knowledge. In *Issues in Cognitive Modeling* (A.M. Aitkenhead & J.M. Slack, eds). Lawrence Erlbaum Associates, Hillsdale, New Jersey.

Russell, J.A. (1980) A circumplex model of affect. *Journal of Personality and Social Psychology, 38*, 1161–1178.

Russell, J.A. (1983) Pancultural aspects of the human conceptual organization of emotions. *Journal of Personality and Social Psychology* **45**, 1281–1288.

Sacks, O. (1989) *Seeing Voices: a Journey into the World of the Deaf*. University of California Press, Berkeley.

Sampson, P. (1993) A better way to measure brand image: positioning, segmentation and the dynamic attributes that drive brands. *Admap,* July.

Schacter, D.L. (1996) *Searching for Memory, the Brain, the Mind, and the Past.* BasicBooks, New York.

Schank, R. (1981) Language and memory. In *Perspectives on Cognitive Science* (D.A. Norman, ed.). Lawrence Erlbaum Associates, Hillsdale, New Jersey.

Schellekens, H. (1993) *Breinboek: Hersenen, Biochemie en de Menselijke Geest.* Aramith, Bloemendaal.

Scherer, K.R. (1984) Emotions as a multi-component process: a model and some cross-cultural data. In *Review of Personality and Social Psychology, vol. 5* (K.R. Scherer & P. Ekman, eds). Sage, Beverly Hills, Calif.

Scherer, K.R. (1996) Emotion. In *Introduction To Social Psychology: A European Perspective* (M. Hewstone, W. Stroebe & G.M. Stephenson, eds), 2nd edn. Blackwell, Oxford.

Schuring, R.J. (1995) *Meten en Verbeteren van uw Marketing- en Verkooprendement: Accountability in Marketingcommunicatie.* Paper presented to the GVR Seminar, Lezing.

Schuring, R.J. & Vogel, M. (1998) Marktsimulatie. In *Merken en Reclame: Hoe Reclame-Effectiviteit Brand-Equity Beïnvloedt* (G. Franzen, ed). Kluwer Bedrijfsinformatie, Deventer.

Scott, L.M. (1994) Images in advertising: the need for a theory of visual rhetoric. *Journal of Consumer Research* **21**, 252–273.

Scroggs, J.R. (1994) *Persoon en Persoonlijkheid: deel 1.* Donker, Rotterdam.

Scroggs, J.R. (1996) *Persoon en Persoonlijkheid: deel 2.* Donker, Rotterdam.

Semon, R. (1923) *Mnemic Psychology.* George Allen & Unwin, London.

Shocker, A.D., Sung Y.J. & Whan Park, C. (1996) Composite branding alliances: an investigation of extension and feedback effects. *Journal of Marketing Research* **33**, November, 453–466.

Sheth, J.N., Newman, B.I. & Gross, B.L. (1991) Why we buy what we buy: a theory of consumption values. *Journal of Business Research* **22**, 159–170.

Signicom (1994) *Onderzoeksrapport.* Confidential document.

Sikkel, D. (1994) *Syllabus Marktanalyse.* University of Amsterdam, Amsterdam.

Sikkel, D. (1999) Personal communication with Centerdata, Tilburg.

Sikkel, D. & Oppenhuisen, J. (1998) *Vrijheid en Gebondenheid: de Woorden van Waarden.* Unpublished.

Sloot, L.M. & Bunt, J. (1996) *BrandWatcher: Meetinstrument voor Merktrouw.* Erasmus University Rotterdam, Rotterdam.

Spence, D.P. (1984) *Narrative Truth and Historical Truth.* Norton, New York.

Standing, L. (1973) Learning 10,000 pictures. *Quarterly Journal of Experimental Psychology* **25**, 207–222.

Stephan, S.K. & Tannenholz, B.L. (1994) The real reason for brand-switching. *Advertising Age* June, 13.

Sutherland, M. (1993) *Adverising and the Mind of the Consumer: What Works, What Doesn't and Why.* Allen & Unwin, St. Leonards, Australia.

Swan, N. (1995) *News from the front line.* Lecture to the Genootschap voor Reclame, Amsterdam.

Swanborn, P.G. (1987) *Methoden van Sociaal-Wetenschappelijk Onderzoek*. Boom, Meppel.

Sylvester, A.K., McQueen, J. & Moore, S.D. (1994) Brand growth and 'phase 4 marketing': new light on the mechanisms of growth and the users that foster it. *Admap*, September.

Taylor, W. (1993) Message and muscle: an interview with Swatch titan Nicolas Hayek. *Harvard Business Review* **71**(2).

Team BBDO (1993) *Categorisatie van wasmiddelen in Oostenrijk*. Team BBDO internal document, Wenen.

Thorson, E. (1991) Consumer processing of advertising. *Current Issues and Research in Advertising* **2**(2).

Tigert, D.J. (1983) Pushing the hot buttons for a successful retailing strategy. In *Patronage Behavior and Retail Management* (W.R. Darken, & R.F. Lusch, eds). North-Holland, New York.

Timmerman, T. (1998) *Attribute Relevance of the Beer Brands Heineken and Grolsch: Report on Experiment 1*. SWOCC dissertation research, University of Amsterdam.

Tomkins, S.S. (1962) *Affect, Imagery, Consciousness, vol. 1: The Positive Affects*. Springer, New York.

Tomkins, S.S. (1963) *Affect, Imagery, Consciousness: vol. 2: The Negative Affects*. Springer, New York.

Tomkins, S.S. (1984) Affect theory. In *Approaches to Emotion* (K.R. Scherer & P. Ekman, eds). Lawrence Erlbaum Associates, Hillsdale, New Jersey.

Trout, J. & Ries, A. (1972) Positioning cuts through chaos in the marketplace. *Advertising Age*, May.

Trout, J. & Ries, A. (1979) The positioning era: a view ten years later. *Advertising Age*, July.

Tversky, A. (1977) Features of similarity. *Psychological Review* **84**(4), 327–350.

Upshaw, L.B. (1995) *Building Brand Identity: a Strategy for Success in a Hostile Marketplace*. John Wiley & Sons, New York.

Valkenburg, P. (1998) Ukkies gáán al helemaal voor Edah. *Volkskrant*, 1/12/1998.

Van de Grind, W.A. (1997) *Natuurlijke Intelligentie: over Denken, Intelligentie en Bewustzijn van Mensen en Andere Dieren*. Uitgeverij Nieuwezijds, Amsterdam.

Van der Ouderaa, I. (1994) Hoezo Merkenbouwen? *Nieuwstribune*, 27/10/1994, 38–39.

Van der Pligt, J. & de Vries, N.K. (1991) Attitudes. In *Cognitieve Sociale Psychologie* (N.K. de Vries & J. van der Pligt, eds). Boom, Meppel.

Van der Ploeg, P.A., ed. (1992) *Geschiedenis en Filosofie van de Sociale Wetenschappen*. Stenfert Kroese, Leiden.

Van Gilst, K. (1999) Ben benieuwd naar de consument. *Adformatie*, 4/2/1999.

Van Ginneken, J. (1999) *Opinie Dynamiek: het Raadsel van Snelle, Radicale en Massale Verschuivingen in de Publieke Perceptie*. SWOCC (University of Amsterdam), Amsterdam.

Van Herk, H., Schelbergen, F., Sikkel, D. & Verhallen, Th. (1995) Positioneringstechnieken. *Tijdschrift voor Marketing*, January/February.

Van Knippenberg, A., van der Kloot, W.A. & Vonk, R. (1991) Methoden, paradigma's en modellen. In *Cognitieve Sociale Psychologie* (N.K. de Vries & J. van Pligt, eds). Boom, Meppel.

Van Tilburg, M.A.L. & Tuitert, A.B.A. (1995) *Kwalitatief Marktonderzoek in Nederland: een Overzicht van Methoden en Technieken uit de Onderzoekspraktijk.* : Catholic University Brabant, Tilburg.

Van Westendorp, P.H. (1996) *Op Weg naar Accountability: GVR-monografie 9.* Genootschap voor Reclame, Amsterdam.

Vaughn, R. (1989) *The projective differential: measuring advertising and image emotions.* Sixth Annual ARF Copy Research Workshop, New York.

Verbeke, W.J.M.I. & Mosmans, A.P. (1990) *Marketingcommunicatie en Chaos.* Kluwer Bedrijfswetenschappen, Deventer.

Verhallen, Th.M.M. (1988) *Psychologisch Marktonderzoek.* Research International Nederland BV/TIAS, Tilburg.

Verheul, M. (1997) *Het Merk als Verhaal.* Afstudeerscriptie Ichtus Hogeschool, Vormgeving & Communicatie, Rotterdam.

Verlinden, R. (1994) Brand personality modelling: a qualitative research method for brand management and brand-extension management. *ESOMAR conference,* October.

Vinson, D.E., Scott, J.E. & Lamont, L.M. (1977) The role of personal values in marketing and consumer behavior. *Journal of Marketing* April.

Visser, H. (1996) Knopen doorhakken. *Wetenschap, Cultuur en Samenleving,* August.

Vroon, P.A. (1991) Reclame: oude hersenen in een nieuwe wereld. *Nieuwstribune,* 21/11/1991, 10–15.

Vyncke, P. (1992) *Imago-Management: Handboek voor Reclamestrategen.* Mys & Breesch, Gent.

Watson, J.B. (1930) *Behaviorism.* University of Chicago Press, Chicago.

Weilbacher, W.M. (1993) *Brand Marketing: Building Winning Brand Strategies That Deliver Value and Customer Satisfaction.* NTC Business Books, Chicago.

Weiner, B. & Graham, S. (1984) An attributional approach to emotional development. In *Emotion, Cognition and Behavior* (C.E. Izard, J. Kagan & R.B. Zajonc, eds). Cambridge University Press, New York.

Whan Park, C., Jun, S.Y. & Shocker, A.D. (1996) Composite branding alliances: an investigation of extension and feedback effects. *Journal of Marketing Research,* November, 453–466.

Williams, T. (1964) *The Milk Train Doesn't Stop Here Anymore.* New Directions, Norfolk, Connecticut.

Witherspoon, D. & Moscovitch, M. (1989) Stochastic independence between two implicit memory tasks. *Journal of Experimental Psychology: Learning, Memory and Cognition* **15,** 22–30.

Wolinsky, S. (1993) *Quantum Consciousness.* Bramble Books, Norfolk, Connecticut.

Woodside, A.G. & Trappey, R.J. (1992) Finding out why customers shop your store and buy your brand. *Journal of Advertising Research* **32**(6).

Wyer, R.S. & Carlston D.E. (1994) The cognitive respresentation of persons and events. In *Handbook of Social Cognition, vol 1* (R.S. Wyer & T.K. Srull, eds). Hillsdale, New Jersey: Lawrence Erlbaum Associates.

Yasin, J. (1996) The effects of advertising on fast-moving consumer goods markets. In *Advertising and Markets: a Collection of Seminal Papers* (J.C. Luik & M.J. Waterson, eds). NTC Publications, Henley-on-Thames.

Zaltman, G. & Higie, R.A. (1993) *Seeing the Voice of the Customer: the Zaltman Metaphor Elicitation Technique.* Marketing Science Institute, Cambridge, Mass.

Zaltman, G. & Higie, R.A. (1995) Seeing the Voice of the Consumer: Metaphor-Based Advertising Research. *Journal of Advertising Research* 35(4).

Zebrowitch, L.A. (1990) *Social Perception.* Open University Press, Buckingham.

Zeitlin, D.M. & Westwood, R.A. (1986) Measuring emotional response. *Journal of Advertising Research* 26(6).

Zijlmans, M. (1998) De muziek was vroeger veel beter. *Volkskrant,* 17/10/1998.

Index

abstraction formation 114
'accessibility of information', hypothesis
    174
action potential 11
activation spreading theory 60–5, 102
    'clearest' and strongest associations 65
    'cocktail party' phenomenon 64–5
    see also automatic and strategic
        activation
'active–passive/positive–negative' model
    225
'advertising and mere exposure effect',
    Bornstein theory 78
advertising associations 215–16
Advertising Response Matrix 145–6
aided brand awareness 171
amygdala 22, 24–7, 30, 33, 47
    sensory perception 220
analogous representations 82, 89
analogue communication 4
anatomical classification, Broadman's
    chart 8
appreciation, and brand relationship
    values 170
area of Broca, memory 41
association chains 56–7
association cortex 7, 22, 24
association laws 52–4
association strength, product
    category/brand 175
association system 55
association theory 49–58
    direction 55
    see also classical associationism; neo-
        associationism
associations 199–200
    and brand functions 162–3

brand name/product category 197–8
category examples 200–11
and congruence 162
differentiation 158
dual structure 149–51
evaluative and differentiative 154–60
mutual interconnectedness 56
networks scope 57–8
product attributes 141, 198–200
strength 52–3, 151–2
and under experiences 199
see also advertising associations;
        core associations; corporate
        associations; cultural
        associations; induced
        associations; service associations;
        unique associations; user
        associations
associative memory, theoretical models
    145
associative network 64, 101–9, 144
    central node 184
    core 152–3
    'dual structure' 150
    multidimensionality 154
    positive 156
associative systems 104–5
    Carslton's theory 104
ASSPAT method, research protection 349
attitude
    habit formation 273
    Van der Pligt & De Vries, definition
        269
attitude scale, Achenbaum's 396
attitude towards the ad (AAD) 277
attitude/behavioural relationship,
        'principle of correspondence' 272

automatic and strategic activation 63–5
automaticity, everyday life 281
automobile brands
    brand meanings/scores 348
    brand positioning 264–6
    dendrogram 142
    functions/relationship technique
        application 389
    hierarchy of meaning 210
    multi-purpose vehicles (MPV), Renault
        Espace 94
axon 12, 14–15, 112

beer market
    market share 331–2
    value positioning 257–8
behavioural brand equity 335
behavioural components, Fishbein &
    Ajzen theory 272
behavioural determinants model 271
'belief'/brand combinations 154
body and mind, emotional memories
    36–8
Bornstein theory, 'advertising and mere
    exposure effect' 78
brain 3–19
    Broadmann's chart, anatomical
        classification 8
    cognitive brain 21–38
    definition 3
    left/right halves 5–8
        interconnectedness 21
        specialisations 6
    scanning studies 40
    sensory categories 46–7
    waves/hemispheric asymmetry research
        376
brain development
    during evolution 3
    embryonic stage 111–12
    memory 111–25
    memory phases 113–21
brain modules 7–9
brand activation 150
brand arrangement/category
    representation 236
brand articles, as 'Gestalts' 330
brand association 64
    and choice factors 161
    and consolidation 48
    direction and intensity 152

mutual connection 56
network formation 105
to product 104
and repetition 54
brand attitudes 236, 269–77, 393–400
    Achenbaum attitude scale 396
    and brand preference 393–4
    durability 295
    Guttman scale 395
    indirect measurements 397
    influences 148, 276–7
    Likert scale 394–5
    to loyalty
        connections 294–6
        relationship 295
    measurement techniques 394
    projective differentiation scale 397
    purchase frequency/buying behaviour
        148
    semantic differentiation scales 396–7
    Thurstone scale 395–6
    unobtrusive measurements 398
    user experience 277
brand awareness 171–5, 275, 365–6
    aided awareness measurement 366
    customer share 324
    extent, intensity and breadth 172–5
    measurement techniques 366
    'naked' spontaneous 172
    spontaneous awareness measurement
        366
    Tachitoscopic research measurement
        366
    top of mind awareness (TOMA)
        measurement 366
brand behavioural tendencies 236,
    279–96, 401–6
    attitude questions 404
    background questions 405
    behavioural questions 404
    brand association questions 405
    brand monitoring 402
    brand watcher 406
    cognitive questions 404
    measurement techniques 402–6
    scale techniques 402–3
brand choice
    bandwagon effect 138
    Engel, Blackwell and Miniard model
        131
    process theory 289–90

brand concepts 210, 240, 242–52, 328
  basic examples 244–5
  lack of clarity 328
brand differentiation, symbolic
    association 238
'Brand Dynamics Pyramid', Millward
    Brown 319–20
brand emotions 34–5, 217–30, 228–30,
    235, 375–9
  bodily responses research 377
  brain waves/hemispheric asymmetry
      research 376
  eye movement research technique 377
  Frijda theory 218–20
  Galvanic skin reaction (GSR) 377
  heartbeat research 376–7
  measurement techniques 376–9
  positive 36
  psychophysiological research 376
  research 229–30
  self assessment manikin (SAM) 379
  verbal research 378
  voice analysis 376
  see also emotions
brand engram, defined 19
brand equity 331–7
brand evaluation 150
  country provenance, relationship 187
brand familiarity 235
'brand fingerprint', Gordon & Restall's
    theory 422–3
Brand Fitness research technique, BBDO
    347
brand function, and associations 162–3
brand ideal, relevance 160–61
brand identification, and perception 115
brand image 326–31
  as concept, groupings 329
  image concept, historical perspective
      326–8
  Poiesz groupings 329
  present day 328–31
  terminology restrictions 330
brand information, hippocampus 30
brand interpretation
  and expectation processes 99
  left/right brain halves 6
brand knowledge, in adolescence 124
'brand learning period', children 124
brand loyalty/consumer share 319
brand meanings 177–216, 235, 367–73

Association Pattern Method (ASSPAT)
    368
Brand Personality Scale (BPS) 370–72
categories 182–4
cognitive response analysis (CRA) 369
cultural associations 180
direct sensory (iconic impressions) 180
goose board method 369–70
hierarchical structure 208–11
idiosyncratic meanings 180
laddering research 211
laddering technique 371–3
level 208–9
measurement techniques 367–73
product related 197–200
repertory grid 367–8
subcultural associations 180
as values 207–8
brand names, and child development
    122–5
brand network, example 179
brand perception, as advertising
    association 215–16
brand personality 201–4, 327
  defined 204
Brand Personality Scale (BPS) 203, 370–2
brand placement, and 'means–goal chain'
    209
brand popularity, consumer usage 138
brand positioning 231–68, 381–91
  allocating attributes 382
  BrandAsset Valuator 389–91
  cube thought model 391
  defined 381
  Delta diagnosis 382–3
  'expressing' vs 'repressing' dimension
      259
  expression/repression instincts 386
  human behaviour 386
  ideal point modelling 384
  Implicit Personality Mapping
      (IMPMAP) 385–7
  Locator technique 383–4
  Market Structure Audit 382
  measurement techniques 382
  natural grouping 382
  quality planning (QP) 384
  research methods into values 259
  social interaction dimension 259
  top of mind image (TOMI) 383
  vector modelling 384

brand preference
  BrandYard 400
  constant sum method 398
  measurement techniques 398
  price trade-off method 399
  ranking 398–9
brand presentation 215
brand purchases, duplication 288–91
brand purchasing behaviour, mental
      brand representation 318
brand ranking 398–9
brand recall 69–70
brand recognition 69–70
  sign system 186
Brand Relationship Quality (BRQ)
      408–10
  technique 307
brand relationships 236, 297–310,
      407–13
  components 306
  conversion model 411–13
    segmented divisions 412
  defined 306
  Lorenz's butterfly 305
  'me map' 410–11
  measurement techniques 408
  network society concept 304
  psychology 297–8
    affinity 299–300
    communication (dominance and
        affinity) 297–301
    continuity 301
    interaction circle 300
    interactions 298
    interpersonal circle 300
    power relationship negotiation 299
    reciprocity 301
  quantum theory 301–5
    Einstein's theory of relativity 303,
        341
    Heisenberg's uncertainty principle
        303, 341
    influences 305
  statements and scales 410
brand relationships schema, meaning
      levels 308
brand repertoire 282–8
  product categories 283
  scope, with category share 283
brand representation 311–37
  development stages 312–22

element interconnectedness 323–4
  and habit 77
  qualitative research 68
  saliency 325–6
brand representation research 343–4
  aids 354–64
  bubble cartoons 361–2
  collage 363
  expression 363–4
  fantasy construction 361
  free association 355–6
  group discussions 351–4
  guided dreams 361
  interviewing methods 349–51
  metaphor and analogy 364
  paint box 360
  personification 360
  phases 345–9
  planet description 360
  projective questioning 361
  projective techniques 355–64
    toolkit 356
  psychodrawings 363
  representation concept 344
  research practice 343–4
  role playing and psychodrama 353–4
  scenario technique 362–3
  secret pooling 356
  sentence completion technique 360–61
  sorting techniques, and examples
        357–9
  stimulus material 355
  synectics 353–4
  Thematic Apperception Test (TAT) 361
  user typology/stereotyping 360
brand representations, development 124
brand research
  behavioural loyalty 296
  vulnerability/low loyalty 296
brand response
  components 146
  interrelatedness 146–9
brand signals 27
brand signs 184–6
brand slogans, associated characters 308
brand stability 313
brand stimuli 42
brand strength, goal cues 336
brand types 168
brand values
  groups 163

underlying constructs 390–1
see also symbolic brand values
brand vision, research technique 342
brand–person relationships 308
BrandAsset Valuator 389–91
brands 168–9
   affective reactions 228
   average score 285
   'big five' personality traits 202–4
   brand 'as a story' 430
   characteristic traits 236
   classification,
        multidimensionality/individual
        strength associations 155
   'clearest' and strong association 65
   cognitions application 178
   cognitive evaluations 33–4
   concepts 239
   consumer brand categorisation 233
   dimensions 423
   distinctiveness 158
   emotional association 33
   expressive function 165
   general typology 267
   impressive function 166
   market position development 316
   memory 171–2
      coding 32
      implicit memory, representation 59
      influencing elements 130–44
      long-term memory 71, 134
      representation 59
      retention 129–70
      sections 145
      specific activation 63
   Moen's general typology of brands
      267–8
   perceived quality 211–13
   relationship values 169–70
   social adaptive function 166
   and sub-brands
      company/manufacturer 187
      country of origin 186–7
      origin 186–97
      with product related meanings 193
   unique position 239–40
   see also identity brands; holistic brand
      research
'brandscape'
   Biel's 381
   self-image/self-ideal 242

BrandWorks, Gordon & Restall's theory
   422–4
'BRANDZ' project
   Millward Brown 320–22
      map 321
breakfast cereals
   brand attributes/consumer view 157
   users'/non-users' belief scores 199
buying behaviour 132
   brand attitudes/purchase frequency 148

categorisation 94, 232–8
   brand–self categorisation 243
   classical theories 232–3
   differentiating traits 236–8
   example 241
   'perceptual maps' 255
   prototype approach 233–8
   subcategory defined 240
category buying, market share vs loyalty
   285
central steering element, memory 41
cerebral hemisphere 5–7
chain conversation, brand representation
   research 351
child development 116–21
   and brand names 122–5
   Piaget's theory 114–15
choice processes 133–44
   choice and alternatives 143
   external information 139
   external/memory information 139
   internal/external interactions 133
   memory information 135, 137
church to brand, religions and pseudo-
   realities 341–2
classical associationism 50
coffee (instant) market
   duplication 289
   share of customer 287
cognitive brain 21–38
cognitive response analysis (CRA), brand
   meanings 369
cognitive stimuli processing, hippocampus
   79
communication, and brands 169
community spirit and belonging, Adler's
   research theory translation 388
compensatory rules 136
computational mind 43
computers, and human mind 37

concept brands 239
concepts
    and categories 91–4
        Tverski contrast model 93
    emotions, Frijda's theory 218
    formation 85
    Frege's theory 90
    hierarchical example 92
    and language 85–8
    'love' 114
    nature 90–1
    units of knowledge 83
conceptual associative model 158
'conceptual primitives' 49
conformity, as human motivator 138
conjunctive decision rule 137
connectionism 49, 106–9
connectionist network models 105–9
    digital watch analogy 105
    parallel distributed processing models
        (PDP) 106
connections 68
    brand use/brand associations 149
    brand use/spontaneous
        awareness 147
    brand/meaning 150
    origin 14–19
    see also recency connection
consciousness 42–5
consideration set 275
    automobiles 142
consolidation
    and brand association 48
    working to long-term memory 47
constant sum method
    brand preference measurement 398
    research 347
consumer brand categorisation 233
consumer brand equity 332–3
consumer brand relationship
    vs relationship through brands 310
    Verlinden's dimensional theory 421–2
consumer choice
    'good product' by 'good company' 197
    semi-scientific models 130–31
consumer share/brand loyalty 319
'Consumer Value Model' 319
contiguity law 52
continuity, and brand relationship values
    169–70
conversion model

brand relationships 411–13
    segmented divisions 412
core associations, defined 57
corporate associations
    categories 194
        characteristics, specific associations
            194–5
corpus callosum 6
cortex 112
    and limbic system 23
    visual cortex 24, 113
country images 188
Cross-Cultural Consumer Characteristics
    (4 Cs) technique, for research 432
cube thought model, brand positioning
    391
cues, influence 67–9
cultural associations 180

decision-making process 33
    phases 131
    positive feelings 35–6
    rules 136–7
declarative memory 77
dendrites 15, 29, 112
determinant associations 159–60
differentiation, 'added value' option 328
direct analogous representations of
    sensory 'sensations' 177
disjunctive decision rule 137
disruption, Dru's theory of disruption 134
'double jeopardy' effect, research 348
driver brands 192
duplication, instant coffee market 289

emotional association 30–4
    brand 33
    heuristics 33
    memory organisation 31
emotional behaviour (adult), analysis 216
emotional brain 21–38, 33
emotional experience
    Frijda's theory 219
    recollection types 34
emotional memories 34–8
    body and mind 36–8
emotional responses, types 225, 229
emotions
    as agents 221
    and autonomy 27
    basic emotions 221–3

combined manifestation, scoring 228
complex 26
concepts 218
  defined 218
  heartbeat research 376–7
  personal regulation 220
  process, role regulation 220
  reasonableness 220–21
  scientific opinion 223
  unconscious/conscious emotions
    26–7
  see also brand emotions
endorsement brands 192
engram 19, 57
epicentre
  Gestalt theory 58–60
  Greenfield's theory 60
episodic memory 77
'established brands', market stability 332
evaluation phase 134–44
evaluative associations 156
evocation phase 139–40
evolution, brain development, MacLean's
    representation 3
explicit memory 77–80
explorer brands 168–9
expressive behaviour 224

Facial Action Coding System (FACS) 224,
    226–7, 229
family resemblance 235
feelings 223–4
feelings and mind, interactions 33
financial-economic brand equity 334–5
firedance, neuron 13
firing disposition, neuron 11
forehead brain (old cortex) 4
forgetfulness 70–72
  the elderly 72–3
  Haitink's memory 73
free format method, for research 416–17

Galvanic skin reaction (GSR), brand
    emotions 377
Gestalt, defined 59
Gestalt psychology 415–16
  brand articles 330
grocery brands 314

habits 279–82
  defined 280

heartbeat research, brand emotions
    376–7
Hebb's theory 17–18, 151
heuristics 33, 35, 64, 138
  brand awareness function 174
hippocampus 22, 24, 27, 29
  cognitive stimuli processing 79
  dry facts storage 34
  long-term memory 47
  memory loss 72
  new information organisation 30
holistic brand research 415–27
  brand fitness 417–18
  explicit method 424–7
  free format method 416–17
  implicit method 417–18
  trance research 416–17
  transactional analysis 418–22
'homunculus' 40, 125
hypothalamus 21–2

icon brands 168–9
identity brands 168–9
implicit memory 78–80
implicit method, holistic brand research
    417–18
Implicit Personality Mapping (IMPMAP)
    347
  brand positioning 385–7
induced associations 152
Information Atomism theory, Fodor's
    83–4
information processing 45–6
information storage 27–30
integrated experiences 26
interaction, brand relationship values 169
involvement and closeness, and brand
    relationship values 170

'knowledge atoms' 49
knowledge structures
  Bartlett's 'scheme theory' 95
  schemata 95–8
'Kompas' value inventory 260–63

language
  brand meaning 180–81
  memory representations 177
  as thought window 86–7
language processing 5
learned habit, purchasing behaviour 132

learning by doing, Piaget theory 115
lexicographic decision rule 137
'likeability', positive attitude towards
	advertisement 277
limbic system 3–4, 22–7
linguistic brain 7
long-term memory 29, 46–8
	brand perception 71, 134
long-term potentiation 27

magnetic resonance imaging (MRI) 32, 73
market laws 291–3
	Dirichlet formula 292
	double-jeopardy/brand loyalty 293
	double-jeopardy phenomenon 291–2
	market share/penetration, connection 293
	penetration importance 292
market position/brand perceived quality
	relationship 213
market share
	beer market 331–2
	change vs share 333
	correlation across 71 brands 331
	'established brands' 332
marketing, 'evoked set' 68
'me map', brand relationships 410–11
meanings
	hierarchy of meaning 159
	and language 83
	see also situational meanings
'means–goal chain', and brand placement
	209
measurement scale, Millward Brown 318
memory 39–73
	area of Broca 41
	basic model 39–40
	and brain development 111–25
	brand coding 32
	brand representation 59
	central processor 41
	central steering element 41
	complexity of processes 73
	emotional 34–8
	long-term memory 29, 46–8
		brand perception 71, 134
	organisation, emotional association 31
	phases, brain development 113–21
	Pribam's theory 47
	retention functions 72
	short-term 39
	working memory model 39–42

see also brand; declarative memory;
	episodic memory; explicit
	memory; implicit memory;
	procedural memory; semantic
	memory
memory organisation, emotional
	association 31
memory organisation packets (MOPS) 96
memory representations 81–99
	examples 177
memory systems 75–80
	habit development 76–7
	processes and files 75–6
mental brand equity 334
mental brand representation, brand
	purchasing behaviour 318
mental brand response, hierarchical
	connection 324
'mentalese', Pinker's theory 86
'mere exposure' hypothesis 174
'modelling', research technique 347
Moen's general typology of brands 267–8
motivated behaviour 224–7
motor nerve cell 15
Multi Dimensional Scaling (MDS) 427
multi-purpose vehicles (MPV), Renault
	Espace 94
mutual interconnectedness, association 56

'naked' spontaneous brand awareness 172
narrative research 429–31
neo-associationism 49–51
neocortex 3–5
networks 13–14
neural brand networks 17
neural circuit 15
neural network 14
	growth 111
	models 108–9
	see also connectionist network models
neuron 9–15, 112
	connections between 12
	types 10
neuronal Gestalts 58–9
neurotransmitter 12
non-compensatory decision rules 137

observation research 431–2
occipital lobe 5
old cortex 3–4
organisational associations 196

paired interviews 350
paleocortex (old cortex) 4
panel research 432–3
parallel distributed processing models
    (PDP) *see* connectionist network
    models
parallelism 106
parietal lobe 5
perceived quality, and market position
    213
perceived quality/value, as separate
    entities 215
perceived (relative) price 214–15
perceived value 214–15
    and quality 215
perception and meaning 81
'perceptual maps', categorisation 255
perceptual representation system (PRS) 78
    Schacter's hypothesis 98
Personal Drive Analysis 417
phenomenological mind 43
phonological circuit 41
phonological loop 41
phonological phase 41
phonological storage system 41
physiological reactions 227
Pleasure Arousal Dominance (PAD)
    379
pluriformity, brand vision 341
positive feelings, efficient decision making
    35–6
positron emission tomography (PET) 32,
    73
postsynaptic dendrite 12
power brands 168
preconscious 43
presynaptic membrane 12
Pribam's theory, memory 47
'principle of correspondence',
    attitude/behavioural relationship
    272
private cars, categorisation 241
proactive interference, forgetfulness 70
procedural memory 76–7
process theory, brand choice 289–90
product brands 239
product category/brand, association
    strength 175
product-related values 163–4
product/brand awareness, top of mind
    awareness (TOMA) 151

'Profit Impact of Market Strategy' (PIMS)
    database 212–13
projective differentiation scale, brand
    attitudes 397
propositional categories 82–3
propositional representations 82, 89,
    108–9, 177
    non-verbal/verbal 84
protein synthesis 29
proto-reptilian brain 3–4
psychodynamic approach, marketing
    analysis 388
psychological closeness, and brand
    relationship values 170
purchasing behaviour
    mental representation 317
    values 166–9
        follow-up 167
        security 167
        simplification 167
purchasing patterns 286

quality/temperature continuum 254

reasoned behaviour theory, Fishbein &
    Ajzen 327
recency connection 53
reciprocity, and brands 169
recollection, defined 418–19
relevance, and brand ideal 160–61
remembering 65–7
repetition, and brand association 54
repetition law 52
representations, origin 112–13
research
    brand as a story 430
    Cross-Cultural Consumer
        Characteristics (4 Cs) technique
        432
    narrative 429–31
    new forms 429–33
    observation 431–2
    panel research 432–3
    VALS segmentation technique 432
retroactive interference, forgetfulness
    71
return on investment (ROI) 213
return on sales (ROS) 213

schemata functioning, Alba and Hasher's
    model 98–9

scheme theory
Bartlett's theory 97, 103
knowledge structures 95
search of associative memory theory 97
semantic differential (ABN/AMRO) 230
semantic memory 77–8
semi-scientific models, consumer choice 130–31
sensory categories, brain 46–7
sensory connections, to amygdala 24
sensory cortex 22, 24
sensory inputs 16
sensory nerve cell 15
sensory perception 17–18, 25
sequential elimination rule 137
serial/parallel processes, thought 44
service associations 199–200
share of customer 284
share of requirements/ratio and market share 287
sign system, brand recognition 186
similarity law 53
single interviews 349–50
single source research 433
situational meanings 200
'social desirability' hypothesis 174
sodium/potassium channel 12
soma 15
statistic analysis techniques 149
stimulus and response principle 279
strong brand, characteristics 334–5
SWOCC value inventory 256–8, 263
symbolic brand values 164–6
synapses 11, 15, 112
increase 113
strengthening 29
synaptic cleft 12

temporal lobe 5
thalamus 21–2, 24, 33

Thematic Apperception Test 361, 430
thought, serial/parallel processes 44
toiletry products, market share 198
'tonal qualifiers', Gordon & Restall's theory 422
toothpaste brands, positioning 256
top of mind awareness (TOMA), product/brand awareness 140, 151, 172
trance research 416–17
transactional analysis (TA), holistic brand research 418–22
transport examples, hierarchical structure 233
triangular interviews, brand representation research 350
Tverski contrast model *see* concepts and categories

unconscious 43
unconscious/conscious emotions 26–7
unconscious information processing 66
unique associations 161
user associations 201

value positioning 256–64
value segmentation 260–63
value systems, definition 204
verbal representations 82
visiospatial sketchpad 40–41
visual cortex 24, 113
vividness law 53

whole brand representation, research 415–27
words, and meanings 88–90

Zaltman Metaphor Elicitation Technique (ZMET) 347, 424–6